HEALTHY THOUGHTS

EUROPEAN PERSPECTIVES ON HEALTH CARE ETHICS

Healthy Thoughts

European Perspectives on Health Care Ethics

Editors

Reidar K. Lie
Paul T. Schotsmans

Bart Hansen
Tom Meulenbergs

PEETERS
LEUVEN - PARIS - STERLING, VIRGINIA
2002

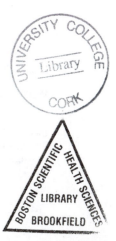

i 19908969

Library of Congress Cataloging-in-Publication Data

Healthy thoughts: European perspectives on health care ethics / editors, Reidar K. Lie ... [et al.].
    p. m.
  Includes bibliographical references.
  ISBN 9042911425
    1. Medical ethics--Europe. 2. Medical care--Moral and ethical aspects--Europe. I. Lie, Reidar Krummradt.

R724.H35 2002
174'.2'094--dc21

2002025345

ISBN 90-429-1142-5
D. 2002/0602/63

© 2002 – Peeters – Bondgenotenlaan 153 – B-3000 Leuven – Belgium

European Ethics Network

Board of Directors

Michel FALISE (Université Catholique de Lille): President ad interim

Johan VERSTRAETEN (K.U.Leuven): Chairman of the Board

Guillaume DE STEXHE (FUSL, Brussels)

Maurice DE WACHTER (Brussels): Representative of the *European Association of Centres of Medical Ethics* (EACME)
José Luis FERNANDEZ-FERNANDEZ (U.P. Comillas, Madrid)
Heidi Hövik-VON WELTZIEN (Norwegian School of Management, Oslo): President *European Business Ethics Network* (Eben)
Walter LESCH, (U.C. Louvain-la-Neuve)
Dirk LIPS (Gent): *European Ethics Network of Institutes of Higher Learning*, (this network will be fully integrated into the EEN)
Lars REUTER (Aarhus University): Secretary General of *Societas Ethica*
Jean-Pierre WILS (K.U. Nijmegen)

Address:

European Ethics Network Coordination Centre
Deberiotstraat 26
B-3000 Leuven
Tel: + 32.16.32.37.95/ 45.34
Fax: + 32.16.32.45.34
Website: http://www.kuleuven.ac.be/een
Email: johan.verstraeten@theo.kuleuven.ac.be

Editorial Team

Editor-in-Chief

Paul T. SCHOTSMANS
CENTRE FOR BIOMEDICAL ETHICS AND LAW
Katholieke Universiteit Leuven

Editor

Reidar K. LIE
DEPARTMENT OF PHILOSOPHY
University of Bergen

Co-editors

Bart HANSEN
CENTRE FOR BIOMEDICAL ETHICS AND LAW
Katholieke Universiteit Leuven

Tom MEULENBERGS
CENTRE FOR BIOMEDICAL ETHICS AND LAW
Katholieke Universiteit Leuven

Addresses:
Centre for Biomedical Ethics and Law
Katholieke Universiteit Leuven
Kapucijnenvoer 35
B-3000 Leuven BELGIUM
Tel. +32 16 33.69.51
Fax. +32 16 33.69.52
website: www.kuleuven.ac.be/cbmer

Department of Philosophy
University of Bergen
Sydnesplassen 7
N-5007 Bergen NORWAY
Tel. +47 952.31.985
Fax. +47 955.50.392
website: www.ethica.uib.no

TABLE OF CONTENTS

FOREWORD

Professional ethics and ethics education
Vision of the core materials project[1]

Johan Verstraeten
Director, European Ethics Network

This book is a result of the core materials project for the development of courses in professional ethics initiated by the *European Ethics Network* and subsidized by the European Commission DG XXII. The target group of this project are lecturers, professors as well as the interest reader. The texts are conceived as a source of inspiration for the development of courses adapted to local situations and personal interpretations. In the first stage the dissemination of the project is realized via the publication of five books:

- Professional Ethics: General Perspectives
- Business Ethics
- Engineering Ethics
- Media Ethics
- Health Care Ethics

The project, in which ethicists from all over Europe have participated, is a response to a real need: a better ethical formation and education of students via (1) an improvement of the courses and (2) the development of an integral life-enabling education project of universities and institutions of higher education.

The project starts from the assumption that the students of today are the professionals of tomorrow. In a world dominated by the power of knowledge, professional experts such as scientists, (bio)engineers, physicians, lawyers, public servants, media experts,

[1] P. VAN TONGEREN, *Ethiek en traditie*, in *Tijdschrift voor Filosofie* 58 (1996) 84-102.

economists and business administrators exercise a crucial influence on the lives and the quality of life of millions of citizens. In the future this will increase under the influence of new (bio)technological, biomedical and managerial developments. Their implementation by professionals will affect the human and natural environment, the solution of problems with regard to life and death, employment and the quality of information and public office.

Very often the actual and future professionals are not sufficiently prepared to deal with the ethical aspects of their professional decisions and with the social consequences of their work. They need a broader education in which their professional knowledge and expertise is completed with the ability to resolve ethical dilemmas and with the capacity to discern the values that are at stake in every professional decision.

Providing students with greater ethical expertise is necessary but not sufficient, since the tendency to hyperspecialization in already quite specialized disciplines goes together with a loss of the ability to integrate everything into a larger and meaningful whole. In such a context, there is need for a broad education in which space is created for an integral interpretation of reality, for initiation into traditions of thought, for the development of the student's civic sense and the configuration of persons as moral subjects.

Learning to interpret

Before one can ethically reflect about the solution to a problem, one must clarify what the problem means, what meanings are connected with the problem and how the problem fits into the wider social context.[2] It would make little sense to pose questions of business ethics if one does not understand what business as a human activity means. It makes little sense to have a technical discussion about euthanasia without asking oneself about the meaning of human life and death. This is confirmed by the European Commission's white paper on *Teaching and Learning: Towards the Learning Society*, where an argument is made, precisely in the context of policy proposals for better technical and scientific education. According to this document professional ethics requires more than simply a transfer of

---

[2] M.C. NUSSBAUM, *Poetic Justice: The Literary Imagination and Public Life*, Boston, 1995, p. 72-78.

ideas from a differentiated ethical discipline or of models of ethical argumentation. It is rather a matter of opening minds and improving the capacity to interpret reality by way of additional education in literature and philosophy. The white paper considers these subjects to be important because, in a world where knowledge is quantitatively increasing, they *'arm the individual with powers of discernment and critical sense. This can provide the best protection against manipulation, enabling people to interpret and understand the information they receive.'*

That a wider and especially a literary education is one of the conditions for acquiring ethical competence, has been suggested by Martha Nussbaum, among others. In her book *Poetic Justice* she shows that it is not enough to initiate students into rational ethical argumentation.[3] One must also educate their emotional intelligence and their capacity to put themselves in the place of others. One of the conditions for this is an initiation into the reading of literary texts. Without an activation of their imaginative powers, according to Nussbaum, future professionals will be unable to put themselves as unprejudiced spectators in the situation of the people about whom they will make decisions in their professional life. Initiation into the reading of literary texts is also a way to liberate future professionals from limited or enclosed circles of interpretation. Their situation is sometimes comparable to that of the cave dwellers in Plato's *Republic*, particularly if they consider a severely limited approach to reality to be the only true one. Sometimes they see only those dimensions of a problem that are considered to be relevant according to the premises of a certain scientific discipline. Especially the applied sciences are apt to get stuck in what Weber called the steel cage of bureaucratic or technical rationality, and what MacIntyre described as a kind of thinking permeated by instrumental rationality and a kind of action reduced to manipulative expertise.

By teaching future scientists and professionals how to deal with new, different, even poetic possibilities for interpreting reality, through an introduction to literary and philosophical texts, one provides them with the means of breaking out of their closed or limited hermeneutic circles. This is not to say that scientific interpretations of reality are meaningless or without value. I mean rather that it is

---

[3] C. Taylor, *Sources of the Self: The Making of Modernity*, Cambridge, 1989, p. 26.

necessary, through initiation into literature and philosophy, to give students access to a horizon of interpretation which is different than the scientific one in which they have been trained. Through a creative confrontation between various possibilities of interpretation, their field of vision expands. One might echo Marcel Proust and say that the *true voyage of discovery is not to seek out new territory, but to learn to see with new eyes*. The most important change that a person can undergo is the change in the way they view reality. One can change studies, job, neighbourhood, country or even continent and yet remain the same. If the fundamental hermeneutic perspective changes, however, then the way in which one experiences reality also changes.

In addition to a specialized course in ethics, something more is needed: the embedding of technical, scientific education within a *universitas* education, a broadly literary, philosophical, and cultural education that provides future professionals with the capacity to 'meaning-fully' interpret the reality in which they live and act.

A purely neutral ethics education is an illusion

The basic philosophy behind the core materials project is not based on the idea of a value neutral ethical expertise. The project also differs from theories in which it has become almost a dogma that ethics should take distance from particular moral or philosophical convictions or religious beliefs if it is to remain meaningful in a pluralistic society. In these theories one starts from a *method of avoidance* or in the best case from the *thinning out of the conflictuous thickness of moral concepts*. The project texts do not deny that overcoming philosophical and religious differences and achieving a reflexive equilibrium or an overlapping consensus is necessary if we are to achieve a minimum consensus regarding difficult questions. But there are doubts about whether a pedagogical process can work with ethical concepts and models that have been *totally* cut off from their original philosophical or religious frame of reference. People do not merely act on the basis of abstract principles or de-natured rational arguments. In making moral decisions, they make use of a scale of values and this is influenced in part by what Charles Taylor would call fundamental frames of reference, i.e., fundamental principles which are not as such rationally justified, but which determine the perspectives on whose basis one attaches importance to specific values.[4] Ultimate frames of reference and meaning, then, have an enormous influence on action. Like it or not, one always belongs to a tradition of thought or belief or, in a fragmented culture, to various traditions from which one draws inspiration. Even when one tries *a priori* to put the influence of traditions out of play, one belongs to a tradition, namely the tradition that uses this conception. This is the reason why it remains of crucial importance to the educational mission of a university to initiate students into tradition(s) of thought and to show them how different particular convictions have ethical implication. According to some scholars such as Alasdair MacIntyre, to be initiated into a tradition is even a precondition for meeting and understanding other cultures.[5] There exists no Archimedean or neutral point from which one can approach these traditions. On the basis of a particular rationality, one can also recognize and clarify the reasonableness of other traditions and, where necessary, even critically integrate their incommensurable aspects into one's own tradition.

Ethics education requires training in civic sense

> *'Par leurs activités de formation et de recherche, les universités sont des acteurs importants de la transformation sociale. Elles peuvent contribuer de façon substantielle à l'évolution des mentalités, des comportements, des structures qui favorisent le renouveau de la citoyenneté...'*
> Colloque 'L'université européenne acteur de citoyenneté'

As a standard-bearer for the knowledge industry, the university is often too one-sidedly oriented towards producing *employable* individuals in the service of the economic system (R. Bellah, *The Good Society*). One then runs the risk of losing sight of an important aspect of education: training in civic sense. Students must also learn to think about their social responsibility and take account of the social

---

[4] We adopt here a standpoint based on A. MacIntyre, *Whose Justice, Which Rationality?*, Notre Dame, 1989, p. 26.

[5] D. Hollenbach, *Intellectual and Social Solidarity: Comment on J.M. Buckley's The Catholic University and the Promise Inherent in its Identity*, in J.P. Langan, L.J. O'Donovan, *Catholic Universities in Church and Society*, Washington, 1993, p. 90-94.

consequences of exercising professional power or knowledge power. Training in civic sense requires not only the transfer of knowledge about political and social ethics, but also the formation of social attitudes such as attention for the least advantaged in society. A university as centre of excellence should not only focus on high points of culture and science, but also the depths of suffering into which a society and its citizens can fall.[6] Every society exhibits the face of its victims, and it is certainly not asking too much of students that they learn as professionals how to recognize that face.

There is no ethical responsibility without personal development

> *The essential mission of education is to help everyone to develop their own potential and become a complete human being, as opposed to a tool at the service of the economy. The acquisition of knowledge and skills should go hand in hand with building up character (...) and accepting one's responsibility in society.*

White Paper, p. 26

Ethics requires more than just knowledge acquisition. An ethical education implies more than providing future professionals with the means to make a critical judgement about problems through rational argumentation. Traditionally ethics has also been viewed as practical wisdom, aimed at the moral development of the acting person. Such a person is not only responsible for what he or she does in specific situations of choice, but also for the moral quality of his or her life, in other words, for the integration of moral choices and actions into a meaningful life that is configured as a narrative unity.

This development of a moral identity has become exceptionally problematic nowadays. In fact, we currently find ourselves in a tension between a modern, liberal illusion of a completely autonomous and self-affirming subject and the factual break-up of the subject by a fragmented existence.[7] The latter implies not merely that the value and meaning systems outside us are breaking up (what the sociologists refer to as the disappearance of plausibility structures), but also

---

[6] J. MORNY, *Reflections on Paul Ricoeur's Soi-même comme un autre*, in R.C. CULLEY, and W. KLEMPA (eds.), *The Three Loves: Theology, Philosophy and World Religions, Essays in Honour of Joseph C. McLelland*, McGill Studies in Religion, Vol. 2, Atlanta, 1994, p. 85.

[7] Cf. P. RICOEUR, *Soi-même comme un autre*, Paris, 1990, p. 137-198.

that the inner life of people is falling apart into a multiplicity of experiences and possibilities. Fragmentation is embedded inside us as a cognitive possibility. In order to get around this impasse, it is necessary to once again offer the conditions of possibility for a new personal configuration. According to Ricoeur, this is primarily a matter of integrating the autonomous ego-identity that maintains itself through the course of time (*idem* identity) and the identity that is built up through the encounter with the other (*ipse* identity).[8] This other is not only the concrete other or the community, but also the texts which offer models in which a person can imaginatively recognize his/her conditions of existence as one step in the direction of a reconfiguration of himself (herself). For Ricoeur, understanding oneself is always a *se comprendre devant le texte*. If this conception is correct, then it means, once again, that initiating students into literary, philosophical and religious texts is a *sine qua non* condition for their moral education. Admittedly these texts have no direct influence on the concrete moral choices that a person must make, but they do open up an entire world of meaning that can stimulate the moral imagination with which moral subjects can recognize new ways of acting and being.

In light of these four points the steering committee of the European Ethics Network holds the opinion that ethical education requires a global pedagogical project. A university is more than an institution devoted to scientific research and education, more than a place where knowledge is acquired and transmitted. It is also a community of professors and students in which life-promoting learning processes are inculcated. As a school of life, the university can make a contribution to the education of citizens with a sense of responsibility.

It is in this broader framework that professional ethics gets its necessary place. The participants in the core materials project do not want to relativize the fact that, in an academic environment, characterized by an increasing number of specializations and hyperspecializations, the rapidly evolving scientific and technological innovations require adequate ethical answers and a permanent adaptation of the law.

---

[8] J. VERSTRAETEN, *De spirituele bronnen van burgerzin en de taak van de katholieke universiteit*, in *Ethische Perspectieven* 8/2 (1998) 59-64.

Before we can even think of excellent courses in professional ethics, we need to consider that first a two-fold expertise is required. On the one hand, there is a need for ethicists with highly specialized knowledge who can function as discussion partners with experts; on the other hand, these experts themselves must learn to discover ethical problems and moral dilemmas in their own field. Ethics is not the application of abstract norms that would be imposed on a discipline like a *deus ex machina*. It begins by uncovering the problems and dilemmas as they present themselves in a specialized domain of knowledge. It is only after an adequate and expert analysis that a reasonably legitimate judgement can be passed. For instance, one cannot say anything meaningful about the ethics of international financial markets without an expert knowledge of derivatives and speculative techniques. It is impossible to pass a legitimate ethical judgement on prenatal diagnosis without a thorough knowledge of the medical aspects of the problem, and the techniques involved. This is why a specialized course in *ethics* for licentiate and postgraduate students is necessary, in addition to training the ethics instructors to be experts in a specific domain. Education in ethics, however, requires more than the introduction of a course in *applied* ethics and a pedagogic relationship between expert ethicists and students. At least as important is dialogue with specialists themselves, not only because ethicists should acquire a better knowledge, but also because the instructors and experts from various disciplines who are not ethicists, should themselves learn to pose ethical questions about their own specialized domain. Whenever *ethics* is restricted to a separate discipline, it is easily perceived by the students to be something standing somewhere outside their own discipline or professional training.

In other words, training in the students' ethical competence demands a simultaneous training in the ethical competence of all the instructors. This is the reason why the texts of the *Core Materials Project* are both destined to ethicists and experts in different fields.

INTRODUCTION

Bioethics, with its historical roots in the US, can be regarded as the mother discipline of applied ethics. It can therefore be no surprise that, since its 'birth' in the late 1960s, bioethics has long been dominated by an Anglo-American approach. Only about ten years after the first Centres for Bioethics were established at American universities (e.g. Georgetown University, Washington DC, and the Hastings Center in New York), European Centres for Bioethics were created for documentation, research and training in the field of Bioethics. At this moment the European Association of Centres of Medical Ethics (EACME) counts more than 60 centres. EACME functions as a broad interdisciplinary network bringing together several cultures in Europe. In this way, bioethics has become fully accepted in Europe and created its own approach inspired by the rich philosophical and theological European heritage with its historical roots in the Graeco-Latin and Judeo-Christian tradition.

The plan to write this textbook is connected with this tradition and must be situated in the context of the Project 'Core Materials for the Development of Courses in Professional Ethics' of the *European Ethics Network* (EEN), endorsed by the Socrates Project of the European Commission (DG XXII) and initiated by Prof. Johan Verstraeten. The European Ethics Network has a very concrete purpose, namely to develop a practical ethics for and as far as possible in cooperation with the world of the professions in several fields. More than 100 universities and schools for higher education such as medical, nursing, business and engineering schools endorse this network. Medical Schools were invited to sponsor the publication of a specific textbook on bioethics. The Steering Committee of EEN gave us the opportunity to function as the editors.

From the beginning, we were aware of the fact that there are many textbooks on medical ethics and bioethics in several language regions of Europe: what new things could then be done? We decided we would not simply write a new textbook, but instead ask key persons in different European countries to reflect on three central areas of importance in current bioethics: the physician-patient relationship, human experimentation and the just allocation of health care resources.

We are indeed convinced that the various European approaches to **the physician-patient relationship** that are presented will complement the 'traditional' Anglo-American approaches in bioethics. As the reader will observe, this part does not present a homogeneous picture of the ethics of the physician-patient relationship, but gives several scholars of different European traditions the chance to explain their ethical view on the relational structure of the medical profession. Latin, German and Nordic cultures present different ideas of how the physician-patient relationship must be understood and function.   In this way, the contributions on the physician-patient relationship are clear manifestations of the diversity of contemporary continental thought in matters of health care ethics.

Another major branch of health care ethics, namely the **just allocation of health care resources**, is also strongly interdependent with national variety and cultural differences. The European democracies stand for a longstanding and strong network of solidarity and social security. The gap with the US seems to be so broad that it may lead to totally different interpretations and even radical misunderstandings. Therefore, we were convinced that also this subject could not be neglected in this European Textbook and needed careful analysis. We hope that the contributions on a just organisation of the health care system will be a helpful guide for bioethicists to receive at first hand the insights of European scholars in this field.

And finally, the subject of **human experimentation** was chosen as a kind of complementary contribution on similar publications in bioethics. Being aware that this field is very international and structured by several – even intercontinental – guidelines, the recent development in Europe (the approval of the European Directive on Good Clinical Practice) needs careful analysis and philosophical clarification. European scholars of different origins and schools are presenting their ideas on the basic presuppositions of human experimentation in medicine. We have therefore placed this section between the two more European oriented subdivisions of this textbook.

By having chosen these three general pathways for presenting European contributions, we are convinced that this book will be an original contribution to the international discussion on medical ethics and health care ethics. With their common European background, the authors want to enrich and encourage the ongoing discussions on the physician-patient relationship, human experimentation and just allocation of health care resources from various perspectives and different points of departure.

The educational approach of this book is both original and constructive. The EEN has set up this project with a clear objective: it was not an attempt to write courses for students, but to write basic material for instructors and lecturers in health care ethics in order to make them less dependent on the classic, predominantly North-American manuals. This is the main reason for the structure of each of the three sections of the book. First, an explanatory introduction will offer the reader a solid basis for a critical reading of the various contributions. In these introductions, a case will be presented to both illustrate the ethical complexity of day-to-day practice and to formulate the ethical questions involved. After the different contributors have shed their light on these questions, each section ends with an epilogue. For this, we asked scholars with experience in the field, to judge the presented material on its merits and to give a few general considerations.

We are indebted to many colleagues who have contributed to this book.. The realisation of this project would not have been possible without the help of our co-editors, Drs. Bart Hansen and Drs. Tom Meulenbergs. We also thank the Coordination Centre of the EEN, and more especially Ms. Maria Duffy and Lucrèce De Becker, for their assistance. We also are very grateful to the members of the Editorial Team who have reviewed the manuscripts and who gave very insightful orientations for the final redaction. Finally, we want to express in a special way our thanks to Dr. Maurice A.M. de Wachter, who was our representative in the Steering Committee of the European Ethics Network.

Thoughts about health care, medical ethics and bioethics will now be presented in various versions and traditions... may they be 'healthy' to all the readers and, in the long run, to those of our common concern, the patients!

Reidar K. Lie
Paul T. Schotsmans

Bergen (Norway) – Leuven (Belgium), March 2002

Part one

THE PHYSICIAN-PATIENT RELATIONSHIP

INTRODUCTION

The relationship between physician and patient is one of the most essential elements of our health care structures. Therefore, it is not surprising that for centuries *the physician-patient relationship* is under examination and various themes from within this relationship are considered time and time again. During the last century, a Copernican revolution has taken place within this relationship: the traditional paternalist model with an omniscient and beneficent doctor has been abandoned in favour of a relationship where the patient's position is consolidated by the move towards more patient autonomy. At the same time, the intimacy of the patient-relationship suffers from the increasing technologisation of health care. In this first part of the book, various authors will bring the physician-patient relationship into perspective. In the first three texts, the framing of the physician-patient relationship in different European cultural contexts is considered, while the following three texts more closely examine some of the basic concepts involved.

In day-to-day practice, the ethics of the physician-patient relationship is a recurrent theme. In the following case of Denise various issues arise that the authors will subsequently elaborate in the following chapters.

An 85 year-old woman, Denise, suffers from a CVA (cerebrovascular accident) which left her partially paralysed (hemiplegic). Besides this, Denise is unable to speak (aphasia) and her swallow reflex is impaired. Because of the CVA, Denise is hospitalised. When her condition is stabilised, she is transferred to the hospital's geriatric department. Without much consultation, artificial feeding and hydration is administered. However, it soon becomes clear that Denise feels uncomfortable with this nasal drip providing the artificial feeding and hydration. She pulls the nasal drip out three times. For medical reasons, however, she is not eligible for a gastrostomy. Besides her CVA-related condition, Denise suffers also from Parkinson's disease. Given the fact that she receives adequate nutrition, her condition can be stabilised and there is a reasonable life expectancy.

During her active life Denise has always been an active and independent woman. She is unmarried and two nieces and a nephew are her only close relatives. The family expresses the wish that Denise's comfort needs to be guaranteed and that her life should not be artificially extended. The relatives claim that before her admission to hospital Denise expressed the wish that she would rather be dead than completely dependent on the care of others. After Denise had pulled out the nasal drip for the third time, the family confirmed her unanimous wish to withdraw artificial feeding and hydration. The family's position is, however, contested by several parties: Nurse A, the social worker and a nephew. Nurse A is a member of the team of caregivers that is responsible for Denise since her admission into the hospital's geriatric department. She believes that the family's decision is based upon their particular interests since their aunt Denise is very well-off. The social worker concerned with the follow-up of Denise's financial situation, cannot exclude these motives either while Denise's nephew has confided to Nurse A his discontent with the wish of Denise's two nieces to terminate the artificial nutrition and hydration.

The attending physician is more inclined to follow the family's wish because she is convinced that the family's wish coincides with Denise's own wish. It is agreed upon that Denise will be asked whether she wishes the artificial nutrition and hydration to be continued or not. When asked by the attending physician, Denise indicates by acquired sign language that she wishes the artificial nutrition and hydration to continue. In accordance with Denise's demand, the physician decides to resume the artificial feeding and hydration. The family reacts with dissent and does not accept that the hospital staff ignores their wish to stop the artificial feeding and hydration. The family members subsequently threaten to move their aunt to the nursing home where no artificial nutrition and hydration will be administered.[1]

The case of Denise consists of various questions and difficulties that the physician-patient relationship is faced with. These issues have to be brought up for discussion and are the object of further ethical reflection in the following chapters: the character of the physician-patient relationship; the manner in which justice is done to the patient's autonomy by the introduction of the concept of 'informed consent'; the various interpretations of autonomy and

---

[1] For a more extensive version of this case, see C. GASTMANS, *Towards an Integrated Clinical Ethics Approach: Caring, Clinical and Organisational*, on p. 81-102 of this volume.

their limits; the necessity of complementing patient autonomy with other concepts such as the concept of care. We invite the reader to take this case description as a referential example in order to apply the different cultural approaches inside the European tradition.

1

THE ETHICS OF THE
PHYSICIAN-PATIENT RELATIONSHIP

The Anglo-American Approach in the European Context

Reidar K. Lie

1.1. The Standard Autonomy Model

It is a remarkable fact about the development of medical ethics from
the 1960s until today that there has been a dramatic shift from a
position where it was taken for granted that the physician knows
best, to a position where much greater emphasis is put on the
patient's treatment preferences. This shift is evident with regard to
physicians' attitudes towards disclosing a cancer diagnosis. For
example, a 1961 survey showed that almost 90% of cancer physicians
reported that their usual policy was not to tell their patients that
they had cancer.[1] The survey was repeated in 1979, and it showed a
complete reversal in attitudes over this 20 year period. 90% of the
physicians reported that their usual policy was to tell their patients
that they had cancer.[2]

One common way of justifying the new approach is to claim that
patients have a right to make their own treatment decisions, referring to the basic value of patient autonomy. However, it is immediately obvious that physicians should not respect all choices made by
patients.

---

[1] D. OKEN, *What to Tell Cancer Patients: A Study of Medical Attitudes*, in *The Journal
of the American Medical Association* 175 (1961) 1120-1128.
[2] D.H. NOVACK, R. PLUMER, R.L. SMITH, H. OCHITILL, G.R. MORROW & JOHN M. BENNET,
Changes in Physicians' Attitudes toward Telling the Cancer Patient, in *The Journal of the
American Medical Association* 241/9 (1979) 897-900.

Consider the following case:

> *A thirty-eight-year-old man with mild upper respiratory infection sud-*
> *denly developed severe headache, stiff neck, and high fever. He went to an*
> *emergency room for help. The diagnosis was pneumococcal meningitis, a*
> *bacterial meningitis almost always fatal if not treated. If treatment is*
> *delayed, permanent neurological damage is likely. A physician told the*
> *patient that urgent treatment was needed to save his life and forestall*
> *brain damage. The patient refused to consent to treatment saying he*
> *wanted to be allowed to die.*[3]

Very few, if any, physicians would respect this person's treatment
choice. The reason is that this patient is not competent to make his
own decisions. Respect for autonomy only requires that the choices
of patients who are competent to make their own decisions, are hon-
oured. Judgements about which patients are competent to make
their own decisions therefore become crucial. There is what might be
called a standard analysis of competence.[4] Judgements about a
patient's competence to make decisions involve the following:

1) Competence is a threshold concept. There cannot be degrees of
   competence. A patient is either competent to make a decision, or
   not. One reason for this requirement is that a competency judgement is the basis for deciding what type of moral principle to
   employ. If the patient is judged to be competent to make his own
   decisions, it automatically follows that his decision should be
   respected. If the patient is judged to be incompetent one has to
   use another decision rule.

2) Even though competence is a threshold concept, competency
   judgements have to be linked to a particular decision. One person
   may be competent to decide what she wants to eat for dinner, yet
   not be competent to make complex financial decisions affecting
   her future.

---

[3] B. MILLER, *Autonomy and the Refusal of Lifesaving Treatment*, in *Hastings Center Report* 11/4 (1981) 22-28.

[4] Cfr. P.S. APPELBAUM & T. GRISSO, *Assessing Patients' Capacities to Consent to Treat-ment*, in *The New England Journal of Medicine* 319/25 (1988) 1635-1638; J.F. DRANE, *Competency to Give an Informed Consent. A Model for Making Clinical Assessments*, in *The Journal of American Medical Association* 252/7 (1984) 925-927; L.H. ROTH, A. MEISEL & C.W. LIDZ, *Tests of Competency to Consent to Treatment*, in *American Journal of Psychiatry* 134/3 (1977) 279-284.

3) When deciding about who is competent for what decisions, one has to take the consequences of the decision into account. If the consequences for the patient are potentially serious, one has to use a strict standard of competence. If the consequences of the decision are trivial, one can use a more lenient standard.

4) The criteria used for competency judgements have to do with how the patient is processing information. For example: is the patient able to understand the information? Does the patient understand the consequences of the various alternatives?, etc.

Consider the following case:

> *A forty-three-year-old man was admitted to the hospital with injuries and internal bleeding caused when a tree fell on him. He needed whole blood for a transfusion but refused to give the necessary consent. His wife also refused. Both were Jehovah's Witnesses, holding religious beliefs that forbid the infusion of blood. The patient's wife, brother and grandfather were present to express his strong religious convictions. The grandfather said that the patient 'wants to live very much ... He wants to live in the Bible's promised new world where life will never end. A few hours here would nowhere compare to everlasting life'. ... [The patient] was conscious, knew what the doctor was saying, was aware of the consequences of his decision, and had with full understanding executed a statement refusing the recommended transfusion.[5]*

This case involves a conflict between the physician's obligation to do what she thinks is in the best interests of the patient (saving his life) and her obligation to respect the patient's choice. However, in the standard analysis of this case one would focus exclusively on the mental capacities of the patient: does he understand that he might die from his condition? How stable is his religious belief? If one decides that the patient truly does not want a blood transfusion, then he should not be treated.

This model of the physician patient relationship takes for granted that physicians should respect the choices made by competent patients. This, of course, has never meant that patients can demand any treatment they want. Issues such as the costs of treatment or whether the treatment violates other social norms will still have to

---

[5] B. MILLER, *op.cit.*

be taken into consideration. But, if no such issues are involved, a patient's decision should be respected, even if that choice means that the patient receives a treatment the physician believes is not in the patient's best interest.

It is probably fair to say that an ethics of autonomy, as it is outlined above, underlies much of current bioethics thinking, as it has developed primarily in the US, with regard to the ethics of the physician-patient relationship. While this thinking has many attractive features, there are also a number of important problems associated with this approach which we would now like to address.

1.2. Difficulties with the Autonomy-Model: Informed Consent in Different Countries

The first problem has to do with its applicability to countries outside of the US. Let us examine this issue by way of how informed consent requirements are dealt with in different countries. In the US, many states have come to accept the so-called 'material risk' standard, or the 'reasonable person' standard. According to this standard, a physician has a duty to disclose 'material risks' associated with the planned procedure. A 'material risk' is a risk a reasonable person would want to know before making a treatment decision. This standard contrasts with a 'professional standard' according to which a physician is obliged to disclose such information that 'a reasonable physician' would disclose. If it can be shown that it is the practice of a reasonable physician not to disclose a certain piece of information, according to this latter standard, a physician would have no obligation to disclose that information.[6] It can be argued that the material risk standard is more in line with an ethics based on patient autonomy. According to the professional standard, it is up to the physicians to decide what information they think is relevant for patients. According to the reasonable person standard, a physician has a duty to ascertain what ordinary reasonable people would want to know

---

[6] L.J. MILLER, Informed Consent: I, in The Journal of the American Medical Association 244/18 (1980) 2100-2103; ID., Informed Consent: II, in The Journal of the American Medical Association 244/20 (1980) 2347-2350; ID., Informed Consent: III, in The Journal of the American Medical Association 244/22 (1980) 2556-2558; ID., Informed Consent: IV, in The Journal of the American Medical Association 244/23 (1980) 2661-2662.

before making treatment decisions. In this way, the shift from a professional standard to a material risk standard is in line with the general shift within medical ethics from an ethics based on paternalism to an ethics based on patient autonomy.

The problem is that the courts of European countries have not followed the US courts in this matter. In the UK the material risk standard has been explicitly rejected.[7] The February 1985 decision in the case of *Sidaway vs. The Board of Governors of the Bethlem Royal Hospital and the Maudsley Hospital* affirmed that:

> *The only effect that mention of risks can have on the patient's mind, if it has any at all, can be in the direction of deterring the patient from undergoing the treatment which in the expert opinion of the doctor is in the patient's interest to undergo. To decide what risks the existence of which a patient would be voluntarily warned and the terms in which such warning, if any, should be given, having regard to the effect that the warning may have, is as much an exercise of professional skill and judgment as any other part of the doctor's comprehensive duty of care to the individual patient, and expert medical evidence on this matter should be treated the same way.*

One can find similar judgements in other countries, such as for example Sweden and Norway. Cases such as these underscore a common criticism of modern bioethics. A number of commentators have claimed that there are important differences in the values accepted in different countries or in different cultures. In the US, according to these commentators, there has been an excessive focus on autonomy as the overriding value.[8] A closer examination, however, reveals that the situation is more complex than that. German courts, for example, accept a subjective standard, which is even more in line with patient autonomy than the US standard. According to this standard, one is obliged to provide the information that a particular patient would want, not just a 'reasonable patient'.[9] One should also note the discussion in *Münchener Medizinische*

---

[7] R. SCHWARTZ & A. GRUBB, *Why Britain Can't Inform Informed Consent*, in *Hastings Center Report* 15/4 (1985) 19-25.

[8] See e.g. the papers in the 14/5 (1984) issue of the *Hastings Center Report*.

[9] For a discussion of this, see D. GIESEN, *International Medical Malpractice Law. A Comparative Law Study of Civil Liability Arising from Medical Care*, Tübingen, 1988 and J. SHAW, *Informed Consent: A German Lesson*, in *International and Comparative Law Journal* 35/4 (1986) 864-890.

Wochenschrift in 1996 showing the range of opinions in a European country.[10] There are actually quite a number of empirical studies which have addressed this issue, and it is worth giving a short overview of some of these. It is readily apparent that there is not a pattern of autonomy in the US, or even in the West in general, and a pattern of community in other countries.

One might, for example compare studies on what physicians disclose to patients in terms of DNR status (Do-Not-Resuscitate status). In the US, it has been found that only 19% of patients who were resuscitated had discussed this with their physicians prior to the episode of cardiac arrest, whereas 68% of the physicians had formed an opinion about the wishes of the patient.[11] A study carried out in Sweden about the same time found that DNR decisions were almost never discussed with patients.[12] A later study in Sweden, although employing somewhat different methodology and being carried out a decade later, found that cardiac resuscitation had been discussed with 33% of the patients.[13] These three studies, in other words, do not warrant the conclusion that autonomy is the dominant value of the US alone. They do, however, demonstrate the general trend towards patient participation in decision-making in all countries. In another case, although it was found that most patients who were to undergo colonscopy wanted information, most physicians did not think that providing such information was necessary.[14] Among women undergoing surgery for breast cancer in Italy, it was found that only 47% of the patients had been told that they had cancer[15], and in in Germany

[10] J. ZANDER, *Für eine Aufklärung über Diagnose und Prognose soweit wie möglich*, in *Münchener Medizinische Wochenschrift* 134 (1996) 412-415; E. WETZELS, *Gegen eine Aufklärung über Diagnose und Prognose soweit wie möglich*, in *Münchener Medizinische Wochenschrift* 134 (1996) 416-419; H.L. SCHREIBER, *Aufklärung – Rechtlicher Zwang zur Wahrheit?*, in *Münchener Medizinische Wochenschrift* 134 (1996) 424-426.

[11] S.E. BEDELL & T.L. DELBANCO, *Choices about Cardiopulmonary Resuscitation in the Hospital. When do phsysicians talk with patients?*, in *The New England Journal of Medicine* 310/17 (1988) 1089-1093.

[12] K. ASPLUND & M. BRITTON, *Do-Not-Resuscitate Orders in Swedish Medical Wards*, in *The Journal of Internal Medicine*, 228/2 (1990) 139-145.

[13] R. LOFMARK & T. NILSUN, *Do-Not-Resuscitate Orders: Should the patient be informed?*, in *The Journal of Internal Medicine*, 241/5 (1997) 421-425.

[14] J.S. MARK & H. SPIRO, *Informed Consent for Colonoscopy. A Prospective Study*, in *Archives of Internal Medicine* 150/4 (1990) 777-780.

[15] P. MOSCONI, B.E. MEYEROWITZ, M.C. LIBERATI & A. LIBERATI, *Disclosure of Breast Cancer Diagnosis: Patient and Physician Reports (Interdisciplinary Group for Cancer Care Evaluation, Italy)*, in *Ann. Oncol.* 2/4 (1991) 273-280.

in the 1970s it was found that an overwhelming majority of patients wanted to be informed about all possible risks of procedures (43%) or the most important ones (49%). Only 8% did not want any information.[16] One should note, however, that at least two studies have found that there are differences between Northern and Southern Europe[17], and yet another study has indeed confirmed the standard view on the differences between the US and Europe.[18] If we go to non-western countries we find a similar picture. In India it has been shown that patients there too want to be informed and are dissatisfied with the information provided[19], and a study in Japan concluded that although most physicians agreed that information should be provided to patients, this was often not done.[20] One commentator has also noted a general trend towards patient participation in Saudi Arabia.[21]

These examples from different countries paint a complex picture and suggest that it may not be the case that differences between different cultures are important when it comes to decision making in medicine. It suggests that there may be forces within medicine itself that determine what ethics predominate in the physician-patient interaction.

1.3. Difficulty with the Autonomy Model: the Conflict with Clinical Medicine

A number of empirical studies have shown that, even in the US, the ethics of patient autonomy is alien to medical culture, and has in

---

[16] L. DEMLING & H. FLUGEL, *Wie steht der Patient zur Aufklärung des Ärtztes?*, in *Deutsch Medisch Wochenschrift* 100/31 (1975) 1587-1589.

[17] O.O. THOMSEN, H.R. WULFF, A. MARTIN & P. SINGER, *What do Gastroenterologists in Europe tell Cancer Patients?*, in *The Lancet* 341/8843 (1993) 473-477; J.L. VINCENT, *Transfusion in the Exsanguinating Jehovah's Witness Patient: The Attitude of Intensive Care Doctors*, in *European Journal of Anaesthesiology* 8/4 (1991) 297-300.

[18] C.B. HOFFMASTER, M.A. STEWART & R.J. CHRISTIE, *Ethical Decision Making by Family Doctors in Canada, Britain and the United States*, in *Social Science and Medicine* 33/6 (1991) 647-653.

[19] T.G. SRIRAM, K.V. KISHORE KUMAR, M.R. JAYAPRAKASH, R. SRIRAM & V. SHANMUGHAM, *Informed Consent: A Study of Experiences and Opinions of Utilizers of Health Services from India*, in *Social Science and Medicine* 32/12 (1991) 1389-1392.

[20] H. HATTORI, S.M. SALZBERG, W.P. KIANG, T. FUYIMIYA, Y. TEJIMA & J. FURONO, *The Patient's Right to Information in Japan: Legal Rules and Doctor's Opinions*, in *Social Science and Medicine* 32/9 (1991) 1007-1016.

[21] D. YOUNG, P. MOREAU, A. EZZAT & A. GRAY, *Communicating with Cancer Patients in Saudi Arabia*, in *Ann N Y Acad Sci* 809 (1997) 309-316.

general not been accepted by clinicians as a basis for their patient interactions. I shall here only mention two such studies. The President's Commission carried out an extensive empirical study of informed consent (President's Commission 1982-1983). Its conclusion was that informed consent is absent from the clinic. It is worth quoting at length from their report:

> We thus undertook to study number of different treatment settings staffed by a range of health care professionals who performed a variety of diagnostic and therapeutic procedures. We hoped to learned what patients are told about particular diagnostic, therapeutic and experimental procedures and by whom (...) we sought to understand how much patients understand, and how their level of understanding is tied to the foregoing variables in the disclosure process; whether patients are perceived by health care providers as capable of understanding (...) This was a rather grand – if not grandiose – research program. However, despite the fact that we have gathered literally reams of data on about 200 patients, 35 doctors, 20 nurses, and countless family members, in a handful of different clinical settings, we have been unable to answer most of the questions we posed for ourselves. This inability amidst a mountain of relevant data is, we think, not a problem of our research strategy. The explanation is simple: informed consent is largely absent from the clinic: it is almost exclusively a creature of law. This is, to some extent, an oversimplification of our findings. But for rhetorical purposes, it is close to the mark. In fact, information is sometimes provided to patients, and patients sometimes make decisions. But when this happens, and it does not very frequently, the explanation for it most likely does not lie in law, but in medical custom. And we are convinced that this medical custom is deeply ingrained and to date has not experienced much change under the influence of law.[21a]

Renée R. Anspach carried out a 16 month fieldwork in two neonatal intensive care units, one associated with a university hospital and the other associated with a 1000 bed County Hospital in the same US state.[22] In the course of this fieldwork she observed a number of treatment decisions with regard to non-treatment decisions for newborn children. From this fieldwork she draws a number of conclusions important for the understanding of the physi-

---

[21a] PRESIDENT'S COMMISSION FOR THE STUDY OF ETHICAL PROBLEMS IN MEDICAL AND BIOMEDICAL AND BEHAVIORAL RESEARCH, *Making Health Care Decisions. A Report on the Ethical and Legal Implications of Informed Consent in the Patient-Practitioner Relationship*, Washington DC, 1982.

[22] R.A. ANSPACH, *Deciding Who Lives. Fateful Choices in the Intensive-Care Nursery*, Berkeley, 1993.

cian-patient relationship in general. Anspach's research confirms that the ideal in medical ethics of the physician giving neutral information to the patient, and the patient then deciding, is seldom fulfilled in actual practice. In most cases, the physicians have made a decision, and the task of the staff is to make the parents accept the decision, in a process Anspach calls 'producing assent'. This is in stark contrast with the ideal that the treatment staff should present the alternatives to the parents who then independently this decide what to do. This does not mean that never happens. Anspach gives the following example of a physician who lets the parents decide:

> *Before we finish, there are two things I want to mention. The first is that sometimes the parents want to hold the baby before he dies, to say good-bye. If you want to do this, we can let you be alone with the baby. We encourage you to do this, but we don't want to pressure you in any way. If not, we can call you when the baby dies. We are here to support you in any way and to respect your wishes. Another thing is, since we want to honor your wishes, sometimes parents prefer that their baby not suffer for a long time, and we will turn off the ventilator that is keeping him alive. Other parents prefer for us to continue to support the baby until he dies. It's entirely up to you.*

Even if Anspach did find cases where the physicians in this way let the parents themselves take responsibility for their decisions, she claims that this happens very rarely. In most cases it is decided what should be done and the physicians see it as their responsibility to make the parents come to accept the decisions. A number of mechanisms are used to achieve this.

Firstly, the unit's staff discusses the cases without the parents being present and before information is given to the parents. Only after the cases have been discussed and a decision reached are the parents involved. This means that the parents are only presented with a subset of the alternatives that were discussed by the staff during their meeting. The uncertainties or disagreements present among the staff are not presented to the parents.

Secondly, the prognosis of the child is often presented to the parents in such a way that the parents will follow the advice given by the physicians. If the physicians want to withhold treatment, the possibilities for survival are, for example, not mentioned. Furthermore, the physicians refer to their expert knowledge, which is difficult to challenge, and they often refer to the possibility that continued treatment will only prolong the suffering of the child. This is of course difficult to challenge.

> *Appeals to expert authority are only one of a number of practices that staff employ to encourage parents to agree to decisions to terminate life support. Other devices commonly used in termination decisions include reviewing test results (thereby appealing to the authority of technology); noting that the baby has failed to improve; assuring the parents that the nursery has done everything in its power to try to help the baby; letting the parents know that the baby is being kept alive by artificial means; either informing the parents of the staff's decision or recommending termination of treat- ment, rather than presenting the parents with options; and finally, closing the discussion with a statement about the moral consequences of keeping the baby alive – that is, prolonging his or her suffering. ... Although pro- fessional constructions shape parent's decisions, so powerful is the public acceptance of expert authority that few parents offer resistance.[23]*

Anspach also analyses how the staff deals with situations where they disagree with the parents concerning which treatment is the best for the child. She claims that physicians and nurses use certain strategies to convince the parents in those cases where there is dis- agreement. I cannot refer to all of these here. Let me only mention what Anspach calls 'psychologising'. Physicians and nurses refer to certain psychological theories about how having a child in a neonatal intensive care unit destroys the natural ties between a mother and child, and that parents go through a mourning process with a series of predictable stages. As a result of this the parents will not be able to evaluate the situation of the child objectively, and it is neces- sary that the health care staff takes responsibility. If the staff disagrees with the position of the parents, they look for signs of the above- mentioned psychological mechanisms, which justifies their disre- garding of the parents' desires. Other types of psychologising are also used. If parents ask too many questions, they are called 'intel- lectualisers' or it is claimed that they have an "almost pathological need to know".[24] Anspach illustrates and documents these claims by a number of cases from her participant observations.

From the results of empirical studies such as these it should be evident that the ideal of an ethics based on patient autonomy is

---

[23] *Ibid.*, p. 97-98.
[24] *Ibid.*, p. 145.

absent from what one finds in actual clinical decision making. There are, however, also some theoretical problems with an autonomy-based ethics.

1.4. Difficulties with the Autonomy Model: Theoretical Problems

There are problems with regard to justification of an autonomy-based medical ethics. The usual justification is in terms of rights. Human beings have a right to make their own choices. This includes a right to make foolish choices or choices that are bad for oneself. If an action only affects that person, he or she should have a right to decide for her or himself. As we have seen above, however, not all choices are protected in this way. Only those choices which are made by competent people, or in Joel Feinberg's terminology, only those choices which are voluntary, are protected. Dan Brock has argued forcefully that the requirements of voluntariness and competency lead to contradictions if anti-paternalism is based on a rights approach.[25]

If we accept a rights-based justification of anti-paternalism we would need a threshold conception of competency. People are either competent to make decisions or they are not. The alternative would be a relativist conception of competency, where competency to make decisions comes in degrees. The question we need to ask, according to Brock, is what the justification is for a threshold conception of competency. That is, why is it that we would not want to respect choices made by incompetent people in this sense, and how do we justify the level where we would distinguish between competency and non-competency. Well, the most natural justification would be that we set the level at a point where we make sure that patients are not exposed to avoidable and unnecessary harm. This is, of course, the reason why, in the standard analysis, competency judgements depend on the consequences of the decision for the patient. Similar arguments can be brought against Feinberg's conception of involuntary choices. Involuntary choices are those choices that are not fully rational, that are based on faulty information or reasoning processes. Again, we make judgements of involuntariness on the basis of a

---

[25] D. BROCK, *Paternalism and Promoting the Good*, in R. SARTORIUS (ed.), *Paternalism*, Minneapolis, 1983.

desire to protect the individual against bad choices, choices that will harm that person.

Brock asks:

> Why should our basic moral principles prevent others from inter-
> fering with our doing what we want when their interfering would
> be for our own good, while our doing what we want would be con-
> trary to our own good?[26]

Brock is quick to point out that the acceptance of this argument does not mean that rights-based language would not be appropriate in other areas of moral life, nor does it mean a general acceptance of consequentialism.

If we accept that the basis for acceptable interventions in patient decision-making is in some sense what is in their best interests, it becomes important to supply a theory of what is in the best interests of patients. Brock is very clear that we still need some kind of protection against interference in a person's actions based on what he calls 'ideal theories' of the good. These are theories of the good that may be accepted by some people, based on certain religious convictions for example, but which are not shared by all. It would be wrong if a physician intervenes in the treatment choices made by patients based on ideas about the good life that are not widely shared in society.

Let me try to sum up the arguments so far. We have noted a dramatic shift from an ethics based on paternalism to an ethics based on patient autonomy. However, we have found that there are a number of difficulties associated with the autonomy approach: it has not really been adopted as a basis for clinical decision making and there are a number of theoretical difficulties associated with the approach. The question now is, where do we go from here?

1.5. Alternatives

During recent years there has been a growing dissatisfaction with the dominant approach to bioethics. In this approach, the task of bioethics is to analyse difficult cases by referring to principles such

---

[26] *Ibid.*, p. 247.

as autonomy, beneficence and justice. One should note, however, that autonomy does not have a supreme place; it is thought to be important to balance the various considerations embodied in the principles accepted, although patient autonomy does have a central place in the analysis. The criticism against this approach has been a criticism of the central role of principles in the model. I shall here only briefly examine some of these alternative approaches and indicate my main criticism of these alternatives.

The critics have pointed out that approaches where principles have a prominent place cannot account for important aspects of moral actions. When dealing with a patient, a health care worker relates to an individual patient and her or his particular needs. The health care worker's main responsibility is to care for the patient, and that which care demands cannot be ascertained from consulting principles but can only be ascertained by regarding the particular needs of this particular patient. Sometimes it would be right to respect the patient's wishes, sometimes not. One would not obtain any guidance as to what to do by consulting principles and attempting to balance them, but would obtain guidance by being concerning with the particular needs of the patient one cares for.[27] Other critics have advocated a revival of casuistry.[28] When contemplating what one should do one would consult paradigmatic cases where one knows what is the right thing to do. Reasoning by analogy one would shed light on the difficult case at hand. Again, not much guidance is obtained by consulting principles.[29]

The problem with alternatives such as an ethics of care and casuistry is that they do not really avoid reference to principles, and when it comes to working with real cases, approaches based on care, casuistry or principlism turn out to be indistinguishable. If an ethics of care or casuistry were going to avoid relativism, they would at

---

[27] N. NODDINGS, *Caring. A Feminine Approach to Ethics and Moral Education*, Berkeley, 1984. For a criticism, see H. KUHSE, *Caring. Nurses, Women and Ethics*, Oxford, Blackwell, 1997. For more on the ethics of care, see also C. Gastmans' contribution in this volume, p. 81-102.

[28] A. JONSEN & S. TOULMIN, *The Abuse of Casuistry*, Berkeley, 1988.

[29] For a discussion of the role of casuistry in bioethics, see e.g. J. ARRAS, *Getting Down to Cases: the Revival of Casuistry in Bioethics*, in *Journal of Medicine and Philosophy* 16/1 (1991) 29-51; ID., *Principles and Particularity: The Role of Cases in Bioethics*, in *Indiana Law Journal* 69/4 (1994) 983-1014; R.B. MILLER, *Narrative and Casuistry: A Response to John Arras*, in *Indiana Law Journal* 69/4 (1994) 1015-1019.

some point have to refer to some general moral principles. Principlism has always maintained that one needs to work back and forth between general principles and the particulars of the cases, and does not rule out extracting general lessons from particular cases where our intuitions about what is the right thing to do are strong and unanimous. A number of commentators have voiced similar critiques against these alternative approaches.[30]

Recently, a number of workers in the field have advocated approaches based on hermeneutics, interpretative theories, or the use of narratives. The virtue of these approaches is also supposed to be the attention to the contextual elements of the decision-making situation.

Jan Marta, for example, criticises what she calls the 'current dominant disclosure model'. In this model "informed consent is comprised of a sequence of acts done *onto* an other: the physician discloses information *to* the patient, the patient consents *to*, or refuses to consent *to*, the physician's execution of the intervention; the physician performs the intervention *on* the consenting patient"[31]. Based on a narrative perspective of Ricoeur, instead, "informed consent is the narratively structured action of patient and physician in relation to each other ... The action of informed consent is open to constant reinterpretation (...). As a Ricoeurian post-structural narrative hermeneutic, informed consent is an experiential, expressive, and interpretative action with sensitivity to the individual, relational, and cultural factors at play in the process and the outcome".[32] There are two problems with this narrative account of informed consent. First, if it only means that one should take into account individual, cultural and relational issues, there is really no conflict with the dominant model. The best work on informed consent has always stressed these elements.[33] Second, if the stress is on the constant reinterpretation of the decision making situation, there is again the

---

[30] J.F. CHILDRESS, *Narrative(s) versus Norm(s): A Misplaced Debate in Bioethics*, in H.L. NELSON (ed.), *Stories and their Limits. Narrative Approaches to Bioethics*, London, 1997; T. TOMLINSON, *Perplexed about Narrative Ethics*, in *Ibid.*.

[31] J. MARTA, *Toward a Bioethics for the Twenty-First Century: A Ricoeurian Post-Structuralist Narrative Hermeneutic Approach to Informed Consent*, in *Ibid.*, p. 205.

[32] *Ibid.*, p. 204, 209.

[33] See e.g. C.W. LIDZ, P.S. APPELBAUM & A. MEISEL, *Two Models of Implementing Informed Consent*, in *Archives of Internal Medicine* 148/6 (1988) 1385-1389.

danger of relativism. The whole point of stressing patient autonomy and informed consent is that the patient should be able to make certain claims against the physician. This approach denies explicitly the idea of a constant reinterpretation, and that is an advantage that should not be given up lightly.

1.6. The Way Forward

I think it is fair to say that, in spite of, or maybe because of, the success of modern medicine, medicine today is in a crisis. This crisis is reflected in major studies undertaking in two countries, one in the North and one in the South of Europe. I shall argue that an examination of the purposes and results of these studies will indicate some of the important tasks of bioethics in the future.

The Norwegian Medical Association has embarked upon an ambitious research project on the working and living conditions of physicians in Norway, called *The Norwegian Research Program on Physician Health and Welfare*. One part of this research program is a questionnaire study sent out to about 9000 of Norway's 14.000 physicians during the Spring and Summer of 1993. The questions concern issues such as job stress and satisfaction, social relations and illness behaviour. One part of the questionnaire concerns health ethics and health policy issues.

One central hypothesis in the project is that a loss of professional autonomy is associated with perceived problems in the daily work of physicians. Professional autonomy is defined as "the ability of the physician to decide diagnostic and therapeutic procedures without approval or challenge by others"[34]. Loss of professional autonomy can be caused by demands from patients, politicians and bureaucrats and other health professionals. Specifically, one factor that is mentioned is the move from a paternalistic medical ethics to an ethics based on patient autonomy, and bureaucratic control over physicians' working conditions.

One publication from the project reparted on the communication pattern between physicians, whether it was based on solidarity,

---

[34] O.G. AASLAND, *Legekårsundersøkelsen: Faglig autonomi*, in *Tidsskrift for den norske lægeforening* 113 (1995) 1155.

mutual support and respect or selfishness and competitiveness.[35] It was found that the communication atmosphere varied significantly with professional autonomy, measured by six questions about the extent to which the respondent could decide about his own working speed, order of tasks, work organisation, plans and taking days off. The authors conclude that the effect of recent retrenchment programmes in the Norwegian health services should be evaluated not only with regard to short-term cost-benefit, but also job satisfaction and professional development. If it is correct that these programmes have increased stress and reduced autonomy and professional energy, they have probably also jeopardised the communication atmosphere needed to secure the continuity of knowledge in the medical profession, i.e. in the long run, they may prove hazardous to the quality of medical care. Similarly it was found that loss of professional autonomy was associated with perceived job stress,[36] and time pressure.[37]

In a series of articles in Norwegian newspapers and professional journals, researchers associated with this project have pointed to perceived problems in today's interaction between physicians, the general public and patients. Patients expect the impossible from physicians and demand treatments for conditions where no treatments have shown documented effects, and demand treatments for life-problems or trivial conditions. As a result more and more areas of life become medicalised. Examples include oestrogen replacement therapy for post-menopausal women.

This study has been funded by the *Norwegian Medical Association* and is carried out by the *Association*. The picture that emerges from the study is a profession under siege, primarily by bureaucrats who demand impossible work schedules and by patients who demand unjustified treatments from the physicians. All of this causes job dissatisfaction, stress, and perhaps even illness and death among

---

[35] V. AKRE, E. FALKUM, B.O. HOFTVEDT & O.G. AASLAND, *The Communication Atmosphere between Physician Colleagues: Competitive Perfectionism or Supportive Dialogue? A Norwegian Study*, in *Social Science and Medicine*, 44/4 (1997) 519-526.

[36] E. FALKUM, *Psychosocial Environment and Job Satisfaction*, in Ø. LARSEN & B.O. OLSEN (eds.), *The Shaping of a Profession. Physicians in Norway,Past and Present*, Cambridge, 1996.

[37] E. FALKUM, E. GJERBERG, D. HOFOSS & O.G. AASLAND, *Tidspress blant norske leger*, in *Tidsskrift for den norske loegeforening*, 117 (1997) 954-959.

physicians. The answer to these perceived problems is that patients and bureaucrats should cease to place these demands on physicians and that the physician's professional autonomy should be restored.

In 1994 the *Catalan Council of Health Sciences Specialties* carried out a survey on future scenarios for the health professions.[38] The survey used discussion groups and the delphi technique to elicit opinions from the participants. A number of interesting observations emerged from this study, paralleling, to a certain extent, the rationale and findings of the Norwegian study. For example, a high number of participants expressed that there is a certain dissatisfaction among the population regarding the health care system. Some pointed out the disparity between the ideals of the profession and the demands of the patients, reflected in the following comment: "it will be difficult to balance professional authority and consumers' preferences. Many patients have a consumerist attitude and many professionals a defensive one."

One of the central obstacles to be overcome is the professionals' perception of losing authority and effectiveness, reflected in the following quotation in the study: "the increase of managers, geared only by economic criteria has created an unsustainable climate for clinicians. Professionals think they are not being listened to." Another quotation sounds as follows: "the technological progress and the working conditions in the health care organisations have contributed to the professional loss of self-esteem and their proletarisation." This perception has direct parallels in the Norwegian study, as indicated above. Other identified concerns were that "the citizen perceives the lack of resources but thinks that social and acceptable mechanisms have not yet been established for its efficient and effective use "resulting in a lack of consensus between citizens, professionals and the Administration about the use of resources". Finally, what is called for is a "re-establishment of trust between doctors and patients based on the perception of professional honesty". This is partly because "traditional values are being challenged, but the new frame of relationships has still to be created".

The picture presented in these two studies is that there are serious problems in the health care professions today. This is partly the

---

[38] M. RODRIGUEZ & C. PILA (eds.), *Professional Competencies on Health Sciences*, Barcelona, 1997.

result of dramatic developments towards increased patient autonomy. There is no question that there are serious difficulties with the
traditional paternalistic medical ethics, and we all welcome developments which have resulted in physicians being more honest and
open about such issues as cancer diagnoses. In general, most of us
would also agree that it is important to involve the patients in the
decision-making process. Changes that increase patient empowerment are generally a good thing. However, as we have seen, despite
the emphasis on patient autonomy, the physician-patient relationship is still dominated by the authority of the physician, and it has
led to increased physician dissatisfaction. I would like to suggest
that an abandonment of an autonomy-based ethics will in fact facilitate patient empowerment. This may sound paradoxical, and needs
some explaining.

Let me more clearly identify the fundamental defect of an autonomy-
based ethics. In this approach, the physician is told to ask whether a
patient is competent to make decisions. My central claim is that the
autonomy model, by focusing on the decision making capacity of the
patient, puts the emphasis in the wrong place if the aim is to increase
patient decision making power. The problem with this approach is that
it will always be possible to come up with reasons why a particular
patient is not competent to make choices in a particular situation, if the
physician does not agree with the decision reached by the patient, and
hence patient empowerment and autonomy are not advanced.

Another reason for the increased level of frustration among health
care workers is found in the conflicts arising out of different organisational arrangements in the health care system. Physicians feel that
their decision making authority has been taken over by managers
and economists, to the detriment of patients. Politicians, on the other
hand, see the need to contain costs and this necessarily involves con-
straining the decision making authority of the physicians. Some of
these conflicts involve the questioning of traditional roles of the state
in the provision of health care services, and the introduction of the
market mechanism, although no satisfactory organisational solution
for the health care system has yet emerged.[39]

---

[39] D.W. LIGHT, Lessons for the United States: Britain's Experience with Managed Competition, in J.D. WILKERSON, K.J. DEVERS & R.S. GIVEN (eds.), Competitive Managed Care.
The Emerging Health Care System, San Francisco, 1997. For more on the organisation of
health care systems, see Part three of this volume, p. 245-340.

Paradoxically, these problems in the current health care system also point to a solution for the problems in defining what the tasks of bioethics should be. What emerges is that there is an urgent need to create new models of the physician-patient relationship. One of the central tasks of bioethics should thus be to propose and test out such new models. Interestingly, this view of ethics is to a certain extent in agreement with some thoughts on ethics expressed by Michel Foucault. Foucault emphasised that there is an intimate connection between knowledge and power, and by analysing how knowledge is used to regulate behaviour we can both understand what is going on and move forward. Such a perspective, I believe, would be immensely fruitful for understanding what is happening in the physician-patient interaction. In addition, in his later works, Foucault tried to develop a new way of doing ethics. Ethics is not about following certain rules or principles, or systematising arguments, in the way it is done in the dominant US bioethics tradition. It is about developing new forms of living, what he called 'ascesis', in a somewhat different sense than usual: it is to work on oneself in order to transform oneself and to invent new forms of being. Transferred to the physician-patient relationship, this would mean to actively explore and experiment with new ways of modelling this relationship, but without a program, or a script to follow. This does not, even according to Foucault, mean relativism, as the following quotation makes clear:

> I think that one of the great experiences we have had since the last war is that all those social and political programs have been a great failure. We have come to realise that things never happen as we expect from a political program, and that a political program has always, or nearly always, led to abuse or political domination from a bloc – be it from technicians or bureaucrats or other people. But one of the developments of the sixties and seventies, which I think has been a good thing, is that certain institutional models have been experimented with without a program. ... being without a program can be very useful and very creative, if it does not mean without a proper reflection about what is going on, or without very careful attention to what is possible.[40]

Although this is only a sketch, I do believe it is a promising way forward. Some of the recent developments within patient advocacy

---

[40] M. FOUCAULT, *Ethics, Subjectivity and Truth*, in P. RABINOW (ed.), *The Essential Works of Michel Foucault. Vol. 1*, New York, 1997, p. 172.

organisation, in particular in the areas of HIV and breast cancer, strengthen this analysis. It is also clear, however, that a lot more theoretical work needs to be done, before we have a satisfactory alternative. What this alternative approach suggests, however, is that much of the current controversy concerning the foundations of bioethics misidentifies the fundamental problem. The problem is not whether principles or particulars should have pre-eminence, or about whether autonomy is the fundamental value or not. All approaches, when it comes down to an analysis of real cases, recognise that both are important, and most of the time, if not all the time, analyses of cases based on rival approaches are indistinguishable. Rather, the fundamental problem is that we are in urgent need of new models of the physician-patient relationship as well as of the role of the physician in the health care system. If this is a correct identification, the main challenge for bioethics is to be creative and propose new models, many of which will not be sustainable, but that is a necessary part of the process.

THE PHYSICIAN-PATIENT RELATIONSHIP WITHIN THE HEALTH CARE STRUCTURE

A Latin-European Approach

Francesc Abel & Francesc Torralba

2.1. Introductory Remarks

When we analyse the physician-patient relationship, we must take into account different considerations. First of all the physician-patient relationship has not been strictly homogeneous throughout history, but rather it has acquired different forms according to differing cultural, social, economic, technological and political developments. In the West, the Hippocratic-Galenic paradigm is essential for understanding the structure of such a relationship throughout its history: Classic Antiquity, Middle Ages, Renaissance and Enlightenment. Greek humanism and afterwards Christian philosophy form the theoretical framework of medical praxis and health care throughout Western civilisation. In the East, on the contrary, the theoretical background should be sought within the cultural context of Hinduism, Buddhism and Confucianism. Secondly, the praxis of such a relationship is closely linked to certain preconceptions of a philosophical and religious nature regarding the figure of the physician and his or her function. Effectively, praxis and theory are very close, although not always explicit. This means that, to understand certain practices, we need to investigate the theoretical foundations of such forms, and, vice versa, in order to understand certain theories we need to analyse their practical implementation. Thirdly, the patient-physician relationship is strongly connected with the health care systems wherein they function. Truly, the patient-physician relationship does not occur in a neutral place, but rather in an institution, whether private or public. At the macro-level, the institution shapes some important aspects that highly influence the micro-level, that is, the interpersonal relationship between the patient and the physician.

The purpose of this contribution is to analyse the physician-patient relationship in the Mediterranean sphere, in the perspective of theoretical and practical transformations of the health care system at both the structural and the policy level.[1]

2.2. The Acknowledgement of the Patient as a Moral Agent

Western Europe has already completed the change from medical paternalism to an attitude of careful attention and respect for the patient, recognised as a moral autonomous agent. This change is the greatest achievement for the physician-patient relationship in the last thirty years. The fact is that for the first time in history, patient rights will be recognised and respected from the very moment of illness or admission to a health care institution.

At the very beginning of this – in T.S. Kuhn's terminology - paradigmatic mutation, we should single out the year 1969, when for the first time the rights of the patient where recognised in a public document. The acknowledgement of every patient as a moral agent, that is, as a subject with his or her rights, constitutes an extraordinary new development in health care involving consequential changes in professional roles. The medical profession had to redefine its role sharing responsibilities with the health care team in a new theoretical framework. Paternalism was strongly criticised. The patient has become conscious of his rights and his or her co-responsibility, and that means he or she requests to be treated as a person and not as a

---

[1] On this subject see: R. GONZALEZ. *La nueva dimensión dela relación médico-paciente en nuestros días*, in *Bioética*, La Habana, 1997; A. GOIG, *Ética de la relación médico-paciente*, in *Cuadernos del programa regional de la Bioética* 1 (1995) 79-90; J. DE LAS HERAS, *La relación médico-paciente*, in *Manual de Bioética General*, Madrid, 1994; A. ALBARRACÍN, *La relacióm médico-paciente, fundamento de la étic médica*, Valladolid, 1987; P. LAÍN ENTRALGO, *Técnica, ética y amistad médica*, in J. GAFO (ed.), *Fundamentación de la bioética y manipulación genética*, Madrid, 1988; D. GRACIA, *La relación médico-paciente en España, balance de los últimos veinticinco años*, in *Todo Hospital* 62 (1989) 23-26.

passive object. Nowadays, paternalism is considered as an exaggeration of the beneficence principle that carries with it the discredit of the patient and his or her fundamental rights: the patient was treated like a minor, as a subject unable to practice his or her autonomy.[2] Criticism of medical paternalism does not involve, however, the rejection of the beneficence principle, but it refers to a disproportionate and exaggerated understanding of beneficence.

As a consequence of their critique on the excesses of medical paternalism, we find certain North American bioethicists defending a radicalisation of the principle of patient autonomy. Such a position is as open to criticism as the previous one on paternalism, and obeys the law of the pendulum, i.e. a comprehensible but unjustifiable reaction to the despotic paternalism that characterised health care before.[3] It should be clear, however, that the autonomy principle has intrinsic and extrinsic limits and should always be closely linked to the beneficence principle.

The confrontation between Hippocratic praxis on the one hand and patient rights legislation on the other, has nevertheless provoked a strong uneasiness among physicians. Legal suits filed against physicians are encroaching upon that very field which the physicians consider exclusively their own: their conduct with their patients.

It may therefore be evident that the equilibrium advocated by Edmund Pellegrino between extreme paternalism and radical autonomy is much more acceptable for physicians who, for the most part, find it difficult to accept what to some non-physicians seems ideal, i.e. complete radical autonomy.[4] Such a position would imply that the physician becomes a servant of the patient's wishes. Only a denial of the true meaning of medical praxis as a profession and vocation could bare such a position.

---

[2] See G. Díaz Pintos, *Autonomía y paternalismo*, Cuenca, 1993.

[3] See G. Díaz Pintos, *Algunos problemas conceptuales del paternalismo y la autonomía moral individual...*, in *Cuadernos de Bioética* 8 (1997) 157-163.

[4] See E. Pellegrino, *To be a Physician*, in N. Abrams & M.D. Buckner (eds.), *Medical Ethics: A Clinical Textbook and Referency for the Health Care Professions*, London, 1983, p. 95-97.

2.3. The Limits of Principlism

Although a new orientation in bioethics, principlism has been strongly criticised in the last decade, since there are many practical problems that cannot be solved through the simple implementation of principles. First of all, the reality of medical practice is charac- terised by a strong complexity. The notion 'complexity' is used today in experimental sciences, physics included, to indicate the plurality of factors and interdependences in which data and events are situ- ated. Contemporary medicine includes many areas: scientific research, technological development, social services and the thera- peutic moment itself, embodied in the physician's person and his/her relationship with the patient. Almost every ethical problem in medicine emerges from the clinical setting. It is therefore neces- sary to highlight the different perspectives of medical practice and the complex origins of ethical problems, precisely because the doctor in his praxis summons the pedagogical and scientific itinerary and places himself in the psychological and social-organisational constraints of the health care system and its limits.

Secondly, the patient is without any doubt autonomous, how- ever not in an absolute sense. In medical practice, it is not easy to determine the competence or incompetence of someone who has to make particular decisions. Although different psychological criteria do exist to determine the degree of autonomy and the person's responsibility, clinical experiences make clear how difficult it is to determine the limits of the autonomy principle. A systematic application of the principle of autonomy without any experiential interpretation may violate the respect for other principles, such as beneficence.

Thirdly, it is impossible to ignore the hermeneutic pluralities in which the four principles are applied. All of them have been the object of many intellectual and practical interpretations. Such a hermeneutic plurality is clear when one compares different bio- ethical projects that have been developed in Europe and the US over the last twenty years. The semantic load of terms like benefi- cence, autonomy, justice or equity changes according to the tra- dition, training and presuppositions of an ethical and/or religious approach to bioethics. Effectively, the conceptualisation of the four principles is not new in philosophical language, but rather they function within the heart of Western ethics to promote a plurality of interpretations of each of the principles. That means that in some cases, the coincidence of principles is merely nominal, since upon a deeper investigation, many differences in interpretation would appear. When we try to understand the meaning of beneficence, justice and the fair distribution of resources, a philosophical background of interpretation emerges, whether of a utilitarian, deontological, consequentialist or teleological nature.

Fourthly, there is the problem of inconsistency among the principles. In applying them to particular problems, the fundamental principles can contradict one another. Such a strained relationship between principles can be exemplified by the possible contradiction between the principle of beneficence and the principle of respect for autonomy. According to the beneficence principle, the physician has a duty to use all available technological and human resources at his disposal to benefit the patient. The intention of the physician's action has to be always and under any circumstance directed towards the patient's good. Nevertheless, the free and responsible patient can reject the therapy proposed by the physician. In such a case there is an obvious conflict between the principle of respect for autonomy and the principle of beneficence. The only possible solution is then to give priority to only one of them.

We may therefore conclude that we have to place principlism in the right perspective: without denying their explanatory and illustrative value, the quoted principles ought to be considered as reference issues, as grammatical means, but never as obvious *formulae* to solve problems. After all, with the same grammatical rules many different texts can be written.

2.4. The Patient-Physician Relationship as a Relationship of Friendship

Essential for the value transmission during the training of physicians are both the climate of trust and the focus on an integral knowledge of the patient. What are the main features of the contemporary patient-physician relationship? It is very difficult to draw up a global perspective, since this relationship changes according to cultural, political and social contexts. According to Pedro Laín Entralgo, the patient-physician relationship can be understood in three different ways.[5] First, there is always a dominant partner in the relationship, namely the physician who is an expert in curing the illness of the patient. Secondly, the patient-physician relationship can be understood as a co-operative relationship. Von Weizsäker, for instance, uses the word *Weggenossenschaft* to refer to the physician-patient relationship. According to him, the physician and the patient should be like fellow-colleagues who walk the same way, towards the same end which is the healing of the ill person. As colleagues, therefore, they help each other. The essence of this companionship is the co-operation at the service of the achievement of the same goal, whether it is political, scientific or industrial. To a certain degree, medicine is a matter of technicality, but these technical aspects are only pre-conditions for the functioning of the patient as a subject. No physician can think about amending the body of an ill person as if it were a car engine. Thirdly, according to Laín's perspective, the physician-patient relationship is a particular type of friendship. Thus, the relationship is not only one of companionship, but even more one of friendship. This approach is very typical for the Latin culture in Europe.

2.4.1. *Entralgo's Contribution to the Ethical Reflection on the Patient-Physician Relationship*

Laín Entralgo argues that friendship as a pattern of the patient-physician relationship requires five activities: "well–saying, i.e. saying well about him; beneficence, i.e. doing well with him and to him; well-trust, i.e. sharing confidently with him and entrusting to him something about oneself by means of words or actions, so that it belongs only to him; cooperation, i.e. trying to achieve the accomplishment of an objective good, to all or to many."[6] He concludes that a correct medical relationship must be friendly, because benevolence, well-saying, beneficence, well-trust in its two facets, confidence and trust, and cooperation are part of it and because it is a relationship established between two unique persons.

The principles that ought to regulate the doctor-patient relationship according to Laín are, firstly, "the principles of the *maximum technical capacity*. Secondly, principles of *beneficence*: do as well as

[5] P. Laín Entralgo, *Técnica, Ética y amistad médica*, in J. Gafo (ed.), *Fundamentación de la bioética y manipulación genética*, Madrid, 1988, p. 115.

[6] P. Laín Entralgo, *Antropología Médica para clínicos*, Madrid, 1985.

possible that what should technically be done. Thirdly, the principles of *goodness and authenticity*: careful adherence to the natural and personal good of the patient."[7]

According to Mediterranean philosophy, a therapy must always be *eros, agapè* and *filia* at the same time. Like any other human action based on vocation, the vocation of the therapist is *eros* in action, namely desire for its own perfection and for the perfection of the world deriving from it. But at the same time, the action of the therapist brings with it the change of *eros* into *agapè*, into love directed towards that which is deficient and needy, *in casu* the patient's condition. Deficiency and need are then changed into the joyful plenitude of health. This love must also be translated into creative acts of *filia*, friendship between the care-taker and the care-giver. Therefore, the therapeutic action is always at the same time *eros, agapè* and *filia*.

As a patient, the ill person is in some manner a disabled being and the physician is the person who can help him out of his disablement. In this setting, the physician has pre-eminence over the patient. Otherwise, his technical relation with the patient will be defective. On the other hand, neglecting the patient as a person will bring about the same problem. This clearly indicates that the patient is not inferior to the physician although he needs the doctor to recover from his illness. In sum, the Mediterranean perspective holds that the adequate medical relationship is *per se* friendly. Medical friendship integrates therefore clearly three virtues: benevolence, beneficence and confidence.

2.4.2. *The Characteristics of the Friendly Relationship*

We affirm that this relationship is different from neighbourly love and companionship. It is a kind of relation through which the doctor seeks the good for the patient. Laín considers two kinds of relationships according to two kinds of illness, namely acute and chronic illness. When illness has taken over a person's life (and becomes a chronic disease), it is far more than a biographical parenthesis but rather affects his very being, then the health care professional has to enter into a confidential relationship with the patient. This particular friendship relies on a medical friendship that is capable of bridging the gap between illness and technique.

---

[7] P. LAÍN ENTRALGO, *ibid.*, p.137.

Laín holds that this friendship is necessary for the perfection of the medical act, and following the American sociologist Riesman, he distinguishes two kinds of persons from a psycho-sociological perspective: 'inner-directed' persons and 'other-directed' persons. The first kind of persons are those who organise and direct their own life. When visiting a doctor they just ask him to give a prescription, but not to intervene in their life. It is a quite common attitude that cannot be kept up indefinitely, because it passes over the fundamental fragility and weakness of our human life. Even the most inner-directed person will need a different kind of relationship than the one built up between provider and consumer. We can see this clearly manifested in cases of chronic disease where the patient has to decide together with the physician and his team about his/her life. For a satisfactory praxis of medicine and nursing, a mutual communication is necessary in these cases. This can only be achieved if a type of peculiar friendship, i.e. medical friendship, is established between the patient on the one hand, and the attending physicians and nurses on the other hand.

Is medical friendship possible within the technological and impersonal world of medicine today? This is not only one of the most pressing problems for medicine, but concerns humanity itself. We must recognise that this is a rather difficult challenge, which requires large economic as well as overwhelmingly technical and personal resources and an adequately educated patient. Our contemporary society is undergoing a transformation of values. This axiological transformation is also affecting the physician-patient relationship. The relationship based on mutual trust between physician and patient has been replaced by one of distrust. The medical profession has turned from a position of privilege as the guardian of health into a totally different situation. The physician has become part of a health care structure in which different professionals are active. Moreover, it is society that determines the defining characteristics of health. Such distrust dramatically erodes friendship since friendship is based on trust. This distrust is the product of the fragmentation of medicine into medical specialities on the one hand, and of the de-personalisation of health care assistance on the other hand. The lack of respect for the autonomy of patients increases the distrust in doctors and their profession.

To recover this friendship a change in attitude is necessary: an attitude of respect towards the patient is strongly needed. Necessary conditions for the recovery of the friendly character of the physician-patient relationship are then tactfulness and kindness in manners, knowledge and acknowledgement of patient rights, the capacity to accept the existence of different hierarchies of values, and professional competency. Apart from that, we can understand that the origin of the social distrust of professional praxis might have its basis and could also be interpreted in terms of the power that results out of the physician's technological superiority. The recovery of the medical friendship is a 'must' in order to avoid that the doctor's image is turned into that of a "biocrat".[8]

The last judgement of Laín is hopeful: he considers it socially and historically possible to develop medical friendship within our health care structures. That implies a re-humanisation of the assisting praxis and a return to the Hippocratic sources, where the doctor is a good man, an expert in science and the art of healing. That is what Hippocrates already meant when he distinguished four characteristics in the healing art: never to disturb, when possible to ease, sometimes to heal and always to reassure. This statement is going radically against the writings of Michel Foucault, who considers the physician-patient relationship as a power relationship where the doctor has the power and the patient is merely an instrument at the service of that power. Foucault made use of the master-slave dialectic structure developed by Hegel in his *Phenomenology of the Spirit* (1807). In such circumstances, the patient has no power to decide, since both the power and knowledge are in the doctor's hands. As suggestive as these essays on power relationships between doctor and patient may be, we consider Hegelian explanations as not consistent with today's reality. Rather, we must recognise that the medicalisation of society and the political and social control of our health care structures have left practically no power for the doctor. In other words: even in a world where medicine is almost omnipresent, doctors have never had so little power in Western Europe as they do have now. Diego Gracia describes this as follows: "Does the doctor still have power today? As an individual subject, less than ever. But medicine as an institution enjoys today a power greater than it could have had in any previous period along its history (...) Never before has

---

[8] F. ABEL, *Actituds i valors en Medicina*, in N., *Quinzè congrés de metges i biòlegs de llengua catalana*, Lleida, 1996, p. 167-172.

the individual's life been so medicalised. Never before was medicine's power greater."[9]

2.5. Conclusion: Friendly Relationship in the Health Care System

The medical friendship must be promoted in the context of our health care system. However, two characteristics of the current social structure of health care seem to make this very difficult to realise. The first one is impersonalisation; the other specialisation. Impersonalisation implies the absence of warmth in the human relationship. Here, the circumstances under which the doctor and the patient meet certainly do influence the medical relationship.[10] It makes a difference whether they meet in the patient's own house or in a clinic, on the battlefield or in a university polyclinic. Centralisation and bureaucratisation are almost unavoidable consequences of the health care globalisation process. Assisting activities are rationalised and become routine in order to allow that professionals can be rotary and moved across the services of the health care centre. It is beyond doubt that the dehumanisation of health care is linked to a more general trend in society. After all, the sphere of health care is not radically autonomous. The same social forces that contribute to the dehumanisation of our economic and political environments have analogous consequences in health care. We are living in a world marked by dehumanisation and medicine is not immune to this trend. Another important factor is connected with the fact that medical services are increasingly becoming instruments in the hand of political leaders and their particular interests. These conflicts of interest constitute major obstacles for an adequate health care management. Because of this, only a forceful ethical reaction will be able to counter the dehumanisation of medicine.

Another factor that endangers the medical friendship is the interdisciplinary structure of medicine. The progressive subdivision and hyper-specialisation of medical knowledge causes epistemological, didactic and ethical problems. Above all, the global perspective, the holistic conception of the patient and his or her personal history fades away. If medicine wants to be ethically acceptable, it is necessary

---

[9] D. GRACIA, *El poder médico*, in N., *Ciencia y poder*, Madrid, 1987, p. 167.

that the patient is approached as a person. Here, the difficulty is to make the person aware of being a subject and not an object of diagnosis. To solve this internal fragmentation of the patient, cooperation is increasingly important as well as coordination between health professionals. Moreover, the family doctor, who helps to read the data given by the patient and who summarises them, must, by means of dialogue, recover in the patient the consciousness of his own condition and the capacity to make decisions that are inalienable to him.

This evolution has led to the translation of the friendly relationship in a societal acknowledgement of patient rights, also in Latin European countries. These rights, today brought together in several declarations, were unthinkable under a medicine controlled by paternalism, understood as the relationship between father and son or master and servant. The fact that doctors were said to have duties mildly acknowledged that they owed something to the patient, but this did not imply the recognition of (legal) rights. The recognition of the rights of the patient is the result of a slow evolution. According to Elizari "many factors contribute to develop the social sensibility towards patient rights. Individuals are learning more about medicine, which then increases their expectations. Their wishes, then, turn into requirements... The increase in the number of malpractice cases indicates that we must clarify the content of patient rights. Scientific research by government institutions and private organisations makes it evident that there is a need for the protection of human subjects. The image of Nazi science demands the creation of a legal framework to avoid such practices in the future. Since the power of medicine is always increasing, this must be compensated by an increasing awareness and participation of the patients."[11]

One of the instruments for the exercise of patient rights has become the right to give 'informed consent'. The acceptance of this right is the result of the convergence of many elements: the sensitivity to freedom that has progressively pervaded social life, the movement for human rights, the development of consumers' rights, the reaction against abuses committed in medical praxis or research, changes in the understanding of the doctor-patient relationship and

[10] M. SANCHEZ BAYLE (ed.), *El sistema sanitario en España*, Madrid, 1996.
[11] F.J. ELIZARI BASTERRA, *Bioética*, Madrid, 1991, p.217.

the increasing importance of research on human subjects. From a regulatory point of view, informed consent has also become relevant in Latin countries, what may be illustrated by various legal initiatives. Therefore, the medical relationship as friendly relationship is fully operational and implemented in the regulation of health care.

HISTORICAL ANALYSIS OF THE CONCEPT OF AUTONOMY FROM A GERMAN PERSPECTIVE

Alberto Bondolfi

3.1. Introduction

The principle of autonomy constitutes a large component of the contemporary bioethical discussion but is at the same time subject to
different interpretations and to a lively debate on its normative
reach. In this essay, we will try to present how this category and its
related ethical principle are interpreted and applied in the philosophical and theological literature in general, and in German biomedical ethics in specific. In keeping with the spirit of this body of
work, we will try to present the problems and discussions in such a
manner as to be accessible to non-specialists and this even with no
direct knowledge of German language and culture.

We start from the very general hypotheses according to which the
principle of autonomy is the subject of a large semantic confusion,
i.e. confusion related to the meaning of the word and even contami-
nated by a series of misunderstandings linked to its undifferentiated
use and application. We would therefore like – in the framework of
this contribution- not really to support a precise thesis but to participate in a sort of operation of 'semantic disinfection' so that the
debate on the principle of autonomy at least gains in clarity.

Our discussion is ordered in the following manner: first, we will
present the historical roots of the concept of autonomy highlighting
the specific contribution of German philosophy. Second, we will present the history of the same category as part of the history of the
medical literature. Next, we will have to examine the use of the term
autonomy within the current discussions on biomedical ethics in the

German-speaking environment. Finally, our essay is an attempt to determine the issues and criticise the normative reach. The whole will stay fragmentary and not at the service of the work of the specialist, but will be rather general in order to give an idea of the fundamental debate.

3.2. A Historical and Philosophical Retrospective

The philosophy of the age of Enlightenment has through the concept of autonomy expressed most precisely and coherently its ideal of human liberty and morality. The work of Immanuel Kant is here foremost. Autonomy represents the essential condition from which true morality derives. According to Kant and the Kantian tradition, there is no true ethics if it is not justified by autonomy.[1] Without willing to enter here into an interpretation of details, one has to notice that, in Kant's view, what has to be proclaimed as necessarily autonomous is first and foremost the human will, which, through the light of practical reason, is capable of deciding the moral good without referring to any external reality.

It is this quality of the will that renders human activity moral. It permits at the same time universalisation, i.e. the general validity of the norms linked to this kind of will. The autonomy of practical reason has thus first and foremost an anthropological connotation, i.e. it is a characteristic of all human life; even before being a quality of a philosophical discipline such as ethics. Since man is free with regard to the laws of nature, he can become a legislator in the reign of the finites. By the same token he only submits to the maxims he has established, declaring them to be a possible basis for a universal

---

[1] Before Kant, the term was mainly used in a legal context, indicating the organisational independence of a personal or collective subject. One notes a certain movement in the evolution of legal and philosophical ideas towards an universalisation of the concept of autonomy. For more on the historical-philosophical evolution, see R. POHLMANN, *Autonomie*, in *Historisches Wörterbuch der Philosophie*, Vol. I, Basel, p. 701-719; G. ROHRMOSER, *Autonomie*, in *Handbuch der philosophischen Grundbegriffe*, Vol. I, München, p. 155-176; G. ROHRMOSER, *Autonomie*, in *Religion in Geschichte und Gegenwart*, Vol. I, Tübingen, p. 788-792; E. AMELUNG, *Autonomie*, in *Theologische Realenzyklopedie*, Vol. V, Berlin, p. 4-17.

legislation.[2] The moral act is autonomous in the sense that Kant wishes to eliminate all influences whether they stem from sentiments or innate tendencies or even from the exterior via parental, political or religious authority. The will only obeys the practical reason and its arguments and is therefore autonomous.

Thinking about this autonomy of the will leads Kant to highly rigid consequences more so than to those elements of emancipation common in 17th century morality.[3] Let us reflect on some practical examples, which are indirectly related to the field of medical ethics: suicide, self-mutilation, and subterfuge for which Kant contemplates only highly rigid responses. These prohibitions or norms in the name of the autonomy of the will are to be considered as absolute and therefore not linked to considerations regarding their effect or consequences, be they factual or ideal.

The post-Kantian tradition gives the concept of autonomy a larger significance. Without wanting to settle here on the more correct interpretation as testified to by the 19th century neo-Kantian literature, one can nevertheless detect some meaning among the most well known opinions.

The idea of the self-determination of a human being, who decides autonomously, liberates himself progressively from the idea that the will is autonomous in relation to external tendencies, such as instincts or sentiments, but only in relation to moral law. Moreover, one always thinks that a human being also determines his goals and values, to which he or she refers. One, therefore, progresses from the 'autonomy of ethics' ('Autonomie *des* Ethischen') to the 'autonomy from ethics' ('Autonomie *aus dem* Ethischen'). John Locke and John Stuart Mill gave the most valuable testimony on the description of autonomy as self-determination. In reference to Locke and his rather implicit acceptance into the literature on bioethics, I can easily agree with Hubert Doucet's exegesis, which maintains that "the Lockian

---

[2] For a global reconstruction of Kant's concept of autonomy, see numerous publications: A. GUNKEL, *Spontaneität und moralische Autonomie: Kants Philosophie der Freiheit*, Bern, 1989; W. MARTIN, *Bestimmung und Abgrenzung von Ethik und Religion: ein Beitrag zur Diskussion über das christlichen Proprium in der Ethik unter besonderer Berücksichtigung der Philosophie Kants*, Pfaffenweiler, 1990; M. SCHEFCZYK, *Moral ohne Nutzen: eine Apologie des Kantischen Formalismus*, St Augustin, 1995; C. SCHILLING, *Moralische Autonomie: anthropologische und diskursstheoretische Gründstrukturen*, Paderborn, 1996.

influence is particularly obvious in the fact that the physician or the researcher can be compared to the sovereign who decides for his subjects, but does not understand their interests; if he understood them then he would not protect them, since he gives priority to his own interests. John Locke immediately joins this pragmatic American vision on autonomy. The English philosopher was pre-occupied with protecting the rights of the individual against the interference by the state. The autonomy favoured by American bioethics is in a large degree identical to the negative liberty of classic liberalism, i.e. to protect the individual against intervention by others."[3] Doucet's interpretation is also valid for German bioethics. Even in this cultural environment, this variation on the liberal tradition is stronger than the one derived directly and exclusively from Kant. The same observations can be made for the philosophy of Mill, which takes on the liberal ideal of autonomy but in an explicitly utilitarian context,[4] undoubtedly, contrary to Kant, but filled with the preoccupation common to all Enlightenment philosophy of liberating the individual from intervention exterior to the subject regarding decisions which fall within the competence of the individual.

From the 19th century onwards, philosophers talked increasingly about another meaning of autonomy where different forms of knowledge are autonomous and methodologically independent. This autonomy is called *Eigengesetzlichkeit* in German.[5] Since the French and English language do not have two specific terms to define autonomy as *Eigengesetzlichkeit*, one has to pay particular attention to the significance of the term autonomy, if possible, to distinguish this term explicitly from the meanings used here above. In this context autonomy is first and foremost medical knowledge with links to other forms of knowledge. Such an interpretation of autonomy has consequences for one's opinion about the relationship between medical and ethical knowledge.

---

[3] H. DOUCET, *Au pays de la bioéthique. L'ethique biomédicale aux Etats-Unis*, Genève, 1996, p. 67.

[4] J.S. MILL, *On Liberty*, Harmondsworth, 1976.

[5] Cf. this terminology see M. HONECKER, *Das Problem der Eigengesetzlichhkeit*, in *Zeitschrift für Theologie und Kirche* 73 (1976) 94-103; A. HAKAMMIES, *Der Begriff Eigengesetzlichkeit in der heutigen Theologie und seine historischen Wurzeln*, in *Studia Teologica* 24 (1970) 117-129.

3.3. The Principle of Autonomy throughout the History of Medical Thinking

Autonomy, which was one of the most original expressions of Enlightenment philosophy, did not have a great reputation in the past theoretical medical literature.[7] The relationship between physician and patient was conceived from the perspective of a paternal bond wherein the will of the patient was not a significant element.[6] The only sphere which seems to introduce a new perspective into this relationship may be 'private life'. One could ask whether the relationship between physician and patient could be reduced to this social sphere. Compared with the English literature since the 17th century, this problem has not been further developed in German medical literature.[7-8]

One can therefore observe a *different sensibility* in the cultural environment of the German language and that of the English language in their respective perception and application of the word 'autonomy'. This is the case even when it comes to discerning the implications for the field of medicine. The Germanic culture tends to accept the principle of autonomy as an *Abwehrrecht*, i.e. the right not to be prohibited from making our own choices; whereas the Anglo-American culture tends to interpret the same principle as an *Anspruchsrecht*, i.e. as a positive and subjective right.

3.4. The German Contemporary Debate on Autonomy in Biomedical Ethics

The contemporary debate confirms on the one hand a difference in sensibility but on the other hand exceeds it, insofar as the influence of the Anglo-American bioethics has become more obvious in the works written in German. Tristram Engelhardt's *The Foundation of*

---

[7] On medical paternalism, see B. ELGAR, *Le concept du paternalisme. Aspects philosophiques et empiriques*, Genève, 1998.

[6] For the reconstruction of the history of this terminology in the domain of medical thinking, see D. GRACIA, *Fundamenti de bioética*, Madrid, 1989.

[8] Gracia evokes for example the debate between Gregory and Cullen at Edinburgh University on the freedom to practice medicine in D. GRACIA, *Fondamenti di bioetica. Sviluppo storica e metodo*, Cineisello Bisamo, 1993, p. 175 ff.

Bioethics[8] has been the subject of debate in Germany despite the fact that this book has not been translated in its entirety.[9] Because of the influence of this author, it is a common conviction in German literature that since it is impossible to obtain a consensus on common moral values which have absolute value therefore one has to orient oneself to the principle of autonomy, which guarantees everyone an equal respect of his or her own personal opinions. This minimalist ethics has its opposing view in the fact that *explicit consent* becomes the moral condition of all medical interventions. No physician could intervene against the patient's will without offending the autonomy principle. But this does not mean that the physician becomes the executor of the patients' wishes and options in Engelhardt's and other German ethicists' opinion.[10] The autonomy principle only requires that one does or does not do as promised in an explicit contract.

In line with European cultural environments, the German bioethics literature also demonstrates the improper but very widespread use of the term autonomy in a purely descriptive sense. In this context, predominately to be found in literature for paramedical personnel, one asserts that a patient is autonomous in the sense that he/she is capable of organising his/her physical needs without assistance from external forces. This interpretation of autonomy can perhaps be accepted in principle but one has to be aware that if this is the case, it looses all moral pertinence because everyone should be able to enjoy this kind of autonomy for as long as possible during his or her lifetime. One could never reproach a person if at some point in time this should be partially or completely lacking. Autonomy in this sense, while organising one's physical existence, has no moral quality and is therefore sufficiently insignificant from an ethi-

---

[9] H.T. ENGELHARDT, *The Foundation of Bioethics*, New York – Boston, 1986.

[10] A partial translation in German has been made: *Die Prinzipien der Bioethik*, in H.M. SASS (ed.), *Medizin und Ethik*, Stuttgart, 1989, p. 96-117. For comment and a critique, see K. STEIGLEDER, *Die Begründung des Moralischen Sollens. Studien zur Möglichkeit einer normativen Ethik*, Tübingen, 1992, p. 36.

[11] See the opinions by N. Hoester, D. Birnbacher, A. Leist and K.P. Rippe. From among their works, the most representative are : N. HOESTER, *Sterbehilfe im säkularen Staat*, Frankfurt, 1998; ID., *Abtreibung im Säkularen Staat*, Frankfurt, 1995; D. BIRNBACHER, *Tun und Unterlassen*, Stuttgart, 1995; A. LEIST, *Eine Frage des Lebens. Ethik der Abtreibung und künstlichen Befruchtung*, Frankfurt, 1990; K.P. RIPPE, *Ethische Relativismus : seine Grenzen – seine Geltung*, Paderborn, 1993.

cal standpoint which is indicated by the fact that the lack of said autonomy is an indirect request for help from the person who is no longer autonomous.

Another dimension in the German debate on the concept of autonomy is that this category has been at the centre of the ethical-theological debate on the ultimate foundation of moral actions since the 1970s.[11] One should not assume that the German speaking culture is so influenced by the reflections of theological ethics that even the interpretation of autonomy in bioethics is directly influenced by it. Its influence is more indirect. Indeed, in the German as in other European cultural environments, the number of theologians engaged in bioethical research is certainly remarkable. Theology has no monopoly on bioethics but it still makes it presence felt. Those authors who have tried to give a theological pertinence to autonomy can certainly not remain indifferent to its significance in bioethics. On the contrary, understanding the multiple meanings of autonomy and those linked to *Eigengesetzlichkeit*, German speaking theologians are well prepared to receive it in a differentiated and critical manner specifically in the domain of medicine and biology. In general, one can observe that the autonomy principle has been accepted into German bioethics literature, but with some reservations.

In my opinion, the most important limitation on the use of autonomy as a category is specifically connected with the fact that the category has to be respected not only when it is empirically present.[13] Autonomy is a constituent principle of human existence as a whole and not just of its particular manifestations. The partial or even definitive lack of autonomy in minors or in persons incapable of understanding and judgement (incapacitated persons) does not signify, for most German authors, that the principle of autonomy does not apply to them. Such application will have to take into account the specific situation of the individual, where charity and

[12] As introduction to this debate, which takes place mainly among Roman Catholic theologians but also has not left the Protestant theologians indifferent, see A. BONDOLFI, *Autonomie et théonomie: une alternative pour la morale chrétienne? Présentation et évaluation du débat en cours entre moralistes de langue allemande*, in *Recherches de sciences religieuse* 70 (1982) 161-180; ID., *Autonomie et 'Morale autonome'. Recherches en cours sur un mot clef*, in *Concilium* (1984) 155-164.

[13] For more details, see A. PIEPER, *Autonomie*, in W. KORFF et al. (eds.), *Lexikon der Bioethik*, Vol 1, Güterloh, 1998, p. 289-293.

justice replace that which autonomy cannot exercise directly. The German debate on the 'Bioethics Convention' and especially on the article that anticipates the regulation of experiments on incapacitated persons has been sufficiently confused precisely since the convention has not been translated. This has prompted confusion between the term 'incapacitated' and 'handicapped'.[14]

Despite these misunderstandings and confusions, one can at any rate note that the German debate on autonomy has nevertheless gained in clarity, insofar as the different authors more or less defend an application of the same principle. They define it as neither the absolute power of self-determination nor as moral autonomy in the Kantian sense of the term. This is pointed out by Birnbacher: "The principle of autonomy has to do less with moral or metaphysical autonomy in the Kantian sense of the term but rather with self-determination in a political and legal sense. This principle demands respect for projects, ideals, the goals and wishes of others, irrespective of the fact that persons have a duty towards those who make these projects, ideals, goals and desires their own."[15]

3.5. Towards a Global Appreciation

What assessment can be drawn from these few major points in a debate that evidently has not yet reached its conclusion? I will try to formulate some strictly personal comments. First and foremost, one can note that the difficulties that the concept of autonomy encounters in the field of bioethics are linked to the fact that liberal thinking has had objective difficulties of asserting itself in the domain of

[14] For a deeper understanding of the problems raised, see A. BONDOLFI, *Autour de la 'Convention Bioéthique' du Conseil de l'Europe : la discussion en milieu germanophone*, in *Ethica Clinica* 13 (1998) 13-20.

[15] See D. BIRNBACHER, *Welche Ethik ist als Bioethik tauglich?*, in J.S. ACH & A. GADT (ed.), *Herausforderungen der Bioethik*, Bad Cannstadt, 1993, p. 45-67, here p. 54: "Das Prinzip der Autonomie hat weniger mit ethischer oder metaphysicher Autonomie in Kantischen Sinne zu tun, dafür aber mehr mit Sebstbestimmung in einem politischen und rechtlichen Sinn. Dieses Prinzip fordert die Respecktierung der Lebenspläne, Ideale, Ziele und Wünsche anderer, unabhängig davon, ob diese Ziele und Wünsche ihrerseits der dadurch Verpflichtete diese Lebenspläne, Ideale, Ziele und Wünsche seinerseits akzeptiert."

clinical practice and biomedical research. On the one hand, liberal thinking was confronted with the classic paternalism of the physician-patient relationship and on the other hand with the alleged objectivity of scientific knowledge regarding pathologies which will not allow a discussion on the rationality of a clinical decision.

Secondly, autonomy runs the risk of leading to highly dubious normative results when confronted only with itself and abstracted from any relationship – whether harmonious or conflicting – with other moral principles. In ethics in general or bioethics in particular, all argumentative monism can only be pernicious. One can therefore not adequately defend the principle of autonomy without expressing an opinion on its relationship with the other bioethical principles, even if the answers regarding the relationship can and must be multiple. They cannot shy away from the debate on the relationship between the principles themselves.

Finally, one cannot defend the principle of autonomy if we do not conceive the latter in a relational context. All human beings are autonomous insofar as one understands him or herself to be free in relation with external constraints. In distancing oneself from these constraints the human being acts morally. But if one understands him or herself to be autonomous in the sense that he or she is the source and producer of all moral values, then autonomy will transform itself into autarky. Our human existence is autonomous within the totality of mutual relationships and therefore cannot by definition think itself to be absolute. A bioethics which has this constantly in mind, is able to contribute to a solution, even if only partially, to our daily conflicts.

Not only do our relationships set limits and bring significance to our autonomy, but our limitations are also linked precisely to our capacity to become ill and to die. Our preferences and desires find their limitations in this morbidity and mortality. Despite all this, we can and must continue to understand our existence as being autonomous. But if one looks more closely, one will see that the latter cannot exist without solidarity.[16]

---

[16] See A. BONDOLFI, *Solidaretà: un valore cristiano secolarizzato?*, in *Servitium* (1987) 42-62.

4

THE IDENTITY OF THE PERSON

Autonomy and Responsibility

M. Patrão-Neves

The overwhelming technological development that we have witnessed during the last few decades has resulted in an increasing artificialisation of human life. It is possible today, by artificial means, to produce human life (e.g. through reproductive technologies), to sustain it (e.g. transplantation), to prolong it (e.g. resuscitation techniques, life supporting systems), and investments are made now to reinvent it through genetic engineering. Either in a framework of the physician-patient relationship, or in a framework of human experimentation – realms where bioethics thrives, specifically as a biomedical ethics[1] – the artificialisation of human life threatens the identity of the person, either when considering the danger of rendering the person an object or when considering the risk of instrumentalisation of the person.[2] I hold that the identity of the person is that which essentially constitutes man in his universality and which each comes to express singularly.

---

[1] Andre Hellegers introduced the word 'bioethics' (by founding, in July 1971, The Joseph and Rose Kennedy Institute for the Study of Human Reproduction and Bioethics) with the meaning of biomedical ethics, an ethics for the sciences of life mainly considered at the human level (medical sciences), the sense in which it was used later. Earlier, however, Potter had already coined the word "bioethics" to refer to a new discipline, a "science of survival", that would combine the knowledge of biology and the knowledge of human values. This wider meaning, of an ecological dimension, of bioethics, is being recovered lately. Cf. W. REICH, *The Word 'Bioethics': Its Birth and the Legacies of those Who Shaped It*, in *Kennedy Institute of Ethics Journal*, 4/4 (1994) 323.

[2] We refer, obviously, to an invasive intervention of biotechnologies in human life.

The recent enunciation of autonomy as an ethical principle that provides an alternative to the traditional medical ethics principle of beneficence[3], in order to preserve the identity of the human, seems to be insufficient. If it is true that the principle of autonomy contributes decisively to the preservation of human dignity in situations of high vulnerability, it is also true that this concept has suffered a generalised semantic misunderstanding, under which a variety of misuses have proliferated. Besides, the nature and reach of most recent biotechnological developments demand another principle to guide human action, determined supra-individually.

We will demonstrate the need to articulate a vindication of autonomy as indispensable for the constitution of the individuality of each being, along with the demand of responsibility as indispensable for the recognition of the status of our humanity, in view of the construction and safeguard of the identity of the person. If autonomy was initially claimed by Anglo-American bioethics, the affirmation of its insufficiency, the relevance given to responsibility and the enhancement of the articulation of both principles, constitute marks of a European perspective on bioethics, which we intend to develop.

Within this context, we will consider first the nature and meaning of the new powers brought about by biotechnologies as a prelude to the claim of the principle of autonomy as a determination of personal identity. Secondly, we will focus on the object and meaning of the duties enunciated by ethics in its application to life in order to propose the principle of responsibility as indispensable to the definition of person. It will be – as we will show – in the combination of autonomy and responsibility that the identity of the person will emerge.

---

[3] At the reflective level, autonomy and beneficence are generally not in opposite, in spite of great promotors of the principle of autonomy, such as J. Childress and T. Beauchamp, ascribing autonomy the primacy in case of conflict between both principles in J. CHILDRESS & T. BEAUCHAMP, *Principles of Biomedical Ethics*, New York – Oxford, 2001. Edmund Pellegrino and David Thomasma try to overcome such dualism by proposing a 'beneficence in trust' which is based simultaneously on healing as the first and most fundamental obligation of the physician and attending the patient's will in E. PELLEGRINO & D. THOMASMA, *For the Patient's Good. The Restoration of Beneficence in Health Care*, New York – Oxford, 1988, p. 51-58.

4.1. Man, between Power and Duty

Let us, then, dwell firstly on the pair power/duty, already much discussed in the history of philosophy. We will treat this pair under the Jonassian implication that power implies duty.[4] The most recent powers conquered by humanity force us to reflect on the deeply intimate and commonly shared reality, this singular universal which is our identity. However, personal identity is not received but achieved through the assumption of our duties, in a continuous process of self-appropriation. Sculptured throughout the centuries by the chisel of power, the image of itself that humanity has been construing resembles today that of the unbound Prometheus.[5] We should, now, use also the concept of duty which, in its smooth and vigorous touch, shall find the trueness of expression, restoring to humanity the dimension of its threatened being.

4.1.1. *The New Powers (or: the Unbound Prometheus)*

At the beginning, and during the process of its hominisation, humanity gradually freed itself from nature's syncretism by mastering it: detachment from nature led gradually to the consciousness of individual beings. This process of detachment from nature, which converts the natural being into a subject of knowledge, by prolonging itself, has led to progressive human self-consciousness through the establishment of a wider anthropocentrism.[6] The ever-growing power that man has achieved over his surrounding reality has contributed decisively to the image he has formed of himself as a being superior to all others and nature's supreme value – of which the

---

[4] H. JONAS, *Le Principe Responsabilité. Essai d'une éthique pour la civilisation technologique*, J. GREISCH (transl.), Paris, 1990, p. 177-178.

[5] We adopt here the image that Hans Jonas makes present in the preface of *Das Prinzip Verantwortung* when referring to the observation that man has endowed science with new forces so powerful that it constitutes danger to man himself.

[6]This dominant anthropocentrism that characterizes the history of humanity, has been progressively denounced during the last decades as corrupt and detrimental to a holistic view of life that is said to respect the wholeness of life in its diversity and to restitute man his right dimension, in his inalienable reintegration in nature. Such an accusation has been headed mainly by ecology – in its commitment to recover the lost unity between man and nature–, and by environmental ethics – realizing that human action within nature is not divorced from ethical meaning.

western humanistic tradition is the reflection.[7] Today, however, the power at human disposal is of a different nature than the traditional one, which points to a corresponding alteration, of a qualitative order, in the concept that humanity has of itself.

Under the previous historical and evolutionist perspective, the new technological powers conquered by humanity would only correspond to a higher degree of complexity and amplitude of the continual progress of civilisation. This does not justify any significant change in this concept. Instead, it strengthens dominant human traits. However, from the point of view of the analysis of technological progress, transformations are obvious, not only in the extension of their range but also in the nature of their procedure, both in the capacity of their exercise and in the object of their action. Technological power is not limited to the construction and use of objects or means of action and their increasingly efficient application to even vaster realities, in the same manner as traditional technoscientific progress, which has always consisted of the instrumentalisation of means for the achievement of pre-planned ends. For example, through genetics, taken in its applied dimension as genetic engineering, humanity is now capable of intervening at the level of life itself either through artificial production and maintenance, or even through its re-creation. It is at the level of the intrinsic constitution of beings, and not solely upon the external surface of objects, that the power of humanity is exercised now in an undeniable transformation of its nature. From the instrumentalisation of reality, we have advanced to the manipulation of life.

This change in the nature of the power of human action (from instrumental to manipulative) carries also with it a new meaning, since technological progress is no longer just the effort to adapt reality to man's needs, a motivation that traditionally guided technological progress. Rather, it is now the desire to reinvent life, serving various interests in the creation of new needs that themselves will come to justify technological progress. When technology began to develop exponentially in the twentieth century (and thus changing into technoscience), philosophical reflection turned its attention to it,

---

[7] The notion 'humanism' is here understood in its widest acceptation, as expressing essentially a faith in man, assuming his theoretical proportion and his ethical defense.

e.g. Gabriel Marcel and Martin Heidegger. Their common denominator is an understanding of technology as a means to enslave humanity and, in this way, an understanding of the preservation of humanity's being, its identifying essence.

Human action is no longer just transformative but also creative. For that reason its newly acquired power seems to correspond not just to a larger development of the human being, but instead to the usurption of God's prerogative, with Prometheus as humanity's prototype. Consequently, the image that humanity projects of itself is also altered: from the creature to creator, now roaming about in a new world fabricated through the illusion of the absence of limits. And because humanity has been converted from a subject into an object of biotechnology, its identity is put in question by its own new powers. Will this unheard of creative power of man ever equal God's creative wisdom, or will we be doomed to witness our own destruction?

4.1.2. *The New duties (or: The Ethical Dimension of Man)*

It is obvious, not only that the image man builds of himself through his newly acquired power has changed, but also that his destiny is threatened. It is important then, to bring into play another dimension constitutive of the human being. We refer, in particular, to the ethical dimension of humanity, which translates into a sense of duty, through the internal experience of a constraint, or obligation which imposes an 'ought-to-be' or an 'ought-to-do'.

We believe that ethics, or the duty by which it expresses itself, has exercised itself under various modalities in the context of the progress of science or the challenges of power: through the imposition of limits, in a repressive action, determined by fear of the unknown; through the elaboration of rules in a normative action demanded by legal imperatives; through the education of conscience in a formative action required by the ethical dimension of our being. In the specific domain of its application to life, ethics was initially seen as setting limits and appeared as a reaction to the excess of interference by technoscience in human existence. In view of the overwhelming progress of biotechnology, we are witnessing a growing artificialisation of life in general and of the human in particular. Thus, we are also witnessing the multiplication of dangers, more or less foreseeable, relative to the well-being or even survival of man –

aspects that nurture a sense of fear traditionally attributed to the unknown. We do not refer necessarily to a "pathologic fear"[8] – a feeling that in its all-encompassing and dominating expression stunts the will and clouds the mind – even if fear, when nurtured by ignorance, can lead to radical, dogmatic or fundamentalist stands which are generally expressed, in the present domain, by the decision totally to ban certain lines of scientific innovation out of the fear of some of its effects. Today, this stand is still widely adopted, particularly among the media. Scientific advancements are often reported in a sensationalist style that magnifies the risks, which are sometimes not yet objectively determinable, bending reality and intending to win a larger audience. In general, the reported information ends with an appeal to ethics to limit such unruly scientific progress.

Ethics applied to life has appeared also as a demand for reflection about the nature, objectives and implications of biotechnology in general, bringing about a deceleration of the irrepressible dynamism of the latter when forcing it to a confrontation with itself, in its investigations, difficulties and presuppositions. There is no attempt to stop progress but, instead, an effort to promote it by re-orienting it. The most common attitude at this level is the attempt to formulate rules or regulations to shape human behavior, or to enunciate principles that address the issue of the foundation of action.

It is this attitude that led to the establishment of centers for bioethics (the first one appeared in the United States, i.e. *The Hastings Center* in 1969, and *The Kennedy Institute of Ethics* in 1971, which were followed by the creation of many others of the same kind, particularly in Europe[9]) and of Healthcare Ethics Committees. These

---

[8] 'Pathological fear' is an expression used by Hans Jonas to bring to mind the meaning that fear assumes as a starting point of Hobbes' ethics – meaning that he himself contradicts, in spite of stating at the same time fear as the basis for the ethics of the future : "Il ne peut donc pas s'agir ici, comme chez Hobbes, d'une peur de type «pathologique» (pour parler comme Kant), qui s'empare de nous de sa propre force, à partir de son objet (...)" in H. JONAS, *Le Principe Responsabilité*, p. 51. 'Pathological fear' is of a selfish nature, fearing but for itself. Hobbes would say, in his study on passions, that fear makes man aggressive, contributing to his anti-social behaviour. On the contrary, for Jonas fear ('heuristics of fear') constitutes a force to act, expression of courage to assume what frightens them, and also a stimulus to research or search of knowledge, if not of the effects, at least of the possibility of the effects.

[9] Many of the existing European centres for bioethics are now gathered under the European Association of Centres of Medical Ethics (EACME).

committees are either of a restricted scope, such as those of the advisory or research type (in line, respectively, with North-American *Institutional Ethics Committees* and *Institutional Review Boards*) whose various functions are sometimes united in a single committee, as some European countries do; or they are of a national dimension which, in the European model, assume a permanent status.[10]

Meanwhile, the effort to pass from the level of advice to that of law-making is increasing lately, namely through the constitution of ethics committees of an increasingly wider scope. The objective is to give the directives issued by ethics committees the force of law so that they will not stay limited to their traditional consultative function, but will come to assume a deliberative, even legislative function. This process is taken to be absolutely necessary, since only the elaboration of legislation on biotechnological research and utilisation can impose respect for those values recognized as determinant for the preservation of the shared image of humanity. Ethical necessity is, thus, converted into legal obligation, of which the elaboration of the *European Convention on Human Rights and Biomedicine* (1997)[11] is a good example. Simultaneously, the risk of shortening the distance or altogether forgetting the difference between 'bioethics' and 'biolaw' arises, due to the intense commitment that the latter has excited (as expressed in various international meetings and in the numerous projects that seek financing by the European Community) to the detriment of the specificity of the former. In this way, what has been characteristic of the European course would be decried as a progression from the ethical level to the juridical level, in which the foundation of the former frames the ruling of the latter and the second guarantees the observance of the first. This is the most common course in the Anglo-American perspective in which, often, through a casuistic approach, court decisions determine which practice to adopt. The weight of the legal dimension is, then, superior and the reflection is more easily centred at the level of biolaw.[12]

---

[10] See the list of National Ethics Committees in the Appendix 'European Perspectives on Health Care Ethics', p. 345.

[11] The *Convention for the Protection of Human Rights and Dignity of the Human Being with Regard to the Application of Biology and Medecine: Convention on Human Rights and Biomedecine* was elaborated within the Ethics Committee of the European Council, and presented to all state members for signature in April 1997, in Oviedo (Spain).

[12] As an example we could refer to the Karen Quinlan, the baby Jane Doe, and the Tarasoff cases.

Ethics, either as setting limits stimulated by fear, or as enunciating norms to be converted into legislation by law, appears still as a new power opposed to biotechnological power.[13] Yet, ethics cannot be reduced to a counter-power.[14] Its authenticity and legitimacy are at the level of duty or good, in which it is primarily expressed as conscience[15] and is exercised usually as practical wisdom.[16] We refer to ethical conscience as a state of (permanent) vigilance relative to action; and to practical wisdom as a reflective and deliberative capacity over the various concrete situations, always new, in the consideration of action in its intention, nature and consequences. It is at this amplified level of reflection, sensitive to the challenges that biotechnologies offer to action, that one finds the necessary broadening of the object of duty: the consideration of humanity as author and end of morality widens now to consider all beings upon which its protean power is exercised. The whole of nature becomes valued and thus an object of duty.[17] By the same token, duty is now exercised not only in respect of humanity in its unconditional value as moral subject, but is opened up to a wider respect to all forms of life, and thus demands for their protection arise.[18]

[13] Hans Jonas, in his work *Das Prinzip Veranvortung*, refers to ethics as a third level of power: the first refers to a domination of man over nature; the second refers to the loss of domination of man over nature; and the third, exercised over the second level power, refers to the self-limitation of domination. Cf. *Le Principe Responsabilité*, pp. 193-194.

[14] If ethics were a counter-power, a "power over power" – as Jonas says – it would still and always be a tool to have or not have, to use or not use. Our scope, however, is to support that ethics constitutes the essential and specific expression of a human being who, by developing it, achieves fulfilment as a person.

[15] Moral conscience – as a universal and atemporal structure (*a priori*) of being, which manifests itself in the spontaneity of every man to apply moral qualities to his action – has developed two different senses to determine action: the "good" and the "obligatory", according to Ricoeur (P. RICOEUR, *Soi-même comme un autre*. Paris, 1990, p. 199) The first would put emphasis on the perfectibility of being; the second, in the regulation of conscience through norms (See. J.-J. WUNENBURGER, *Questions d'éthique*. Paris, 1993, p. 38-39).

[16] Aristotle's term is *phronèsis* which we want to evoke as the true essence of ethics.

[17] Jonas is a herald of this new dimension (not specifically ecological) of ethics.

[18] Contemporary ethics (and particularly applied ethics) surpasses its traditional boundaries of intersubjectivity and expands in the just measure of the reach of human action. One example is environmental ethics, which extends duty to all living beings in general and also, in some of its tendencies (eco-ethics), to the habitats of the living beings.

In this perspective, in which the ethical dimension is presented as constitutive of the specificity of the human being (the anthropological difference is ethical), one should acknowledge that restrictions of duty on power are not imposed from the outside as something artificial, but are demanded from the inside. Humanity requires such restrictions during the course of its development, as an indispensable condition for the fulfilment of the self and as an obligation of respect for human dignity. In fact there is not, and there cannot be a real contradiction between the exercise of power and the claim of duty. Both constitute inalienable dimensions of the human being which articulate at the level of conscience the domain in which a person can be fulfilled as a moral being in the construction of ones personal identity.

4.2. The Identity of the Person

The relationship of mutual and necessary presence that we have now established between power and duty as indelible traces of humanity's image of itself reflects (correspondingly) on the relationship present between 'autonomy' and 'responsibility'. These are inalienable principles constituting the identity of the person, that is, of that specific character which one acquires through his or her action. In this sense, we can propose that autonomy is an expression of the person's power through which the person affirms itself in its individuality and that responsibility is an expression of duty through which the person integrates and interacts in the community to which he or she belongs. One should stress, once more, the specificity of European bioethical thought which, in its more markedly social and communitarian trend (here exhibited through the application of the principle of responsibility), surpasses the strong individualism characteristic of the Anglo-American perspective. In the convergence of these two principles one finds the identity of the person, that is, the essential unitary trace that characterizes a person as a singular being and that defines him or her as a member of humanity.

4.2.1. *Autonomy (or: About the Power of Humanity)*

Autonomy, designating etymologically the human authorship of the law to which it submits itself, has been through time the dominant trait of the identity of humanity itself and the foundation of its very dignity.[19] Human law ('*nomos*') has appeared beside nature's law ('*physis*') ever since the first forms of society government,[20] and this new order, the human order, tends progressively to separate itself from the order of nature, attempting even to dominate it in the course of history. Mainly, since the anthropological period of ancient philosophy, humanity has been urged to conduct itself according to the most excellent part of the soul, that is, according to his essence (Plato), according to its specific substance (Aristotle) as a trait identifier of the human and foundation of the value which is attributed or recognized. Reason as the rational part of the soul that, under a still deeply vitalist conception of a universal soul, is generically tripartite, is, then, identified as the specific difference of humanity, the faculty that knows the principles and guides the action in accordance to those truths (in the exercise of the theoretical use and the practical use of reason that only appears in Aristotle). Clearly with the Stoics, and particularly with Seneca, man who conducts himself by reason is he who lives a truly human existence and is worthy of respect. Man, the rational being, possesses an absolute value, says Seneca, and ought to be sacred to himself ("*homo sacra res homini*").

Reason is always the principle of universal intelligibility, for instance in Greek antiquity, where it reflects the harmony of the cosmos (*logos*), or in medieval Christianity, where divine law shines through it (natural law), or still in the modern and contemporary world, where it impersonates objective truth (science). Valuation of the personal, singular element in man's selfdetermination occurs with the introduction of the notion of will, already under the influence of Christianity and, particularly with St Augustine. The power of human will (now determined not only by reason, as in antiquity, but also by love) develops from the intensification of the interior life of man. Will, as the expression of an individual wish, is then associated with the universality of reason in the irreducible unity of the

[19] The notion of 'autonomy' appears first in the political context, meaning the independence or self-determination of a state, and only later came to receive a predominantly moral connotation, which we privilege here.

[20] It will be interesting to point out that, from the exclusive attention to '*physis*' to the joint reference to *nomos* (with all the meaning of "conventional" or "arbitrary" it carries), the passage from a stronger incidence of the physical domain to the ethical is remarked.

moral act. It is this mutual and indispensable concourse of reason and will in the ambit of morality that, already in the beginning of Modernity, Kant will establish in his classical concept of autonomy.

Kantian autonomy expresses that the will (the good will) has to be its own law in a complete identification between itself and reason. The good will is the will which is free from all interest and determined by reason alone. Acting out of the necessity of the respect for the law, the value of this rational will is found solely in its intentions. Only in this sense does autonomy constitute itself as a supreme principle of morality. That is, only in this sense does the concept of autonomy express the universality of the law that commands all singularly in the perfect coincidence of the most rigorous submission and of the most absolute freedom. This way, the human being is converted into the universal legislator, and assuming an unconditional value (not only as author of moral law, but also as end of morality itself) which Kant designates by dignity – the quality of being an end in himself, common to every rational being.

The concept of autonomy, i.e. full use of reason and extensive exercise of freedom, is perpetuated in the occidental tradition as a fundamental principle of moral life and of the identity of the person. However, it is important to acknowledge that the genuine Kantian sense that legitimates autonomy as principle of morality is fading away. Autonomy is being converted into a moral ideal, losing its meaning as the condition of morality; it is being converted into a psychological capacity, fading away as a condition of the person. Besides, since it articulates in its concept the demand for reason and freedom, autonomy will be strongly shaped by the moral and political theory of liberal individualism, which is commonly expressed in the language of rights. This is a process that increases as liberal revolutions occur (England, United States, France, etc.) and their ideals are spread (the common recognition of fundamental human rights, either of sociopolitical or individual nature, emerges from that of freedom). But then it becomes the object of a claim, loosing its meaning as trait of the identity of the person which proves to reduce and impoverish the concept in question.

Such liberalism will become strongly marked and expressed in an overpowering way in bioethics during the decade of the 1960s in the United States. In this perspective we should refer to the decisive importance of the *Belmont Report* (1978). This report of the *National Commission for the Protection of Human Subjects and Behavioral*

Research, appointed by the U.S. Congress in 1974, systematises three fundamental principles that legitimate research, namely respect for people, beneficence and justice. Respect for persons implies the recognition of their autonomy, which appears, then, in general terms, as the capacity for the individual, rational and free, to make decisions about him or herself. In this context, Paul Ramsey's work *The Patient as a Person* was precursory.[21]

Still at a theoretical level, Beauchamp and Childress' model, since the first edition of the *Principles of Biomedical Ethics* in 1979, presents four principles as *prima facie* duties, i.e. beneficence, non-maleficence, justice and respect for autonomy. In case of conflict, the principle of respect for autonomy gains preponderance. The autonomous choices of the individual must be made under certain conditions (more or less rigorously established) that function as the criteria of autonomy. This concept refers, then, univocally, to the capacity of the self-determination of the individual, a meaning by which the autonomy principle would be widely expressed and strongly implanted in the Anglo-American tradition with also a strong influence on the bioethical debate in many European countries. Autonomy is assumed as a fundamental value and a basic right of every individual. What seems clear here is the transition of the autonomy principle from a universal dimension to a purely individual dimension. The autonomy of the person is no longer the coincidence of the individual maxims with the universal law, but the individual power of decision, i.e. self-determination.

At the practical level, and specifically regarding human experimentation and clinical practice, the practice of autonomy ensures that every rational, free and well-informed individual, can choose his or her own course of action. This principle was fundamental for the overcoming of the paternalistic model of medicine, which started to appear with increasing relevance since the decade of the 1950s. This opened the way to the professional-patient relationship which we summarise, paraphrasing Ramsey, as the patient as a partner. Progressively, the principle of autonomy itself becomes hegemonic, which leads to the paradoxical situation of being invoked to justify procedures of that contradict sense. For instance, one may refuse

---

[21] P. RAMSEY, *The Patient as a Person: Explorations in Medical Ethics*, New Haven, 1970.

treatment and in doing so either speed an avoidable death or simply deny the relief of suffering.

In brief, we can say that, in the context of the bioethical debate, the right to exercise autonomy is found in the act of informed consent, which the individual allows or denies; and that autonomy, since it is a principle, is recognized by respecting the decision that the individual takes. We admit, though, the important restriction that is designated by incompetence, which is applied in the absence of appropriate rational capacity and/or free exercise of will. The mentally handicapped and individuals suffering from depression are not treated as competent and are thus denied their dignity as persons. The fact that some individuals are diminished or even destitute of autonomy was widely treated, for example, by Tristam Engelhardt, in the first edition of *The Foundations of Bioethics* (1986).[22] He thus excluded these individuals from the bonds of obligations in which the moral community consists. More recently the author has adopted a less extreme position. However, Engelhardt's original position prevails still in other authors, either in the enunciation of principles (for example, the capacity of suffering as a criterion of moral obligation as defended by Peter Singer) or in clinical practice (for example, the possibility of adoption of the neo-cortical death criterion, described by R. Veatch).

The autonomy principle, as it has been taught in bioethics and, definitively, when radicalised (i.e. taken as isolated) has not only been used for various individual interests, but has also become a factor in the exclusion or destitution of some individuals from the personhood – thus radically contradicting the Kantian sense of the term. In this context, it is important to take into consideration another principle, one which tends to neglect interests or benefits derived from autonomy and which thus tends to widen the extension of moral community, hereby cancelling the excesses of autonomy. This principle appears to be that of responsibility.

4.2.2. *Responsibility (or: the Duty of the Human Being)*

The idea of responsibility has a long history, although the concept is relatively recent, and has gained only during this century a specific moral dimension. The attribution of responsibility as a quality (as an

---

[22] H. T. ENGELHARDT, *The Foundations of Bioethics.* New York – Oxford, 1986.

adjective: the 'responsible being') is already common during the Middle Ages; however, the notion 'responsibility' appears only by the end of the 18th century, as a characteristic of a juridical language. The concept of responsibility is then translated by the notion of 'imputability', that is, in general terms, the attribution of an action freely carried out to a subject who is its author or cause. The etymological sense of the term is thus kept in its suffix and root ('*re-spondeo*', to present oneself as a token for a promise, a commitment), responsibility meaning literally the capacity to answer for one's own actions. We see, then, that the concept of responsibility, as primarily defined by law, does not refer to or create a new reality, but instead formalises an already ancient idea in the history of philosophy that was originally presented under the notion of "cause". Indeed, the term 'aítos', meaning cause, appears in Plato's Republic (*Republica*, X, 617e), as well as in Aristotle's *Nicomachean Ethics* (*Ethica Nicomacheia* III, 7, 1113b), referring to the same reality we translate today as the notion of imputability or of responsibility[23]. This sense prevails in Kant's *Grundlegung zur Metaphysik der Sitten*, in the statement that imputation in the moral sense is the judgement by which someone is considered as the author of an action (which is then called a fact and submitted to laws). This idea that connects the subject, as cause, to his free action, passes by the history of philosophy, but responsibility will only find the conditions necessary to assume a moral dimension following the systematic study of freedom, which we are witnessing in contemporary culture. Responsibility then is clarified as a consequence of the person's freedom.

However, keeping in mind the unfolding of its constitutive moral dimension, responsibility has surpassed its traditional meaning of imputability and now appears as an appeal. If, while under its previous meaning, responsibility would relate immediately to subjectivity in its individual character and to freedom in its absolute character, today responsibility is no longer mainly a choice but mostly a commitment, an attribution to which we all are bound, a task or mission to which we all are committed. For that reason, it no longer strictly depends on the freedom that we recognise in each of the acts we perform, nor does it simply put the individual in confrontation

---

[23] J. HENRIOT, *Responsabilité*, in *Encyclopédie Philosophique Universelle*, Vol II. Les Notions Philosophiques, Paris, 1990.

with himself. Rather, it flows from the human condition itself, from an existence shared in the community, from the dimension of alterity constituent of subjectivity itself that establishes an unbreakable bound between all persons.

This new meaning of responsibility is mainly treated and developed by Emmanuel Levinas, particularly in *Autrement qu'être ou au-delà de l'essence* (1974).[24] Levinas presents responsibility as the essential, primary, fundamental structure of subjectivity, a subjectivity which is both de-position and ex-position, the most passive passivity in a total and gratuitous gift of one to the other. Subjectivity is openness and openness is vulnerability of the person who, naked of any disguise, exposes oneself to the wound and outrage of the other. Confronted with the face of the other, the only ethical relation is that of non-violence to violence to which the vulnerability of the other's face invites; the ethical relation is responsibility, the answer of subjectivity to the call of the other, the neighbour, humanity. In this sense, responsibility no longer exhausts itself in the duty to answer for one's actions, but opens up a vaster duty to answer for what penetrates the human being, one's very humanity. The etymology of the word is preserved and its meaning is amplified, in a clear accentuation of its inter-subjective nature. One is responsible for and before, one answers for and before, which implies that we are not alone.[25]

This widening of the concept of responsibility, from the strict sense of imputability to the broader sense of answerability, marks a decentralisation from that individualism attendant with the inseparability of freedom and responsibility. Each individual is held responsible for himself, for his action, for his freedom. Hopefully this leads away from the autonomous subject toward the consideration of questions regarding one's responsibility.[26] This is a new cen-

[24] E. LEVINAS, *Autrement qu'être ou au-delà de l'essence*, Paris, 1990.

[25] Alain Etchegoyen says that "the notion of responsibility is directly intersubjective. It cannot be elaborated in an unrealistic 'solipsism'. Responsibility can only put on a moral dimension when it confronts the responsible man with a look that surpasses the limits of his own territory: whether is it the other, or the immanence of the other to his own conscience." In A. ETCHEGOYEN, *Le temps des responsables*, Paris, 1993.

[26] In this new meaning, responsibility does no longer necessarily flow from freedom (as its natural and inevitable consequence, as the 'reverse of the coin'), but can even precede it (as it is defended by E. Lévinas and H. Jonas), once it relates to man's own condition or, as Jean Ladrière says referring more widely to ethics as the "dimension qui appartient constitutivement à l'existence, [...] le constitutif le plus essentiel." J. LADRIÈRE, *L'éthique dans l'univers de la rationalité*, Québec, 1997, p. 145).

tering, like a Copernican revolution, and it in fact corresponds to a particularly significant inversion: the inversion of the Kantian understanding of power through duty to the Jonas' understanding of duty through power.

For Kant, duty, expressed by moral law determines the power of the autonomy of will. However, within the context of the new understanding of responsibility, eminently represented by Hans Jonas (*Das Prinzip Verantwortung*, 1979), it is the power of technology that implies duty (solicitude). Jonas will say that the more techno-logical power one has, one has that much more responsibility, that much more duty. Kant's and Jonas' concepts of power do not have the same meaning but the inversion of the relationship between power and duty is still significant when revealing power as a corol-lary of morality under the sign of autonomy, and a corollary of duty under the sign of responsibility[27].

For Hans Jonas, the responsibility by which duty is expressed con-stitutes the foundation of all human relationships, whose archetype consists in the parental relationship: it is the new-born that, out of the most absolute absence of power, appeals to the responsibility of the parents, who have all the power. Responsibility expresses the obligation placed upon the action determined by power. Only he who can, ought to; and those who can do nothing, have no duty – the latter are object of the responsibility of those who can, they are those to whom everything is due. Jonas, thence, breaks away from the traditional correlation between rights and duties – a terminology that strongly shapes the expression of Anglo-American bioethics, and that weakens in the European scenario. The European bioethical expression is more committed to the establishment of equity, and therefore is not restricted to the search for the individual good, but rather aspires to the realisation of the common good. Simultane-ously, the philosopher chooses vulnerability as the object of respon-sibility.

---

[27] Contradicting Kant's position that duty precedes power – "you ought, then you can", Hans Jonas would say: "you can, then you ought". Power is the root of duty – in the Jonassian point of view – a power while final causal force, emancipated by knowledge and freedom (power that chooses ends with knowledge) and duty is "a certain correlate of power such that the amplitude and the type of power determine the amplitude and type of responsibility." H. JONAS, *Le principe responsabilité*, Paris, 1995, p. 177.

The vulnerable person is now the object of responsibility in this new, and at the same time original, willingness to answer the call of he who lacks power (Jonas), and of passivity (Levinas). For Levinas, vulnerability is the expression of the nakedness of the face (of what escapes my power) and of the obsession for the other; it is an expression of a subjectivity without interiority, without identity, which as such goes as far as the substitution of the other, taking responsibility for the other. For Jonas, vulnerability is the perishable character of life, of the being that, in its frailty, calls for care, for solicitude, for duty, for responsibility of the other. With this new conception of responsibility the links of obligation are tightened within the moral community, from which no one is excluded.

The principle of responsibility is not widely applied as a bioethical position. For instance, Levinas never addresses bioethics, although it may be possible for us to apply his thinking to bioethical problems. Following his line of thought abortion and euthanasia would be absolutely prohibited due to the first command of the face of the other: "Thou shall not kill". Moreover, our infinite duty to the other in his weakness would address issues arising from the commercialisation and depersonalisation of health care, and from our obligation to care for terminally ill patients.

Jonas, on the other hand, refers specifically to bioethical issues, particularly to human experimentation. He condemns all experiments that have as their only goal the increase of knowledge. He also refers to the unacceptability of abortion, except in the case of a positive genetic diagnosis and the child's best interest. Moreover, he condemns positive eugenics and cloning. He refers to the maximalist definition of death with the consideration of the possibility of organ transplantation. He considers the progress of genetics, and in doing so, considers safeguarding the integrity of man and of living beings in general. Due to the preponderance of duty over power and the new object of responsibility, Jonas extends the traditional domain of the human to all living beings in nature, and projects responsibility beyond the here-and-now of the present to a distant future that contemplates the coming generations. Responsibility exercises itself, invariably, toward protecting threatened life and preserving the 'being-as-such' (way of being) of the existent.

However, it should be recognised that this Jonassian responsibility for every form of life, present and future, appears not only as vague – in that we do not know well enough the distant effects of our actions of today –, but as also extremely demanding, for it only can be fulfilled collectively. In order to become effective, responsibility must be shared by the community, becoming an insertion factor of the individual into the collectivity by rendering uniform the meaning of action. The principle of responsibility, as it is recognised by Jonas, expresses a duty that is never merely individual, but instead demands a wider political organisation to assure its execution. In this sense, personal responsibility tends to be diluted. This aspect is taken to the extreme by Levinas through a reversed process: it is subjectivity that is always responsible; however, being unlimited and *a priori* responsible for everything and for all, causes the weight of the actions to fade.[28]

A wider reflection on the various ethical perspectives that developed in the second half of the 20th century in Europe, will most certainly show the inflection, more and more marked, of the direction of action: from the imperative of power to the imperative of duty; from the demand for freedom to the demand for responsibility. This reorientation of action seems positive to us, even necessary, not as an alternative but as a search for an equilibrium among different expressions of the human and considering the establishment of the best conditions for the realisation of man's ethical vocation.

In the past, we gave pride of place to the principle of autonomy in human development, but now we see that it is impossible to consider the principle of responsibility in isolation. Autonomy, in the absence of responsibility, tends to restrict itself into a self-centered and autistic individualism; responsibility, in the absence of autonomy, tends to fade into the anonymity of impersonal collectivity. Autonomy without responsibility is sterile; responsibility without autonomy is inconsistent. In the same way, power without duty becomes oppressive and duty without power becomes subservient. In fact, each of these elements of the binomial calls for the other and fulfills itself in the other.

It is important, then, to demand and to safeguard the necessary indissolubility between the autonomy principle and the responsibility principle: the former as indispensable for the constitution of the

---

[28] Levinassian responsibility (always extra responsibility and responsibility for the other's responsibility) in its infinitude proportionate to election, is more easily seen as formal than foreseen as authenticity to fulfil (utopic character of Levinassian responsibility).

person as a rational and free individual; the latter as indispensable for the constitution of the person as a solidary being. The identity of the person is constructed in the crossing, intertwining, interweaving of the dimensions of power and duty, of the sense of individual freedom and communitarian obligations, of the principles of autonomy and responsibility, in the singular fulfillment of the universal humanity – the essential unity that makes the identity of the person.

THE PHYSICIAN-PATIENT RELATIONSHIP

A Hermeneutic Perspective

Guy A.M. Widdershoven

5.1. Introduction

The physician-patient relationship has long been regarded as asymmetric. The physician was supposed to have knowledge about the patient's condition, whereas the patient was seen as someone who lacked insight in her own situation. The physician was considered to be rational, the patient emotional. In the last few decades this picture has changed fundamentally. With the upsurge of patient rights, the physician is no longer supposed to have control over the situation. The physician's role is to provide information about treatment options, and to help the patient to make her own choice. The patient is no longer seen as someone who lacks the possibility to make reasonable choices. A good patient is someone who takes decisions about treatment, based upon sufficient knowledge of risks and outcomes. The traditional asymmetry seems to have been reversed. Whereas the patient used to be regarded as passive, following the doctor's orders obediently, she is now seen as the person who is in charge of the process, while the physician merely provides the information which the patient needs in order to make an informed choice.

These changes in the physician-patient relationship have lead to new forms of cooperation and new solutions in case of conflicts. Whereas formerly cooperation between physician and patient implied that the patient helped to realise the course of action laid out by the doctor, nowadays cooperation between physician and patient means that the doctor enables the patient to make a choice and helps to put the chosen treatment into effect. While conflicts between doctors and patients used to be solved on the basis of the physician's authority, now the emphasis is on respect for the patient's right to refuse. This is especially clear in psychiatry. Here the traditional idea that the patient might and even should be overruled for her own best interest has been replaced by the rule that patient's refusals have to be respected, even if this is harmful to the patient's own health, as long as there is no serious danger for the patient or the environment.

This reversal of roles in the physician-patient relationship certainly has had positive consequences. Physicians are nowadays less inclined to think they know what is best for the patient. Patients are more active and have more opportunities to influence treatment. Yet the new situation also has its disadvantages. Physicians feel they have little room to bring to the fore their own perspective of the situation, and do not know how to act in cases in which the patient's preferences may seriously be doubted. Patients experience little support from physicians who merely formulate risks and benefits and indicate that it is up to the patient to make the choice. Several authors make a plea for a more mutual physician-patient relationship.[1] They introduce notions such as partnership, conversation and negotiation. Such notions clearly appeal to both doctors and patients, since they tend to do away with asymmetries and give room for equal input of both parties in the decision-making process.

In this contribution I will present an approach to the physician-patient relationship emphasising mutuality. This approach focuses on dialogue and deliberation as basic constituents of interpersonal relationships. This approach has been elaborated by Emanuel and Emanuel, who compare what they call the deliberative model of the physician-patient relationship to other models, amongst which the traditional paternalist model and the informed consent model. Gadamer's analysis of human understanding can further elucidate the philosophical foundations of the deliberative model. Gadamer distinguishes between three forms of understanding. According to Gadamer, the third, hermeneutic form of understanding implies a

---

[1] See e.g. J. KATZ, *The Silent World of Doctor and Patient*, New York, 1984; H. BRODY, *The Healer's Power*, Yale, 1992; H.R. MOODY, *Ethics in an Aging Society*, Baltimore, 1992; G.J. AGICH, *Autonomy and Long-Term Care*, New York - Oxford, 1993.

dialogue in which both parties change their views. I will illustrate the discussion of the various approaches to the physician-patient relationship with a case story from the field of psychiatry.

5.2. A Case Story

In her autobiographic book *An Unquiet Mind*, the psychiatrist Kay Redfield Jamison tells her history of coping with her own psychiatric disease, manic depression. She vividly describes both the fascination of being manic and the misery of being depressed. She shows the impact of the illness on her life and work. Her life is a constant struggle, fighting against the dramatic consequences of the disease. Yet her life and work also depend upon her moods, since in manic phases she is actually able to be productive, intense and effervescent. She knows medication is necessary to keep her alive, but on the other hand she fears the negative consequences of taking lithium, and losing her energy and creativity. She is constantly tempted to stop taking pills, and actually does away with them several times, only to find herself in a state of utter misery. Jamison makes clear that there is no simple solution for her, although there is a drug that in a sense is able to cure. Taking the drug is difficult for her, because she feels that she thereby loses what makes her personal as well as her academic life fruitful: her creativity. She somehow has to find a way to be able to avoid the extremes of madness, without losing all of the inspiring aspects of her moods. She is only able to keep on try-ing, and in the end partly succeeding to find a balance, by the con-stant support and attention of caring others. One of them is her psy-chiatrist, who both helps her to struggle with her disease, and acts as a role model and inspiration for her own professional practice as a psychiatrist. In her book she describes her relationship with him as follows:

> *Over the next many years (...) I saw him at least once a week; when I was extremely depressed and suicidal I saw him more often. He kept me alive a thousand times over. He saw me through madness, despair, wonderful and terrible love affairs, disillusionments and triumphs, recurrence of illness, an almost fatal suicide attempt, the death of a man I greatly loved, and the enormous pleasures and aggravations of my professional life – in short he saw me through the beginnings and endings of virtually every aspect of my psychological and emotional life. He was very tough, as well as very*

*kind, and even though he understood more than anyone how much I felt
I was losing – in energy, vivacity, and originality – by taking medication,
he never was seduced into losing sight of the overall perspective of how
costly, damaging, and life threatening my illness was. He was at ease with
ambiguity, had a comfort with complexity, and was able to be decisive in
the midst of chaos and uncertainty. He treated me with respect, a decisive
professionalism, wit, and an unshakable belief in my ability to get well,
complete, and make a difference.[2]*

5.3. Four Models of the Physician-Patient Relationship

The traditional view of the physician-patient relationship was that of
the doctor knowing what was good for the patient and acting in the
patient's interest. This view is clearly expressed in the Hippocratic
oath. With the development of medical ethics in the second half of
the twentieth century, the patient became more prominently posi-
tioned. Patient autonomy (in the sense of self-determination) became
regarded as an important element of medical practice and patients
acquired the right to refuse treatment. This gave rise to the doctrine
of informed consent. Paternalism and informed consent are two fundamentally different ways of conceptualising the physician-patient
relationship. These two conceptualisations are, however, not exhaus-
tive. Emanuel and Emanuel discuss four models of the physician-
patient relationship.[3] For each of these models, they describe the
goals of physician-patient interaction, the physician's obligations,
the role of patient's values and the conception of patient autonomy.
    The first is the paternalistic model. In this model, the goal of
physician-patient interaction is to ensure that the patient receives the
best treatment. The physician's obligation is to promote the patient's
well-being, irrespective of the patient's expressed preferences. The
physician provides selected information in order to encourage the
patient's cooperation. In this model the doctor is the guardian of the
patient. The process is guided by objective values, foremost the
value of health. The physician has knowledge about these values
and about what is needed to realise them. The patient is supposed to

---

[2] K.J. JAMISON, *An Unquiet Mind*. London, 1996, p. 87-88.
[3] E.J. EMANUEL & L.L. EMANUEL, *Four Models of the Physician-Patient Relationship*, in
JAMA 267 (1992) 2221-2226.

share these values. If the patient expresses wishes or preferences that are not in conformity with those values, the physician may disregard them. The patient is considered autonomous when she assents to the physician's determination of what is best. Autonomy here is to go along with what is in one's own interest.

The second model is the informative, or consumer model. The aim of physician-patient interaction in this model is to enable the patient to make an informed choice about treatment. The physician has to provide relevant information and to help the patient to choose. This implies that the physician should not act in a directive way; he should refrain from influencing the patient. After the patient has made her choice, the physician should implement the selected intervention. In this model the doctor is the technical expert and patient values are central. The values are supposed to be clear-cut, stable, and known to the patient. The physician's values are not relevant to the process of selecting the desired intervention. The patient is seen as autonomous if she is able to formulate her own choices, without external interference. Patient autonomy in this model can be defined as negative freedom: one is autonomous if one is free from outside influences.[4]

The third model is the interpretive model. It aims at interpreting the patient's values and implementing the patient's selected intervention. Contrary to the informative model, the patient's values are not supposed to be fixed and clear. The values of the patient are seen as inchoate and conflicting, and in need of interpretation. It is the physician's role to help to elucidate the patient's values. In this model the doctor is a counsellor or adviser. Patient autonomy is more than freedom from external pressure. In order to be autonomous in choosing a course of treatment, the patient has to gain self-understanding. The patient comes to know more clearly who she is and how she should evaluate various medical options in the light of her identity. This implies a conception of autonomy as positive freedom: one is free if one's actions contribute to make one's life a meaningful whole.

The fourth model is the deliberative model. It is based upon the presupposition that the patient's values are not only in need of interpretation, but also of discussion and deliberation. The doctor is regarded as a friend or teacher. His role is to engage the patient in a

---

[4] I. BERLIN, *Four Essays on Liberty*, Oxford, 1969.

dialogue about what is best. In such a dialogue, the physician may introduce other values than those of the patient, in order to make the patient consider alternative ways of evaluating the situation. Thus, the physician's own values become relevant, not because the physician knows best what is good (as in the paternalist model), but because the patient may learn what is worthwhile by being confronted with the physician's views. Patient autonomy in this model is moral self-development: "the patient is empowered not simply to follow unexamined preferences or examined values, but to consider, through dialogue, alternative health-related values, their worthiness and their implications for treatment."[5] Autonomy is again seen as positive freedom. The patient is autonomous if she develops new values and integrates them into her own identity. In contrast to the interpretive model, this process of self-development is not just a growth of awareness into what one already was, but a change into a new personality on the basis of interpersonal relations with others, amongst which the healthcare professionals.

According to Emanuel and Emanuel the models may all be appropriate depending on the situation. Thus, in an emergency the paternalist model may be suitable. If physician and patient interact shortly over a simple issue, the informative model may be adequate. Interpretive or deliberative elements may be useful if the patient's wishes need further investigation. This is not just a matter of eclecticism. Emanuel and Emanuel argue that normally one of the models will be the basic or paradigmatic approach. This means that the use of another model requires justification on the part of the physician. In healthcare law, the informative model is mostly regarded as the standard. Paternalism is not wrong per se, but one has to give specific arguments to defend such behaviour, by referring for instance to the patient's incompetence. Emanuel and Emanuel regard the deliberative model as the ideal model, and argue that this should be the paradigmatic approach in health care. According to them, it fits best with what people expect physicians to do. It gives the physician a role, not only as an expert on medical facts, but also as a participant in the process of finding out which values are relevant to one's health. It entails a rich notion of autonomy. Autonomy is more than just choosing for oneself; to be autonomous requires that individuals critically assess their own values and realise them in their actions.

[5] E.J. EMANUEL & L.L. EMANUEL, op.cit., p. 2222.

What kind of model is characteristic of the psychiatrist in the case of Jamison? He is clearly not paternalistic, since he puts much energy in understanding the patient. Although he does insist on the use of medication, he is open to the doubts of the patient. He does not express an attitude of 'doctor knows best', but acknowledges that the right solution is not easily found. He also indicates that it is the patient who has to solve the problems in order to get well, not the doctor. This insistence on the role of the patient does not mean that the psychiatrist adheres to the informative model. Giving information is clearly not the central element of his relation with the patient. Moreover, he does not go along with the patient's expressed wishes, but resists them if they are not in the interest of the patient's health. He does not give in to the patient although he understands her position. The psychiatrist's behaviour does show distinctive elements of the interpretive model. He is aware of the complexities in the patient's situation and tries to help her to find out what really matters to her. He supports her in developing her own identity, as a person who has a disease, but is still able to achieve her own goals in life. Yet his role goes further than illuminating and making explicit given values of the patient. He is described as both understanding and decisive in the midst of chaos and uncertainty. By being open as well as firm, he helps her to find new ways of dealing with her situation and valuing her life. These activities refer to the deliberative model. The physician does not so much help her to find out who she already is, but supports her in finding new values in life and developing into a new person.

5.4. Three Kinds of Interpersonal Understanding

Traditionally, hermeneutics deals with human understanding. For Dilthey, understanding is for the cultural sciences what explanation is for the natural sciences. One can only know the products of human action by looking for meaning, not for causes. Hermeneutics aims to make clear what is involved in understanding. For Gadamer, following Heidegger, hermeneutics does not only concern the methodology of the human and cultural sciences, as it did for Dilthey. Understanding meaning is characteristic of ordinary life. Thus, hermeneutics as a theory of human understanding has to analyse what is characteristic of everyday life. According to

Gadamer, understanding in everyday life is primarily being engaged in the situation. It is not a matter of reflection, but of response. Understanding is based upon silent pre-understandings. Yet, this does not mean that everything is moulded into an existing framework. Understanding also means openness towards aspects that do not fit into one's pre-understandings. Although understanding requires a horizon of pre-understanding, this horizon is not fixed, but develops through the process of understanding itself. Hermeneutic understanding is essentially a process of self-development through confrontation with the other. The basic model of hermeneutic understanding is to be found in the realm of intersubjectivity, that is in interpersonal understanding.

In elaborating the notion of hermeneutic interpersonal understanding, Gadamer distinguishes three kinds of experience of the other.[6] The first entails an explanation of the other's behaviour by applying knowledge of human nature. This is not interpersonal understanding in the strict sense of the term, since the other is seen as an object. The other is seen as predictable, on the basis of general insight into human nature. The attitude towards the other is strategic. The other is not really regarded as a moral subject.

The second kind of experience of the other is to know the other in his uniqueness. In this case one claims to be able to understand the other exactly as he is. The person who approaches the other in this way claims to know him truly, even to know him better than he knows himself. The one who knows in this way, does not consider himself part of the relationship with the other. He is superior to the other, and cannot be touched by whatever the other brings to the fore. This kind of understanding is characteristic of historicism. The aim of historicism is to understand every epoch from the inside. This means that the one who knows (the historian) has no special position or interest himself. He is distanced and superior, knowing the other, but unattainable by him.

The third kind of understanding of the other is to be really open to what the other has to say. This means that one does not put oneself above the other, but is prepared to hear what he has to say, and to acknowledge that it may be necessary to change one's own views about the matter. Gadamer explains this third, specifically

---

[6] H.-G. GADAMER, *Wahrheit und Methode*, Tübingen, 1960, p. 340 ff.

hermeneutic, kind of understanding of the other thus: "When two people understand one another, this does not mean that one 'understands' the other in such a way that he sees the other from above, and thus oversees him ('überschaut'). Likewise, to 'hear someone and respond to him' ('auf jemanden hören') does not mean to execute blindly what the other wants. A person who acts in such a way is called slavish ('hörig'). Openness towards the other entails the recognition that I myself will have to accept things that are against me, even if no one else pushes me to do so."[7]

The first kind of understanding of the other aims at manipulation; the other person is used to serve one's own purposes. The second kind of understanding focuses upon the other's point of view. It aims to find out what is really important for the other. The third kind of understanding is mutual: it involves dialogue. According to Gadamer, in dialogue both of the participants change. "To reach an understanding in a dialogue is not merely a matter of asserting one's own point of view, but a change into a communion in which one does not remain what one was."[8] Two points should be added: in the first place, this process of understanding through dialogue is not necessarily (not even primarily) an intellectual process. Understanding is not based upon a conscious decision (although deliberations may very well be apart of it), but upon a preconscious engagement with a common movement. In the second place, the mutuality reached is never a total union; in a dialogue, a common point of view may be reached, but this is always partial (since the perspectives of the participants will never fully overlap), and in danger of breakdown.

Following Gadamer's analysis of human understanding, one may distinguish two radically different ways of understanding the other person as a concrete human being. The first form of understanding aims to know the other person directly, from the inside. This kind of understanding puts the interpreter in a superior position over the person who is understood. The interpreter ideally knows what the world looks like for the other person. This knowledge is in no way influenced by his own worldview, nor does it influence the latter. The second kind of interpersonal understanding is based upon openness and dialogue. It aims at a mutual agreement between the

---

[7] *Ibid.*, p. 343.
[8] *Ibid.*, p. 379.

interpreter and the person who is understood. The interpreter does not have a special insight into what has to be done; this is negotiated between the participants. In this hermeneutic conception of under-standing, both parties are involved in a process of change.

The two kinds of interpersonal understanding entail different views regarding the nature of human values. In the historicist kind of understanding, the values of the other are seen as given, to be uncovered by the interpreter. In principle, the interpreter can fully understand the values of the other person, which means that total knowledge of the other is (ideally) possible. In hermeneutic under-standing, the values of the other are not seen as given. They do not exist apart from the relation with the interpreter. Through mutual interaction, values become expressed, and thereby get a concrete shape. In this process of making explicit what really matters, some aspects of the other's way of viewing the world come more to the fore, and others are obscured. Thus, the values of the other are developed in the process of communication. This means that total knowledge of the other is impossible, since every act of understan-ding changes the situation. The other is never fully known; there is always a gap; the other presents himself as evading.

Let's return once again to Jamison's story. What kind of under-standing is characteristic for her psychiatrist? Clearly he does not just apply laws of human nature in order to help his patient. He is not primarily interested in seeing similarities between this patient and the next; his patient is for him an individual person, with her own life history. She is aware of the fact that he knows her more than anybody else. He knows about her feelings, her frustrations and hopes. Yet, his knowledge is not strictly historicist. He does not just notice what is important for her, but also acknowledges his own responsibilities. Even though he understands that she looses a lot by taking medica-tion, he does not just let her stop taking it. This, on the other hand, does not mean that he keeps her claims at a distance. He takes seri-ously her need to be emotional, vivid and energetic. By being respon-sive, he helps her to find a new balance between being overwhelmed by emotions and killing them totally with drugs. Through interaction and negotiation, the physician succeeds in bringing about a mutual adjustment of his own values and those of the patient.[9] He is not just

---

[9] H.R. MOODY, *Ethics in an Aging Society*, p. 135 ff.

attentive to the patient's history, but actually takes part in it, making it into a joint history of finding new ways of valuing life and dealing with its ambiguities and complexities. The physician is not just empathic in a historicist sense (putting himself in the position of the other), but also in the hermeneutic sense (communicating with the other). To quote Frank: "If people could believe that each of us lacks something that only an other can fill – if we could be communicative bodies – then empathy would no longer be spoken of as something one 'has for' another. Instead empathy is what a person 'is with' another: a relationship in which each understands herself as requiring completion by the other".[10]

5.5. Conclusion

The physician-patient relationship is not necessarily one-sided, with either the physician being active and the patient passive (as in traditional paternalism), or the other way around (as in the contemporary informed consent model). Emanuel and Emanuel sketch the outlines of a deliberative model of the physician-patient relationship, in which the physician helps the patient to examine critically her values and develop new ways of leading a meaningful life. The hermeneutic approach to interpersonal understanding shows that this implies a mutual interaction, in which both the participants change.

Hermeneutics can elucidate what is at stake in the deliberative model of the physician-patient relationship. It can also provide a correction to the way in which Emanuel and Emanuel describe the deliberation process. In the first place, hermeneutics emphasises that self-development is not primarily a matter of reflection.[11] Negotiations about values do not have to take the form of rational argumentation. Confrontation and persuasion may be more relevant to the process of broadening one's horizon than critical analysis or debate.[12] This implies that the deliberative model of the physician-patient relationship is not only adequate for competent patients, but may also be applicable in cases where the patient is less prone to

---

[10] A.W. FRANK, *The Wounded Storyteller*, Chicago - London, 1995, p. 150.
[11] G.J. AGICH, *Autonomy and Long-Term Care*.
[12] H.R. MOODY, *Ethics in an Aging Society*.

conscious reflection, for instance in psychiatry or in the care for people with a mental handicap.[13] As the case of Jamison shows, personal development is not necessarily the result of argumentation, but of engagement, trust and support. In the second place, hermeneutics stresses that in dialogue both participants change. Thus the process of moral development envisaged in the deliberative model should not only concern the patient, but also involve the physician. The physician will have to realise that his values can also be in need of change. He will have to see that there are more ways than one to deal with the disease, and that new approaches are needed when for example effective medication destroys the patient's creativity, as in the case of Jamison. In the third place, hermeneutics involves a conception of autonomy that is explicitly relational. Self-development is always a process of being in relation to others. Autonomy is not the opposite of dependency, since people are always interdependent.[14] Jamison may be able to find a balance in her life, but in doing so she is dependent upon the constant attention and care of others.

From a hermeneutic perspective, the physician-patient relationship is a mutual process of learning to deal with the disease in such a way that one can live, and in a certain sense, even live a better life than before. This will not be an ideal life: rather it will entail the realisation that former ideals are in need of correction. It will be a life expressing more clearly the importance of interpersonal relationships as well as emotions and material conditions. To quote Jamison once again:

> *Although I went to him to be treated for an illness, he taught me, by example, for my own patients, the total beholdenness of brain to mind and mind to brain. My temperament, moods, and illness clearly, and deeply, affected the relationships I had with others and the fabric of my work. But my moods were themselves powerfully shaped by the same relationships and work. The challenge was in learning to understand the complexity of this mutual beholdenness and in learning to distinguish the roles of lithium, will, and insight in getting well and leading a meaningful life.*[15]

---

[13] G. Widdershoven & C. Sohl, *Interpretation, Action, and Communication: Four Stories about a Supported Employment Program*, in T.A. Abma (ed.). *Telling Tales: On Evaluation and Narrative*, Stanford, 1999, p. 109-130.

[14] J.C. TRONTO, *Moral Boundaries. A Political Argument for an Ethic of Care*, New York - London, 1993.

[15] K.J. JAMISON, *An Unquiet Mind*, London, 1996, p. 88.

TOWARDS INTEGRATED CLINICAL ETHICS APPROACH: CARING, CLINICAL AND ORGANISATIONAL

Chris Gastmans

6.1. Introduction

Since the 1980s, a movement within health care ethics has pushed the clinical reality, with the physician-patient relationship as one of its main constituents, to the forefront. This style of health care ethics is referred to as 'clinical ethics'. In clinical ethics, the focus is on the ethical aspects of the factual clinical situation with attention to all the relevant clinical factors involved such as the situation of the patient with his/her expectations, pain, fears, etc., as well as the professional and personal experiences of the caregivers. These are not bare facts but are in need of a normative interpretation. This normative interpretation of a clinical reality – the ultimate goal of clinical ethics – is reached using specific methods, concepts, argument trees, etc. One can therefore note that for the past 20 years, the so-called principle-framework of Beauchamp and Childress has had a major influence on clinical ethics in the Anglo-American culture.[1] According to this approach, a clinical-ethical problem is considered to be a conflict between abstract, universalised ethical principles. According to Beauchamp and Childress, respect for autonomy, beneficence, nonmaleficence and justice are the major principles through which clinical-ethical problems can be conceptualised and interpreted. The aforementioned principles can be used to develop possible standard procedures, which – when followed strictly – can result in a

---

[1] T. BEAUCHAMP & J. CHILDRESS, *Principles of Biomedical Ethics*, 5th ed., Oxford, 2001.

defendable solution for the clinical-ethical problem. Principlism exhibits all the characteristics of an ethical spirit of abstraction, that focuses on identifying, categorising and solving problems, the abstraction of actual persons, etc. The major advantage of such 'neutral language', this *lingua franca* of a number of principles which should lead to a consensus, is that it has given rise to a sort of procedural pattern of thought that facilitates decision-making in a pluralistic context.

The frequently applied principlist approach in clinical ethics undoubtedly has many disadvantages.[2] First of all, one of the most fundamental criticisms regarding this approach is the lack of content regarding the underlying concept of humanity. Principlism lacks a fundamental anthropological framework, a lack which carries the risk that fundamental aspects of moral experience are overlooked. For example, within this ethical framework, hardly any attention is given to basic ethical intuitions or to the attitudes of the caregivers, which, when confronted with actual ethical problems, form the basis of their ethical thinking and subsequent action. Secondly, clinical-ethical reflections based on principles largely ignore the larger context wherein caregivers have to make their decisions.[3] Current clinical debate mainly states that the essence of clinical care can be reduced to a number of isolated medical decisions. Such 'medical-clinical' ethics overlooks the fact that human beings (e.g. the chronically ill and the elderly) go through a whole process of care, during which they, in close interaction with caregivers (physicians, nurses, therapists etc.) and members of their family, continually have to make minor and major decisions.[4] Such a process of care situates itself within a well defined relational (e.g. physician-nurse-patient relationship), institutional (hospital, nursing home, home care etc.) and social context (e.g. society's (dis)respect regarding care) that has a profound influence on clinical-ethical decision-making.

---

[2] For an overview of the various criticisms, see E. DUBOSE, R. HAMEL & L.O. CONNEL (ed.), *A Matter of Principles. Ferment in U.S. Bioethics*, Valley Forge, 1994; T. DAVIS, *The Principlism Debate. A Critical Review*, in *The Journal of Medicine and Philosophy* 20 (1995) 85-105.

[3] R. SIEDER & C. CLEMENTS, *The New Medical Ethics. A Second Opinion*, in *Archives of Internal Medicine* 145 (1985) 2169-2173.

[4] G. WIDDERSHOVEN, *Ethiek in de kliniek. Hedendaagse benaderingen in de gezondheidsethiek*, Amsterdam, 2000.

Starting from the above-mentioned one-sided principlist-approach, we want to explore some new ways of thinking that may broaden the clinical-ethical debate. We were inspired by a relatively new way of thinking in health care ethics that presents itself as a partial alternative to principlism, namely the ethics of care. We state that the complexity of the contemporary clinical reality demands an integrated ethical interpretation where clinical as well as organisational viewpoints are taken into account.

6.2. Different Perspectives on Man, Care and Ethics

The ethics of care evolved out of the Kohlberg-Gilligan debate on moral psychology and from the work done by such social scientists as Joan Tronto in the United States of America and Selma Sevenhuijsen in the Netherlands.[5] For philosophical-ethical research regarding care and its application in health care, one can refer to the work of Warren Reich in the United States, and Henk Manschot, Marian Verkerk and Guy Widdershoven in the Netherlands, among others.[6] The methodology of the ethics of care in health care has until now been primarily applied in nursing[7], elderly care[8], mental health care[9] and in prenatal diagnosis and abortion[10].

---

[5] C. GILLIGAN, *In a Different Voice. Psychological Theory and Women's Development*, Cambridge, 1982; J. TRONTO, *Moral Boundaries. A Political Argument for an Ethic of Care*, London, 1993; S. SEVENHUIJSEN, *Oordelen met zorg. Feministische beschouwingen over recht, moraal en politiek*, Amsterdam, 1996.

[6] W. REICH, *Care*, in W. REICH (ed.), *Encyclopedia of Bioethics*, New York, 1995, p. 319-344; H. MANSCHOT, *Kwetsbare autonomie. Over afhankelijkheid en onafhankelijkheid in de ethiek van de zorg*, in H. MANSCHOT & M. VERKERK (ed.), *Ethiek van de zorg. Een discussie*, Amsterdam, 1994, p. 97-118; M. VERKERK, *Zorg of contract*, in H. MANSCHOT and M. VERKERK (ed.), *Ethiek van de zorg. Een discussie*, Amsterdam, 1994, p. 53-73; M. VERKERK (ed.), *Denken over zorg. Concepten en Praktijken*, Maarssen, 1997; G. WIDDERSHOVEN, *Ethiek in de kliniek. Hedendaagse benaderingen in de gezondheidsethiek*, Amsterdam, 2000.

[7] C. GASTMANS, B. DIERCKX DE CASTERLÉ & P. SCHOTSMANS, *Nursing Considered as Moral Practice. A Philosophical-Ethical Interpretation of Nursing*, in *The Kennedy Institute of Ethics Journal* 8/1 (1998) 43-69.

[8] J.M.M. VAN DELDEN, C.M.P.M. HERTOGH & H.A.M. MANSCHOT, *Morele problemen in de ouderenzorg*, Assen, 1999.

[9] J. GRASTE & D. BAUDUIN (ed.), *Waardenvol werk. Ethiek in de geestelijke gezondheidszorg*, Assen, 2000.

[10] E. GATENS-ROBINSON, *A Defence of Women's Choice. Abortion and the Ethics of Care*, in *Southern Journal of Philosophy* 30/3 (1992) 39-66.

When one looks closely at the origins of clinical ethics and the ethics of care, one comes to the conclusion that both categories of ethics were developed during approximately the same period of time i.e. the beginning of the 1980s, with a definite breakthrough in the 1990s.[11] In the first edition of the *Encyclopedia of Bioethics* published in 1978, clinical ethics and ethics of care were not included as separate topics. However, in the second edition (1995) a lot of attention was given to these topics; both are referred to as very promising developments in health care ethics.[12] Before one can illustrate the contribution of the ethics of care to clinical ethics, the issue of the ethics of care has to be clarified. Therefore, we will reflect on the concept of the person and the concept of care that underly the ethics of care and how these are connected to ethical problems.

6.2.1. *The Human Being as a Subject of Care*

Contrary to the principlist approach of clinical ethics, the ethics of care attends to the anthropology that underlies ethical thinking in health care. The concept of the person utilised by care ethicists is characterised by a great emphasis on the relationship between human beings on the one hand, and the integration of human actions and being on the other hand.

Contrary to those who advocate the individualistic concept of the person where autonomy and caring for others are scarcely linked, care-ethicists opt for a perspective where the relationship between human beings, viewed in terms of bonding and responsability, is paramount.[13] Of optimal importance is the fact that humans are born into a state of dependence upon others and until they reach adulthood they need intensive care. But adults also have a need for caring and bonding with their fellow human beings. Consequently, every human being is a part of a complicated network of relationships, which is often created without any initiative on his part. A caring human being does not always choose his relationships; he discovers his relational anchors through caring involvement. Each person

---

[11] J. FLETCHER & H. BRODY, *Clinical Ethics. Elements and Methodologies*, in W. REICH (ed), *op. cit.*, p. 399-402.

[12] B. KOCZWARA & T. MADIGAN, *The Heterogeneity of Clinical Ethics*, in *The Journal of Medicine and Philosophy* 22 (1997) 75-88.

[13] M. VERKERK, *Zorg of contract*, in H. MANSCHOT & M. VERKERK (ed.), *Ethiek van de zorg. Een discussie*, Amsterdam, 1994, p. 53-73.

always holds a piece of another's life of or is replied given a piece. Every day, always in new variations, every human being is dependent upon others, but is also upon. In short, the total sum of daily human activity is a complex network of mutual dependency. As a result, human beings experience their life as a project where others play a crucial role and share joint responsibility.

Another important characteristic of the total concept of the person as described by care ethicists is related to the concept of virtues and links the integration of being and actions on the one hand and the cognitive and affective abilities of human beings on the other hand. Within the ethics of care an adequate analysis of human action is as important as the clarification of the internal disposition where human actions take form. Actions, dispositions, and attitudes have a lot in common. These behavioural components are mutually inspiring and motivating. Moreover, human behaviour may not be divided up into rational and irrational components. If a human being acts, he/she acts as a whole using his rational as well as his affective abilities.[14] Emotions and intuitions should be cultivated since they fulfil a dual purpose in creating an integral personality. For the first time emotions have a discerning function: insights into the morally relevant aspects of a situation regarding a fellow human being demands, beyond the intellectual discerning mind, an affective attachment and emotional sensitivity, which express themselves in attitudes of care, altruism and compassion. Moreover, emotions have an expressive function: the quality of ethical actions not only depends on the contents of the action but also on the manner in which the action is executed.[15] The way in which one person approaches another shows a certain 'colour'. One should be able to listen, ask questions, have a conversation, pay attention to the other person's well-being, and be attentive and responsive. These qualities are precisely those that make a human being a caring person. We wish in this regard to defend the need to enlarge the definition of the concept of care, and hence to make an attitude of care an integral element of the understanding of ourselves and of our relationships.

[14] H. REINDERS, *De grenzen van het rechtendiscours*, in H. MANSCHOT & M. VERKERK (ed.), *op. cit.*, p. 74-96.

[15] E. CARSE, *The 'Voice of Care'. Implications for Bio-Ethical Education*, in *The Journal of Medicine and Philosophy* 16/1 (1991) 5-28.

6.2.2. *Care as a Fundamental Human Activity*

The most remarkable characteristic of the integral concept of humanity is without a doubt the great emphasis on the concept of care in order to describe the essence of human life. According to care ethicists, the concept of care can be defined as a fundamental way of life. This 'way of life' expresses itself in specific behaviour (actions and attitudes) that focuses on maintaining, continuing and repairing 'our world', so that we can live in it as well as possible: "Our world includes our bodies, our selves and our environment (fellow human beings, animals, nature etc.) which we try to interweave in a life-sustaining web".[16] Care is, thus, an active as well as a passive form of involvement in our world along with our fellow human beings in order to preserve it as much as possible. According to this viewpoint, care is not just a necessary but uninteresting irrelevance which happens to be part of life. It is, on the contrary, a practice that permeates all human actions from the beginning to the end and without which human life is impossible. Care is oriented towards improving the quality of life. From this angle, care is an ethically relevant concept.

Joan Tronto distinguishes four dimensions of care.[17] The first dimension is worrying about someone or something (being troubled, being anxious, paying attention to, being aware of). Without this attitude the request for care is not perceived. The corresponding ethical attitude is 'attentive rapport'. Rollo May considers this basic caring attitude as the most essential condition for ethical actions.[18] An attitude of indifference can never co-exist with this basic ethical attitude of attentive rapport. The second dimension of care is 'taking care of' (looking after, providing care); however this does not imply that one executes actual tasks of caring. One only takes responsibility for improving the condition of the other person. Responsibility is thus the corresponding ethical attitude. The third dimension of care concerns the actual caregiving. This dimension of care requires the necessary competence. Finally, there is the dimension of care-receiving. This dimension distinguishes itself from the previous three since

---

[16] B. FISHER & J. TRONTO, *Toward a Feminist Theory of Care*, in E. ABEL & M. NELSON (ed.), *Circles of Care. Work and Identity in Women's Lives*, Albany, 1991, p. 40; J. TRONTO, *Moral Boundaries. A Political Argument for an Ethic of Care*, London, 1993, p. 103.

[17] J. TRONTO, *op. cit.*.

[18] R. MAY, *Love and Will*, New York, 1969.

the focus here is on the viewpoint of the person receiving care and not on that of the caregiver. To receive care demands from the receiver an attitude of responsiveness towards the caregiver.

The above-mentioned concept of care corresponds to at least two levels of the integral concept of the person. Firstly, care in itself is a relational activity. The act of caring always takes place within the framework of a relationship wherein the caregiver and the care-taker are reciprocally involved. Even when the person receiving care cannot give verbal or conscious expression to his/her request for care, his/her presence alone is the motivating factor for a caring human being to assume the giving of care to a person in need of care. If the person receiving care is conscious, then the process of care can only be considered as 'completed' if the offered care is affirmed by that person. The fundamental reciprocity of a relation-ship of care can be found in the dynamic interaction of giving care and receiving care.[19] Secondly, the four dimensions of care illustrate most convincingly that empirical acts of care as much as caring atti-tudes and intuitions form a part of the integral concept of care. Therefore, according to Tronto, concrete acts of care can only be exe-cuted if the caregiver has paid attention to the request for care in the first place and consequently felt responsible to change the situation. The person receiving care for his or her part has to be responsive to the offered care. According to Tronto, attention, responsibility and responsiveness are the essential attitudes that those involved in the process of care must acquire if care is to be optimal. This integral concept of care corresponds with the concept of the person wherein not only objective aspects of actions but also affective, intuitive and virtuous capabilities of human beings have to be taken into consi-deration.

6.2.3. Ethical Problems

The integral concept of the person and care which forms the basis of the care approach has a fundamental influence on the manner in which ethical problems are detected, interpreted and solved. Contrary to the approach based on principles wherein ethical problems are considered conflicts between abstract, universal ethical principles, the ethics of care understands ethical problems as linked

---

[19] G. WIDDERSHOVEN, op. cit..

to tensions and breakdowns in the relational care network of human beings. These conflicts, anchored in relationships, cannot be solved by logical arguments whereby abstract ethical principles are being linked to one another. On the contrary, attention has to be focused rather on the diverse components that together constitute the concrete context wherein the conflict takes place. All persons involved are in a well-defined relationship and bond to a lesser or greater extent. From the perspective of care, the nature and quality of the bond between people forms the basis for ethical interpretation. This relationship, however, does not stand on its own. It is situated in time, in a continuous life story, where others also play a part. It is therefore of the utmost importance to attach great value to detecting, interpreting and comparing the viewpoints of all those involved in the conflict. One has to judge from the perspective of real people involved in personal relationships. Thus, we must promote solutions to ethical problems that search for the bonds of care, attention and responsibility while we must discourage relationships accompanied by helplessness, indifference, and pain.[20] In other words, ethical conflicts should take a narrative form that requires an interpretative approach.

6.3. The Ethics of Care and the Physician-Patient relationship: a Case of Artificial Feeding and Hydration

The aforementioned aspects of the ethics of care, namely the integral concept of the person and care on the one hand and the subsequently deduced narrative-hermeneutic concept of ethical problems on the other hand, open new perspectives in tackling clinical-ethical problems. We will illustrate the ethics of care approach based on clinical-ethical decision making as it relates to artificial feeding and hydration of a geriatric patient: please consider the following case of Denise.

Denise is 85 years old and has for the past 7 years been a resident in a nursing home. The management considers good nutritional care to be one

---

[20] M. VERKERK, *Zorg of contract. Een andere ethiek*, in H. MANSCHOT & M. VERKERK (ed.), *Ethiek van de zorg*, Amsterdam, 1994, p. 53-73.

of their top priorities. They invest a lot of man-hours and resources towards this end. The underlying goal of this policy is to delay as long as possible artificial feeding and hydration. And, if possible, to avoid administering it altogether. At this nursing home, artificial feeding and hydration are given only very exceptionally.

Denise's functional condition was relatively good but she needed assistance with some activities of everyday life. She was recently transferred to a nearby general hospital for hip surgery. Before the operation could take place, Denise suffered a CVA (cerebrovascular accident) which left her partially paralysed (hemiplegic), unable to speak (aphasia) and her swallow reflex was impaired. When her condition stabilised somewhat, she was transferred to the hospital's geriatric department where she is still a patient. The physicians did not expect her functional status to improve to such an extent as to enable her to leave the hospital. Five years ago, the hospital created an Ethics Committee, but until now it has focused primarily on reviewing clinical trial protocols. The hospital therefore has no policy on ethics (protocols, opinions, guidelines etc.) relating to medical decisions at the end of life.

Without much consultation, artificial feeding and hydration (via nasal drip) are immediately administered. But it is soon obvious that the drip is making Denise uncomfortable. She has pulled it out three times already. She is not eligible, for medical reasons, for a gastrostomy. Denise also suffers from Parkinson's disease, but has no other underlying pathologies. She still has a reasonable life expectancy provided she is well cared for and receives adequate nourishment. The nurses have ascertained that Denise is sometimes alert but more and more often experiences periods of confusion. Denise cannot speak but the nurses have managed to let her indicate yes or no using simple gestures.

Denise during her active life was an independent woman. She did not marry and her only close relatives are two nieces and a nephew. Earlier, the family had already expressed the wish that Denise's comfort is to be guaranteed, but not to artificially extend her life. The family confided to the team of caregivers that Denise – just before her admission to hospital – told them that she would rather be dead than completely dependent on the care of others. The family informed the team of caregivers in writing – after Denise had pulled out the drip for the third time – that it is their unanimous wish to withdraw artificial feeding and hydration. They are of the opinion that the autonomous wish of the patient needs to be respected.

Nurse A, who has cared for Denise since the start of her admission to the geriatric department, voices her concern regarding the family's viewpoint. She feels that the family has not reached its decision out of concern for the well-being of Denise. She is very uncomfortable because she thinks her patient 'is being abandoned' by her family. She sees it as degrading to deny artificial feeding and hydration. She sees the granting of the family's wish as an attack upon her professional and moral identity. She deems it possible that the family's decision stems from interested motives; their aunt is very affluent. The social worker, who in the past has spoken several times with the family regarding organisational and financial aspects of their aunt's stay in hospital, cannot quite exclude conflicts of interests.

Denise's nephew has confided to Nurse A his discontent with the so-called 'unanimous wish of the family'. In his opinion, his aunt's life has still a certain value, be it only on a affective and spiritual level. Nurse A uses this viewpoint as proof to demonstrate the lack of unanimity within the family.

Denise's attending physician is more inclined to follow the family's wish. She declares that their viewpoint is maybe the closest one to what Denise would have wanted. She thinks that Nurse A exaggerates the discomfort caused by the withdrawing of artificial feeding and hydration. The doctor also states that this possible discomfort has to be weighed against the discomfort of continuing artificial feeding and hydration (since the nasal drip has been pulled out three times). Moreover, the attending physician is irritated by the conviction with which Nurse A states her opinion. She makes it perfectly clear that in the end it is the doctor who decides.

It is agreed upon that Denise will be asked if she wishes artificial feeding and hydration to be continued. Nurse A was not quite sure about what should be done if Denise should refuse artificial feeding and hydration. In the end, it was decided to respect Denise's wishes, regardless.

Denise indicates by acquired sign language to her team of caregivers (present are the attending physician, nurse A and two other Nurses) that she wishes artificial feeding and hydration to continue. The family is informed of Denise's wish. They react with dissent, anger even. The family refuses to accept the fact that the hospital has not taken its wishes into account. They threaten to move their aunt from the hospital to the nursing home, where according to them artificial feeding and hydration will not be administered. They communicate their displeasure to the hospital's director and inform him of their plans. They also demand that this conversation with Denise should be repeated in their presence and in the presence of the family doctor. Nurses fear that the presence of the family will put pressure on Denise. Moreover, the case has become somewhat urgent since Denise has not received any nourishment for the last few days. Taking into account the recently expressed wish by Denise and the possible fatal consequences of not providing nutrition, the attending physician decides to resume artificial feeding and hydration until Denise has unequivocally expressed her wish in the presence of her family.

Some days later, Denise's cognitive abilities have seriously deteriorated. The patient moans during treatment and clutches her head. It is not clear what is making her uncomfortable. A physical examination provides no explanation for her symptoms. When she, in the presence of her relatives and family doctor, is asked if she wishes artificial feeding and hydration, Denise reacts with a violent crying-fit and restless plucking at the nasal drip. To the caregivers it is not clear anymore whether they have to interpret this behaviour as a purely impulsive reaction or as a clear refusal. Consequently, all those involved reaffirm their previous opinions. Moreover, they defend them more vehemently. Nurse A is still of the opinion that administering nourishment is a moral duty and she cannot justify " letting this patient down". The attending physician was initially inclined (based on information provided by the family) not to resume artificial feeding and hydration. The subsequent wish of the patient expressed to her caregivers, made her doubt her decision, which resulted in a temporarily resuming of artificial feeding and hydration. Since the patient is unable to confirm or deny this wish and the repeated attempts to pull out the nasal drip, the doctor is not clear what should be done. She asks herself whether to continue artificial feeding and hydration should not be considered futile treatment (therapeutic obstenicy). The family interprets Denise's restless behaviour as a confirmation of their viewpoint. They demand the immediate cessation of the artificial feeding and hydration and a transfer to the nursing home which, according to them, is the only place where their aunt can die with dignity.

6.3.1. Ethical Considerations

From the viewpoint of principlism, the ethical problem pertaining to the case of Denise could be considered as one of rights and duties, whereby Denise's claims, those of her family, and caregivers are either in balance or in conflict. These rights and duties can be expressed at a theoretical level as conflicting principles, namely those of respect for the autonomy of the patient, nonmaleficence, beneficence and justice. One can imagine that the use of these theoretical principles allows the construal of arguments both for and against the withdrawing of the artificial feeding and hydration. These theoretical principles form the basis for finding a solution and for determining what is or is not relevant. In this way of reasoning, it is for example plausible that to determine Denise's wishes is of the utmost importance, since in this way respect for the autonomy of Denise can be realised.

According to the ethics of care approach, however, the ethical problem as it relates to the case of Denise cannot be reduced to a theoretical conflict between two or more principles. On the contrary, clinical-ethical problems are related to concrete patients who are a part of a network of relationships. In other words, each clinical-ethical problem is hidden behind a relational web of the persons concerned. In the case of Denise, this relational web entails, in the first place, Denise herself, her family (two nieces and a nephew), the attending physician, the nursing team (that manifests itself mainly in the person of nurse A), the directors of the institution (of the hospital and the nursing home where Denise has lived for the past seven years). Because of the very difficult decision that had to be taken, this relational network has been put under severe pressure. In order to reduce the pressure, a solution will have to be found that satisfies all parties. This implies that all those concerned can find themselves in agreement as much as possible on the proposed solution. Much attention needs to be paid to the opinions, viewpoints and experiences of all interested parties. The idea that all those concerned can lay claim to certain rights is not a deciding factor. Attention should not be paid to Denise's claim alone, or the possible claim of her family, or her caregivers (or to the balance between all these claims), but to a compound given: the relational bond. All the parties in this case are in a relationship with one another. These relationships have a strong influence on the opinions expressed in this case. Thus, Denise's 'silent wishes' can only be construed and understood against the background of her personal life story. This means that the ethics of care approach demands great skill from all those involved in ethical decision making when interpreting opinions and viewpoints which manifest themselves in the guise of stories: clinical ethics reveals itself as a form of narrative and interpretative ethics.

6.3.2. *Clinical-Ethical Decision Making as an Interpretative Dialogue*

From the ethics of care approach, two important characteristics can be deduced: on the one hand the hermeneutic-interpretative aspect and on the other hand the dialogical aspect. We will illustrate these two aspects with elements from the case of Denise. The analysis of a problem according to the ethics of care approach is characterised by the large amount of attention paid to interpreting the different viewpoints of those involved with the ethical problem. One assumes that these viewpoints are never completely clear to those concerned. Even the person who voices a certain opinion is never totally aware of the complete contents or consequences of his/her opinion. What a person exactly wants is never really clear, especially when confronted with life-threatening situations. It is therefore obvious that Denise's wishes cannot be considered as a given whose contents can easily be deduced from the case study and which clarifies for all those involved what must be done for Denise throughout the consecutive stages of her care. What Denise would have wanted under the specific circumstances needs to be construed based on what we know of her life, previous pronouncements and actual reactions from Denise to concrete proposals. This information from Denise does not reach us directly or without a mediator, but is told by third parties that knew Denise more or less well. This case deals mainly with Denise's family, which opines that they are able to tell us something about Denise's past. From conflicting information communicated by family members and from background information provided by a social worker, it becomes clear that this information is not impartial. On the contrary, the disagreement of Denise's nephew illustrates that the concrete relational bonds that the family members have with their aunt influence all viewpoints. This case clearly shows that there is no such thing as direct access to Denise's wishes. Furthermore, it has never been clear whether Denise ever stated 'clearly formulated wishes' in regard to what should be done if she ever found herself in her present situation.

What does apply to Denise's wishes, namely that these cannot be considered to be a given but need to be gradually construed, developed and then interpreted, is also valid to a certain extent with regards to the opinions, ideas and viewpoints as formulated by all those concerned with this case. Let us take the wishes of Nurse A as an example to illustrate this point. What does she really want? On what information is her opinion based? Does she – at whatever cost – want to continue the artificial feeding and hydration or does she not want to let Denise down? If she wanted the latter – which we can assume in view of her strong commitment to Denise – one could imagine her radically changing her opinion in regards to continue the artificial feeding and hydration if she was to receive and be receptive to recent clinical findings on the therapeutic value of artificial feeding and hydrating terminally ill patients.[21] These studies show that under these circumstances artificial feeding and hydration cause more disadvantages than advantages for the patient and that other forms of palliative care more accurately show a caring presence to the patient. Taking into account the possibility of incomplete and/or incorrect information on the part of Nurse A, we could deduce that the accurate content of the nurse's wishes is not a static but dynamic given and thus continually has to be explored and developed. It is only through the process of joint exploration and consultation that the wishes of Nurse A gradually become clear. In view of the aforementioned, it is a pity that the attending physician did not take the time to have a conversation with Nurse A during which he could have clarified the recent clinical findings on artificial feeding and hydration (which presumably she already knew). The physician avoided the conversation by stating that "in the end it is a doctor who decides whether or not artificial feeding and hydration will cease". By using an argument of power, the ethical question of what is in Denise's best interest slips into the background in favour of the pseudo-ethical question of who has the right to decide. The goal of the process of interpretation, which is to purify ethical viewpoints, is abruptly broken off and replaced by an external question about decision making authority. The dialogic aspect of clinical-ethical decision making is thus ignored. We will illustrate this below.

If we are to consider seriously the hermeneutic-narrative aspect of clinical-ethical decision making, then it automatically follows that this process also has a dialogical aspect. This dialogical dimension of the clinical-ethical decision making process can be interpreted from two different angles. On the one hand, there is the perspective of interdisciplinary co-operation, while, on the other hand, there is the perspective of the integral concept of the person and the concept of care. First of all, several parties are always involved in caring for others. Beside the patient and the patient's family, there is the team of caregivers, usually of an interdisciplinary composition. For the clinical-ethical dialogue to succeed, it is necessary that all those involved are motivated to explore jointly the possible alternatives.

---

[21] T. FINUCANE, C. CHRISTMAS & K. TRAVIS, *Tube Feeding in Patients with Advanced Dementia*, in *The Journal of the American Medical Association* 282 (1999) 1365-1370; M. GILLICK, *Rethinking the Role of Tube Feeding in Patients with Advanced Dementia*, in *The New England Journal of Medicine* 342 (2000) 206-210.

Hereby, one assumes that it is not known in advance what is objectively right in a given situation. This can only be discovered by linking all the different (e.g. personal, familial, medical, nursing) viewpoints. Via this confrontation, one can identify pseudo-questions and solutions based on incomplete or incorrect information. We have already referred to the possibility of refining Nurse A's opinion by giving her access to correct and comprehensible information on the therapeutic value of artificial feeding and hydrating terminally ill patients.

Secondly, the dialogical model in clinical-ethical decision making corresponds much better with the integral concept of care and the person that underlies the ethics of care approach. Seen from an ethics of care perspective, it should be a misconception to think that in the search for what is best for Denise, all attention should be focused on Denise's wishes as an isolated individual. What is best for Denise is that which can be meaningfully integrated into her life and life history; this manifests itself in the form of stories of mutual bonding, responsibility and dependence on human beings. The presence of so many concerned parties at Denise's bedside aptly illustrates the relational web in which she is caught until the end of her life. In order to do justice to the relational dimension of Denise's life during the decision making process, one has to take into account the opinions and ideas of all those involved in her care (with the exclusion of those whose opinions are not based on a positive bond with Denise). The ethics of care approach does not prefer self-determination as such (whether as a patient, a family-member or a caregiver) but rather the 'joint' decision. Organising consultations, where all those concerned get a chance to express their opinion on the ethical problem posed by Denise's care, is essential in order to reach the right decision. It is imperative to listen to the stories told by Denise, her family, her physician, her nurse and the institutional-policy formulators because they outline the narrative context in which Denise's care has to take shape. It is necessary to put great emphasis on those efforts contributing to a joint decision. The goal of this joint decision making is to reduce as much as possible the pressure on the relational network, caused by the ethical problem. Doctors and nurses should be able to function again as a team. All parties involved should be able to face each other again and continue to build an authentic relationship.

6.4. A View on Moral Perception and Institutional Policy

Before we conclude this study, we want to draw attention to two aspects of ethical decision making, which care ethicists increasingly emphasise as topics that have a strong influence on the physician-patient relationship. The first aspect relates to the underpinnings of the actual ethical deliberation process, namely moral perception. The second aspect deals with the influence of contextual factors (inter-disciplinary, institutional, social, etc) upon the contents and process of ethical decision making.

6.4.1. *Moral Perception and Moral Sensitivity*

We have illustrated above, how, according to the ethics of care approach, the clinical-ethical decision making process can be viewed as a sort of interpretative dialogue. Based on a reciprocal dialogue, all those involved in the clinical-ethical decision-making process commit themselves as accurately as possible to an evaluation and interpretation of a clinical care situation from an ethical perspective. The essential condition for such a narrative-hermeneutic dialogue is the caregivers' perception of a problem that is both clinical and ethical. Hence clinical ethics unavoidably begins with a good moral perception.[22] According to Joan Tronto, moral perception situates itself in the first phase of the caring process.[23] During this exploratory phase, a caring person is 'morally sensitive' to his/her surroundings. He/she is attentive to what happens around him/her and tries to detect situations where the life-sustaining web containing the others is weakened. By this morally sensitive attitude, a caring person clears the path in order to 'be touched by' and subsequently to 'be concerned' by the situation of the other who is in need of care.

A sensitive moral perception or an attentive moral outlook determines to a large extent what is relevant to observe and reflect on to the ethical level. In this way, an accurate perception of the ethical components of this specific clinical problem is the only possible condition to ensure adequate clarification of the ethical problem. Based on their moral perception, we can state that all those involved in

---

[22] L. BLUM, *Friendship, Altruism and Morality*, London, 1980; L. BLUM, *Moral Perception and Particularity*, in *Ethics* 101 (1991) 701-725.

[23] J. TRONTO, *op.cit.*.

caring for Denise arrive at different ethical points of order. The family sees it as a problem that Denise's autonomous wishes are not being met. The nurse, on the contrary, thinks that withdrawing artificial feeding and hydration is irreconcilable with the patient's dignity because she has interpreted this option of care as letting the patient down. The attending physician's first concern is not to cause any more harm. It is remarkable that many of those involved view the ethical problem posed by this case as a battle of conflicting principles, i.e. the principle of autonomy (family), the principle of non-maleficence (physician) and the principle of beneficence (nurse). As the case further develops, we notice how every participant clings increasingly tenaciously to his or her principle and is less and less interested in interpreting the viewpoints of others.

As soon as one detects that this conflict is in fact difficult to solve, the ethical discussion regarding what is best for Denise gets broken off very quickly and is replaced by a more procedural approach that focusses on who has the right to decide. Such an evolution during an ethical deliberation process is linked to the perception of the ethical problem as a conflict between principles, obligations, rights and claims and to the way in which to handle this (procedural instead of contentual-interpretative). An ethics of care perspective in the case of Denise would have probably unearthed completely different relevant ethical aspects (i.e. the relationship between Denise and her family). Moreover, it would have led to a different approach (dialogical and interpretative).

The American philosopher Laurence Blum writes that a good moral perception is characterised by attention to the particular.[24] An accurate insight into a particular situation should enable the caregiver to discern which ethical factors are relevant in a clinical case. By paying attention to the particular, the moral observer learns that each situation is different. This so-called 'particularistic attitude' prevents the caregiver from making irresponsible generalisations and can therefore be used as a tool when searching for the correct moral interpretation of a specific patient related situation. It is obvious that such a particularistic attitude is of paramount importance in clinical ethics. The participants in the clinical-ethical decision making are expected to become as aware as possible of the particularity of the

---

[24] L. BLUM, *Friendship, Altruism and Morality*, 1991.

case under discussion. Even if Denise's artificial feeding problem can be linked to general pathologies, the specific existential and relational framework wherein a solution must be found necessitates, nevertheless, an individual approach to Denise's case.

The particular character of moral perception is reflected not only in its object (the immutable clinical reality) but also in the subject. A moral outlook is an ability that should be associated not so much with the intellect as with the moral person as a whole. Moral perception is not limited to one segment of a human being, e.g. his rational ability. On the contrary, different aspects of a person's unique personality are activated while perceiving and interpreting a concrete clinical- ethical problem. It is therefore the unique and integral personality of the caregiver that participates in the ethical discussion regarding a concrete patient. The caregiver's medical-technical knowledge is only one aspect of his/her personality. Other equally important factors that influence the moral interpretation-process are the caregiver's implicit, intuitive moral ideas (regarding e.g. the quality of life, suffering, human dignity and death), his/her emotional, relational and communicative abilities (empathy, emotional intelligence etc.), his/her personality traits (altruism, dialogical or introvert), and his/her moral background (his/her own personal set of values, ideology, theoretical knowledge of ethics, experience with ethical dilemmas).[25] In the case of Denise, this entails that we can assume that the contents and interpretation of ethical tensions are strongly coloured by the existential, psychological, relational and moral 'housekeeping' of all those involved.

The emphasis on the particularistic aspect of moral perception indicates that clinical-ethical decision-making in practice may never be reduced to a form of 'moral engineering' whereby ethical principles are linked in an abstract-theoretical manner.[26] In our opinion, the role of the morally perceptive person should be larger than applying formal principles and detecting the most ethical course of action. The morally motivated caregiver should absorb the case with which he or she is confronted, identify the morally relevant aspects and assume an attitude – supported by factual actions – which will (as much as

---

[25] *Ibid.*

[26] A. CAPLAN, *Applying Morality to Advances in Biomedicine. Can and should this be done?*, in W.B. BONDESON (ed.), *New Knowledge in the Biomedical Sciences*, Dordrecht, 1982, p. 155-168.

possible) develop the inherent moral possibilities of a particular situation or *'le meilleur humain possible'* according to Paul Ricoeur.[27] This whole process requires a high degree of moral sensitivity on the part of the caregiver. One refers here to the ability to develop a great sensitivity to the moral background present within a particular situation and to subsequently react appropriately.[28]

6.4.2. *The Institutional Dimension of Care*

Clinical ethics is often regarded as a sort of micro-ethics that orients medical actions within the framework of the individual doctor-patient relationship. Clinical ethics has this association with micro-ethics in common with the ethics of care, which is also mainly seen as the ethics of individual relationships (between family members, neighbours, colleagues, friends, etc.).[29] In our opinion this demonstrates a severe lack of insight into the different aspects of clinical care; it implies that clinical-ethical decision making is locked up in the intimacy of the doctor-patient relationship.

A careful reading of Denise's case teaches us that the doctor-patient relationship cannot be seen as an isolated form of interaction, but is situated in the global care process, which is realised through the co-ordinated activities of a team of caregivers (physicians, nurses, social workers etc.), who are also a part of a health care institution (general hospital, nursing home). This team of caregivers is interdisciplinary in make-up, therefore the ethical dialogue in the team acquires an interdisciplinary dimension. The institutional context of the nursing home and the hospital where Denise resides, is partially outlined in the existence of concrete opinions and policies on care or lack thereof. The case of Denise is to a large extent marked by the tension between the existence of a carefully thought out policy on nutritional care at the nursing home, on the one hand, and the lack of such policy at the hospital, on the other hand. Also typical for the institutional culture in which the case of Denise unfolds, is the observation that, although the hospital has a medical ethics committee

---

[27] P. RICOEUR, *Le problème du fondement de la morale*, in *Sapienza* 28 (1975) 313-337.

[28] P. VAN TONGEREN, *Ethical Manipulations. An Evaluation of the Debate Surrounding Genetic Screening*, in *Human Gene Therapy* 2 (1991) 71-75; P. VAN TONGEREN, *Morele passiviteit*, in *Wijsgerig Perspectief* 33 (1992-1993) 108-112.

[29] N. JECKER & W. REICH, *Contemporary Ethics of Care*, in W. REICH (ed.), *op. cit.*, p. 336-344.

at its disposal, the committee has barely begun making headway in developing an institutional policy regarding dignified care at the end of life. This contextual information together with the fact that at the hospital without a lot of consultation, one immediately started artificial feeding and hydration via a nasal drip, gives us the opportunity to form a rather detailed image of the institutional circumstances wherein the clinical-ethical dialogue about Denise unfolds. The hospital has barely any experience with structured interdisciplinary ethical consultations. Also the team that treats Denise has obviously not been systematically attentive to the ethical dimensions related to the chosen treatment options, such as artificial food and fluid administration. All these contextual factors greatly influence the questions asked (or not), the problems signalled (or not), the solutions proposed (or not) or simply how Denise is treated.

A good observer of the clinical-ethical dialogue will quickly note that the process and outcome of ethical reflection is influenced not only by the above mentioned institutional factors, but also by other external factors, such as, for example, the position of power between doctors and nurses, the concrete working relationship within the team and in the hospital, the relationship between caregiver and hospital directors, etc. The influence of professional relationships and positions on the ethical decision making process is expressed in the concept of the 'moral position of the caregiver'. This means that the actual position of caregivers in an institution of care is crucially important for the way in which they deal with ethical problems and participate (or not) in ethical consultations.[30] In reference to the case here presented, one can suspect that in view of the physician's irritation with Nurse A, she will only moderately appreciate the assertive attitude of nurses in the ethical debate. Is the attending physician convinced of the contribution supplied by an interdisciplinary ethical dialogue in the search for what is humanly possible for Denise? This difficult ethical dialogue between all those concerned with the case illustrates how ethical problems, next to clinical ones, are also predominantly anchored in institutional, professional and relational dimensions. Ethical problems occur in an atmosphere of power-

---

[30] A. VAN DER AREND & C. GASTMANS, *Ethik für Pflegende*, Bern, 1996; V. JAMES, *Who Has the Power? Some Problems and Issues Affecting the Nursing Care of Dying Patients*, in *European Journal of Cancer Care* 5 (1996) 73-80.

lesness, helplesness, emotional concern, indifference, efficiency and cost-efficiency, pressure at work, (in)competence etc. This atmosphere determines who expresses which moral convictions and the kind of influence they will have on care.[31] For a few years, the framework of 'organisational ethics' has led to extensive research into the institutional influences on clinical ethics.[32] One could describe the link between organisational and clinical ethics as the critical and systematic reflection on values which underlie organisational and policy-based options and which have a direct influence on the process and quality of patient care.[33] A concrete example: reflections on the statutes of the charter, the patient-oriented institution, possibility of patient-oriented (i.e. guarantees for patient safety) and yet cost- efficient care, the organisation of care (patient-oriented or task-oriented), handling tension between professional groups (such as doctors and nurses), the involvement of and the stimulating role of policy formulators in formal ethical consultation channels (i.e. Ethics Committees), criteria for hiring caregivers, etc.

We could state that with the organisational-policy-based component of care, we are increasingly confronted with a "third" party, which, using its direct or indirect influence, orchestrates the clinical-ethical dialogue. A characteristic of this third party is that it deploys initiatives, outside the caregiver-patient relationship which determine the circumstances and peripheral conditions of clinical practice. Recent research indicates that clinical-ethical decision-making is to a large extent influenced by institutional-organisational choices. However, it is problematic that these institutional-organisational factors mostly do not become explicit as such, hence the absence of an ethical touchstone. Consequently, a development has taken place whereby an increasingly important role is attributed to management in ethical care questions. Discussing ethics is no longer a matter for caregivers alone, but also for institutions of care as a whole, including the policy makers. This means that those responsible for policy have to be explicit about ethical questions and the choices made. Further-

---

[31] M. VERKERK, *De organisatie als praktijk van verantwoordelijkheid*, in J. GRASTE & D. BAUDUIN (ed.), *ibid.*, 2000.

[32] R. SPENCER, A. MILLS, M. RORTY & P. WERHANE, *Organizational Ethics in Health Care*, Oxford, 2000; R. HALL, *An Introduction to Healthcare Organizational Ethics*, Oxford, 2000.

[33] R. POTTER, *On Our Way to Integrated Bioethics. Clinical, Organizational, Communal*, in *The Journal of Clinical Ethics* 10/3 (1999) 171-177.

more, they should create forums to discuss norms and values that could give guidance during the making of those choices. For all these tasks institutional policy needs to develop tools. One of those tools is an Ethics Committee. Thus ethics can become an integral part of institutional policy.

6.5. Conclusion

When we reflect on the field of ethics of care from afar, the approach seems to be connected with a specific underlying approach to (health) care and also with a specific philosophical-ethical viewpoint on human beings and a dignified life. Defenders and opponents of the ethics of care not only have a different opinion on care, but also refer to different concepts of the person and even to diverging methodologies of ethical analysis. In this contribution we have reflected on three elements from the ethic of care approach which in our opinion could open up the current clinical-ethical debate. Firstly, we outlined the importance of the relational network wherein an ethical problem occurs. Clarifying and solving ethical problems will require an interpretation of the stories of those involved and how those stories can be linked to one another. Secondly, the ethics of care draws our attention to the fact that this interpretative dialogue begins with a good moral perception, which is attentive to the particularity of a concrete case. Finally, the growing convergence between the ethics of care and organisational ethics, which points out to the clinical ethicist that attentiveness to the specific always has to be accompanied by a realistic evaluation of the contextual factors on an institutional level, can drastically influence the ethical decision making process. In calling these three topics to attention, we hope to have made a modest contribution to what could be called an integral clinical ethics: an ethics anchored in clinical practice, based upon an integral concept of care and sensitive to the larger context wherein clinical practice takes place.

7

EPILOGUE

The Physician-Patient Relationship

Maurice A.M. De Wachter

After everything has been said by various authors, the epilogue is meant to recall the original design envisioned by the planning committee concerning the physician-patient relationship, to see how the authors acquitted themselves, and to suggest lines for further exploration by teachers of medical ethics with professionals and students.

The six chapters of Part One were meant to highlight the Western, more particularly the European characteristics of the doctor-patient relationship. The authors, one dare say, have done just that, and they have done it well. Half of them has written about the state of the art, more particularly about the context of the doctor-patient relationship in a given region of Europe. The other half has offered more philosophical reflections on core concepts such as autonomy and respect for the totality of the human person. Together they have focused on the elements and the dynamics of that relationship.

The physician-patient relationship had been chosen because it is a major, if not the most basic theme in the literature of medicine, reflecting its unique role in medical practice. In fact, it is the only area where medicine may fulfill its mission of bringing the greatest benefit to mankind. For thousands of years numerous facets of medicine have been linked to that relationship, some on the side of the physician, others on the patient's side. Thus, respect, empathy, availability by always 'being there', truthfulness, compassion until the end, to name a few qualities expected from the physician. From the patient's side, trust, compliance, information and communication are rightly expected. Together, physician and patient may prevent or cure disease, together they may be able to face the final moments of one's life. This is a tall order, especially after the original intimacy of the personal relationship was cooled of by 'scientific' medicine and technology.[1] Nowadays, the personal tradition of bedside medicine has been definitively challenged and changed by a more instrumental way of treating the patient. The GP has been replaced by specialists. In our rapidly developing and global societies, we find that patient autonomy is becoming a dominant value worldwide. What then, are the main points our authors have brought to the fore?

The trend towards autonomy may have been set in the United States of America but is, by no means, restricted to that country, not even to the Western world. Paternalism is being replaced by patient autonomy. Nevertheless, R. Lie, in a somewhat contrary fashion, argues both practically and theoretically against this widely accepted proposition. He shows that, in the United States, informed consent is largely absent from the clinic. Moreover, he exposes theoretical problems intrinsic to the autonomy model.[2] He, then, looks for alternatives but realizes that none of the suggested ones will do. So, what might the way forward be? Not unexpectedly, recent studies in Northern as well as Southern Europe have shown that professional autonomy of the doctors is in dire need of repair, having been damaged by the destructive pressure of consumer's preferences. Rather than submitting to the widespread view of doctor-patient rivalry for autonomy, R. Lie believes that time must be taken for experimenting with new models of the physician-patient relationship.

It so happens that the next chapter is written by authors from Southern Europe. F. Abel and F. Torralba analyse the doctor-patient relationship in the Mediterranean sphere, more particularly in Spain. They have no doubt about patient autonomy being a progress in the

---

[1] About the influence of science on the doctor-patient relationship, see R. PORTER, *The Greatest Benefit to Mankind*, London, 1997, especially p. 9-10 and p. 668-709.

[2] An earlier, shorter version of R. Lie's chapter appeared in *Ethical Perspectives* 4/4 (1997) 263-270. Approving as well as critical comments appeared by X. ETXEBERRIA MAULEON, *op. cit.*, p. 271-273 and by G. KINSMA, *op. cit.*, p. 274-279.

doctor-patient relationship. But, then, they define the relationship in quite different terms than the Anglo-Saxon model of principlism. In line with Laín Entralgo they explore the doctor-patient relationship as a friendship.

Within the range of European languages, Bondolfi makes several important points about 'autonomy' in German speaking countries. First, he shows the different meanings of autonomy in various professions, even in medical ones, for instance nursing as opposed to other medical groups. But, even more important, is the particular notion of 'Eigengesetzlichkeit' which is being used in the tradition of positivism, that is scientific and disciplinary independence. This notion may have been of influence upon medical paternalism in the German speaking context. Another point of importance, albeit not limited to German speaking countries, is the prevalence of political and legal uses of autonomy, namely as self-determination rather than as an ethical notion in the Kantian sense.[3] At the level of philosophical reflection M. Patrão-Neves uses both Western history and a comparative method to highlight her concern for personal identity. She deplores that persons are loosing their identity in the artificial context of medical technology. What we need to do, according to her, is to complement the widely acclaimed autonomy principle by a sense of responsibility, both individual and communitarian. She builds her case by referring to the major masters of Western philosophy, and she succeeds in showing, time and again, the mutual need of autonomy and responsibility as integral parts of personal identity.

From a perspective of hermeneutics, G. Widdershoven highlighs the doctor-patient relationship as mutual. Today, the physician-patient relationship is not seldom the reverse of paternalism: now, the patient is in charge. But more refined models are also being proposed. Thus, models based on partnerships, conversation, delibera-

---

[3] I should like to draw the reader's attention to volume I of the present series of Core materials for the development of courses in professional ethics, namely G. DE STEXHE & J. VERSTRAETEN (eds.), *Matter of Breath. Foundations for Professional Ethics*, Leuven, 2000. In particular chapter 10 on *Autonomy*, p. 159-170, will be of interest. There, X. ETXEBERRIA covers both the views on autonomy as held by Kant and Mill.

tion and mutuality. Widdershoven focuses on mutuality. Here, dialogue and deliberation bring parties to change their views. Both patients and doctors critically assess their own values and, subsequently, implement those in their actions. The hermeneutic perspective throws light on the doctor-patient relationship, revealing its basis in intersubjectivity, and confirming it to be mutually formative to the point where, to put it with Gadamer, 'one does not remain what one was'.

The last chapter on care ethics is an important one. In line with Widdershoven, C. Gastmans completes the picture of doctor-patient relationship by bringing it to its full human dimension. Starting from the main criticism of principlism, viz. its lack of a concrete anthropology and its reductionistic tendency to submit to abstract principles, Gastmans believes that, next to reason and rationality, attention must be given to feeling, emotion, intuition. All of those aspects will effectuate a bonding relationship with the patient, who now can be seen as a person. Rather than decide on which of the conflicting principles prevails, care ethics pursues an ongoing interpretative dialogue within a network of caring relations, that should allow to agree upon what is really best for the patient.

Future editions of this handbook may consider some additonal topics which may, in time, prove to be decisive for the doctor-patient relationship. One example is the influence of hospital ethics committees on this relationship. What if patients shall not be treated for infertility unless an ethics committee has evaluated their aptness for proper parenthood? What if an ethics committee has to evaluate a patient's request for euthanasia or assisted suicide? What if hospitals require approvement by an ethics committee of newly developed treatment protocols? Next to what Porter called the invasion of 'science' into the doctor-patient territory, one would discover, in all of the just mentioned examples, the imposition of institutional norms upon activities that once would have come exclusively under the 'colloque singulier' between a doctor and a patient. These issues ought to be looked into.

Part two

HUMAN EXPERIMENTATION

INTRODUCTION

The international character of clinical trials involving human subjects makes it hard to present a specific European ethical perspective. Nevertheless, we invited European philosophers and bioethicists to elaborate in the following part some typically European approaches to this field. Probably the most important notion comes from the French philosopher, Paul Ricoeur (cf. M.L. Delfosse). His concept of *solicitude* proofs to be a useful guidance when controversy emerges in collaborations among people regarding the distribution of benefits in medical research. Such controversies occur particularly when the nations involved do not share the same cultural, political, ethical or economic perspectives and when they are at different stages of development (cf. R. Lie: the discussion on HIV trials). *'Solicitude'* aims at setting up equality in a relationship that could be unequal, which is mostly the case in a research setting. Moreover, Ricoeur links this notion with the European philosophical tradition. He points out that the intuition of true otherness inherent in *'solicitude'* goes together with the well known Kantian categorical imperative ("Act in such a way that you treat humanity as well in your own person as in that of any other always at the same time as an end and never simply as a means."). This is only one illustration of an ethical foundation of medical research. Other authors give similar examples of the need to reflect much more deeply on the presuppositions of research ethics.

In order to apply these insights, we better start with a case presentation. The research protocol carried out to lower the rate of maternal-to-infant transmission of HIV, focuses on using placebo-controlled trials when an effective treatment already exists. This means that individuals in the control groups in developing countries are being treated differently than those in control groups of developed nations (where the control is an established treatment). This may imply that human research subjects are not always and everywhere considered equally worthy.

A National Institutes of Health (NIH) sponsored study conducted in the United States and France (called 'Aids Clinical Trials Group Protocol [ACTG] 076', after the number of the NIH protocol), demonstrated that maternal-to-infant transmission of HIV could be reduced by two-thirds when a particular regimen of the antiretroviral drug zidovudine (AZT) is administered. The so-called 'triple combination therapy' involves three stages: (1) an oral dose of AZT five times a day for an average of 11 weeks during pregnancy; (2) intravenous treatment during labour and (3) oral treatment of the child for 6 weeks after birth.

Although this treatment became the standard of care in the United States and other industrialised countries, several factors made it impossible to follow the regimen in developing countries, primarily cost and the lack of a health care infrastructure to administer the regimen. As a result, some of the clinical trials conducted in Thailand and Africa were designed to test a lower dose of AZT in HIV-positive women, which was much less expensive than the standard dose (the wholesale drug costs for the AZT in the 076 regimen are estimated to be in excess of $800, an amount that is 600 times the annual per capita allocation for healthcare in Malawi), in a placebo-controlled trial. The use of a placebo-controlled trial means that only half of the women who were HIV-positive actually receive the drug. The other half of the women involved in the trial received a placebo. In addition, these studies initiated the treatment much later in pregnancy, since women in these countries do not receive early prenatal care, and the AZT was administered orally rather than intravenously, in line with the availability of medical facilities. Moreover, newborns did not receive full treatment. These departures from the proven ACTG 076 regimen aimed to establish a course of treatment that could reasonably be implemented for HIV-positive pregnant women in resource-poor countries.

For ethical reasons, placebo-controlled trials testing this experimental treatment regimen could not have been conducted in the United States and other developed countries once the efficacy of the ACGT 076 regimen had been established. In other words, it would be considered unethical to withhold from women in a research study an effective treatment that they could obtain as part of their routine medical care. The justification for conducting the research in developing countries was that it compared a new regimen with the existing level of care in those countries, which means: no treatment at all.[1]

---

[1] Paraphrased from NATIONAL BIOETHICS ADVISORY COMMISSION, *Ethical and Policy Issues in International Research: Clinical Trials in Developing Countries*, Bethesda, 2001, p. 2. (http://bioethics.georgetown.edu/nbac/pubs.html)

This case presentation may be a guide to the reading of the contributions of several authors in this second part of our book. The unique character of this second part may be that essentially European authors try to clarify various controversies in international medical research settings. To cite some of these controversies: can research that is beneficial and to which valid consent has been given, still be unethical? M.L. Delfosse will explore whether it is ever possible to answer 'yes' to this question. According to her, asking 'simple' questions as a starting point of ethical reflection will enable to tackle more complex situations in the future (e.g. the case of persons suffering from illnesses at present incurable such as AIDS). Secondly, does the HIV-transmission-case highlight new ethical issues? J.-N. Missa provides us with some striking historical comparisons were physicians arbitrarily planned research activities with little respect for research subjects. Thirdly, is there a conflict between the need to protect the interests of research subjects and the desire to carry out Randomised Clinical Trials (RCTs) which will benefit future patients (e.g. children)? This will be analysed by R. Lie. Finally, the latter will give an overview of the arguments for and against carrying out HIV placebo-controlled trials.

Research ethics has provided the international community with some very important international guidelines. Their importance is that large that we enclose the latest revision of the Helsinki Declaration, together with the European Directive on Good Clinical Practice.

We want to present an ethical clarification of the presuppositions of current research ethics rather than a practical guide for those involved in human research. For the reader it may be a different approach to a field where procedural ethics has taken the lead.

1

EXPERIMENTS CARRIED OUT ON HUMAN SUBJECTS AND THE DOCTOR-PATIENT RELATIONSHIP

Epistemology and Ethics

Marie-Luce Delfosse

It was due to the development and the putting into practice of practical testing methods for physiological and pathological phenomena that medicine gradually became a science as from the 19th century, whereas up to then it was essentially defined as 'the art of healing'. In the place of empirical acts, based on trial and error, or acts based on logical reasoning, there is now a tendency to substitute experimental methods combining inductive and deductive reasoning, a respect for facts, together with their interpretation, a desire both to explain and to care for the patient. What is the impact of this evolution on the relationship of doctors with their patients, and on the standards of professional ethics that regulate this relationship? These are the questions to which this contribution tries to find an answer by setting out the criteria allowing case studies to be analysed, and thereby making clear the ethical considerations. Firstly, the status of medical activities will be studied: is it useful to distinguish between those relating to treatment and those relating to research? If so, how can this be done? Subsequently, the status of those involved in the doctor-patient relationship will be studied: in what manner does experimentation alter this? A reflection is then made on the repercussions of these changes on the way in which ethical problems are posed. Finally, the rules of professional ethics regarding human experimentation will be studied.

Before starting, it is necessary to make clear that in the present text a distinction will be made between ethics as a philosophical reflection and professional ethics, an ensemble of recommendations made to a professional group by a body whose authority it recognises. Ethics as philosophy aims at offering a coherent viewpoint to guide action in general, or a particular type of action. Professional ethics makes possible the exercise of different aspects of a profession, in this case the medical profession, while respecting values that were recognised as important from the beginning (e.g. not to do harm to the patient), and at specific points of its history (e.g. the valorisation of science since the 19th century, or, at the present time, a growing insistence on a respect of the autonomy of the patient). An important difference here becomes apparent: ethics as philosophy is based on, or implies, a certain vision of mankind and the world, while the recommendations of professional ethics combine several sources of ethical interpretation. These recommendations, taking the form of declarations, of guidelines, or of an oath, are directed to the conscience of doctors. This means that their violation does not incur sanctions, except for indirect ones, for example, as regards tests carried out on human beings, the rule forbidding the publication of research results not in conformity with the recognised ethical principles. The latter often inspire the deontological rules. They acquire a legal status when they are integrated into a rule of law. The declarations and guiding lines in any case make it clear that doctors are not exempt from their penal, civil and deontological responsibility under the internal laws and rules of their native country.

To bring the projected line of reflection to a proper conclusion, it is important to regulate the analysis properly, that is to say to allow oneself the possibility of finding the specific questions raised by carrying out experiments on human beings *as such*. This is difficult, as experimental situations are complex and their study can be biased. To approach them immediately under their ethical dimension is to reach a dead end, due to not having rigorously separated the different elements that in real life are mixed. For this reason two priorities underpin the method to be followed: one should begin with an *epistemological analysis*, the only one capable of discerning the nature of the activities being studied; and one should favour an analysis of situations seen as *the most simple,* insofar as these are least subject to pre-judgement by values capable of masking the perception of what is being judged in experimenting on human beings as such. This second priority leads to two choices being made. In the first place, our reflection will be confined to one case, that of *experiments on free and responsible adults*. This choice does not ignore questions raised by experiments carried out on categories of the population requiring special protection: embryos, children, pregnant women, those mentally ill or handicapped, prisoners, persons suffering from illnesses at present incurable such as AIDS, the dying... On the contrary, its aim is to give the reader a basis of reflection that will enable him later to envisage more complex situations, on the basis that the questions raised by experimenting on human beings as such will have been previously studied very carefully. Next, the different steps in the study will be illustrated by examples taken from one special type of experiments, that of *clinical trials of drugs*. This method, whose details have been well worked out, and that has as to its main lines the approval of researchers, offers the possibility of isolating the various stages in the analysis, since several phases have been defined that are fairly clearly distinguished. It also permits a realisation of the diversity of the problems met with in the process of experimentation, and does this better than with other examples during which the different phases cannot be so easily distinguished. It is certain that some of these problems are specific to the trials of drugs. However, this is not the case with all, and even those that are specific give indications that are enlightening for an approach to other lines of experiments on human beings, even when these use methods and means that are special and specific to their subject. For this reason, clinical drug trials are a particularly favourable example. In addition, they are widely practiced, and therefore constitute a representative share of medical experiments carried out on humans. Nevertheless, they are only an *example*. Whatever its heuristic value, the part should not be confounded with the whole.

1.1. The Status of Medical Acts

"To speak of experimenting on human beings is to place oneself frankly and brutally at the interior of scientific discussion."[1] H. Atlan

---

[1] H. ATLAN, *Distinctions nécessaires : l'innovation thérapeutique, l'expérimentation sur l'adulte, l'expérimentation sur l'embryon. Intervention sur le rapport de J. Ladrière*, in J. ILLIOPOULOS-STRANGAS (ed.), *Expérimentation biomédicale et Droits de l'Homme*, Paris, 1988, p. 207.

here introduces a net distinction in a domain where both language and practice constantly favour an overlap between the arts of healing and scientific research. In fact, one speaks of *clinical trials* to cover all the planned steps by which research leading to the fine-tuning of new drugs is carried out.[2] These trials are also called *therapeutic*, because their final aim is certainly to enlarge and consolidate the range of drugs available, even if the method employed is that of research, and not strictly speaking that of treatment.[3] R. Flamant, together with many others, gives an explanation for the use of these expressions: "It is still normal to avoid the use of the term 'experimentation', by analogy with the actions of Nazi doctors".[4] This analogy has gradually lost its force, mainly due to the greater and greater recognition by the public of experimentation being carried out on human beings, and the accent put on the necessity of those involved giving their informed consent. Nevertheless, doctors continue to use the term "trials" to designate experiments. This shift in the use of language is also connected to two convictions that are deeply entrenched in doctors. On the one hand, they know from experience that they can never be totally certain of the effects produced by their treatment, and also that they can never a priori be certain of the results of a piece of research; in their eyes treatment and research acts both amount to trials; in different degrees, uncertainty is an inherent dimension. On the other hand, doctors see such a close link between the different aspects of their actions that they esteem that "there is a continuum between experimentation on human beings, biomedical research, and the treatment of patients, passing by clinical and therapeutic research". From this point of view, experimentation is seen as "the most rigorous method of acquiring experience". In short, "research is part of medical practice".[5]

---

[2] Cf. notably J.P. GIROUD, G. MATHE, G. MEYNIEL et al., *Pharmacologie clinique. Bases de la thérapeutique*, 2ième ed., Paris, 1998, p. 77.

[3] Cf. notably D. SCHWARZ, R. FLAMANT AND J. LELLOUCH, *L'essai thérapeutique chez l'homme*, 2ième ed., Paris, 1985 ; E. ESCHWEGE, G. BOUVENOT, F. DOYON & A. LACROIX, *Essais thérapeutiques: mode d'emploi*, (Le Quotidien du médecin-INSERM), 1990.

[4] R. FLAMANT, *Malade ou cobaye. Plaidoyer pour les essais thérapeutiques*, Paris, 1994, p. 106.

[5] Y. KENIS, *Expérimentation, recherche, soins. L'expérience d'un cancérologue*, in J.-N. MISSA (ed.), *Le devoir d'expérimenter*, Bruxelles, 1996, p. 83-84.

This overlapping of treatment and research suggests two comments, at first sight contradictory. In the first place, it can be seen that, at the present, medicine consists indissolubly of the art of healing and the science of illnesses and remedies; art and science mutually support and stimulate each other, in a search for treatments becoming always more efficient and better adapted. It would be both useless and artificial to separate what is so well united. However, this strong unity is the result of a collaboration between activities whose epistemological statute is distinct. Moreover, this epistemological difference is of great ethical importance since it defines specific modalities in the doctor-patient relationship. To take account of this is an indispensable preliminary to any ethical analysis. Even more radically, it can be said that it is the only method really allowing for the recognition of the ethical stakes in the doctor-patient relationship in the framework of experimentation.

What is at stake? Insofar as what is involved is the art of healing, a medical act aims above all at finding the method, or methods, capable of producing a cure for a specific patient. In this framework, to 'experiment' is to try a treatment or a medicine without being sure of the result, it involves doing something for the first time. Whatever the background of knowledge used by the doctor on this occasion, and even if he innovates hoping to be even more effective, his line of conduct is essentially practical, and is centred on a particular patient; how can the best treatment result be arrived at for that patient? When the medical act is aimed at obtaining a contribution to science, its aim is different. What is involved is the evaluation or the understanding of the effect of a treatment or a substance, their method of action, or possibly the pathological process as such, usually as applied to a group of patients.[6] In order to work in a rigorous

---

[6] It is necessary to remember that present day medical research is a continuation and radicalization of the trends of the past, even if new aspects emerge. It thus inherits the epistemological duality of empiricism/rationalism. This duality goes hand in hand, although it does not completely coincide, with the pragmatic/explanatory duality of aims that were exposed in clinical drug tests by D. Schwarz, R. Flamant & J. Lellouch (*L'essai thérapeutique chez l'homme*, p. 36). The explanatory attitude aims to provide an answer in the realm of understanding or 'knowledge'. The pragmatic attitude has as its objective the definition of the interest of a new treatment compared to classical treatments; the approach is therefore more global, and the aim is to provide elements for the decision of the practicing doctor as to treatment. The adoption of the one or the other influences the planning and the carrying out of the experiment, and thereby also influences the conditions imposed on patients. Moreover, a different

manner, doctors and research teams follow a certain procedure; they draw up a hypothesis on the basis of the knowledge available, and draw up a programme of tests that permit the hypothesis to be tested. The test programme aims at creating a situation where such relevant variables are considered as strictly controlled as possible. In this framework, the experiment – taken here in its strict sense – consists in introducing variables, also controlled, into the situation to see if the hypothesis can be confirmed. An attentive analysis will lead to two types of objective, and correlatively two types of activity, being defined: the *therapeutic* intention of the act of treatment that falls into the field of *medical practice* and the *cognitive* intention of the act, carried out in the framework of *research*. However, as has been said, these two intentions and these two fields of action are very closely linked, and, in many respects, cannot objectively be separated; they take place in the same context, with the same personnel, and include many of the same acts. However, the *process* of which they form a part is different. This difference is clearly perceived when what happens before and afterwards is taken into account. The process into which the act of healing carried out by the practitioner is inserted is well described by R. Flamant: "Obviously, the attitude that should be apparent in good medical practice is that of a rational course of action, based on interrogation and a systematic clinical examination, additional x-ray and biological examinations, in order to arrive at a diagnosis. Then, in function of this, the different possible methods of treatment should be reviewed, and the one chosen that is at the same time the most efficient and the best tolerated, in function of the medical and scientific knowledge available at that time."[7] Research follows a different path. Before undertaking a medical act aimed at research, it is necessary to draw up a hypothesis, and to draw up a programme of tests, subject to specific conditions as to the number of patients, the length of the trials, the products

kind of epistemological validity is given to the results; tests that are carried out with a pragmatic approach are more limited. These two attitudes are in fact extremes that can in certain cases be adapted to the case in point. However, in most cases, clinical trials have an aim that is neither purely pragmatic nor purely explanatory. The distinction between these two attitudes, however, does permit the unmasking of compromises that are unsatisfying from the epistemological viewpoint. In this sense the attention paid to it may favour obtaining more precise information.

[7] R. FLAMANT, *Malade ou cobaye*, p. 16.

to be administered, the means chosen, etc. When the experiment has taken place, its results must be interpreted so as to see whether or not the hypothesis was confirmed.[8] A big difference thus appears between the process having the aim of healing and the process into which research acts are inserted. In fact, an act undertaken with the aim of research takes place within an experimental plan that is laid down in advance, a plan that, in the name of scientific rigour, should (except in special cases) be followed without any alterations. On the other hand, a medical act that is strictly therapeutic, even if experimental, both permits and requires a much greater freedom to change so as to adapt better to the needs and characteristics of the patient. Already, at this as yet elementary level of analysis, it is obvious that the process within which the act takes place involves specific modalities in its relation to the patient. If ethical problems are to be correctly posed, it is important to take this into account.

In order to do this, a global approach to medical activities and its opposite, an approach limited to the act itself, are both found to be inappropriate since both the one and the other fail to bring this specific point into evidence. A global approach puts the accent on the final intention of the treatment and research processes, and this is always definitely therapeutic, whatever the steps taken to achieve it. A limited approach puts the accent on the appearance, or possibly the material nature of the acts carried out; it thus neglects the process of which they form part, whereas this process may even be decisive to the nature of the acts. To put this in a more concrete fashion, the prescription given to a patient in a purely therapeutic framework may be identical to that given to a patient included in a research project. In the first case what is involved is an individual prescription, motivated by the desire to adapt as far as possible to the needs of the patient, whereas in the second case the prescription will have been settled in advance within the plan of the experiment. In order to remedy the limitations of these two approaches, it is important to favour a *differentiated analysis* of the different elements of medical activities. Such an analysis consists of distinguishing what, within the always complex case of a medical treatment, has a strictly therapeutic intention and is included within the framework of medical practice, and what has a cognitive intention and is

---

[8] For further explanation, cf. the methodological works already cited.

included within the framework of research. In function of the intention, it is possible to decide what ethical demands should be satisfied, in other terms when it is appropriate to follow the ethical standards special to the medical profession, aimed at the health of the patient and at not harming him, and when it is appropriate to respect the specific demands of the ethics of experimentation on human beings as they can be deduced from the various declarations and texts published by international medical organisations and national institutions.[9]

1.2. The Status of Research Subjects

The carrying out of experimental acts aimed at research profoundly changes the relationship between a doctor and his patient. In fact, as long as the relationship remains placed under the exclusive heading of healing, the primary intention is therapeutic, even if at the same time it gives the doctor the possibility of enlarging his knowledge empirically by observation and reflection on the case he is treating. However, when it also comes under the heading of research, a cognitive objective is *added*[10] to the therapeutic one. The doctor therefore plays a *double role* as regards his patient. He is the doctor trying to find the most beneficial effect for the health of a particular patient; he is

[9] For up to date international texts, see *infra*, note 25. Among national texts, cf. notably: in the United States, THE NATIONAL COMMISSION FOR THE PROTECTION OF HUMAN SUBJECTS OF BIOMEDICAL AND BEHAVIOURAL RESEARCH, *The Belmont Report. Ethical Principles and Guidelines for the Protection of Human Subjects of Research*, Bethesda, Maryland, 1979; in France, COMITÉ CONSULTATIF NATIONAL D'ÉTHIQUE POUR LES SCIENCES DE LA VIE ET DE LA SANTÉ (CCNE), *Avis sur les essais de nouveaux traitements chez l'homme*, no. 2, 9 October, 1984, in CCNE, *Xe anniversaire. Les avis de 1983 à 1993*, Paris, 1993, p. 19-23 (in this text, "consent to treatment" is distinguished from "consent to trials" for patients taking part in research); in Canada, THE MEDICAL RESEARCH COUNCIL OF CANADA, THE NATURAL SCIENCES AND ENGINEERING RESEARCH COUNCIL OF CANADA, THE SOCIAL SCIENCES AND HUMANITIES RESEARCH COUNCIL OF CANADA, *Code of Ethical Conduct for Research Involving Humans*, Ottawa, 1998; in Belgium, COMITÉ CONSULTATIF DE BIOÉTHIQUE, *Avis no. 13 du 9 juillet 2001 relatif aux expérimentations sur l'homme, et rapport introductif*, Bruxelles, 2001 (www.health.fgov.be/bioeth). The two national texts first cited above are reprinted in M.-L. DELFOSSE, *L'expérimentation médicale sur l'être humain. Construire les normes, construire l'éthique*, Bruxelles, 1993, p. 311-327.

[10] On the impact of this 'addition' on the manner of considering the act, cf. the primacy of the cognitive over the therapeutic objective in experiments that also have a therapeutic aspect (end of section 2).

also the researcher who, while carrying out this specific act of treatment, is taking part in a research plan as previously defined, that normally includes several people and whose aim is to test a hypothesis.

As can be seen, each of these roles implies a different mode of attention to the patient. In the therapeutic relationship, the doctor attempts to find the special characteristics of the patient so as to treat him as well as possible. The attention paid to the individual, within the moral tradition special to the medical profession, is therefore intimately linked to medical knowledge and technique, and takes its form in the choice of a surgical intervention or a treatment. Carrying out a research plan, on the contrary, implies the scrupulous following of rules previously decided upon, so as to gather data that will allow the confirmation or the refutation of the initial hypothesis. In the name of scientific rigour, this path should be followed in preference to the taking into consideration of the characteristics of the individual. This is clearly underlined by H. Atlan: "In scientific phraseology, the experimentation in question is one that must be carried out in accordance with scientific rules, and that has no other criterion than these rules." He continues: "Put differently, by definition, scientific experimentation is one dealing with the objects of tests, and it is vital that these should only be the objects of tests. If they are to a greater or lesser extent something other than the objects of tests, it is no longer a scientific experiment, but becomes a subjective experiment. The principle of objectivity is no longer respected, since subjective considerations, in the wide sense of the term (moral considerations, etc.) enter into the experiment, and it is well known that this is a catastrophe from the viewpoint of the experimental method. Consequently, when speaking of experimentation on humans, what is meant is that human beings are the objects of the experiments."[11]

Several methods used for the drawing up and realisation of controlled tests in phases II and III of clinical drug trials[12] show this

---

[11] H. ATLAN, *Distinctions nécessaires*, p. 207. On his side, H. Jonas (*Réflexions philosophiques sur l'expérimentation humaine*, in M.A.M. DE WACHTER, *Médecine et expérimentation* (Cahiers de bioéthique, 4), Quebec, 1982, p. 325) defines the status of persons involved in a research by the term 'sample'.

[12] Clinical tests of drugs are one of the stages in the research and fine-tuning of new drugs. They are carried out after laboratory research and testing on animals. They include four phases, generally presented as follows, and which can be resumed thus: an evaluation of the product on a small number of healthy volunteers (I), on a small group of ill people (II), on a large group of ill people (III), and finally, after

alteration in the status of the patient. This appears especially in the decision to attribute a particular treatment to the patient, by a system of drawing lots or randomly, as well as double blind testing.

In spite of the ethical problems raised, drawing lots seems definitely the most rigorous from the scientific point of view, in order to constitute groups of patients who are as similar as possible. According to the constantly affirmed principle that "what is not scientific is not ethical", this is also the method that is most acceptable ethically.[13] Before using this method, however, a large number of points must be clarified, ensuring the scientific quality of the trials: a rigorous definition of the objectives of each of the phases of the trials, which implies a definition of the treatments being compared, the conditions and context in which they are administered; the drawing up of criteria for judgement, a decision as the time at which the measurements will be carried out and their quality (objective, subjective, rudimentary or not); and finally a definition of the illness, or the particular form of the disease that is in question, as well as of the subjects on which the tests will be carried out, that is to say a list of the criteria for exclusion and inclusion – notably the "ambivalence clause"[14] – in function of which patients will be chosen. The criteria for exclusion and inclusion allow the assurance that the treatment given to the patient will not be detrimental to him. The treatment is, however, carried out at random. Moreover, in the absence of circumstances beyond control, it must be continued up to the moment

---

commercialization, epidemiological studies of rare side effects, or effects that only appear after a certain time (IV). The trials are said to be controlled when two groups of patients are set up, in a rigorous manner, the two groups to be as similar as possible, and the effects of the product being tested are compared with those of a known drug or a placebo, following a set method for the administration of the products.

[13] On the drawing of lots, cf. notably D. SCHWARZ, R. FLAMANT & J. LELLOUCH, L'essai thérapeutique chez l'homme, p. 15. The authors give a survey of the various possible methods for the formation of groups during comparative tests, and underline their advantages and disadvantages. See also E. ESCHWEGE et al., Essais thérapeutiques, p. 13-20. The principle 'What is not scientific is not ethical' implies that ethical research on humans is only ethical if it is acceptable on scientific grounds, viz. scientifically necessary and strictly carried out. Nevertheless, the link between ethics and scientific rigour is not an absolute one; it has to take human factors into account, e.g. the condition of the patients on whom experiments are being carried out (cf. section 4). H. Atlan (Distinctions nécessaires, p. 208-209) however, proposes a different interpretation of the principle, 'what is scientifically incorrect, is unethical'.

[14] The 'ambivalence clause' consists of only including in a comparative test those patients who can undergo without harm either of the treatments to be compared.

when there are results that are statistically significant. It can therefore not be changed while the test continues, unless there are serious circumstances that cause the patient to be taken out of the trials. In fact, the doctor may not depart from the path laid down under the research protocol. With relevance to this, R. Flamant underlines that the doctor may feel himself a slave to the constraints of the trials, but, together with H. Atlan, he believes that only the acceptance of these constraints allows a scientifically valuable result to be obtained.[15]

Controlled tests carried out under phases II and III of clinical drug trials are generally carried out 'blindly', or 'double blindly' wherever this is possible.[16] This method permits increased objectivity: that is the elimination of inequality of judgement as to the course of the illness, whether this is made by the patient himself (simple blind test), or by the doctor (double blind), and the elimination of inequalities in the evolution of the illness, due either to extrinsic or intrinsic factors (auto-suggestion of the patient in the case of single blind tests, hetero-suggestion on the part of the doctor in the case of double blind).[17] These gains in objectivity are particularly important from the scientific viewpoint, but the methods used to obtain them make it clear that the patient is here only a 'sample', and that the doctor for his part is only a link in a chain, a link contributing only to a limited, if important, part in a piece of teamwork, whose details he does not necessarily know, something which is possibly desirable.

The use of these methods has the same aim as that of the trials, that do not attempt to find the most effective treatment for a particular patient, but, for example, might serve to ascertain the percentage of efficiency of a medicine or of a treatment as regards a chosen population group.[18] The attention of the doctor, centred on the patient in a

---

[15] R. FLAMANT, *Malade ou cobaye*, p. 91.

[16] In a single blind test, the doctor is aware of the exact type of product administered, but the patient does not know. In a double blind test, the patient does not know which product he is taking, and the doctor does not know which patients receive the test product. In both cases the products to be compared are made indistinguishable both in appearance and in the way in which they are to be taken.

[17] For a table of the advantages and problems of 'blind' tests, cf. notably D. SCHWARZ, R. FLAMANT & J. LELLOUCH, *L'essai thérapeutique chez l'homme*, p. 80.

[18] On the introduction of statistics into the experimental process, cf. notably F.-A. ISAMBERT, *L'expérimentation sur l'homme comme pratique et comme représentation*, in *Actes de la recherche en sciences sociales* 68 (1987) 26.

therapeutic relationship, passes, in a research situation, from the individual to the group; and at this moment "another type of ethics appears"[19] that in the name of scientific rigour, favours taking account of the group and not the individual. Consequently, if the roles of the doctor as healer and as researcher seem to converge because they lead to taking actions that, as acts, are the same, they must nevertheless be distinguished, because the actions taken follow two different systems of logic. These lead to two incompatible attitudes towards the patient, and therefore assign to the doctor roles that are completely incompatible, even if they are combined in practice. This incompatibility does not however have the last word. To take the matter further, it is important to remember that the conditions imposed by research will take precedence over the strictly therapeutic medical acts. There follows from this an epistemological consequence of overriding importance, and one whose ethical repercussions are also very important: from the moment that a medical activity pursues a cognitive aim within the framework of a research, this aim should be recognised as the principal aim, since it is finally this aim that will dictate the conditions that must be followed. In other words, an experiment carried out on patients with an intention that is cognitive cannot as such be called a therapeutic act only on the grounds of the benefit it will bring to these patients. On the contrary, it must be recognised as an act of research. It is only on these conditions that research can be carried on rigorously, and that respect and protection can be adequately given to those involved. In addition, if the people included in experiments should be considered as the 'objects tested', as H. Atlan clearly points out, it is now considered that, in view of the dimension of uncertainty inherent in experimentation, they should also become 'partners', cooperating in a limited but effective manner in the elucidation of the matter being studied.

1.3. Ethical Repercussions

For reasons of scientific rigour, the doctor carrying out tests should regard the patients or persons involved in research trials as 'experimental objects'. He should also regard them as partners or collaborators. Ethically, what are the implications of this change of status?

---

[19] D. SCHWARZ, R. FLAMANT & J. LELLOUCH, *L'essai thérapeutique chez l'homme*, p. 259.

This question is very difficult, and opens up a line of reflection where professional and philosophical ethics interact. In the preceding sections it has been seen that therapeutic and research medical activities act under two systems of logic that are not only different but, more radically, also incompatible. These two systems also involve two systems of professional ethics that are in many respects contradictory. To the practitioner, the patient is an end in itself, and what must be done is to use the knowledge available, and the experience that he has acquired, to give that patient the care that is most appropriate to his state, to his specific needs. In health care ethics, thus, there is a principle of beneficence – and non-maleficence –, as well as of paying attention to patients in their individuality, which can act as a first step along the road to the respect of persons. For the researcher, the primary objective is to advance knowledge in a rigorous manner, and the patients – or the healthy persons – are first of all a means to this end, even if they are also regarded as partners. While the practitioner takes his stand within the moral tradition of the medical profession – I will consider the health of my patient as my first care[20] – the researcher for his part follows another ethical perspective, in which there is a strong link between an ethic of knowledge, putting an accent on the objectivity indispensable to acquiring scientific knowledge and its necessary progress and an ethic of collective utility that accentuates the benefit to all humanity brought about by research carried out on a small number. Attention paid to individuals is thus rivalled on the one hand by the requirements of science, and on the other by taking of collective utility into consideration. Beneficence and non-maleficence take on a special aspect in the context of research, since risks and benefits are judged not only by reference to the persons involved in the experiment, but also by reference to potential beneficiaries. Experimentation therefore gives rise to tension between three sets of values: a respect for individuals, the objectivity of scientific knowledge, and the public good. It is the sharpness of this tension that inspired Jean Bernard to give this lapidary and striking comment, "Experimentation on human beings is morally necessary and necessarily immoral".

---

[20] WORLD MEDICAL ASSOCIATION, *Serment de Genève*, in WORLD MEDICAL ASSOCIATION, *Handbook of Declarations*, Farnborough, Hampshire, 1985, p. 31; also reprinted in M.-L. DELFOSSE, *L'expérimentation médicale sur les êtres humains*, p. 298.

It is most important to be aware of the radical nature of this tension so as to avoid shaky compromises in the scientific or the ethical field.[21] However, it is not possible to directly oppose respect for persons and experimental research on human beings. This would lead to all research being stopped, which would be the negation of beneficence, and would not even amount to showing respect for persons. What is therefore needed is a closer examination of the opposing viewpoints. In order to do this the question of the treatment of human beings as objects will be more closely examined. On the basis of what has been previously said, it is tempting to couple on the one hand an attention to patients, a characteristic of healing, with respect for persons, and on the other hand treating people merely as objects. It must however be admitted that the practice of medicine always acts by treating people as objects. For example, treatment often takes the form of acting upon the body with the help of a chemical substance. The body is then treated as an object; but this happens only temporarily, since the objective aimed at is that of restoring health to the patient. In this context, treatment as an object is only the means towards an end, the subject himself. In the opposite case, in the relationship established in experimental research, the objective aimed at is primarily cognitive, even if it may, in a subsidiary manner, also be therapeutic; what is intended is to carry out a scientifically valid experiment. To do this, the doctor must consider the body as a complex biological system, and not as the existence in the world of a subject. Objectification, a temporary methodological stage in any relationship between a doctor and a patient, thus becomes the sole mode in the relationship, and, as H. Atlan underlines, this is necessary in the name of scientific rigour. The accent put today on the partnership between the doctor and the patient serves to modify this demand, particularly in borderline cases, but it does not abolish it.

In such conditions, how should respect for persons be envisaged? So as to give a considered answer to the question, it is useful to think of experimental research as a process that not only includes several stages, but also has a scientific and an ethical aspect, the two coming together and interacting all the time. The scientific viewpoint has already been touched upon: the concept of the research project

---

[21] About this, cf. supra, the remark of H. Atlan (note 11) and the primacy of the cognitive intention in all experiments.

– elaboration of a hypothesis, and the drawing up of a plan of experiments –, the carrying out of the experiments (that is properly speaking the experimentation), and then the interpretation of the results. The details have also been mentioned that need to be settled before the experimentation is carried out, notably the criteria of exclusion and inclusion according to which patients will be selected. All of this work of elaboration, scientific realisation and interpretation has a specific ethical dimension, as will be seen in section 4. In particular, constant vigilance on the part of the doctors is demanded, so as to master and control the entire process as tightly as possible. However, this constant control, exercised notably over the definition of criteria of exclusion and inclusion, comes to an end when, on the basis of these criteria, doctors reach the stage of inviting those selected to take part in the tests. In fact, what is then asked of these research subjects is to express their consent to take part in a process that will treat them as objects. This step, preceding the experimentation in the strict sense, is of particular importance with regard to the ethics of respect for persons. It is this that allows the patients, selected to have their say in the matter, to have a voice as intelligent human beings with free will. Respect for persons here takes the form of a respect for subjects in the sense of human beings capable of auto-determination. It imposes a double and correlative obligation on the doctors carrying out research, that of telling the patient to what it is intended to subject him, and of thereafter asking for his consent, that is to say, to put the matter clearly, to allow him to decide, in an autonomous manner, and being fully aware of what is involved, whether he will agree to allow his body to take part in something that will treat him as an object, and that, going beyond his own interests, will aim at the common good. Certainly, within the course of the experimentation, an appeal will be made to the will and intelligence of the human subjects in involved, notably when they are asked to follow rigorously the conditions decided upon in the research, and to communicate their reactions to the products being tested. This cooperation, however, will be strictly controlled by the research plan and the controls it necessitates, even if, should it prove desirable, the plan should become subject to change during the tests. Informed consent, as an expression of respect for persons, is not only a condition that precedes the beginning of the research. It also gives rise to the necessity for continued information, the doctor-patient relationship being thereby viewed as an agreement that evolves and is subject to constant renegotiation.

This double requirement of information and consent is conceived primarily as applying to experiments carried out on free and responsible adults. However, many other population groups are today included in tests; some are deprived of physical liberty (prisoners, for example), others do not have the ability to speak reasonably and with free will (notably embryos, those seriously ill and the mentally disabled). The greater the vulnerability of those on whom it is intended to carry out experiments, the more radical is the ethical debate. The question of principle is posed in new terms; can one experiment on, that is to say, to include in a process of objectification, persons who are incapable of understanding what is involved and of giving their considered consent to it? In view of the fact that such tests can prove themselves of benefit to the categories of populations concerned, other modalities of respect for persons are sought, notably other means of giving information and obtaining consent. The requirements drawn up for the test case of free and responsible adults serve thus as a guide in the search for specially adapted requirements, but still retain their radical character in the name of respect for persons.

How can the radical nature of the relationship with free and responsible adults be asserted? Informing and getting consent can quickly become routines that lose their sense if what is in question is not properly recognised. It has already been pointed out that they both introduce a break in continuity in the objectification demanded by the scientific procedure. In addition, they constitute moments of reciprocal dependence; the patient knows that he is dependent on the doctor (and hospital practice often serves to underline this dependence), but the doctor is also dependent on the patient and the consent that he will give. Although they take place against a background of the patient's dependence on the doctor, these moments of reciprocal dependence set up a kind of equality between the partners; each of them needs something from the other, and each has something to give the other. The awareness and acceptance, without evasion, of this situation on both their parts make it possible to abandon, at least briefly, the stereotyped roles the illness and the hospital institution, or the organisation of the health system, have given the protagonists. A real meeting of minds becomes possible, the sole capable of giving to the demands of information and consent the sense of an exchange between two free wills. The partnership thereby takes on the real meaning of a reciprocal agreement, fashioned in accordance with the different stages of the experimentation and the different types of experimental situations.

In order to examine what such an encounter might entail, looked at from the doctor's viewpoint, the ethical step proposed by P. Ricoeur in *Oneself as Another* will be followed, more particularly the notion of *solicitude*.[22] For Ricoeur, *solicitude* describes a wish to do good that is spontaneous, intuitive, and according to which we try to help the other in preference to the following of any rule. What characterises it is the engagement of oneself in favour of the other; *solicitude* is therefore not pity "where the self is secretly happy to be spared".[23] On the contrary, it aims at setting up equality in a relationship that could be unequal, for example because of the context in which it arises. *Solicitude* is therefore viewed as an exchange between two beings perceiving each other as equals, as sources of self-esteem.

Self-esteem is, however, founded on the fact of considering oneself as a being capable of acting intentionally, and of turning one's intentions into concrete acts. I cannot prove that I am free, I can only show it by my acts. And *solicitude* leads me to recognise freedom in others, on the same basis as in myself. It follows from this that it is only if I think myself free that I can believe in the liberty of others. If I consider that my actions are pre-determined, others can expect no action of mine towards them to be responsible. This fact is particularly significant in the situation here envisaged, a situation that puts in relation a doctor who wishes to know more about the behaviour of bodies and a subject whom he asks to agree to lending his body for an investigation of this.

Solicitude should however submit to the test of universality so as to become free of inclinations that might affect it or alter its nature. It is then confronted by the formal requirement of respect for persons, as expressed in the Kantian imperative, "act in such a way that you treat humanity as well in your own person as in that of any other always at the same time as an end and never simply as a means". Ricoeur points out the affinity of these two notions; respect due to people is *solicitude* under the regime of the moral law. In this optic he shows how the imperative prolongs the intuition of true otherness inherent in *solicitude*. In fact, while making reference to a

---

[22] P. RICOEUR, *Soi-même comme un autre*, Paris, 1990, p. 199-344.
[23] *Ibid.*, p. 223.

unitary notion of humanity, the imperative takes into account the plurality of persons seen as ends in themselves. But plurality is viewed in the perspective of universality; quite apart from their diversity, persons should be respected in reason of the intrinsic dignity conferred on them by their humanity. In addition, like *solicitude*, but at the level of a rule of form of universal applicability, the imperative aims to establish equality into the relationship, however dissymmetric this may have been initially. In fact, by refusing that the other should ever be treated only as a means, it forbids one to do violence to another. Again, these observations are particularly relevant to the experimental relationship. The very aim of this is that the will of one person should be able to act on another as an object. Consent gives legitimacy to this fundamentally non-respectful relationship. But it has this value only if it has been given within a process in which the autonomy of the other has been entirely respected; no influence, no misleading, no tempting, but a respect for the other as a person, as an end in himself, that is to say notably there must be a preoccupation with informing him sufficiently in language that he can understand. And even during the course of the experimentation the imperative keeps all its force; what is thereby forbidden is that the experimentation should interfere with the self-respect of every human being.

However, formal conformity with the imperative of respect for persons is not sufficient to ensure the quality of the experimental relationship. In fact, at the moment of information and consent, ill people, and also the healthy, cannot only be considered under the angle of their common participation in the human race; account must also be taken of their individuality. Apart from the imperative of respect for persons, what must here be returned to is *solicitude*, the qualities of kindness and a spontaneous wish to help, which, beyond all conformity to a rule, are brought into being by the interpellation of the other. But what is here in question is no longer a naïve *solicitude*. Having been submitted to the test of universality in its confrontation with the imperative, *solicitude* will be freed of inclinations that might darken it. Having become a "critical" *solicitude*, it can guide the moral judgement in the situation in question and inspire an attention to persons proceeding from an authentic practical wisdom, far from any 'situationism'.

Up to the present, attention has been centred on the relationship between the doctor and the patient who is being asked to take part in experimental research. However, the context into which this relationship is inserted cannot be ignored. This will only be briefly mentioned. In contemporary societies, the progress of scientific knowledge, particularly of medical knowledge, is regarded as beneficial in itself to humanity, in spite of an increasingly lively awareness of its ambivalence in view of the "regressions" that accompany it in all fields.[24] This state of mind has led to the thinking, as expressed in Jean Bernard's formula cited above, that experimentation on human beings is morally necessary. Consequently, while insisting on the necessity of information and consent as well as what is involved in the relationship whose establishment they permit, account must be taken of the fact that the background against which they take place is socially predetermined by a positive appreciation of scientific knowledge. The necessity for 'informed consent' is not thereby limited as such. But the extent of the expression of free will is nevertheless limited.

1.4. What Kind of Professional Ethics?

The ethical reflection just made is echoed in the recommendations by international medical organisations or national institutions made to doctors carrying out research.[25] These have progressively defined a

---

[24] Cf. as to this notably C. MENDES (ed.), *Le mythe du développement*, Paris, 1977; J. HABERMAS, *Après Marx*, translated from the German by J.D. LADMIRAL & M.B. DE LAUNAY, Paris, 1985; A. GORZ, *Métamorphoses du travail. Quête de sens. Critique de la raison économique*, Paris, 1988, p. 138-220. In recent publications, the same themes are found.

[25] We cite here the principal international texts on ethics that give these conditions at the moment: WORLD MEDICAL ASSOCIATION, *Declaration of Helsinki*, adopted in June 1964 and amended in 1975, 1983, 1989, 1996 and also at the 52nd General Assembly, Edinburgh, 2000; having the same attributions: INTERNATIONAL CONFERENCE OF ORDERS AND ORGANISMS OF THE EUROPEAN COMMUNITY, *Guide européen d'éthique médicale*, in ORDRE DES MÉDECINS, *Bulletin du Conseil national* 35 (1987) 36-40; COUNCIL FOR INTERNATIONAL ORGANISATIONS OF MEDICAL SCIENCES (CIOMS) & WORLD HEALTH ASSOCIATION (WHO), *International Guidelines for Biomedical Research Involving Human Subjects*, Geneva, 1993. For a general presentation of the texts published at that date, cf. A. FAGOT-LAREGEAULT, *L'homme bio-éthique. Pour une déontologie de la recherche sur le vivant*, Paris, 1985. For a more detailed analysis, and an account of the relationships between these texts and their importance, cf. M.-L. DELFOSSE, *L'expérimentation médicale sur l'être humain*, p. 311-327.

general set of rules so as make it ethically acceptable to carry out
human experimentation with a cognitive intention. These guidelines
are centred on ethical principles whose relevance is largely recognised by the medical profession, even if the interpretations given
sometimes differ. Let us briefly set out these principles. Experimental research on humans is ethical only if it is scientifically acceptable,
that is to say if it is capable of leading to progress in knowledge, and
if it is carried out under rigorous conditions. In addition, a constant
search for therapeutic progress constitutes a moral obligation, as
does the fact of allowing patients to profit from it. Nevertheless, the
desire for scientific progress cannot take precedence over the well-
being and interest of patients. These principles are expressed in a
series of conditions that constitute the questions that Ethics Committees should discuss when they evaluate research protocols.

- Firstly, is the project scientifically rigorous? Is it based on adequate
  pre-requisites: laboratory experimentation, in vitro and on several
  species of animals, in a sufficiently large number? Will it take place
  in an appropriate context, with a competent team? Is the objective
  well defined?
- Secondly, have the known or possible risks been evaluated, as well
  as the expected benefits? Are these benefits capable of counter-
  balancing the risks their participation in the research implies for
  those taking part? Do the methods employed minimise the damage
  and maximise the benefits?
- Thirdly, are the proposed procedures for the selection of subjects
  fair?
- Fourthly, will the subjects be informed, and will their consent be
  obtained? Are the conditions for obtaining this satisfactory?
- Fifthly, has the project been assessed by an Ethics Committee? Was
  the assessment positive?

There are some texts that say that these different elements of appreciation should be taken in a pre-determined order and that if a condition is not fulfilled it is not necessary to examine those that follow.[26] This is very important, since it reinforces the guarantees aimed
at ensuring the scientific quality of the project, and gives protection

---

[26] Cf. as to this, CIOMS, *International Guidelines for Biomedical Research Involving Human Subjects*, p. 38-39. See also CCNE, *Avis sur les essais de nouveaux traitements chez l'homme*, p. 22.

against the abusive interpretation of consent as being an authority to carry out a research project, even one badly defined scientifically. However, the conditions are not found exactly as such in all the texts. Some give greater importance to one or the other, while being vague or silent to others. Strictly speaking, therefore, there is no unanimity.[27] This is why the ensemble of texts on human experimentation should be considered as an *inspiration*, and not as a body of rules laying down unequivocally how different problems should be handled. What the texts allow is rather that of working out a generally common way of treating such problems. They are also based on a common recognition that experimentation on human subjects poses moral problems that can never have a totally satisfactory solution. In fact, the whole problem of human experimentation is subject to the tension between two requirements that at first sight seem contradictory: the progress of knowledge requires the use of human subjects as material to be studied; respect for persons requires that they be protected in this context. The different texts each try to define an acceptable compromise, through conditions that are more or less detailed. However, these conditions do not constitute an ensemble that holds together harmoniously; on the contrary tensions exist between them that cannot be entirely resolved. For this reason, a *dialectic approach* must be adopted; it is by the confrontation between the principles and the conditions in which these are expressed, *taken as a whole*, that it is possible, dealing with a particular research project, to try to define the attitude or the method which will be the most ethical. In other terms, any formalistic or partial interpretation of the conditions will deform the spirit that underlies them. In addition, the sense and the scope of the conditions should be viewed *in the specific conditions of the test in question*. The ethical question in front of researchers today is no longer: under what conditions can one experiment on humans? It is rather: how, in the tests that are envisaged, can one apply in practice the general conditions set out in the texts defining the rules of professional ethics in human experimentation?

Let us consider a typical situation. The texts on medical ethics that treat human experimentation underline the necessity of proceeding

---

[27] All the texts insist that the advice of an Ethics Committee should be asked for; some insist that it should be favourable.

in a rigorous manner, using the methods best adapted to this end. In spite of the ethical difficulties it raises, the use of a placebo in comparative tests[28] appears to be one of these methods, since it allows significant differences to be brought to light, better than a comparison of active substances. For his part, H. Atlan criticises a mechanical recourse to this method.[29] He judges that in certain situations, for example tests on the terminally ill, it is not admissible to give a placebo to one group of patients so as to compare them with another group receiving active treatment. For him "It is purely and simply a crime", even if, to his colleagues it is "an ethical attitude". He considers that the terminally ill should have the benefit of all the treatments that could benefit them. Consequently, at this stage of life, a method of acquiring knowledge that takes the state of patients into account must be worked out. For H. Atlan this means in concrete terms that one must give up comparative testing, even though this method is the most rigorous, and proceed by innovation in treatment; even if the result is not certain, the new treatment gives a chance to the patients and possibly puts off the condemnation to which they are subjects. In any case, observation of the patients given the new treatment will allow information to be gained, even if it does not have the status of scientific knowledge.

This example is worthy of reflection. In the first place it shows that all situations are not suitable for experimentation. In spite of the conviction that progress must always be made in the knowledge and the scientific evaluation of therapeutic processes, there are cases where a different line of conduct must be followed. Here, scientific certainty will not be arrived at, but there will nevertheless be indications giving guidance to therapeutic practice. As is underlined in the last version of the Declaration of Helsinki, these indications should, as far as possible, be the object of a study whose aim is to evaluate their

---

[28] The use of a placebo in comparative tests allows results to be obtained that have greater contrast, and are therefore more meaningful, while involving a smaller number of people than the comparison of a product to be tested with an already known active product, which can demand the involvement of a large number of people. The counterpart to this benefit is that active medicine is not given to some patients. This is why, when the problem of giving a placebo is considered, strict conditions are generally imposed, cf. notably CCNE, *Avis sur l'utilisation de placebo dans les essais thérapeutiques d'antidépresseurs*, in CCNE, *Xe anniversaire. Les avis de 1983 à 1993*, Paris, 1993, p. 359-364.

[29] H. ATLAN, *Distinctions necessaires*, p. 208.

security and efficiency.[30] In addition, it is known that the texts on medical ethics lay down the following conditions: a research project should not be undertaken unless the risks and benefits have been previously weighed and unless there is a reasonable balance between them. The well-being of those involved in the test should always have precedence over the interests of science and of society; "The advantages, risks, constraints and efficiency of a new method should always be evaluated in accordance with the best diagnostic and therapeutic methods, and the best methods of prevention, in current use."[31] The latest version of the Helsinki Declaration adds, "This excludes neither the use of a placebo nor an absence of treatment in studies where no proved diagnostic or therapeutic method, or method of prevention, exists". Nevertheless it can be taken that these conditions were not respected in the case taken as an example; the balance between risks and benefits is not acceptable; the interests of science manifestly take precedence over the interests of the patient; the terminally ill patient is not being given the best available treatment.

A lesson appears here. To respect *one* of the conditions defined by the medical ethics approach of human experimentation – here, the requirement of scientific rigour – while ignoring the other conditions does not permit the adoption of an ethical state of mind. In reality, as has been said above, it is the *ensemble* of principles and conditions laid down by these codes of professional ethics that must be taken into consideration in order to attempt to define the most ethical attitude or method.

Another lesson is that the texts on medical ethics relating to human experimentation bring into question conditions and concepts inspired by the ethics of care. This applies to the evaluation of risks and benefits and to the respect of a balance between them, and to the priority to be given to the well-being and health of the patient.[32] It can therefore be seen that there is a certain connection between an ethics of care and an ethics of human experimentation. Would this connection allow it to be said that an ethics of care is sufficient to overcome the problems posed by human experimentation? A positive reply would explain that the specificity of acts of medical

---

[30] Cf. WORLD MEDICAL ASSOCIATION, *Declaration of Helsinki*, C. 32.
[31] *Ibid.*, A.5, B.16,17,18, C. 29.
[32] Cf. as in the Hippocratic Oath.

research has not been recognised. This specificity implies the pursuit of a cognitive objective, and the exigencies that this implies, particularly, as R. Flamant (as already quoted) underlines, the fact that the point of view shifts from the individual to the group, that is to say that the perspective of collective utility takes precedence over considering the interests of the individual patient, who moreover becomes, in the context of the research, a sample. It is because of these modifications that in spite of the similarity of concepts and conditions posed by an ethics of care and an ethics of experimentation, it has to be admitted that these concepts and conditions acquire a new meaning in the case of experimentation. This must be recognised if it is wished to really ensure a respect for persons within an experimental situation that is not, as we have seen, purely and simply identifiable to the relationship of care. Nevertheless, this recognition should not lead to a radical cutting off of the ethics of research from that of care. They both draw upon the same sources: attention to patients is primordial, even if, in the setting of research, it should be combined with, and very often be hidden behind, the scientific demands put forward, under certain conditions, as having priority. But the fact that they are hidden behind does not imply that they are being denied: they simply are hidden but remain present.

ETHICS OF EXPERIMENTATION ON HUMAN BEINGS

J.-N. Missa

2.1. The Duty to Experiment

The history of experimentation in medicine coincides with the progressive apprenticeship of a suitable method of carrying out experiments on humans, both at the level of methodology and at that of ethics. Methods of experimentation have gradually been improved: comparative experiments, planning of experiments, the random assignment of patients between those given "treatment" and those in a control group, the use of placebos, the method of double blind testing, the use of statistics... These scientifically carried out experiments give much better results towards the progress of knowledge than the empirical trial and error methods of previous centuries. There is therefore a duty to experiment, so as to offer patients the best treatment and the best knowledge. However, it is obvious that experimentation cannot simply be carried out under any type of conditions. Certain rules must be followed.

2.2. Self-Regulation of Research

It was the public revelation of abuses of medical experimentation that led to a reflection on the ethical rules to be followed in the case of human experimentation. The Nuremberg trials, by unveiling the barbarous practices of Nazi doctors, demonstrated the necessity of establishing the rules for human experimentation. The World Medical Association's Nuremberg code (1947), and then the Declaration of Helsinki (1964, and amended in 1975, 1983, 1989, 1996 and also at the 52nd General Assembly, Edinburgh, 2000), make the voluntary consent of the patient the touchstone of medical ethics. However, before the sixties, the attitude of the medical profession was still strongly paternalistic. In the thinking of the experimenter of that time, obtaining the informed consent of the patient was often completely secondary to the scientific interest of the experimentation. In 1966, Henry Beecher, research professor in anaesthesiology at the Harvard Medical School, revealed numerous cases of abusive experiments, carried out on patients who had not given their consent.[1] Mentalities changed at the end of the sixties. Nevertheless, the practice of systematically obtaining the informed consent of the patient when carrying out experimental research was not generalised until the beginning of the seventies.

At the end of the sixties and the beginning of the seventies, several scandals linked to experiments on human subjects were denounced in the American press. Let us give two famous examples. In the affair of the Jewish Chronic Disease Hospital, cancerous cells were injected into patients, so as to discover the immunity reactions of transplant rejection. In the Tuskegee Syphilis Study[2], doctors failed to prescribe Penicillin to Afro-American males suffering from syphilis, with the aim of following the natural long-term evolution of the disease. These affairs led the American authorities to set up structures allowing for the control of experimentation on human beings. In introducing the Institutional Review Board (IRB) system, the precursors of the currently widespread Ethics Committees, the Americans put into place a regulation of experimental research based on a control carried out by members of the profession and representatives of the public. The development of Ethics Committees (composed of physicians, nurses and members with general ethical and legal interests, and also members exterior to the institution), represents a flexible system allowing for the management in a pragmatic but vigilant manner of the ethical problems raised by human experimentation,

---

[1] H.K. BEECHER, Ethics and Clinical Research, in The New England Journal of Medicine 274 (1966) 1354-1360.

[2] See on this subject the documentation Twenty Years After. The Legacy of the Tuskegee Syphilis Study, in Hastings Center Report 22 (1992) 29-35; see also J. H. JONES, Bad Blood: The Tuskegee Syphilis Experiment, New York, 1981.

while remaining close to clinical reality. Within this system of regulation, the research project must be clearly defined in a research protocol, and must be submitted for examination to the Ethics Committee. This procedure considerably improves the guarantees for those who will be the subjects of the research.

2.3. Freedom of Research, Respect for the Autonomy of the Individual and Partnership while Refining Bio-Medical Knowledge

At the roots of the ethics of experimentation on human beings, there is a tension between two fundamental principles: the freedom to carry out research and the protection of the autonomy of the individual. From this point of view the rule of informed consent definitely plays a fundamental role in the ethics of medical research. It is the non-respect of this rule that underlies the main scandals linked to human experimentation. The true practice of informed consent implies the abandonment of medical paternalism. The doctor cannot decide alone what is good for the patient. He must take the time to inform his partner/patient fully. An individual freely taking part in a research project is not an object being manipulated in order to carry out an aim to which he is alien. Ideally he should be an individual cooperating, in a limited but effective manner, in the improvement of medical practice and the furthering of the scientific knowledge of human beings.

2.4. The Ethics of Neuroscience: the Example of Experimental Brain Surgery

I will illustrate my theoretical point of view by studying, from an ethical and historical point of view, the evolution of two controversial experimental practices in the fields of neurosurgical psychiatry and functional neurosurgery: psychosurgery and the intracerebral transplant of foetal cells.

2.4.1. *Psychosurgery*

Psychosurgery is a practice aimed at treating mental health problems by carrying out surgical operations on the brain. At the end of the

19th and the beginning of the 20th century, the Swiss G. Burckhardt[3] and the Russian L. Puusep made isolated attempts at psychosurgery. However, the history of psychosurgery really starts in 1935, the year that the first prefrontal leucotomy was thought of by the Portuguese psychiatrist Egas Moniz, and carried out by the neurosurgeon Almeida Lima.

At the beginning of the 20th century, psychiatrists had no really effective biological methods of treatment. As from 1917, they invented a series of desperate forms of treatment, in order to cure the mentally ill vegetating in lunatic asylums. New and daring practices put an end to the "curative nihilism" that dominated psychiatry at the beginning of the century. The introduction of shock methods opened a new era. Beginning in 1917 with the malaria therapy of Wagner von Jauregg (a febrile shock practiced on patients suffering from general paralysis, a mental illness of syphilitic origin), it was followed by the insulin shock of Manfred Sakel (1927), then by Meduna's cardiazol shock (1934), and finally by Cerletti and Bini's electroshock. Psychosurgery is the most radical of these radical treatments, of these "great and desperate cures".[4]

2.4.1.1. Moniz and the Beginning of Psychosurgery

Its history starts in London, in 1935, at the second international neurology congress, when two American professors (Fulton and Jacobsen) described the effects of the ablation of the frontal lobes on the behaviour of two chimpanzees. The animals showed a placidity that was remarkable in contrast to their previous choleric behaviour. On the basis of this information, E. Moniz, a Portuguese psychiatrist present at the congress, used a technique aimed at partially destroying the prefrontal region of the brain on the patients of the Lisbon mental hospital.[5] In this procedure, known as leucotomy or

---

[3] G. BURCKHARDT, Über Rindenexcizionen, als Beitrag zur operativen Therapie der Psychosen, in Allgemeine Zeitschrift fur Psychiatrie und psychisch-gerichtliche Medizin (1891) 463-548.

[4] E.S. VALENSTEIN, Great and Desperate Cures: The Rise and Decline of Psychosurgery and Other Radical Treatments for Mental Illness, New York, 1986.

[5] "Although in his memoirs Moniz downplayed the influence of this report, stating that he had conceived the idea of a neurosurgical approach two years before, most observers, including Fulton and Freeman, believed that the animal results were the primary impetus for his taking such a bold step in November 1935." (www.nobe.se/medicine/articles/moniz); E. MONIZ, How I Succeeded in Performing the Prefrontal Leukotomy, in Q. Rev. Psychiatry and Neurology 15 (1954) 373-379.

lobotomy, the connections between the prefrontal cortex and the rest of the brain are cut. Moniz, a psychiatrist and not a surgeon, had operations carried out on the first patients by Almeida Lima following two techniques. The first is the introduction of alcohol into various parts of the two prefrontal lobes, a technique that was quickly abandoned because of its imprecision and the dangers of the diffusion of the alcohol. The second is the practice of lesions made by the rotation of an instrument furnished with a metallic loop, the "cerebral leucotome". This technique was later judged "imprecise and relatively blind".[6] The first operation took place on November 12, 1935.

In his book *Tentatives opératoires dans le traitement de certaines psychoses* (Surgical Trials in the Treatment of Certain Psychoses), published in Paris in 1936, Moniz describes the beginnings of this experimental treatment. The book takes the form of a report on the attempts of the Portuguese psychiatrist to treat certain psychiatric problems by means of surgery. Moniz is aware of the problems posed by human experimentation. "Scientific investigation in a clinical field is often very difficult, because it puts the life of patients at risk, something that for us doctors has the highest value. Much reflection is required before making attempts that could be harmful to patients. All the circumstances must be taken into account, and all hypotheses weighed and meditated."[7] He regrets that prior experimentation on animals is hardly possible in the case of mental illness, affirms the necessity of experimenting on people, and defines his ethical principles: "Even if our theory is exact, we act as if blind in this therapeutic practice. We have to feel our way carefully, but also decisively, as soon as we are certain that the life of patients is in no danger. The first attempts should be made on cases considered incurable, as then what we can change in the mental life of these patients is of no consequence. In the worst hypothesis, they will continue to be mentally insane."[8]

For Moniz, it is by following an orientation that is organicistic that psychiatry will make real progress: "Psychiatry has entered a phase that is organicistic (a better name is neurologic)."[9] According to him, experiments on animals, clinical observations of brain tumours and

---

[6] J. Le Beau, *Psychochirurgie et fonctions mentales*, Paris, 1954, p. 61.
[7] E. Moniz, *Tentatives opératoires dans le traitement de certaines psychoses*, Paris, 1936, p. 6.
[8] *Ibid.*, p. 49.
[9] *Ibid.*, p. 10.

surgical ablations (unilateral or bilateral) of the frontal lobes show that these lobes are the seat of the elaboration of "mental syntheses". Moniz believes that the multiple links between brain cells play a fundamental role in the production of mental phenomena. To cure the mentally ill, one must destroy "the arrangement of more or less fixed cellular connections that must exist in their brains, and particularly those connected with their frontal lobes"[10].

Moniz found the first results "rather encouraging". This led him to continue the experiments "with the persistence needed for work of this type". While honestly admitting his probable partiality in the estimation of results, Moniz invited others to continue his work: "We leave appreciation of the method to those prepared to try it."[11] His technique first aroused the interest of American neuropsychiatrists. In the United States, Freeman and Watts, the two doctors who have contributed the most to the spread of the use of psychosurgery, carried out the first operation on September 14, 1936. A little later, Freeman and Watts introduced a new type of operation, "standard prefrontal lobotomy". In France, the beginnings of psychosurgery were less invasive. David and Claude made some attempts before the war. However, French psychiatrists preferred to use shock therapies: Sakel's cure, cardiozol therapy, or electro shocks. It was only after 1945 that psychosurgery became established in France with David, Talairach, Puech and above all Le Beau. After the Second World War, psychosurgery spread throughout the whole world.

2.4.1.2. The Standard Lobotomy of Walter Freeman and Transorbital Leucotomy

In 1942, Freeman and Watts published their fundamental work, "Psychosurgery: Intelligence, Emotion and Social Behavior following Prefrontal Lobotomy for Mental Disorders".[12] They described a new technique of prefrontal leucotomy, the "standard lobotomy", which consists of a severing of the frontal lobes in front of the coronal suture of the cranial dome. It is a closed technique: after

---

[10] E. MONIZ, Les premières tentatives opératoires dans le traitement de certaines psychoses, in L'Encéphale 91 (1936) 1-29.

[11] ID., Tentatives opératoires dans le traitement de certaines psychoses, p. 7.

[12] W. FREEMAN, J.W. WATTS, Psychosurgery: Intelligence, Emotion and Social Behavior Following Prefrontal Lobotomy for Mental Disorders, Springfield, 1942.

trepanation, the neural fibres are cut by a special leucotomy. The surgeon cuts the white fibres to disconnect the frontal lobe from the thalamus.

In the preface to their book, the authors acknowledge that the frontal lobes are essential to satisfactory social adaptation. Postulating that the activity of the frontal cortex is disturbed in the mentally ill, they judge that a partial inactivation of the frontal lobe resulting from an operation would allow for a better social adaptation. According to them, it is the perturbed activity of the frontal lobe that is responsible for the psychosis. It follows from this that the psychosis will disappear when the prefrontal cortex is inactivated: "Without the frontal lobes there could be no functional psychoses."[13]

Freeman and Watts advance the hypothesis that the frontal lobes are especially concerned with insight and foresight. The emotional components associated with these functions, however, are under the control of the thalamus. Accordingly, when the frontal/thalamic connections are cut, the intellectual functions (insight and foresight) are deprived of their emotional content. Freeman and Watts judge that the neurosurgeon is justified in carrying out an operation that perturbs the patient's intellectual sphere insofar as it is the link between an exaggerated emotional sensibility and perturbed intellectual faculties which is the cause of psychotic behaviour. The prefrontal lobotomy cuts off the emotions associated with delirious ideas, thereby relieving the mental suffering.

For Freeman and Watts, prefrontal lobotomy is a treatment of last resource. It should be carried out only on patients with no hope of spontaneous recovery, and who show a risk of suicide or permanent incapacity. It is necessary to be aware of the personality changes that will certainly follow if the operation succeeds. The potential secondary effects of lobotomy must also be borne in mind: permanent apathy, epileptic fits, incontinence, aggressive behaviour. In the preface to their 1942 book, Freeman and Watts honestly give a warning to the reader of the dangers of standard lobotomy: "Not always does the operation succeed; and sometimes it succeeds too well, in that it abolishes the finer sentiments that have kept the sick individual within the bounds of adequate social behaviour. What may be satisfactory for the patient may be ruinous to the family."[14]

---

[13] *Ibid*, p. vii.
[14] W. FREEMAN, J.W. WATTS, *loc. cit.*

After the war, Freeman[15] introduced into the United States, and popularised, a technique perfected by the Italian Fiamberti in 1937: transorbital leucotomy.[16] The technique consists in introducing a metal point under the upper eyelid, perforating the orbital dome, making the instrument penetrate the brain several centimetres deep, and, finally, turning the instrument sideways to cut the white fibres of the prefrontal region. According to its Italian promoter, this technique is characterised by its extreme simplicity, and can be used in psychiatric institutions that do not have real surgical installations. At the beginning it was not really successful, but as from 1946 Walter Freeman practiced it on a large scale and made it popular. He modified the technique to make it even faster. As anaesthesiologist, he used the period of unconsciousness following an electric shock. He limited aseptic measures to the hands and the leucotome. Other surgeons, such as Almeida Lima, the collaborator of Moniz, moreover reproached him with not respecting "the most elementary rules of asepsis that should characterise intracranial operations".[17] With Freeman, the operation was carried out, on both sides, in a few minutes. Thanks to this new procedure that he judged "more simple and more rapid"[18], he could carry out up to fifteen operations in a morning. Due to its great simplicity, its facility and the speed of its execution, transorbital leucotomy did not require any special surgical talent, and could therefore be carried out by any doctor. Practitioners without experience were therefore tempted to carry it out, thereby adding to its risks.

At the beginnings of psychosurgery, the psychological observation of patients before and after operations was more or less rudimentary. As to results, surgeons limited themselves to counting the number of patients who returned home, as well as giving a rough review of their general psychological evolution. The results given often seem caricatural, some psychiatrists going so far as to put photos of their

---

[15] W. FREEMAN, Transorbital Lobotomy, in American Journal of Psychiatry 105 (1949) 734-739.

[16] A.M. FIAMBERTI, La méthode transorbitaire de la leucotomie préfrontale, in Encéphale 41 (1952) 1-13.

[17] Ibid., p. 8.

[18] W. FREEMAN, Transorbital Lobotomy, in American Journal of Psychiatry, p. 738: "Transorbital lobotomy is simple, quick and safe. It is recommended particularly for psychiatrists in mental hospitals where major neurosurgical procedures are not available."

patients before and after the operation in their articles, having taken care to put on make-up and to dress them elegantly.

2.4.1.3. The Situation of Psychosurgery at the Turn of the Forties and Fifties

The first international psychosurgery congress took place in Lisbon, from August 4-8, 1948.[19] Most of the pioneers of psychosurgery attended, in order to pay homage to Moniz. A year later, Moniz received the Nobel Prize for Medicine "for his discovery of the therapeutic value of prefrontal leucotomy in certain psychoses". He was not the first psychiatrist to receive this prestigious prize. The Nobel jury had already given the prize to the Austrian Wagner-Jauregg for his work on malaria therapy. At the end of the forties, psychosurgery had its golden age. Operations continued, in greater and greater numbers.

However, at this period there were some psychosurgeons, such as J.L. Pool in New York, G. Rylander in Stockholm, W. Scoville in Hartford and J. Lebeau in Paris, who already realised the limits and dangers of psychosurgery, and who attempted to carry out operations more selectively. It was also at this period that the first stereotaxic operations took place. The starting point of this surgery was Horsley and Clarke's stereotaxic equipment (the "stereoencephalotome"), already used in animal physiology. The founders of stereotaxic neurosurgery, Spiegel and Wycis, produced limited lesions in the brain by means of electrodes whose direction and position were determined with exactitude by mechanical procedures. The first operation was carried out in 1947. The fundamental principle of the technique is an exact calculation of, on the one hand, the position of the electrode based on the determination of a reference point by means of a standard X-ray, and on the other hand, on an exact knowledge of the region to be destroyed, in relation to the point of reference. Around 1950, stereotaxic equipment was still a little too complicated to be easily used clinically on humans. At the end of the 60's, stereotaxic surgery would play a fundamental role in the renaissance of psychosurgery.

2.4.1.4. Decline and Criticism

The period of euphoria for psychosurgery did not last long. It came to a definite end in 1955 with the arrival of psychopharmacology. It is

---

[19] H.J. BARAHONA FERNANDEZ, *Anatomo-physiologie cérébrale et fonctions psychiques dans la leucotomie frontale*, Paris, 1950, p. 1-62.

time to take a critical look at whether psychiatric surgery has a valid foundation. At the beginning of the 50's, a number of retrospective studies were undertaken to evaluate the effects of standard lobotomy. The judgement was far from being positive.[20] By 1955, tens of thousands of people (including children) had received psychosurgical treatment. These operations posed obvious ethical problems. They were based on physiological knowledge that was very poor. The criteria for surgery were often applied without discernment, and included almost all mental pathologies. In addition, the results were disappointing: few cases of improvement, a large proportion of surgical deaths, and major secondary effects (apathy, loss of spontaneity, amnesia, different personality changes...). The effects of the operation on the patient's personality were often deplorable. Massive frontal lobotomy often caused a syndrome that Barahona Fernandez[21] described in a general manner under the name of "frontal syndrome", assigning certain common characteristics to the modifications to patients' personalities: a tendency to euphoria, changeability, egocentricity, a lack of tact, troubles of judgement, changes in symbolic values. It was the onset of this syndrome that largely contributed to reticence towards psychosurgery, or even to its total rejection.

From its beginnings, psychosurgery has been seriously criticised. The enthusiasm of the Nobel jury for psychosurgery has not always been shared. According to its adversaries, the deleterious effects of psychosurgery were underestimated. A recurrent problem of psychosurgery is the difficulty of an objective evaluation of its results. Some critics of leucotomy, such as C.E. Allen, thought that the publication of good results came always from those a priori favourable to psychosurgery. Others, like D.W. Stanley and W.J. Atkinson, were persuaded that the majority of surgeons ignored the disastrous effects of the operation on their patients.[22]

---

[20] J. LE BEAU, Psychochirurgie et fonctions mentales, Paris, 1954; M. Partridge, Prefrontal Leucotomy, Oxford, 1950; M. GREENBLATT, H.C. SOLOMON, Studies of Lobotomy, New York, 1950; ID., Frontal Lobes and Schizophrenia, New York, 1950; A. PETRIE, Personality and the Frontal Lobes, London, 1952; F.M. ROBINSON, W. FREEMAN, Psychosurgery and the Self, New York, 1954; P.M. TOW, Personality Changes Following Frontal Leucotomy, London, 1955; N.D.L. LEWIS, C. LANDIS, H.E. KING, Studies in Topectomy, London, 1956.

[21] H.J. BARAHONA FERNANDEZ, Anatomo-physiologie cérébrale et fonctions psychiques dans la leucotomie frontale, Paris, 1950, p. 1-62.

[22] The authors mentioned in this paragraph published their studies in the 1955 issues of The British Medical Journal.

Still others think that psychiatric surgery is morally reprehensible. This is the case of the psychoanalyst D.W. Winnicot, who affirms that "the new physical treatment of mental troubles is socially dangerous, and that a surgical intrusion into the brains of the mentally ill is never justified."[23] In a letter addressed to the *British Medical Journal* in 1956, in which he underlines that psychosurgery consists of a deliberate destruction of parts of a healthy brain, with the aim of provoking an improvement in the mental state of the patient, Winnicott reproaches psychosurgeons with never defining what this "improvement" consists of. He notes the often devastating effects of prefrontal leucotomy on the personality. According to him, psychosurgeons create definitive psychic perturbations in patients who, before the operation, suffered from pathologies that were spontaneously reversible or that could be treated by less radical means. For Winnicot, the existence of leucotomy is detrimental to the whole medical and paramedical profession. The practice furnishes an extreme example of a psychiatry that has become blinded and disinterested in human nature. "Nothing better than leucotomy divides psychiatry as a blind therapy from psychiatry as a complex but interesting concern for the human being who finds life difficult and whose problems we can feel to be represented in ourselves."[24]

Some authors are convinced that the medical profession would gain much by abandoning leucotomy, a gain of such importance as to render insignificant the possible loss, in some cases, of a hypothetical therapeutic effect from surgery. The arguments of e.g. the French psychiatrist Baruk go in the same direction. Baruk remarks that a superficial examination of the patient who has been operated – even where psychological tests are carried out – can sometimes lead one to believe that there has been an improvement. However, when the doctor takes the trouble to follow the patients more closely and to observe how they live, he can often see the dire consequences that had not at first been noticed. Baruk calls for the moral interdiction of psychosurgery that changes a functional trouble into an incurable illness. Even some supporters of biological psychiatry, like Manfred Sakel, the inventor of insulin therapy, expressed reservations

---

[23] Cited by P. PUECH, P. GUILLY, G.C. LAIRY-BOUNES, *Introduction à la psychochirurgie*, Paris, 1950.

[24] D.W. WINNICOT, *Prefrontal Leucotomy*, in *British Medical Journal* 1 (1956) 230.

with regard to psychiatric surgery. "Properly speaking, these operations are not treatments. They are more like amputations"[25], writes
Sakel, who notes that it is often impossible to remedy the bad effects
of psychosurgery.

After a period of great expansion about 1950, psychotherapy
declined at the end of the 50's due to the growth of psychopharmacology. The appearance, and then the multiplication, of chemo-
therapies relegated shock treatment and psychosurgery rapidly to a
position of secondary importance. After 1955, the number of operations diminished significantly. As from 1960, the death of psychosurgery could be seen to be at hand. In the 60's, it was still practiced, but with a limited field of action and at a slower rhythm.

2.4.1.5. *The Improvement of Stereotaxic Surgery and the Renaissance of Psychosurgery at the Beginning of the Seventies*

Because of the relative stagnation of psychopharmacology, the discovery of secondary psychotropic effects and the improvement of
stereotaxic techniques (in particular, those that target the limbic
system), psychosurgery again became more active at the end of the
60's. A sign of this renaissance was the holding of the second International Congress of Psychosurgery in Copenhagen in 1970. The
new generation of psychosurgeons improved both stereotaxic techniques and operations aimed at the temporal lobe, the limbic system and the mesencephalic structures. The operations diversified:
selective stereotaxic destruction of the hypothalamus, of the thalamus, of the amygdale, of the callus matter, of the cingulum, of the
frontal lobes, and of the temporal lobes. This "stereotaxic" surgery
was practiced massively not only to treat traditional psychiatric
syndromes (depressions, psychoses…) but also to suppress deviant
behaviour (delinquency, pathological aggression, sexual perver-
sion…) and to "treat" troubles whose limits are ill defined such as
the syndrome of "child's hyperactivity". These "stereotaxic" techniques are more sophisticated, and cause surgical lesions that are
more discrete, but the lack of a theoretical foundation is equally
serious.

---

[25] M. SAKEL, *The Classical Sakel Shock Treatment: A Reappraisal*, in *Journal of Clinical and Experimental Psychopathology* 15 (1954) 311.

Amygdalectomies and posterior hypothalamotomies were carried out on children or adults showing "pathological aggression."[26] Destruction of the anterior hypothalamus is carried out on sexual perverts (paedophiles,...).[27] Without doubt it is the doctors of Madras (India) who have practiced destruction of the hypothalamus and the amygdale with the most enthusiasm. Following the path traced by the Japanese Sano and Narabayashi, the Indians Balasubramaniam and Ramamurthi carried out an impressive number of these operations on children judged aggressive or "hyperactive".[28] In 1988, Ramamurthi summed up the results of these operations. Out of 1774 stereotaxic operations carried out over 28 years, the aim of 603 was to treat children under fifteen whose behaviour was judged aggressive. At the beginning, Ramamurthi operated only on adolescents, but, helped by his growing experience, he began to exercise his art on children of six or seven who had already received a medical treatment, unsuccessfully, for at least two years. With Sano, Ramamurthi judges that it is not helpful to postpone the operation, as an early operation gives the child better chances of reinsertion. First of all, a bilateral amygdalotomy is carried out. If this does not calm the child, the treatment is completed by a unilateral posterior hypothalamotomy. The results were judged good in 39% of cases, moderate in 37%. For Ramamurthi, "the results are considered good or excellent when the patient continued to be calm and quiet, despite provocation", or when the family of the patient showed that it was satisfied by the operation: "The immeasurable value for the family is indicated by the response from parents and relatives, whose quality of life suddenly improved, and also from the increasing demand for such operations." In brief, Ramamurthi is convinced of the therapeutic value of the technique, and, with a certain can... he asks why this operation does not have more success in... "With this experience, it is strange to note that in the W..." surgical world these operations have not become r

[26] K. SANO, Sedative Stereoencephalotomy: Fornicatomy... Mesencephalic Reticulotomy and Posteromedial Hypothalamotomy, in Progres... Research 21b (1966) 350; K. VAEMET, A. MADSEN, Stereotaxic Amygdalecto... sofrontal Tractotomy in Psy-chotics with Aggressive Behavior, in Journal of... Neurosurgery and Psychiatry 33 (1970) 858. ...hereum in Sexual Deviates, in Confin.

[27] F. ROEDER, Stereotaxic Lesion of ... in Behaviour Disorders, Amygdalotomy and Neurol., 27 (1966) 102. ... (Suppl.) 44 (1988) 152-157.

[28] B. RAMAMAURTHI, Stereot... Hypothalamotomy, in Acta N...

2.4.1.6. New Hostile Reactions

Stereotaxic surgery was intensively practiced at the end of the 60's
and the beginning of the 70's. Operations carried out on prisoners,
aggressive delinquents and sexual perverts were the cause of violent
reactions towards all psychosurgery. There were violent manifestations against psychosurgery in many countries, in particular in the
United States. One of the principal leaders of the protest movement
was the psychiatrist Peter Breggin, who, in February 1972, laid two
reports before the American Congress that were extremely critical
towards psychosurgery.[29] Breggin asked that psychosurgery be forbidden in the United States. Several countries took measures to for-
bid or limit the practice of psychiatric surgery, notably the United
States, Germany and Japan.

2.4.1.7. Psychosurgery Today (1980-1997)

Although psychosurgery experienced a definite decline at the beginning of the 80's, it is still practiced. Today, the return to this treatment among some psychiatrists and the appearance of new surgical
instruments – for example, the "gamma knife" – could lead to a new
return to grace of psychosurgery. In Europe and the United States,
four stereotaxic surgical procedures that were developed during the
60's are still being used to treat anxiety syndromes, obsessions and
severe depressions: anterior capsulotomy, subcaudal tractotomy, cingulotomy, limbic leucotomy.
- Anterior capsulotomy consists of cutting the connections between
  the frontal cortex and the thalamus at the level of the internal capsule. Herner perfected this psychosurgical operation at the beginning of the 60's to treat anxiety disorders that were resistant to normal treatments.[30] Today, the frontal limbic connections of the

---

29 P.K. BREGGIN, *turn of Lobotomy and Psychosurgery*, Congressional Record,
92nd Cong., 2nd session, Congressional ... 118, pt. 5: 5567-5577; ID., *Psychosurgery for the Control of*
Violence, ID., *Psychosurgery for Politic* 92nd Cong., 2nd session, 1972, 118, pt. 9, 11396-11402;
The Return of Lobotomy and Ps...es, in *Duquesne Law Review* 13 (1975) 841-862; ID.,
New York, 1982; S. CHAVKIN, ...ry, in R. EDWARDS (ed.), *Psychiatry and Ethics*,
Boston, 1978.   *Stealers: Psychosurgery and Mind Control*,
   30 T. HERNER, *Treatment of Mental* ... in *Acta* ...
A Follow-Up Study of 116 Cases,   *ith Frontal Stereotaxic Thermo-Lesions.*
                                                        urol. Scand. (Suppl.) 158 (1961) 36.

anterior region of the internal capsule are destroyed by radio-surgery (gamma rays).[31]
- Subcaudal tractotomy: Knight described this procedure in 1964.[32] The lesion is practiced bilaterally in the medio-posterior part of the frontal lobes. It is a stereotaxic version of Scoville's orbital under-cutting.
- Cingulotomy: Ballantine in the United States made this operation popular.[33] By the section of the anterior supracallous fibres, it aims at changing some connections within the limbic system.
- Limbic leucotomy: this combines cingulotomy and subcaudal trac-totomy; Alan Richardson was the first to introduce it.[34]

2.4.1.8. Psychosurgery: an Experimental Practice

The history of psychosurgery is the history of a treatment that is experimental. It permits an attempt to be made at a better under-standing of the functions of different regions of the central nervous system. This purpose has, moreover, always been admitted by psy-chosurgeons (Moniz, Freeman, Le Beau, Lewin, Fulton...) even if today they are somewhat more discrete about it.

Despite technological advances, psychiatric surgery remains an experimental practice whose results are irreversible. The term experi-mentation has two distinct senses. In its first sense (experimentation with a cognitive intention), the experimentation is carried out with-out a therapeutic purpose; its only aim is the progress of knowledge. In the field of psychiatric surgery, this type of experimentation should be severely rejected. In the second sense (experimentation with a therapeutic intention), a practice is said to be experimental when its effects are unpredictable, its risks very variable, its method of action little understood and its utility subject to debate in the sci-entific community. By reference to this second sense, psychosurgery has always been, and still is, a form of experimentation on human beings (Moniz, Freeman, Scoville, Herner, Knight...).

[31] L. LEKSEL, Stereotactic Radiosurgery, in Journal of Neurology, Neurosurgery and Psychiatry 46 (1983) 797-803.

[32] G. KNIGHT, Stereotactic Tractotomy in the Surgical Treatment of Mental Illness, in Journal of Neurology, Neurosurgery and Psychiatry 28 (1965) 304-310.

[33] H.T. BALLANTINE et al., Stereotaxic Anterior Cingulotomy for Neuropsychiatric Illness and Intractable Pain, in Journal of Neurosurgery 26 (1967) 488-495.

[34] A. RICHARDSON, Stereotactic Limbic Leucotomy: Surgical Technique, in Postgrad. Med. J. 49 (1973) 860-864; cited by H. HANSEN, et al., Stereotactic Psychosurgery, in Acta Psychiatrica Scandinavica 66 (1982) 121.

- Therapeutic Effects of Psychosurgery

The therapeutic effects of psychosurgery have always been very unpredictable. In addition, an operation on the brain causes risks that are far from being negligible. The first operations often menaced the life of patients and caused strong personality changes. Now, with the development of new stereotaxic techniques (anterior capsulotomy, subcaudal tractotomy...), somatic complications have diminished; secondary effects on personality characteristics have also been reduced. Nevertheless, undesirable behaviour troubles still subsist. Perseverance in the same behaviour patterns is often observed after capsulotomy. The patient tends to repeat old behaviour patterns even when circumstances demand a different course of action. A neuropsychological examination shows failures (with repeated errors) in tests for problem solving where the rules change in the course of the test. This effect on behaviour is hardly surprising since capsulotomy cuts the connections between the thalamus and the prefrontal cortex.[35]

- Mechanisms of the Therapeutic Effects of Psychiatric Surgery

The mechanisms of the possible therapeutic effects of psychiatric surgery are not known. In fact, as regards the neurophysiological mechanisms that are supposed to explain the effects of the operation, today's neurosurgeons are hardly further advanced than Moniz. The explanations are still rudimentary. There are still questions as to the nature of the effects of the operation. The same operations have been used to treat the most diverse neuro-psychiatric symptoms (depression, obsessions, phobias, psychotic deliria, pain, aggression...).

---

[35] J. FUSTER, The Prefrontal Cortex, 2nd edition, New York, 1989: "The most distinctive disorder arising from prefrontal damage is the inability to initiate and carry out new and goal-directed patterns of behavior. The patient encounters trouble when forced to develop a new form of behavior based on deliberation and choice, especially if in order to reach the goal that behavior requires the organisation of a novel sequence of acts. The frontal patient tends to repeat old patterns of behavior even in circumstances that demand change. Perseveration in old but inappropriate behavior is a distinctive trait of the performance of frontal patients in cognitive tasks" (The Wisconsin Card Sorting Test makes perseverance behaviour very obvious in patients who suffer from prefrontal lesions.)

"There is no universally accepted comprehension of the mode of action of psychosurgery, but, it is obvious, psychosurgery produces modifications in the patient, and reduces some of his biological vulnerabilities", claims the Belgian neurosurgeon P. Cosyns.[36] In fact, neurosurgeons do not know the exact functions of the brain zones that they destroy (prefrontal cortex, amygdala[37] ...). This is one of the most disturbing aspects of psychosurgery. A. Waltregny shares this opinion: "From the neurophysiological point of view, a bilateral destruction of the amygdala does not have a well determined effect on behaviour. Nevertheless, in our experience, this destruction gives valuable results in spite of our inability to assign specific functions to the amygdala (...). No specific data from experiments on animals gives any foundation to the neurophysiological bases of psychosurgery. For psychiatric illnesses, there is no adequate animal model. Consequently, our duty as surgeons is to collect experimental data in humans by adopting an appropriate methodology and to respect the rules of ethics."[38]

Despite the formidable growth in the neurosciences over the last years, our knowledge of the brain is still very imperfect. Today, we know that the prefrontal cortex plays a part in the "superior mental functions", in planning and in the temporal organisation of behaviour. Nevertheless the precise role of different areas of the prefrontal cortex remains little known.[39] As M. Jeannerod notes, psychosurgery of the frontal lobe is its own justification. "It was a very curious scientific reasoning that stated that a trouble of mood or behaviour

---

[36] P. COSYNS, *Psychosurgery and Personality Disorders*, in *Personality and Neurosurgery, Acta Neurochirurgica (Suppl.)* 44 (1988) 124.

[37] See J.P. AGGLETON, *The Functional Effects of Amygdala Lesions in Humans: A Comparison with Findings from Monkeys*, in ID. (ed.), *The Amygdala*, New York, 1992, p. 499: "In spite of the shortage of systematic data and the limitations imposed by the nature of many of the subjects, it is evident that there are many important similarities between the effects of amygdala damage in man and other primates. (...) There is preliminary evidence that while amygdala damage does not disrupt verbal memory, it may impair some aspects of visuospatial memory. (...) Damage to the amygdala is responsible for changes in emotion. As it is the case in monkeys, it is not that humans with amygdala damage are unable to make appropriate responses, it is that the threshold for such responses is altered."

[38] A. WALTREGNY, *Regarding the Experimental Neurophysiological Basis of Psychosurgery, Psychosurgery and Personality Disorders*, in *Personality and Neurosurgery, Acta Neurochirurgica (Suppl.)* 44 (1988) 134.

[39] See, for example, J. FUSTER, *The Prefrontal Cortex*, 2nd edition, New York, 1989.

caused (in principle) by a functional disorder of the frontal lobe would disappear if this frontal lobe were to disappear. Many examples exist in medicine where the therapeutic intervention aims at reducing the hyperactive functioning of an organ. In the domain of neurosurgery, one could cite attempts at the section of the pallido-thalamic fasciculus in order to reduce trembling in Parkinson's disease. However, this ideal of a surgery that is "functional" is limited by our level of knowledge of the system in which we wish to intervene. To exclude a part of the frontal lobes under the pretext that they were over-functioning, or that their dysfunction threatened to contaminate the rest of the system, is a bit as though one advised the ablation of the occipital lobe of a patient complaining of visual hallucinations, or of the temporal lobe of someone with auditory hallucinations![40] Recently, the Dutch neuro-anatomist Groenewegen defended a reasoning similar to that attacked by Jeannerod to explain the neuro-functional bases of obsessions and to justify psychosurgery.[41] According to him, it is a malfunctioning of the cortical-striatal system that is responsible for the behavioural symptoms suffered by patients with obsessions. Groenewegen notes that lesions of the sensori-motor systems of the basal ganglia can lead to "hyperkinetic or hypokinetic syndromes". By analogy, he esteems that disturbances of "the associational or limbic parts of the basal ganglia may lead to similar symptomatology in the affective or behavioural

---

[40] M. JEANNEROD, *Organisation et désorganisation des fonctions mentales: le syndrome frontal*, in *Revue de Métaphysique et de Morale* 2 (1992) 251.

[41] H.J. GROENEWEGEN (*Recent Insights in the Frontal Cortical-Basal Ganglia Relationships, Relevance for Obsessive-Compulsive Disorders, Abstract Presented at the 6th Meeting on Controversial Topics: The Use of Psychosurgery in OCD and Related Disorders*, Belgian College of Neuropsychopharmacology and Biological Psychiatry, Antwerp, 26 November 1993) thinks that the frontal cortex and the basal ganglia play a preponderant role in obsessions. "Functionally different frontal cortical areas (i.e. sensori-motor, association, and limbic) are connected with distinct parts of the basal ganglia and the thalamus forming the neural basis for functionally different circuits. In sensori-motor circuits, the basal ganglia and connectionally related frontal cortical and thalamic areas are thought to play a major role in the planning and sequencing of movements. Similarly, the association and limbic parts of the basal ganglia and their related parts of the (pre)frontal cortex and ventral and medial thalamus are considered to be concerned with the planning and sequencing of mental processes and complex behavior." "Lesions of the sensori-motor parts of the basal ganglia may lead to either hyperkinetic or hypokinetic syndromes", thinks Groenewegen. By analogy, he esteems that "disturbances of the associational or limbic parts of the basal ganglia may lead to similar symptomatology in the behavioral, cognitive or affective realm."

realm." This type of reasoning is very hypothetical. Moreover it concerns a theory that is somewhat simplistic to explain a disorder as complex as an obsessive neurosis.

- The Utility of Psychiatric Surgery is Far from Being Unanimously Accepted

The therapeutic results of psychosurgery have never been clearly identified. As Marc Jeannerod notes again: "The appreciation given by the first neurosurgeons as to the future of the patients they have themselves treated by lobotomy, often carried out by reference to post-operational evolution in the short term, or founded on a summary classification, should be treated with caution."[42] Today the results of operations are subject to much stricter evaluation than previously. However, despite the use of diverse scales of evaluation, the evolution of a mental problem is often extremely difficult to quantify.

The utility of psychosurgery is the object of serious debate within the medical community. H. Hansen, R. Anderson, A. Theilgaard and V. Lunn, of the psychiatric service of the Copenhagen Righospitalet, have re-evaluated the positive and negative effects of psychosurgery, giving particular attention to the global evolution of the personality and the social life of the patient. The results of this in depth enquiry were published in 1982.[43] This study is the result of a retrospective study of people who had been the subjects of stereotaxic operations at the University Hospital of Copenhagen between 1965 and 1974. The authors were thus able to verify their intuitive hypothesis, according to which the results of the operation are much more controversial than is generally admitted by psychosurgeons. According to them, the results appear good when the enquiry is limited to a study of the evolution of the patient's symptoms after the operation. Surgical treatment can reduce the pathological symptoms of the patient and, in consequence, cut down on the length of hospitalisation and the need for treatment. However, an evaluation centred only on the evolution of symptoms is insufficient. In fact, the improvement in symptoms could have been obtained at the expense of a deterioration of the emotional and intellectual qualities of the

---

[42] M. JEANNEROD, *Organisation et désorganisation des fonctions mentales: le syndrome frontal*, p. 249.

[43] H. HANSEN et al., *Stereotactic Psychosurgery*, in *Acta Psychiatrica Scandinavica* 66 (1982) 7-123.

individual. In order to evaluate the results of the operation correctly, the global evolution of the personality must be taken into account. In an evaluation, psychological tests certainly play a useful and important role; but they should not be the only criteria.

Heidi Hansen underlines the necessarily subjective nature of the evaluation: the appreciation of the results varies with the observer. Nowadays, psychosurgery is no longer a normal treatment. Recent psychiatric textbooks rarely mention it. This radical treatment continues to be used only in a few rare hospitals. The large majority of psychiatrists have given up this form of treatment. In most hospitals, psychosurgery has disappeared from the choice of treatments, As to those psychiatrists who are still convinced of its use, they do not agree on its applicability. Most judge that psychosurgery should be reserved for "highly disturbed and suffering therapy-resistant patients". For others its field of application is much wider. The Danish psychiatrist Haaijman, for example, believes that "psychosurgery may be a good indication for patients with post traumatic stress disorder."[44] He judges the point of view whereby psychosurgery is the treatment of last resort to be out of date.[45]

- Towards More Effective Ethical Regulation of Psychiatric Surgery

Psychiatric surgery has always constituted a form of experimentation on human beings. Today, in spite of the techno-scientific progress that has been made, the procedures employed in psychiatric surgery remain experimental. A procedure is experimental if its effects are unpredictable, its risks very variable, its mechanisms ill understood and its utility the subject of wide debate in the medical community.[46] Psychosurgery unites all these conditions.

Nowadays psychosurgery is a rare treatment. Two factors could play a role in the probable new development of psychiatric surgery. The first factor is the appearance of new surgical instruments – an

---

[44] W.P. HAAIJMAN, *Psychotherapy in Patients with Anxiety Disorders: the Supportive Influence of Psychosurgery*, Abstract Presented at the 6th Meeting on Controversial Topics: *The Use of Psychosurgery in OCD and Related Disorders*, Belgian College of Neuropsychopharmacology and Biological Psychiatry, Antwerp, 26 November 1993.

[45] W.P. HAAIJMAN, *loc. cit.*: "Psychosurgery as ultimate resort is an out-of-date standpoint."

[46] H. HANSEN *et al.*, *loc. cit.*

example is the "gamma knife"[47] – that could lead to a renewal of psychosurgery similar to that experienced with the appearance of stereotaxic methods. The "gamma knife" is a new radio-surgical instrument that allows selective lesions of the brain to be made without opening the scalp.

The second factor is that psychosurgery has again become popular with some psychiatrists. During the sixties, surgery for mental troubles experienced a strong decline. At the beginning of the eighties, it was possible to believe that psychosurgery had disappeared.[48] Nowadays, however, some psychiatrists think that the treatment is still useful to treat severe psychiatric disorders, resistant to normal treatments. Over the next few years it is possible that there will be a notable increase in the number of psychosurgical operations. Psychosurgery has always been a very controversial treatment. In view of its strong symbolic charge, this treatment, by nature experimental, should be subject to strict regulation.

2.4.2. Intracerebral Grafts of Foetal Cells

Grafts within the central nervous system are a promising experimental technique, where cells are transplanted within the nervous system so as to restore a function that is perturbed. While the first brain grafts were carried out on animals as from the end of the 19th century, it was only during the sixties that scientists (Olson, Lund, Björklund, Perlow…) took up this type of work again seriously, and envisaged its application on humans.[49] The rational basis for brain transplants for those suffering from Parkinson's disease rests on an experimental animal model of the disease. In 1979, Perlow[50] and

---

[47] L. LEKSELL (Stereotactic Radiosurgery, in Journal of Neurology, Neurosurgery and Psychiatry 46 (1983) 797-803.) perfected stereotaxic radiosurgery in 1951. Over the last ten years, this technique has been considerably developed and made more complex. The "gamma-knife" allows one to send a high dose of radiation, capable of destroying selectively a small, localised region of the brain. See also S. BLOND et al., Stereotactically Guided Radiosurgery Using the Linear Accelerator, in Acta Neurochirurgica (Suppl.) 124 (1993) 40-43.

[48] In 1980, an article in the Nouvelle Presse Médicale gave the obituary of psychosurgery.

[49] See on this subject S. WOERLY & R. MARCHAND, 100 ans de neurotransplantation chez les mammifères, in Journal de Neurochirurgie 36 (1990) 71-95.

[50] M.F. PERLOW, W.F. FREED et al., Brain Grafts Reduce Motor Abnormalities Produced by the Destruction of Nigrostriatal Dopamine System, in Science 204 (1979) 643-647.

Björklund[51] showed that grafts of immature dopamine producing cells can compensate for a motor deficit artificially induced in a rodent by a selective destruction of the dopamine producing cells of a limited region of the central nervous system: the black substance, or *locus niger*.

As from 1982, brain grafts have been carried out in order to treat patients suffering from Parkinson's disease. This disease is the result of degeneration of the dopamine neurons of the locus niger. The axons of these neurons, situated in the locus niger, innerve the striatum – a sub-cortical region consisting of the caudal nucleus and the putamen – and thereby form the nigrostriatal pathway. From a functional point of view, this pathway is concerned in the control of voluntary movements and in the regulation of muscular tones. The absence of control, normally provided by the liberation of dopamine into the striatum, is responsible for the characteristic motor symptoms of Parkinson's disease: muscular rigidity, slowness of movement and trembling. To compensate for the dopamine deficit, neurobiologists had the idea of grafting dopamine cells directly into the brains of Parkinson patients. To do this, two different techniques are used: in the first, cells from one of the adrenal medulla glands of the patient are grafted; in the second, dopamine producing cells are used, coming from the mesencephalon – a region situated at the base of the brain – of about nine week old human foetuses.

At the beginning of the eighties, adrenal medullary grafts were carried out much more often because, on the one hand, these autografts do not cause immunological problems, and, on the other hand, do not a priori raise ethical problems as acute as the method using foetal tissue. It was Backlund[52] and his collaborators who attempted the first human application, implanting, by a stereotaxic technique, adrenal medullary tissue into the striatum of Parkinson patients. Between 1982 and 1984, four patients received this type of graft; the results were disappointing.

---

[51] A. BJÖRKLUND, U. STENEVI, *Reconstruction of the Nigrostriatal Dopamine Pathway by Intracerebral Nigral Transplant*, in *Brain Research* 177 (1979) 555-560.

[52] E.L. BACKLUND et al., *Transplantation of Adrenal Medullary Tissue to Striatum in Parkinsonism; First Clinical Trials*, in *Journal of Neurosurgery* 62 (1985) 169-173; O. LINVALL, E.O. BACKLUND, L. FARDE, et al., *Transplantation in Parkinson's Disease: Two Cases of Adrenal Medullary Grafts to the Putamen*, in *Annals of Neurology* 22 (1987) 457-468.

Doctor Madrazo later took up the technique of an autograft of adrenal medullary tissue, carried out unsuccessfully by the Swedish team.[53] This Mexican clinician's method is not the same; the adrenal medullary graft is fixed to the caudate nucleus during open surgery. The spectacular results obtained by Madrazo were at first received with enthusiasm, and were abundantly commented upon by the media. Many hundreds of patients suffering from Parkinson's disease received adrenal medullary grafts. Soon, however, the enthusiasm was lost. At the Ninth International Congress on Parkinson's disease, held at Jerusalem in June 1988, a very negative assessment of the results was presented. In the vast majority of cases, the state of the patients had not improved. In addition, there were many postsurgical complications. In consequence, Madrazo himself asked the medical body to adopt a moratorium on intracerebral grafts on humans.[54] It should be noted that this graft, that at first view does not pose any particular problem since it consists of the implantation of cells belonging to the patient himself, had not previously been the object of many animal tests.

The other procedure uses cells coming from the mesencephalon of a human foetus. Here, numerous experiments have been carried out on animals of grafts of foetal cells, not only on rodents but also on primates suffering from artificially induced Parkinson's disease following the injection of a neurotoxin, MTPT (1-methyl-4-phenyl-1,2,3,6-tetrahydropyrdine).[55] They show that the grafts insert themselves into the host's nervous system and thus compensate for certain functional deficits. As from 1988, grafts of foetal cells into the brain started to be carried out on humans.[56] In the first stage, mesencephalic tissue is removed from approximately nine-week-old foetuses (at this age, the neural cells in the process of differentiation are

---

[53] I. MADRAZO, et al., Open Microsurgical Autograft of Adrenal Medulla to the Right Caudate Nucleus in Two Patients with Intractable Parkinson's Disease, in New England Journal of Medicine 316 (1987) 831-834.

[54] See on this subject M. PESCHANSKI, Le cerveau réparé?, Paris, 1989.

[55] D.H. REDMOND JR., J.R. SLADEK JR., R.H. ROTH et al., Fetal Neuronal Grafts in Monkeys Given Methylphenyltetradropyridine, in Lancet 338 (1986) 1125-1127.

[56] E.R. HITCHCOCK et al., Embryos and Parkinson's Disease, in Lancet 340 (1988) 1274; I. MADRAZO, V. LEON, C. TORRES et al., Transplantation of Fetal Substantia Nigra and Adrenal Medulla to the Caudate Nucleus in Two Patients with Parkinson's disease, in New England Journal of Medicine 318 (1988) 51; O. LINDVALL, Transplantation Into the Human Brain: Present States and Future Possibilities, in Journal of Neurology, Neurosurgery, Psychiatric Special Supplement (1989) 39-54.

at the optimal age for a graft); secondly, the neural cells are injected into the brain of the patient, after separation of the foetal brain tissue. The first results of these operations were also disappointing. Nevertheless, in 1990, a graft of foetal cells into a patient suffering from Parkinson's disease gave a positive result. Olle Lindvall, Anders Björklund and their colleagues introduced foetal brain tissue (coming from four aborted foetuses) into the brain of a forty nine year old man.[57] Eight weeks after the operation, the patient, suffering from a severe form of Parkinson's disease, was in a considerably better state. Observation of the brain structures by positron tomography, a new medical imaging technique, showed that the graft had "taken" well, and had re-established the brain functions that had been changed. Since 1990, experiments have multiplied: more than a hundred patients have received grafts of foetal cells into their brains.[58] Various operating techniques have been tried: unilateral or bilateral injection into the striatum; injection into the caudal nucleus and/or into the putamen; the use of fresh or frozen foetal tissue; variations in the quantity of tissue grafted (tissue from one to eight foetuses as appropriate).... The transplant does not cure the patients, but it improves their clinical state: they show fewer periods of immobility ("off" periods); they speak and move more easily; they remain under medication but the doses of levadopa can be reduced. The results are encouraging to those neurosurgeons who are working at the development of this type of graft, and give credence to the hopes legitimately held today as to the efficiency of this surgical approach in the treatment of Parkinson's disease.

In addition, neurotransplantation offers interesting perspectives in the treatment of other diseases of the central nervous system. The treatment is most efficient when the brain damage is localised, and preferably has struck only a given system of neurotransmitters.

---

[57] O. LINDVALL et al., Grafts of Fetal Dopamine Neurons Survive and Improve Motor Function in Parkinson's Disease, in Science 247 (1990) 574-577; J. MARX, Fetal Nerve Grafts Show Promise in Parkinson's Disease, in Science 247 (1990) 529.

[58] C.R. FREED, R.E. BREEZE, N.L. ROSENBERG et al., Survival of Implanted Fetal Dopamine Cells and Neurologic Improvement 12 to 46 Months After Transplantation for Parkinson's Disease, in New England Journal of Medicine 327 (1992) 1549-1555; D.D. SPENCER, R.J. ROBBINS, F. NARTOLIN et al., Unilateral Transplantation of Human Fetal Mesencephalic Tissue Into the Caudate Nucleus of Patients with Parkinson's Disease, in New England Journal of Medicine 327 (1992) 1541-1548; H. WIDNER, J. TETRUD, S. REHN-CRONA et al., Bilateral Fetal Mesencephalic Grafting in Two Patients with Parkinsonism Induced by MPTP, in New England Journal of Medicine 327 (1992) 1556-1563.

These conditions are all found in Huntington's chorea, a dominant genetic disease, characterised by the progressive arrival, between the ages of thirty and forty, of abnormal choreiform movements and intellectual difficulties. Graft experiments are being carried out now on animal models of Huntington's disease, and a European programme has been set up so that human experimentation should start soon. Traumatisms of the spinal cord could also, in the future, be a major indication for neurotransplantation: the grafts would supply a replacement for the paths interrupted by focal lesions of the nervous system. On the other hand, it seems improbable that neurotransplantation would be an appropriate treatment when, as in Alzheimer's disease, the lesions are diffuse and affect several nervous systems.

To sum up, neurotransplantations are a promising technique, susceptible of improving the condition of those suffering from severe neurological complaints. They do not, however, yet constitute a common clinical treatment.[59] Neurotransplantation remains an experimental treatment that raises a certain number of moral dilemmas. These dilemmas will now be examined, starting with the most sensitive, the use of foetal tissue.

2.4.2.1. *Transplantation of Foetal Tissue: a Problem that is Both Ethical and Political*

Grafts of foetal nerve tissue raise the question of whether the current utilisation of nervous tissue from human foetuses poses objections from the ethical point of view. On this point there are, in broad terms, two different positions. The first, on moral, philosophical or religious grounds, is totally hostile to the use of embryonic or foetal tissue, because of the controversial status given to the embryo. In the United States, following a decision of the federal government taken under pressure from those opposed to the practice of abortion, the NIH (National Institutes of Health) has for a long time given no subsidies to research that employs human foetal tissue.[60] The moratorium

---

[59] G.W. PAULSON, *Therapy of Patients with Parkinson's Disease*, in *Archives of Neurology* 51 (1994) 754-756; D.C. GOETZ et al., *Neurosurgical Horizons in Parkinson's Disease*, in *Neurology* 43 (1993) 1-7.

[60] See J.P. KASSIRER, M. ANGEL, *The Use of Fetal Tissue in Research on Parkinson's Disease*, in *The New England Journal of Medicine* 327 (1992) 1591-1592; B.J. HOFFER & L. OLSON, *Ethical Issues in Brain-Cell Transplantation*, in *Trends in Neuroscience* 14 (1991) 384-385.

was indirectly provoked by a demand from James Wijngarden, director of the NIH, to the Health Department. Robert Wisdom, at that time Assistant Secretary of Health, imposed a temporary moratorium in this research field, while waiting for the consultative committee of the NIH to give its opinion on the ethical questions raised by intracerebral grafts of foetal tissue. At the end of 1988, the Human Fetal Tissue Transplantation Research Panel, composed of 21 experts in different fields, published a report that was favourable to the financing of experiments on the transplantation of foetal tissue, and drew up a number of rules to be followed. In spite of this positive report, the Bush administration maintained the moratorium, which finally lasted five years. The first American experiments were therefore carried out with private funding.[61] It was necessary to wait for Clinton's accession to the presidency to see the lifting, in 1993, of the ethical/political moratorium on the public finance of foetal tissue transplantations.

The second position, believing that the transplantation of foetal tissue could be of great service to those suffering from severe neurological troubles, encourages the use of foetal tissue subject to certain conditions: anonymity between the donor and the recipient, the exclusion of any financial dealings, careful study of the validity of the project.... Having settled the rules of conduct to be respected in neurotransplantation, the Swedish ethical authorities authorised the first tests of intracerebral grafts of foetal tissue in 1986. The French National Consultative Committee on Ethics had an attitude that was more qualified, more hesitant. In 1989, it advised against the practice of grafts of nervous tissue.[62] A year later, the same committee changed its mind and authorised the experimental practice of brain grafts: the first two French intracerebral grafts were carried out on Parkinson patients in June 1991 and January 1992[63]. It judged that the use of foetal tissue for therapeutic purposes was justified provided that "this utilisation is of an exceptional character and is controlled by an Ethics Committee". The exceptional character is

---

[61] This was the case with the first intracerebral transplantation of foetal tissue in the United States, carried out by Freed in 1988.

[62] CCNE, *Avis sur les greffes de cellules nerveuses dans le traitement de la maladie de Parkinson*, 16 October, 1989. (www.ccne-ethique.org).

[63] CCNE, *Avis concernant des greffes intracérébrales de tissus mésencéphaliques d'embryons humains chez cinq malades parkinsoniens dans un but d'expérimentation thérapeutique*, 13 December 1990. (www.ccne-ethique.org).

advisable "so as to avoid such utilisation becoming a factor of pressure in favour of massive abortions, and becoming a routine and generalised technique". A drift in this direction is possible. Since the tissue must be taken from a foetus of a specific age (seven to eleven weeks), the practice of intracerebral grafts could lead to planned pregnancies and to abortions provoked at appropriate dates. The Swedish Ethics Committee, which authorised the first transplantation experiments, for its part insists on the fact that the experiment should in no way influence the procedure, the timing or the motivation of the abortion.

In the United States, as from 1988, the NIH Human Fetal Tissue Transplantation Research Panel laid down a series of recommendations concerning the use of foetal tissue[64]:

- The decision to terminate a pregnancy and to have an abortion should be taken independently of any recuperation or potential use of the foetus.
- The timing of and the method used for the abortion should not be influenced by the use of the foetal tissue for the purposes of transplantation or medical research.
- The foetal tissue obtained by the voluntary interruption of pregnancy must not be used for medical research without the prior consent of the mother.
- The decision and consent to abort should precede any discussion about the potential utilisation of the foetus.
- The pregnant women cannot designate the receiver of the transplant.
- Any payment or other form of remuneration or compensation, following the obtaining of foetal tissue, should be forbidden, with the exception of reasonable expenses resulting from the recuperation, stocking, preparation and transport of the tissue.
- Any potential receiver of foetal tissue should be informed of the nature of the graft, as should the medical and research teams concerned.

[64] It should be remembered that this committee, charged by the NIH with the examination of the ethical questions linked to the use of foetal cells, judged, in 1988, that the transplantation of foetal cells was acceptable provided that its recommendations were followed. In spite of this favourable opinion, the moratorium continued until 1993.

- The foetal tissue should be treated with the same respect as that given to other tissues coming from human corpses."[65] It should be added that, since 1988, the National Organ Transplant Act forbids the purchase and sale of foetal tissue.

Today, after the end of the moratorium and of the French hesitations, protocols for intracerebral grafts are being drawn up in most Western countries. Since 1990, the various European teams specialised in intracerebral transplantations collaborate within the NECTAR network (Network of European CNS – Central Nervous System – Transplantation and Restoration) and have set up their own code of conduct. [66] At the beginning of 1994 the NIH gave its financial support to a new American transplantation test on Parkinson patients.

Since the utilisation of foetal tissue coming from elective abortions is the main source of contention, it would be useful to dispose of other sources of graft material. Foetal tissue from ectopic pregnancies or spontaneous abortions does not have the qualities necessary for transplantation.[67] In any case, in the future, technical demands will doubtless make the discovery of an alternative solution to the use of foetal tissue indispensable. In spite of the positive results of grafts, the symptoms of Parkinson's disease do not disappear completely. Present day grafts do not supply a sufficient number of dopamine cells. The dopamine producing neurons represent only a feeble proportion of the cell population of the foetal mesencephalon used as a graft. To obtain better results in treatment it would be necessary to be able to inject bilaterally into the striatum a larger number of dopamine producing neurons. In these conditions, Björklund, one of the pioneers of neurografts, judges that the mesencephalic tissue from ten to fifteen foetuses could prove necessary for the carrying out of one useful transplant.[68] If brain transplantations are going

---

[65] NATIONAL INSTITUTES OF HEALTH, *Report of the Human Fetal Tissue Transplantation Research Panel*, Bethesda, Maryland, 1988; cited by J. BROTCHI, & M. LEVIVIER, *Ethique et recherche en neurochirurgie*, in *Revue Médicale de Bruxelles* 12 (1991) 204.

[66] See G.J. BOER, *Ethical Guidelines for the Use of Human Embryonic or Fetal Tissue for Experimental and Clinical Neurotransplantation and Research*, in *Journal of Neurology* 242 (1994) 1-13.

[67] D. GARRY, *Are there Really Alternatives to the Use of Fetal Tissue from Elective Abortions in Transplantation Research?*, in *The New England Journal of Medicine* 327 (1992) 1592-1594.

[68] A. BJÖRKLUND, *Better Cells for Brain Repair*, in *Nature* 362 (1993) 414-415; ID., *Neural Transplantation – An Experimental Tool with Clinical Possibilities*, in *Trends in Neuroscience* 14 (1991) 319-322, 328-334.

to be carried out on a larger scale, other sources of cells will definitely need to be found (cells genetically modified to produce dopamine, the creation of cultures of human dopamine producing cells using neural cells that are not yet differentiated...). Already, researchers are experimenting with these new grafting techniques on animals.[69] The possible creation and use of cell banks of dopamine producing cells would no doubt raise fewer ethical questions than the removal of neural tissue from human foetuses of a specific age coming from elective abortions.

2.4.2.2. High Technology and the Allocation of Resources

As a medical technique that is sophisticated and therefore relatively expensive, neurotransplantation raises the problem of the allocation of resources. The public funding dedicated to health care and medical research is not unlimited. It seems fitting to favour techniques giving a good cost/benefit return for health care, and that are likely to treat a large number of patients, or improve their quality of life. At the present state of experimentation it is difficult to predict the future and the possible applications of neurografts, which could have unsuspected consequences for other research sectors. Today it therefore seems legitimate to encourage the development of neurotransplantation. Nevertheless, if neurografts were one day to become a routine means of treatment, the question of the allocation of resources would become a more pressing problem. In the future there could be many cases where an effective treatment, available and technically possible to carry out, could not be offered to all patients who could benefit from it, for economic reasons. To take the example of Alzheimer's disease, it is possible that neurografts might soon become effective to attenuate the symptoms of senile dementia. Financial constraints would no doubt make the idea of systematically giving grafts to those suffering from Alzheimer's disease unrealistic. A public health policy establishing priorities for treatments given public funding is entirely indispensable.[70]

---

[69] F. GAGE, M.D. KAWAJA, L.J. FISHER, Genetically Modified Cells: Applications for Intracerebral Grafting, in Trends in Neuroscience 14 (1991) 328-334.

[70] See A.M. CAPRON, Oregon's Disability, in Hastings Center Report 22 (1992) 18-20; P.T. MENZEL, Oregon's Denial, in Hastings Center Report 22 (1992) 21-25. The Oregon Public Health Plan furnishes a good example of an attempt to plan medical requirements. Set up at the end of the eighties, it establishes priorities for medical treatment,

The choice of these priorities is nevertheless extremely delicate, and inevitably gives rise to moral dilemmas.[71]

2.4.2.3. *Neurotransplantation and Brainwashing: a Fear that is Unfounded*

Brain grafts raise another question. Would it be possible, with the help of these intracerebral grafts, to manipulate the mind? Is there not a risk of using grafts of neural tissue in the future not only to treat illnesses that are really incapacitating but also to manipulate the mind, to modify behaviour, or even to rejuvenate? Experiments on the nervous system, and more particularly the carrying out of grafts in the brain, "the seat of thought", have fascinated human imagination for a long time. Writers and philosophers have created more or less frightening science fiction, in which "mad scientists" have striven to graft human brains. But what really happens? It must be underlined that, at the moment, a graft of the entire brain is quite impossible; it is in the realm of science fiction. There is another point: is it possible for a graft of neural cells coming from the nervous system of another human, even if it is only a foetus, to cause the transfer of a part of the mind? There again, the reply is clear: the risks of manipulation of the mind in the course of an intracerebral graft are non-existent. In fact, on the one hand, the neuroanatomical correlations of human thought are largely unknown; on the other hand, under current practice, unconnected neural cells only are injected, while it would appear that mental functions develop through a slow and gradual structuring of the neural network as the individual grows. Nevertheless, it cannot be excluded that grafts carried out in several regions of the central nervous system could, like some psychotropic medicines, have secondary effects on the cerebral functions

---

based on the concept of quality of life. The least efficient treatments are not funded. This programme for the rationalisation of health services has been criticised as unjust towards some people suffering from specific handicaps.

[71] On this subject see D. CALAHAN, *What Kind of Life?: The Limits of Medical Progress*, New York, 1990: "Life has no price." From an idealistic point of view, everyone would wish to support this popular adage. Public opinion polls confirm this credo. "Everyone has the right to receive the best health care." "Medical insurance should cover all life-saving treatments, even if they cost a million dollars", claim those Americans questioned in a public opinion poll. Idealism is nevertheless tempered by realism when the economic consequences of this attitude are explained. Those who favour unlimited access to health care are not ready to assume the cost of their convictions.

of the patient, and possibly on his personality.[72] In no case, however, can intracerebral grafts lead to a planned manipulation of the mind.

2.4.2.4. Prudence and Auto-Regulation of Research

Have there not been transplantations carried out prematurely, when sufficient data from animal experimentation was not available? This question touches upon the current state of knowledge; the history of adrenal medullary grafts shows that experimentation on humans has sometimes been too rapid, and that scientific teams do not always take sufficient precautions. Recently, a neurobiologist discovered with surprise that more patients had received an adrenal medullary graft than monkeys had received a similar operation! One can therefore reproach neurosurgeons who have carried out adrenal medullary grafts with having acted too quickly, and with not having had the patience to wait for the results of animal experiments to accumulate.

We think that research on grafts of foetal tissue to the brain should be encouraged. Nevertheless, it is necessary to move with prudence and without precipitation, so as not to reach situations similar to those arrived at by the unfortunate experiments of medullar-adrenal grafts. From this point of view, the initiative of the NIH (National Institutes of Health) to subsidise experiments on a large scale is perhaps premature, even in the opinion of a number of intracerebral transplantation specialists. In fact, at the beginning of 1994, after the moratorium on the public funding of foetal tissue transplants in the United States had been lifted, the NIH decided to give a large grant to the team of Kurt Freed (University of Colorado Health Sciences Center) to carry out an experimental study of foetal grafts on 40 Parkinson patients. This was an ambitious experiment, on a large

---

[72] Some patients who received grafts showed post-surgical psychiatric troubles. See M.A. MENZA, L.I. GOLBE, Hypomania in a Patient Receiving Deprenyl (Selegilin) After Adrenal-Striatal Implantation for Parkinson's Disease, in Clin. Neuropharmacol. 11 (1988) 549-551; C.G. GOETZ, C.W. OLANOW, W.C. KOLLER et al., Multicenter Study of Autologous Adrenal Medullary Transplantation to the Corpus Striatum in Patients with Advanced Parkinson's Disease, in The New England Journal of Medicine 320 (1989) 337-341. Neuropsychological changes have also been noted. See F. OSTROSKY-SOLIS et al., Neuropsychological Effects of Brain Autografts of Adrenal Medullary Tissue for the Treatment of Parkinson's Disease: Clinical Observations in Five Patients, in Neurosurgery 22 (1988) 999-1004; D.D. SPENCER, R.J. ROBBINS, F. NARTOLIN, et al., Unilateral Transplantation of Human Fetal Mesencephalic Tissue Into the Caudate Nucleus of Patients with Parkinson's Disease, in New England Journal of Medicine 327 (1992) 1541-1548.

number of patients. The European researchers from the NECTAR network wrote an open letter to the revue Science in order to express their concern. At the present state of research, they consider that it would be preferable to finance a number of small clinical tests, using different techniques, rather than one large-scale experiment. In addition, what is involved is a double blind test, which in the case of neural grafts poses ethical problems. Twenty patients would receive a graft. The twenty others would act as a control group, so as to detect a possible placebo effect. Initially, they would not receive a graft, but holes would nevertheless be made in their cranium, so as to follow the methodology of double blind tests. Not agreeing with the ethical foundation of this project, some neurotransplantation specialists have protested, so as to avoid a hazardous test compromising the future of grafts to the brain.

This episode is an example of an attempt of autoregulation of research, since it was the researchers themselves who were the first to react, so as to prevent a badly thought out experiment discrediting their field of research. In the domain, perpetually evolving, of intracerebral grafts, we believe that, above all, it is the role of researchers themselves, and of the Ethics Committees examining the protocols, to ensure the regulation of research.

2.5. Conclusion

It should be remembered that it was the public revelation of abuses in medical experimentation that engendered reflection on the ethical rules to be respected within the framework of human experimentation, and that led to a system of peer regulation. By introducing, in the sixties, the IRB system, the Americans arrived at a regulation of experimental research based on control exercised by peers and informed representatives of the public. The creation of Ethics Committees was a flexible instrument, allowing for the ethical problems raised by human experimentation to be managed in a pragmatic but vigilant manner, while remaining close to clinical reality. Under this system of regulation, every research project should be clearly defined in an experimental protocol and should be submitted to an Ethics Committee for examination. This procedure gives good guarantees to the subject of the experiment. However, because of their social, political and economic implications, some ethical problems are not within the competence of local Ethics Committees. For this reason it should be possible for the fundamental ethical questions to be examined by consultative committees of ethics, national or international, who would undertake, after consulting experts, the drawing up of reports capable of serving as guidelines to local committees of ethics. Any system of self-regulation of research should be supple, and should allow for a rapid adaptation of decisions in function of the progress of research. The rapid evolution of the research context and the necessity of having a flexible system of regulation are well illustrated by the hesitations and changes of position of the French Comité Consultatif National d'Ethique (CCNE) (National Consultative Committee of Ethics), concerning intracerebral grafts of foetal cells. In October 1989, the CCNE refused its support, and recommended "that therapeutic trials (of grafts of dopamine producing neurons of human embryos) should not be undertaken in France". Only a year later, in December 1990, the CCNE gave a new opinion, this time favourable, and decided to authorise a French medico-surgical team to carry out intracerebral grafts of foetal cells. For the CCNE, the situation had changed "since a Swedish team had carried out remarkable work". The publication in February 1990, by Lindvall and Björklund's team, of only one case, showing favourable results, of a patient who had received an intracerebral graft of foetal cells, was sufficient to convince the CCNE of the utility of carrying out human experiments in France. The system of self-regulation of research based on the action of local committees of ethics, made up in the majority of doctors and researchers close to clinical reality, and of consultative committees, seems to us to be the best adapted to the changing reality of medical experimentation, and the most likely to conciliate the interests of patients and the necessities of research.

3

RANDOMISED CLINICAL TRIALS: A CONFLICT BETWEEN INDIVIDUAL AND COLLECTIVE VALUES?

Reidar K. Lie

During the mid-1960's, two classics of research ethics were published. One was Henry Beecher's famous article, which documented the widespread inattention to ethical principles among top level biomedical researchers.[1] Some of the cases in Beecher's article were actually provided by Pappworth, who published a book in the UK one year later, also documenting widespread lack of concern for ethics among researchers.[2] Based on the public discussion after the publication of these works, Research Ethics Committees (RECs) were introduced in the US and UK, and later in other countries.

In these two early publications an important conflict in research is indicated that remains with us today. This is the conflict between the need to protect the interests of research subjects and the desire to carry out research which will benefit future patients. As Beecher pointed out, there are different types of clinical research. Research may be carried out on healthy subjects, and sometimes patients are offered innovative therapies, the efficacy of which has not been documented but which nevertheless are hoped to provide some benefit to the patient. Beecher is concerned with "experimentation on a patient not for his benefit but for that, at least in theory, of patients in general". Beecher also pointed out that patients are willing to

---

[1] H.K. BEECHER, *Ethics and Clinical Research*, in *New England Journal of Medicine* 274 (1966) 1354-1360.

[2] M.H. PAPPWORTH, *Human Guinea Pigs: Experimentation on Man*, London, 1967; ID., *Human Guinea Pigs – a History*, in *British Medical Journal* 301 (1990) 1456-1460.

undergo some discomforts for the sake of future patients, but will not undergo significant risks to health and life. The ethical requirement is that one should ensure that patients do not undergo unacceptable risks for the sake of future patients. There are at least three different ways one can ensure that this is the case. One has to require a fully informed consent from the patients before they are enrolled in a research project. Interestingly enough, Beecher is very sceptical of the role of informed consent, but instead recommends as an alternative reliance on the personal responsibility of the researcher:

> If suitably approached, patients will accede, on the basis of trust, to about any request their physician may make. ... There is the more reliable safeguard provided by the presence of an intelligent, informed, conscientious, compassionate, responsible investigator.

Subsequent developments introduced a third way of ensuring the safety of research subjects. Pappworth points out that there were various attempts after the Second World War to regulate clinical research in the UK, all of which were largely unsuccessful. The objections from physicians and researchers were that regulations would make clinical research impossible, and that the conduct of research was essentially a matter of medical ethics, not the matter of legislative or other regulatory bodies, in a sense supporting Beecher's point. However, as a result of the works of Beecher and Pappworth, regulations and external review through Research Ethics Committees were introduced in the two countries.

In the subsequent development of research ethics codes and regulations, there has been an implicit assumption that it is not permissible to expose patients participating in research to any harm with the justification that this is done to benefit future patients. This is most clearly seen in the Helsinki declaration, which forbids this explicitly, but is implicit in the way research regulations are formulated. Jay Katz, who was a member of the advisory panel investigating the Tuskegee experiments in the US, has argued that we still have not come to grips with "the value conflicts inherent in research" and that we need to make choices "about the priorities to be given to competing values". Katz further argues that

> The mandate conferred on physicians at the beginning of this century to practice medicine with few constraints cannot be readily transported into research settings. Policymakers must confront their responsibility to formulate a distinctly separate social mandate for

the conduct of research that specifies the lengths to which a democratic society like ours can go in compromising citizen subjects' rights to autonomy and physical integrity for the sake of medical science.[3]

He argues here that we still do not understand that there is an inherent value conflict in research medicine, and that we need to confront that value conflict. Later in the same article he argues that research ethics nevertheless has still not taken seriously the rights of the individual research subject. Although he recognizes that there is a value conflict, Katz comes down firmly on the side of autonomy, but allows for exceptions sometimes:

> It is important to remember that at the dawn of bioethics, respect for human rights, autonomy, self-determination was foremost in the minds of the philosophers, theologians, and the many others who created this new discipline. ... Twenty years later respect for the principle of autonomy is once again going out of favour, and it is time to be astonished once again about the principle's short life. ... After reflecting about where we began and where we now are, I want to argue more uncompromisingly than I ever have done that respect for autonomy and self-determination in clinical research, whenever human beings serve as means to others' ends, should be a binding commitment, except under the most exceptional and well-defined circumstances, and then only with societal approval.[4]

In this paper I shall examine this inherent conflict in research ethics between the value of individual autonomy and the value of conducting research for the benefit of society. This value conflict needs to be confronted prior to one's reflection on issues such as informed consent and ethics review procedures, and the way one deals with this value conflict, will have consequences for proposals concerning research ethics guidelines. I shall argue, as Katz has done, that this value conflict is still to be resolved, and that we urgently need to address it. I shall examine the value conflict through a discussion of the ethics of randomised clinical trials (RCT). It is widely accepted today that the randomised controlled clinical trial is the gold standard for justifying clinical interventions, and is in many ways today

---

[3] J. KATZ,. *Ethics and Clinical Research Revisited*, in *Hastings Center Report* 23 (1993) 31-39, p. 37.
[4] *Ibid.*, p. 38-39.

the paradigmatic way of carrying out clinical research. In such a trial, ideally, one group of patients, chosen at random, will receive either a placebo, or the best current treatment, and another group of patients, also chosen at random, will receive the promising new treatment.[5] Some additional ethical issues need to be discussed with regard to placebo controlled trials which I shall not touch upon here. I shall assume that placebos are only justified when there is no accepted treatment for the patients in the study, and will not further discuss the issue that this sometimes may result in carrying out trials that may not be as efficient as a placebo controlled trial.

The standard justification for initiating a controlled clinical trial is the following: on the basis of the best current knowledge, which includes past clinical trials and knowledge gained from basic research, we truly do not know which of the two treatments is the best treatment. In such a situation, the only acceptable course of action is to randomise the whole patient group into two groups, each group receiving one of the two treatments in question. In this way, we are ensured that, if one treatment is superior, then at least half the patients will receive it, and if they are of equal value, no harm has been done.

From the very beginning, the ethical issues associated with the methodology have been discussed. It was noticed that RCTs represented a potential conflict between the interests of the individuals taking part in the trial and the interests of science in getting reliable data.

3.1. The Conflict between Individual and Collective Ethics

According to Austin Bradford Hill an RCT can only be justified if the physicians have no preference one way or the other concerning the superiority of one or the other treatments. The potential conflict is solved by only allowing randomisation when there is indifference between two treatments. For example, Hill argued that:

---

[5] D.P. BYAR et al., Randomised Clinical Trials. Perspectives on Some Recent Ideas, in New England Journal of Medicine 295 (1976) 74-80; T.C. CHALMERS et al., A Method for Assessing the Quality of a Randomised Control Trial, in Controlled Clinical Trials 2 (1981) 31-49.

If the doctor ... thinks even in the absence of any evidence that for the patient's benefit he ought to give one treatment rather than the other, then the patient should not be admitted to the trial. Only if, in his state of ignorance, he believes the treatment given to be a matter of indifference can he accept a random distribution of patients to the different groups.[6]

Another prominent person in the movement to introduce RCTs, Thomas Chalmers, also noted the conflict between individual ethics and collective ethics. He, however, at least initially, was less certain about how one should solve this conflict:

But what about the rights of the patient who enters a study at a time when one treatment is leading the other, but when the study is being continued because the difference is not significant? One can easily argue that since the difference is not significant, the results can be reversed by future experience. But one can also argue that the welfare of that patient is more assured if he receives the treatment that is ahead rather than the one that is currently behind in the evaluation. In other words, randomisation would be unfair to him because he might be assigned to a treatment that has less than 50 percent chance of being shown to be the correct one. ... To this problem I can see no solution.[7]

Chalmers later recommended data monitoring committees as a solution to this conflict, but this of course does not solve the problem of on what basis a data monitoring committee would be justified in terminating a clinical trial. Both Hill and Chalmers are convinced that the potential conflict between individual ethics and collective ethics is solvable, while ensuring that the best interests of patients taking part in the trial are not jeopardized.

A number of people have, beginning in the 1970's, pointed out apparent deficiencies in the argument that the conflict between individual ethics and collective ethics, or between a physician's therapeutic obligation and her research obligation, can be solved, while still protecting individual interests.[8]

---

[6] A.B. HILL, *Medical Ethics and Controlled Trials*, in *British Medical Journal* i (1963) 1043-1049, p. 1047.

[7] B. BRODY, *Ethical Issues in Drug Testing, Approval and Pricing. The Clot-Dissolving Drugs*, New York, 1995, p. 120.

[8] J. LELLOUCH & D. SCHWARTZ, *L'essai thérapeutique; éthique individuelle ou éthique collective?*, in *Rev. Inst. Int. Statist.* 39 (1971) 127-136 ; D. MARQUIS, *Leaving Therapy to*

Central to this position is the claim that there is always evidence available before one initiates a trial which indicates that one or the other treatment may be superior. Although this evidence is not conclusive, it may be sufficient to convince some investigators or patients that it is in the patient's best interest to choose one particular treatment rather than be randomised into one of the treatments under investigation. Randomisation can only be justified, the argument goes, in terms of the altruistic interests one may have in obtaining more secure knowledge that may benefit future patients. This would mean that if the primary obligation of a physician is to act in the best interests of her patients, a physician would usually not be justified in randomising patients into one of the two treatment alternatives.

If this argument is correct, it would make it difficult to justify RCTs. A fundamental principle of research ethics is that research on human beings should not be carried out if it is not in the best interests of the patients taking part in the research (cf. Helsinki Declaration). Specifically, one cannot argue that it is legitimate to expose patients taking part in clinical research to some risk for the sole reason that the knowledge gained from the study may benefit future patients. Although there may be some risk in taking part in a clinical trial, on balance, the participants in a clinical trial should benefit from taking part in the trial. If trials can only be justified in terms of possible benefit for future patients, this would make all RCTs ethically problematic.

Different writers have drawn different conclusions from this. In Germany, Burkhardt and Kienle raised these ethical objections as part of a larger critique of the methodology of randomised clinical trials, and concluded that RCTs are not justified both from

---

Chance, in Hastings Center Report 13 (1983) 40-47; ID., *An Argument That All Pre-randomised Clinical Trials Are Unethical*, in Journal of Medicine and Philosophy 11 (1986) 367-384; S. J. POCOCK, *Clinical Trials*, Chichester, 1983. L. KOPELMAN, *Consent and Randomised Clinical Trials: Are There Moral or Design Problems?* in Journal of Medicine and Philosophy 11 (1986) 317-346; F. GIFFORD, *The Conflict Between Randomised Clinical Trials and the Therapeutic Obligation*, in Journal of Medicine and Philosophy 11 (1986) 347-366; S. BOTROS, *Equipoise, Consent and the Ethics of Randomised Clinical Trials*, in P. BYRNE (ed.), *Ethics and Law in Health Care and Research*, Chichester, 1990, p. 9-24; S. HELLMANN & D.S. HELLMAN, *Of Mice but not Men*, in New England Journal of Medicine 324 (1991) 1585-89.

methodological and ethical reasons.[9] Others have taken a less extreme view and argued that RCTs are necessary, but one should accept justifications in terms of societal or collective benefit.[10]

There is yet another reason why some have been critical of the possibility of justifying RCTs.[11] It is pointed out that a clinical intervention seldom has only one effect of interest to patients. Although there may be uncertainty as to whether an intervention is beneficial in terms of one consequence, such as survival, the intervention may have other effects that will ensure that patients will not be indifferent towards a choice of interventions. In the choice between mastectomy and lumpectomy for breast cancer, for example, there may be uncertainty as to the effect of these two interventions on survival. The two treatments, however, differ in their effects on disfigurement. Patients will probably differ in their evaluation of the various outcomes, and the overall balance of risks and benefits may therefore differ from patient to patient. Even though one may not know whether lumpectomy increases survival compared with mastectomy, patients may still choose one treatment rather than randomisation based on other considerations than survival.

Similar arguments have been made with regard to benign prostatic hyperplasia. As a result, John E. Wennberg and his colleagues studying treatments for benign prostatic hyperplasia, have introduced the notion of the preference clinical trial. Patients are presented with the various treatment options, their possible outcomes, and associated probabilities, based on the prognostic subgroup the patient belongs to. Based on this knowledge, the physician and patient select the treatment that they feel is the best. The patients are then followed up. The data gathered are also used to update the information presented to future patients. The study groups are thus based on informed patient choice rather than on randomisation. It is felt that this is appropriate in the case of the study of benign prostatic hyperplasia because the known outcomes are asymmetric with

[9] R. BURKHARDT & G. KIENLE, *Ethical Problems of Controlled Clinical Trials*, in *Journal of Medical Ethics* 9 (1983) 80-89. G. KIENLE & R. BURKHARDT, *Der Wirksamkeitsnachweis für Arzneimittel. Analyse einer Illusion*, Stuttgart, 1983.

[10] F. GIFFORD, *The Conflict Between Randomised Clinical Trials and the Therapeutic Obligation*, in *Journal of Medicine and Philosophy* 11 (1986) 347-366; D. MARQUIS, *An Argument That All Pre-Randomised Clinical Trials Are Unethical*, p. 367-384; S. J. POCOCK, *loc. cit.*

[11] S. BOTROS, *Equipoise, Consent and the Ethics of Randomised Clinical Trials*, p. 9-24.

regard to important endpoints. Operation carries with it a risk of death, impotence and incontinence. Not all patients would want to take this risk in order to increase their quality of life, but would prefer the alternative of 'watchful waiting'. They have also suggested the possibility of letting patients choose between randomisation and open choice of the two treatment alternatives. The advantage of this design is that we will find out whether patients who opt for randomisation are significantly different from patients who do not want to take part in a randomised clinical trial.[12] The proposed design has some similarities with those proposed by J. Kadane.[13] There are of course also marked differences between these proposals. One should also mention the less radical proposals made by M. Zelen and others to modify the standard way of doing clinical trials.[14]

The existence of such multiplicity of outcomes undoubtedly complicates things. It shows that it may be difficult to justify a clinical trial. However, one may assume that there are patients who are indifferent concerning the other outcomes of intervention, and are only concerned about the outcome being studied in the trial. This argument from the multiplicity of outcomes is therefore not in itself an argument against the ethical justification of RCTs, but in conjunction with the argument presented above, it does of course strengthen the case against the ethical justifiability of RCTs.

In addition to the question of how to justify the initiation of clinical trials, there is the issue of when to stop a clinical trial as interim data from that trial becomes available, or data from other trials become available (see Chalmers' quotation above). Many of the criticisms against clinical trials have been in terms of the conflicts inherent in the question of premature termination of RCTs. It is pointed out that data may become available showing that one treatment is superior. Although one may ideally want to continue the trial in order to have full confidence in the results, the principle that one should do what is in the best interests of patients, taking part in the trial, again dictates that one should terminate the trial before one has

[12] J.E. WENNBERG, *What Outcomes Research?* in A.C. GELIJNS (ed.), *Modern Methods of Clinical Investigation*, Washington, 1990, p. 33-46.

[13] J.B. KADANE, *Progress Toward a More Ethical Method for Clinical Trials*, in *Journal of Medicine and Philosophy* 11 (1986) 385-404.

[14] For a discussion, see L. KOPELMAN, *Consent and Randomised Clinical Trials*, p. 317-346.

results that could be used reliably to treat future patients. Although termination of clinical trials may raise a number of important issues of statistical method, from the point of view of the ethics of trials, termination does not raise any new issues of principle.

During the 1980's, then, some kind of consensus was reached that there is a conflict between the interests of the individuals taking part in the trial and the interests of science in getting reliable data to treat future patients. Furthermore, many argued that RCTs can only be justified in terms of collective benefit. One would have to argue that it could be legitimate that the individuals taking part in the trial would be exposed to some individual risk, which needed to be balanced against the possibility of future benefit for other patients.

3.2. Benjamin Freedman's Notion of 'Clinical Equipoise'

In 1987, Benjamin Freedman introduced the notion of 'clinical equipoise' to answer the argument that RCTs involve an inherent conflict between individual and collective ethics, and claimed that this move solves some of the ethical problems identified in earlier criticism. Freedman's aim is to show that there is no conflict between individual ethics and the methodology of RCTs. In fact, he argues strongly that it would be a mistake to give up the requirement that participants in clinical trials should not be exposed to any risk in order for researchers to obtain knowledge that can be used to treat future patients. He consequently does not believe that RCTs can only be justified in terms of collective benefit. His article has been so influential that it is important to examine it in some detail.

> These proposals seem to be frank counsels of desperation. ... would their approach allow clinical trials to be conducted? I think this may fairly be doubted. Although many people are presumably altruistic enough to forgo the best medical treatment in the interest of the progress of science, many are not.[15]

In a later article he is even more explicit:

> Proponents of clinical trials ... often ... argue that there is a need to balance the rights of subjects against the needs of society. By this

---

[15] B. FREEDMAN, *Equipoise and the Ethics of Clinical Research*, in *New England Journal of Medicine* 317 (1987) 141-145, p. 142-143.

tactic, the proponents of clinical trials have implicitly surrendered, for to admit that something is a right is to admit that it represents a domain of action protected from the claims or interests of other individuals or of society itself.. ... Closer examination and finer distinctions reveal, however, that the conflict between patients' rights and social interests is not at all at issue in controlled clinical trials.[16]

Freedman's argument goes as follows. Although an individual clinician may believe that one or the other treatment is superior, clinical equipoise means that "there is no consensus within the expert clinical community about the comparative merits of the alternatives to be tested".[17] Freedman argues that it is not unethical to randomise patients if clinical equipoise exists, because evidence in medicine is supposed to be public. The fact that the clinical expert community is divided concerning the superiority of one or the other treatment shows that there is no publicly available evidence in favour of one or the other treatment. If that is the case, it is justifiable to randomise patients to the two treatments.

Freedman maintains that if clinical equipoise exists one would not jeopardize patients' best interests by randomising them to the interventions being studied in the RCT. For this argument to work, he therefore has to deny that it is the case that we know, before the initiation of an RCT, that the new treatment is possibly better than the old at the same time as it is no worse than the old.

One should note that there is some ambiguity in the way Freedman defines clinical equipoise. On the one hand clinical equipoise is characterised in terms of the actual beliefs in the clinical expert community. Freedman uses notions such as

> ... there is a split in the clinical community, with some clinicians favouring A and others favouring B. ... there is no consensus within the expert clinical community about the comparative merits of the alternatives to be tested.[18]

This is a characterization of 'clinical equipoise' as a description of the actual states of affairs in the clinical community. Freedman seems to argue that if there is disagreement, then there is clinical equipoise.

---

[16] ID., *A Response to a Purported Ethical Difficulty with Randomised Clinical Trials Involving Cancer Patients*, in *Journal of Clinical Ethics* 193 (1992) 231-234.

[17] ID., *Equipoise and the Ethics of Clinical Research*, p. 144.

[18] *Ibid.*, p. 144.

Baruch Brody has criticized this 'sociological' approach.[19] There can be all kinds of reasons why some clinicians do not think that one treatment is better than another, including reasons based on financial considerations. We would therefore want some reference to the evidence for one or the other treatments, which Freedman also provides, in phrases such as

> ... when the accumulated evidence in favour of B is so strong that ... no open-minded clinician informed of the results would still favour A, clinical equipoise has been disturbed. ... The ethics of medical practice grants no ethical or normative meaning to a treatment preference, however, powerful, that is based on a hunch or on anything less than evidence publicly presented and convincing to the clinical community.

In this quotation the emphasis is on the publicly available evidence in favour of one or the other treatment, which is clearly preferable to the first descriptive approach. In this set of quotations there is a distinction between treatment preferences based on public evidence and treatment preferences based on 'anything less than' public evidence.

By using this distinction between preferences based on evidence and preferences based on 'anything less than' evidence, Freedman believes that he can answer the argument that we have some preference before the initiation of a clinical trial that one treatment may be superior. Freedman maintains that unless this preference is based on evidence one cannot maintain that it would be rational for all patients to choose the preferred treatment. In the argument against RCTs presented above, some evidence is assumed in favour of one or the other of the treatments, although this evidence may not be conclusive. Freedman argues that this is a mistaken characterisation of the situation. There is no evidence, only treatment preferences based on 'anything less than' public evidence. Implicit in this argument is the assumption that evidence does not come in degrees. Either there is public evidence for one or the other treatment, or there is not. If there is not, there is clinical equipoise, and one can justify a clinical trial. If there is, one should choose one of the treatments. Interestingly, however, Freedman uses a third set of statements, where he seems to recognise that evidence comes in degrees.

---

[19] B. BRODY, *Ethical Issues in Drug Testing, Approval and Pricing. The Clot-Dissolving Drugs*, New York, 1995, p. 120.

This is of course the basis for the criticism of RCTs presented above. I shall in a moment suggest that this is indeed the natural characterisation of the situation before one initiates an RCT, and that therefore Freedman has not shown that RCTs do not violate the best interests of clinical trial participants:

> ... There exists an honest, professional disagreement among expert clinicians about the preferred treatment. ... Each side recognizes that the opposing side has evidence to support its position, yet each still thinks that overall its own view is correct.

From these statements we get the idea that although there is some evidence in favour of one or the other treatment, this evidence is not conclusive, precisely as the critics of RCTs have maintained.

Let me summarise the arguments so far. Critics have pointed out there often may be evidence, although not conclusive, before a clinical trial that one alternative is preferable to the other. Freedman has criticized this argument, pointing out that if one wants to show that RCTs are ethically problematic, one needs to point to publicly available evidence. Although one may have hunches that one treatment is superior, this is not in itself enough to conclude that randomisation would be unethical.

3.3. Criticism of Benjamin Freedman

Freedman is undoubtedly right in claiming that we need to refer to evidence that is more than a personal hunch to show that a planned RCT is ethically problematic. It therefore cannot be an argument against RCTs that there might be evidence, not yet conclusive, in favour of one of the treatments under study.

There is, however, one element missing in this account. The action of randomisation also needs to be justified. We not only need to justify treating patients with one or the other of the treatments under study by referring to publicly available evidence. In order to justify the initiation of a clinical trial we also need to have publicly available evidence that patients who enroll in the clinical trial will not be harmed, if we accept that a clinical trial can only be justified in terms of harms and benefits to the study subjects, which Freedman does. Mere hunches will not do, for the same reason that mere hunches will not justify one of the interventions as superior. I shall now attempt to show that if we can obtain enough publicly available evidence to justify the initiation of an RCT in terms of the benefits to the individuals participating, we would also have enough publicly available evidence to justify choosing one or the other treatment.

Let us begin by attempting to characterize the evidence that we need to have available more precisely. We would want to maintain something like the following: the risk to the participants is in proportion to the possible benefits. There are of course known risks and benefits associated with the established treatment. We also need to know something about the new treatment. Clearly, one could not justify an RCT if one knew nothing about the new treatment. Therefore, there has to be some evidence that the new treatment might be effective, although one may agree that this evidence is not convincing. The usual way of putting this is that one has some reason to believe that the new treatment might be as effective as the old, but one does not know this for sure. The new treatment might of course also be less effective than the established treatment. The problem is how one should understand this statement in terms of publicly available evidence strong enough to justify the conclusion that the patients taking part in the trial, and thereby being randomised to one or the other of the treatments, will not be taking greater risks than those who could choose one specific treatment. One might be tempted to suggest that one knows that the two treatments are of equal effectiveness. If that were the case, one would have no objections to being randomised. The problem with this position is that, if one really knows this before the trial, one knows this in a stronger sense than merely hypothetical, and thus there would be no need to carry out the trial.

The important point here is that the ethical requirement that we need to justify clinical trials in terms of benefits for the individuals taking part in the trial, demands that we can know that those taking part in the trial will not be taking greater risks than those who do not participate in the trial. I fail to see any way to characterize the knowledge we then would have that would not at the same time entail that one of the two treatments is superior. If we merely have personal hunches about the relative benefits of the two treatments we would not be able to justify the randomisation of the patients. If we have something more than a hunch, we would also not be justified in carrying out the trial.

The reason for the impossibility of justifying an RCT only in terms of the interests of those who participate in the trial should be readily apparent. If we are only allowed to refer to the risks and benefits of those who take part in the trial, the choice of strategy, either randomisation or the choice of one or the other of the treatment alternatives, is the same as any other clinical decision. We are faced with a choice between three alternatives: treatment A, treatment B, or randomisation between treatments A and B. Justification of the third alternative requires that we justify by publicly available evidence that it is better than the two other alternatives, which cannot be done if we are restricted to do so in terms of the benefits for patients taking part in the trial.

Let me briefly note that a response in terms of pointing out that patients usually do better in clinical trials than outside clinical trials will not do. If we have evidence to that effect it would mean that we could not use the results from clinical trials to predict what will happen in actual clinical practice.

Another way of putting this argument is in terms of a dilemma. We need to know something about the two treatments in order to justify the initiation of a clinical trial. Specifically, we need to know that we are not harming the subjects of the trial by the act of randomisation. This knowledge would have to come from some other source of knowledge than the results of a clinical trial, precisely because we now want to do a clinical trial. But if we can know this much without a clinical trial, what is to prevent us from knowing that one treatment is superior without carrying out a clinical trial? If we can know this much without a clinical trial, the trial is unnecessary. If we cannot know this much, the trial is unethical. Therefore, given the premise that a trial should be justified in terms of the benefits of the participants taking part in the trial, the clinical trial is either unnecessary or unethical. My conclusion is therefore that if we accept that RCTs can only be justified in terms of the risks and benefits of the individuals taking part in the trial, RCTs can never be ethically justified.

3.4. What Should We Do?

There are two ways out of this dilemma. One can either accept that RCTs should and can be justified in terms of collective benefit, which is the common position, or one can accept that there will always be other ways of gaining reliable clinical knowledge (we all accept that there are sometimes other ways of gaining reliable clinical knowledge). Both of these options are today problematic for the following reasons: the first is that we do not have any fully worked out alternatives to the RCT. There are of course alternatives, such as those based on Bayesian statistics. Whatever merits one may think these have, I think it is fair to say that there is general agreement, both among friends and foes, that they are not yet fully worked out alternatives.

Milton Weinstein proposed back in 1974 that one should explore alternatives to randomisation.[20] David Eddy has recently pointed out that there are biases in all trial designs, and argued that one should explicitly correct the estimates based on the known biases of the designs used.[21] In his proposal a randomised clinical trial is no longer the gold standard, but has its own biases compared with other study designs. This analysis is based on Bayesian statistical theory[22], as are Kadane's proposals.[23] I do not, however, think that this is presently a particularly promising way forward. For one, it will likely take a long time before any of these alternative methods become accepted in the clinical research community. The second reason is that currently accepted research ethics rejects the justifications in terms of collective benefit. As argued in the introduction, modern research ethics is based on the acceptance that it is never justified to use a research subject as merely a means to improve treatments of future patients. I think that it might be possible to work out such an ethical justification. The problem is that we do not have one that is adequate today.

One should note that to work out alternatives to justifications in terms of societal benefit in the way we do today, or to develop alternative methods of evaluating clinical interventions, is not only a theoretical problem. Increasingly, criticism has been voiced in terms of actual patient expectations. Hazel Thornton in the United Kingdom, for example, has related her frustrating experience of having to

---

[20] M.C. WEINSTEIN, *Allocation of Subjects in Medical Experiments*, in *New England Journal of Medicine* 291 (1974) 1278-1285.

[21] D.M. EDDY, *Should we Change the Rules for Evaluation Medical Technologies?*, in A.C. GELIJNS (ed.), *Modern Methods of Clinical Investigation*, Washington, 1990, p. 117-134.

[22] D.M. EDDY, V. HASSELBLAD & R. SHACHTER, *An Introduction to a Bayesian Method for Meta-Analysis: The Confidence Profile Method*, in A.C. GELIJNS (ed.), *Modern Methods of Clinical Investigation*, p. 101-116.

[23] J.B. KADANE (ed.), *Bayesian Methods and Ethics in a Clinical Trial Design*, New York, 1996.

decide whether to take part in a controlled clinical trial for Ductal Carcinoma in situ.[24] One of her main complaints was that she felt that her interests as a patient were abandoned in the interest of scientific investigation. This particular case raises a number of other important issues, such as the role of the informed consent process in clinical trials and in particular the issue of how information is presented to prospective clinical trial participants. For the purposes of this paper, however, the important point that Mrs. Thornton made was that she felt that, given the rigid requirements of the clinical trial protocol, it would be difficult or impossible to individualize the treatment plan in a way that would be in her best interest, pointing to the conflict between science and individual best interests.

We return, then, to Katz' point mentioned in the introduction of this paper. We still have not, as a society, come to grips with how to deal with the inherent value conflict in clinical research. Although there is no question that research ethics review procedures and informed consent guidelines are important, the discussion has shown that there is an underlying, unresolved issue, which needs to be addressed if we are to move the field of research ethics forward. I also think that only then we will be able to resolve some of the current particular controversies, such as the permissibility of carrying out research in developing countries not carried out in one's own country.

One way to address this issue might be to return to another classic of research ethics, Hans Jonas' article of 1969, which he revised in 1974.[25] Jonas here notes also the inherent conflict between the individual and society in research ethics, and argues that research involves sacrifice and conscription:

> Not for a moment do I wish to suggest that medical experimentation on human subjects, sick or healthy, is to be likened to primeval human sacrifices. Yet something sacrificial is involved in the selective abrogation of personal inviolability and the ritualised exposure

---

[24] H. THORNTON, *Breast Cancer Trials: a Patient's Viewpoint*, in *Lancet* 339 (1992) 44-45; ID., *Clinical Trials – a Brave New Partnership?*, in *Journal of Medical Ethics* 20 (1994) 19-22; M. BAUM, *Clinical Trials – a Brave New Partnership: a Response to Mrs. Thornton*, in *Journal of Medical Ethics*, 20 (1994) 23-25. R. GILLON, *Recruitment for Clinical Trials: the Need for Public-Professional Co-Operation*, in *Journal of Medical Ethics* 20 (1994) 3-4.

[25] H. JONAS, *Philosophical Reflections on Experimenting with Human Subjects*, in *Daedalus* 98 (1969) 219-247; H. JONAS, *Philosophical Reflections on Experimenting with Human Subjects*, in ID. (ed.), *Philosophical Essays. From Ancient Creed to Technological Man*, Chicago, 1974, p. 105-131.

to gratuitous risk of health and life, justified by a presumed greater, social good. ... We must realize that the mere issuing of the appeal, the calling for volunteers, with the moral and social pressures it inevitably generates, amounts even under the most meticulous rules of consent to a sort of *conscripting*.[26]

In closing, I would submit that Jonas' proposed solution is still worth considering, when we consider the inherent conflict in clinical research. Jonas argues that mere consent is not enough; what is essential is that the research subjects *identify* with the research project, in such a way that the research subject can be seen as *willing* to be used as a means for the good of others. In Jonas' words: "Ultimately, the appeal for volunteers should seek this free and generous endorsement, the appropriation of the research purpose into the person's own scheme of ends."[27]

If we followed Jonas' advice, there need to be dramatic changes in the current review procedures and in the informed consent process. This is, however, what we would need to do in order to solve the conflict between individual and collective values inherent in clinical research.

---

[26] ID., *Philosophical Reflections on Experimenting with Human Subjects*, in *Daedalus* 98 (1969) 224, 233.

[27] *Ibid.*, p. 236.

4

THE HIV PERINATAL TRANSMISSION STUDIES
AND THE DEBATE ABOUT THE REVISION
OF THE HELSINKI DECLARATION

Reidar K. Lie

In 1994, the so-called ACTG (AIDS Clinical Trials Group) protocol 076 showed that treatment with AZT (Antiretroviral Zidovudine) five times a day for an average of 11 weeks before giving birth, intravenous treatment during labour, as well as treatment of the child for 6 weeks after birth, resulted in a reduction in HIV-transmission from 25% to 8%. The treatment regimen costs at least $800. It is recognized that it is not possible to introduce this treatment in developing countries, both because of its cost and for logistical reasons. Because of this, a number of clinical trials started with shorter course of AZT treatment. Most of these trials were carried out in developing countries, and used a placebo trial in the control group. The US Center for Disease Control (CDC) has justified the trials in a document publicly available on the Internet. It is worth quoting at length from this document:

> The CDC is not using the ACTG-076 regimen in the current studies because although those results have changed the standard of care in the United States and other industrialized countries, the standard of care for treating HIV infected pregnancies in most developing countries remains 'no intervention'. The intent in the current studies is to answer the question which is most relevant for public health decision makers in developing countries: "Does AZT, when given at this specific dose for four weeks, result in a lower perinatal HIV transmission rate compared to untreated women?" There is consensus at WHO, UNAIDS, and in countries where these trials are being conducted that the full regimen of ACTG-076 could not currently be implemented as standard of care. Another reason that

placebo trials have been recommended is because it is necessary to change multiple parameters from the ACTG-076 regimen ... A placebo trial is the most scientifically valid way to determine the effect of these changes. Moreover, a placebo design ... allows for a 'streamlined study' which can provide an answer within one to two years after the start of the study. ... A study design that compares a short AZT regimen with the long ACTG-076 AZT regiment would not meet the study objectives, in other words, it would not answer the question, "Does short course AZT work to prevent perinatal transmission?" This would not indicate whether the short AZT regimen was better than the currently available intervention – nothing at all. ...One of the most important ethical considerations in conducting clinical trial research is that participants in the research should not receive less care than would be available to them if they were not involved in the research. Since AZT is not currently available for perinatal HIV prevention in Thailand and Ivory Coast, the placebo-controlled trial design is consistent with that principle.

Not everyone shared this opinion, however. As early as in 1995, the investigators responsible for one non-placebo controlled trial in Thailand wrote in a letter to *Science*:

We firmly believe that it would be unethical to incorporate a placebo arm in our study in Thailand. ... Adding a placebo arm to our study design could provide added reassurance that the 076 regimen is as effective in the Thai population as in the original study and a more definite estimate of the degree of efficacy of the shortened regimen over no treatment. However, we believe that this scientific justification does not outweigh the ethical imperative to provide all subjects with a treatment that is consistent with current scientific knowledge about the efficacy of AZT in preventing transmission and with the emerging standard of care in the country in which the study is undertaken.[1]

Although the criticism of the placebo studies was voiced in the literature as early as 1995[2], not much happened until the Public Citizens' Health Research Group criticized the trials in a congressional hearing on bioethics May 8, 1997.[3] The story was picked up by a variety of news agencies in the countries concerned. The placebo trials were criticised by for example Robert Kuttner in the *Singapore Straits*

---

[1] M. LALLEMANT et al., *AZT Trial in Thailand*, in *Science* 270 (1995) 899-900.
[2] J. COHEN, *Bringing AZT to Poor Countries*, in *Science* 269 (1995) 624-626.
[3] ID., *Ethics of AZT Studies in Poorer Countries Attacked*, in *Science* 276 (1997) 1022.

Times[4], in Uganda and in Thailand.[5] The placebo trials were compared with the Tuskegee syphilis studies, and it was argued that more than 1000 children in developing countries would die unnecessarily. The hearing was also picked up by press reports in North Carolina[6] where the NGO Family Health International involved in the study and Glaxo Wellcome both are located. The NGO was clearly troubled by the criticism. In this press report it was also apparent that at least the bioethicists interviewed at that time to a large degree were sympathetic to the claims by the Public Citizens Health Research Group, although they found it difficult to draw firm conclusions. It was also clear [7] that a number of officials from the developing countries themselves supported the trials. Jon Cohen, for example, writes that: "Edward Mbidde, chair of Uganda's AIDS Research Committee ... wrote that he read Public Citizen's arguments with 'dismay and disbelief'. He described their attacks as 'patronizing' and said it reeked of 'ethical imperialism'." He also re-iterated the argument that a placebo trial is necessary to find out whether a short course is better than nothing. The alternative trial without placebo might conclude that a shorter treatment is inferior, although it in fact might be better than placebo.

4.1. The Criticism by Angell, Lurie and Wolf

These stories went largely unnoticed by the general media until Marcia Angell criticized the trials in an Editorial in the *New England Journal of Medicine*, September 18, 1997.[8] The editorial was accompanied by a Sounding Board article by Lurie and Wolfe from the Public Citizens' Health Research Group.[9] They argued that the

---

[4] R. KUTTNER, *US Double Standards Hurt Ordinary Folk*, in *Singapore Straits Times*, May 7, 1997.

[5] A. BHATIASEVI, *Testing AZT on Pregnant Thai Women – Critics Accuse US of Double Standards*, in *Bangkok Post*, April 25, 1997.

[6] T. READY, *AIDS Research in Africa Raises Thorny Questions for RTP Group*, in *News and Observer*, June 30, 1997.

[7] J. COHEN, *Ethics of AZT Studies in Poorer Countries Attacked*, p. 1022.

[8] M. ANGELL, *The Ethics of Clinical Research in the Third World*, in *New England Journal of Medicine* 337 (1997) 847-849.

[9] P. LURIE & S.M. WOLFE, *Unethical Trials of Interventions to Reduce Perinatal Transmission of the Human Immunodeficiency Virus in Developing Countries*, in *New England Journal of Medicine* 337 (1997) 853-856.

placebo-controlled trials are unethical as they deny the control group a proven beneficial treatment. According to the previous version of the Helsinki-declaration, all the participants "should be assured of the best proven diagnostic and therapeutic method". They also demonstrated that a placebo trial might not require fewer subjects nor would it take longer to get the necessary results. In their article, Lurie and Wolf countered the arguments that, as no treatment is the standard of care in developing countries, research subjects in the placebo group would not be denied the available treatments in that country. They point out that the reason for this standard of care is economic. However, it would not be economically difficult to provide the participants in the study with AZT in the required amount: this would not add much to the cost of the study. They recognized that it may not be justifiable to provide more expensive forms of care, such as treatment in coronary care units.

The *New England Journal of Medicine* Editorial was picked up by newspapers such as *the New York Times*.[10] In a subsequent Op-Ed letter Joseph Saba of UNAIDS and Arthur Amman of the American Foundation for AIDS research defended the trials.[11] They argued that the trials conformed to international guidelines, had been approved by Ethics Committees in the countries concerned, and were necessary in order to find an effective intervention for huge health problems. Critics would be guilty of "imposing their standards of care on developing countries. Local health experts, bioethicists and affected groups are best qualified to judge the risks and benefits of any medical research", and the trials "adhere to one of the basic ethical principles of any study, regardless of locale: that the planned intervention can be applied in the country in which it is tested". In a reply, Marcia Angell pointed out that the trials did not conform to the Helsinki Declaration and cited the passage quoted above; it was therefore not a matter of imposing US standards on others, but breaking an international agreement. She also maintained that: "Researchers knowingly consign many newborns to HIV."[12] A member of the *New England*

---

[10] S.G. STOLBERG, *U.S. AIDS Research Abroad Sets off Outcry over Ethics*, in *New York Times*, September 18, 1997.

[11] J. SABA & A. AMMAN, *A Cultural Divide on AIDS Research*, in *New York Times*, September 20, 1997.

[12] M. ANGELL, *AIDS Studies Violate Helsinki Rights Accord*, in *New York Times*, September 24, 1997.

Journal of Medicine editorial board, David Ho, criticised the editorial by Marcia Angell, and he subsequently resigned from the Editorial Board in protest against the editorial.[13] The editorial was defended in a subsequent editorial authored by both the editor in chief and Marcia Angell.[14] Varmus and Satcher clarified the position of the CDC and NIH in a subsequent article.[15] In this article they argued that

> the most compelling reason to use a placebo-controlled study is that it provides definite answers to questions about safety and value of an intervention in the setting in which the study is performed, and these answers are the point of research ... comparing an intervention of unknown benefit – especially one that is affordable in a developing country – with the only intervention with a known benefit (the 076 regimen) may provide information that is not useful to patients. If the affordable intervention is less effective than the 076 regimen – not an unlikely outcome – this information will be of little use in a country where the more effective regimen is unavailable. Equally important, it will still be unclear whether the affordable intervention is better than nothing and worth the investment of scarce resources.

4.2. Arguments For and Against the Trials with Placebo Controls

From the above, we can identify the following arguments in favour of carrying out trials with placebos in developing countries:
- The benefit to future millions of babies exposed to HIV outweighs the possible risks to the few babies in the placebo controlled clinical trials.
- The participants in the clinical trials receive the standard of care in their own countries. They are not denied treatment they would otherwise get.
- The trials have been approved by local Ethics Committees and local community representatives. Refusing to carry out these trials would be an imposition of external values.

---

[13] D. HO., *It's AIDS, not Tuskegee. Inflammatory Comparisons Won't Save Lives in Africa*, in *Newsweek*, September 29, 1997.

[14] J.P. KASSIRER & M. ANGELL, *Controversial Journal Editorials*, in *New England Journal of Medicine* 337 (1997) 1460-1461.

[15] H. VARMUS & D. SATCHER, *Ethical Complexities of Conducting Research in Developing Countries*, in *New England Journal of Medicine* 337 (1997) 1003-1005.

- These trials differ from the Tuskegee trial in that the women have given their informed consent to participate.
- The placebo trials are the only way to get results that are truly useful for the countries themselves. As such they conform to the principle that research should be responsive to the health needs of the country.

The following are the main arguments against carrying out the placebo trials:
- The trials violate international guidelines.
- The trials knowingly expose children to risk of HIV infection that could be avoided.
- Valid results can be obtained from alternative designs that do not use placebo as the controls.

4.3. Can Useful Results Be Obtained with a Non-Placebo Controlled Trial?

The central claim by Lurie and Wolf in their article is that it would be possible to obtain useful results by carrying out an equivalence trial comparing the current treatment against the treatment with a reduced dosage.[16] In order to do so, one would use as the null hypothesis the claim that the standard treatment reduces perinatal transmission by at least a specified percentage over the experimental treatment. The claim could, for example, be that the standard treatment reduces perinatal transmission by more than 5 percent compared with the experimental treatment. If this null hypothesis is true, then the two treatments are not equivalent; if it is false then the two treatments are equivalent. Based on this, one can calculate the necessary sample size associated with desired error probabilities. Lurie and Wolf claim that it is possible to carry out such a trial using the same number of participants as a placebo controlled trial. If the trial results in a rejection of the null hypothesis, i.e. an acceptance of the two treatments as equivalent, we can conclude that the two treatments do not differ by more than 5 percent. If the trial results in

---

[16] For a discussion on equivalence trials, see J.H. WARE & E.M. ANTMAN, *Equivalence Trials*, in *New England Journal of Medicine* 337 (1997) 1159-1161.

an acceptance of the null hypothesis, we can conclude that there is at least a 5 percent difference between the two treatments. It is at this point that the arguments made by people such as Mbidde, Satcher and Varmus become important. According to them, if we accept that the two treatments are not equivalent in this sense, the experimental treatment may still be useful to developing countries. If we assume that the perinatal transmission rate is 25% without any treatment, the experimental treatment may have a transmission rate of 15%, which represents a significant reduction in transmission that would still be of interest to developing countries, although it is larger than the transmission rate of 8% in the 076 regimen.

One obvious answer to this worry would be to redefine the null hypothesis as a difference by more than 10 percentage points, or whatever transmission rate would be of value to a developing country. The problem with this strategy is that in order to determine the transmission rate that would be of value for the experimental treatment, one would have to give an estimate for the transmission rate without treatment. But that estimate could be wrong by a number of percentage points for the population under study, and this cannot be known if a placebo controlled trial is not carried out.

The controversy over whether a non-placebo controlled study can yield useful results thus boils down to a controversy over whether one judges it to be likely that the experimental treatment will reduce perinatal transmission close to what was found in the ACTG 076 regimen, and whether one can make reliable judgements about the perinatal transmission rate if no treatment is given.

This particular controversy reflects a larger controversy regarding the general acceptability of placebo controlled trials. It is, of course, generally accepted that if there exists a treatment for a serious or life-threatening condition, it would be unethical to deny participants in a trial that treatment, if it were available to them outside the trial. Some have argued, however, that for less serious conditions, under certain circumstances, it might be permissible to withdraw accepted therapy for the period of the trial. This general argument for the acceptability of placebo control trials even when effective treatments exist, is motivated by the 'assay sensitivity': proven effective therapies may show a wide variation in their effects in different clinical trials. When a new treatment is shown to be equivalent to an established, known effective treatment, this therefore does not necessarily show that the new treatment is effective, because the established treatment could be ineffective in that particular trial. In the absence of a placebo arm, one simply does not know.[17] This argument is a variation of the argument that an equivalence trial cannot show whether a treatment is better than placebo.

The argument in favour of placebo controlled trials even in the presence of known, effective treatment, has been criticised.[18] The two articles by Freedman et al. mainly argue against the position that equivalence trials are difficult to analyse from a statistical point of view. They, however, accept the argument that equivalence trials can establish only with difficulty that the new treatment is better than placebo:

> Evidence for the effectiveness of standard therapy must, therefore, be carefully evaluated before an equivalence study is initiated. If strong evidence exists that standard therapy is effective in the population to be studied, the assumption of efficacy is reasonable. Temple's point, therefore, indicates the need for proper caution when constructing an active-control trial, rather than pointing to any intrinsic theoretical problem associated with its use.[19]

Weijer has provided specific arguments against the problem of 'assay sensitivity'. He argues that the observed variation in response rates may be due to the small size of the trials, and therefore the answer is to conduct larger trials. Second, the selection of participants to trials may be influenced by the fact that they are placebo controlled, with a higher likelihood that treatment resistant patients will enter these trials than would enter equivalence trials. Placebo controlled trials are therefore the problem, not the solution.[20]

---

[17] S.S., ELLENBERG & R. TEMPLE, *Placebo-Controlled Trials and Active-Control Trials in the Evaluation of New Treatments. Part II: Practical Issues and Specific Cases*, in *Annals of Internal Medicine* 133 (2000) 464-470; ID., *Placebo-Controlled Trials and Active-Control Trials in the Evaluation of New Treatments. Part I: Ethical and Scientific Issues*, in *Annals of Internal Medicine* 133 (2000) 455-463.

[18] K.J. ROTHMAN & K.B. MICHELS, *The Continuing Unethical Use of Placebo Controls*, in *New England Journal of Medicine* 331 (1994) 394-398; B. FREEDMAN, K.C. GLASS & C. WEIJER, *Placebo Orthodoxy in Clinical Research II: Ethical, Legal and Regulatory Myths*, in *Journal of Law, Medicine and Ethics* 24 (1996) 252-259; ID., *Placebo Orthodoxy in Clinical Research I: Empirical and Methodological Myths*, in *Journal of Law, Medicine and Ethics* 24 (1996) 243-251; C. WEIJER, *Placebo Controlled Trials in Schizophrenia. Are they Ethical? Are they Necessary?*, in *Schizophrenia Research* 35 (1999) 211-218.

[19] B. FREEDMAN, K.C. GLASS & C. WEIJER, *art. cit.*, p. 243-251.

[20] C. WEIJER, *loc. cit.*

How should one evaluate these arguments in the context of the perinatal transmission studies? There clearly is agreement that one has to assume reliable data about the response rate in an untreated population in order to conclude that both of two equivalent trials are effective. If one treatment is shown to be superior, one has reliable evidence for the superiority of one of the two treatments. One would, however, again have to have reliable evidence about the response rate in an untreated population in order to conclude that the inferior treatment is better than placebo.

When deciding whether to initiate these trials or not, the relevant issue is, of course, what could be known about this before the trial starts. Evidence from the various trials can, however, tell us about how reasonable the assumption would have been concerning variability in response rates. The placebo transmission rates in the studies vary from around 19 to 30%. If therefore the result of an equivalence trial showed a transmission of 12% in a short course group, this might or might not be significantly better than placebo, depending on what the placebo transmission rate would have been in that trial. These data do therefore lend some support to those who claim that the placebo controlled trials are necessary in order to obtain results useful to developing countries.

4.4. Can the Equivalence Trials Be Justified?

Those who have criticised the placebo controlled studies have advocated trials where the ACTG 076 regimen is used as the control group. The problem with this suggestion is that this trial design may also be contrary to the Helsinki Declaration's demand that all trial subjects should receive the best current treatment.

Usually, when a trial is initiated it is because the currently available treatment is unsatisfactory in one way or another. It may be that it is not particularly effective, and a new experimental treatment may be more effective. Or it may be that the currently available treatment has unacceptable side-effects, and a new experimental treatment may have fewer side-effects, although it may not necessarily be more effective. Or, of course, it may be a combination of both. According to the commonly accepted position, in such a situation of genuine uncertainty as to which treatment is better for the patient, it would not be unethical to randomise the patient group to standard treatment and experimental treatment. A completely different situation would arise, however, if the currently available treatment is unacceptable 'because it is too expensive'. If there is no reason to expect that the new treatment is better, or has fewer side-effects, than the currently available treatment, and that the most that one could hope for is that it is equivalent in terms of efficacy and side-effects, how can one then justify the trial in terms of clinical equipoise? This would seem to be exactly the case with regard to the protocol using the 076 regimen as control. The main argument against the placebo trials was that one knowingly exposed identifiable women to a treatment, known to be inferior (placebo), or put another way, one withholds a known superior treatment from one group of women (the 076 regimen). In the alternative case one does exactly the same things. One withholds a known effective treatment from one group of women, providing a treatment that is cheaper, but with no reason to expect any benefit to the participants in the trial over and beyond the benefit provided by the known effective treatment. Of course, it might be the case that some women would prefer a shorter regimen because of the possibility that this would give them a lower chance of developing AZT resistant strains. That is, there may be some women for whom the choice between the shorter course vs. the longer course of treatment would make no difference. But that is not the type of trial the defenders of equivalence trials have been advocating.

The defenders of the equivalence trials also argued that more useful results would be possible from these trials. When, however, looking at the results from the Thai equivalence trial, and comparing these with the results from the three placebo controlled trials, it is uncertain whether the equivalence trial produced more useful results. From the Thai trial, one would not have known that the short course trial used the placebo. The Thai trial had four arms. Interim analysis discontinued the short-short arm as it found that it was significantly less effective than the long-long arm: 4.1% transmission vs. 10.5%. The final analysis showed a 6.6% transmission in the long-long arm, a 4.7% transmission in the long-short arm, and a 8.6% transmission in the short-long arm (and this is borderline significant). Here the two short arms were not equivalent to the long arms, as feared by the defenders of the placebo controlled trials. From this trial one could therefore only conclude that the two long treatment arms are equivalent, and possibly the short-long arm, but one would not know whether the short-short arm would be better than placebo. Had one not done a placebo controlled trial in Thailand, one might have erroneously assumed that the placebo transmission rate was in the 20s, rather than below 20% as was indeed the case in the placebo controlled trial done in that country.

The justification for carrying out the equivalence study in Thailand was the argument that AZT treatment would be available to pregnant women in that country. In fact, it would seem that even in Thailand AZT was not yet generally available to HIV positive pregnant mothers during the course of these studies. According to a news report on March 27, 1997 (*Emerging Markets Datafile Nation*), Dr. Virat Sirisanthana of Chiang Mai University argued that because of price reductions AZT should now be offered to all infected pregnant women. However, senior medical officers of the Ministry of Health, Dr. Viwat Rojanapitayakom and Dr. Vichai Chokeviwat, pointed out problems such as testing one million pregnant mothers a year, and concluded that they would wait the results of ongoing studies before making AZT available. This observation would tend to support the official CDC and NIH position against the position of the Harvard group proposing a non-placebo controlled trial in Thailand.

One may therefore reasonably conclude that carrying out a placebo controlled trial is the only way to obtain knowledge about a treatment that can be useful for developing countries, and that *any* study of a cheaper regimen would violate the Helsinki Declaration. If this is correct, it would mean that acceptance of the Helsinki Declaration would entail that useful studies for developing countries cannot be carried out. This may, of course, be a conclusion we would want to embrace, but we need arguments to that effect, or arguments that the Helsinki Declaration should be rejected. One cannot simply reject the trial because it does not conform to international guidelines. Although the fact that a proposed trial is not in accordance with international guidelines is something that should be taken seriously, one has to take into account that the guidelines may be inadequate or that the guidelines may have to be modified in light of new information. One needs to provide an argument that it is correct to follow the guidelines as well as to provide arguments for why it is justifiable to violate the guidelines. Having said that, however, one should also recognize that only in unusual circumstances one should violate international agreed standards for the conduct of clinical trials. Examples such as the perinatal transmission studies may show that the guidelines need revision. Ideally, though, this revision should take place before the trials in question are initiated. Let us now examine some of these arguments.

4.5. Arguments For and Against the Helsinki Declaration

The debate about the perinatal HIV transmission studies led to a debate about the acceptability of the previous version of the Helsinki Declaration. Those who defended the trial argued that the Helsinki Declaration should be changed to 'allow for a local standard of care', pointing out that this would make possible studies of relevance to developing countries.[21] Those who criticised the trial pointed out that a change in the Helsinki Declaration would inevitably lead to exploitation of developing countries by introducing a double standard.[22] At a meeting in Edinburgh in October 2000, the World Medical Association did revise the Helsinki Declaration, by stating that: "The benefits, risks and effectiveness of a new method should be tested against those of *the best current* prophylactic, diagnostic and therapeutic methods." The World Medical Association therefore essentially affirmed the previous standard of the Helsinki Declaration. The controversy is, however, not over, as new revisions are being considered. The controversy over these trials is based partly on disagreements about fundamental ethical theories, such as the acceptability of a general consequentialist approach versus an approach that takes it to be morally wrong to perform certain actions, such as directly causing preventable harm to an identifiable individual. This shows that there is still a need to reconsider the arguments.

Let us now therefore try to reconstruct the main argument *in favour* of placebo controlled trials. It depends crucially on the judgement that carrying out a placebo controlled trial is the only way to gain useful knowledge, on the claim that people taking part in the

---

[21] For a defense of this position, see R.J. LEVINE, *The Need to Revise the Declaration of Helsinki*, in *New England Journal of Medicine* 341 (1999) 531-534.

[22] T.A. BRENNAN, *Proposed Revisions to the Declaration of Helsinki – Will they Weaken the Ethical Principles Underlying Human Research*, in *New England Journal of Medicine* 341 (1999) 527-531

trial are not made worse off than they would be if they did not take part in the trial, and on the judgment on balance, the good consequences of carrying out the trial far outweigh the bad consequences of doing nothing. Although the argument in that sense is a consequentialist one, it is not incompatible with maintaining that some actions are wrong independent of their consequences. As will be seen below, the argument is not necessarily incompatible with the fundamental tenet of modern research ethics that one cannot inflict harm on research participants for the sake of benefit to future patients.

The argument, then, is the following: everybody agrees that perinatal transmission of HIV is a huge problem, and that an effective, affordable and suitable therapy for developing countries is urgently needed. The only way to find out if a short course AZT treatment is effective is to do a placebo controlled trial. This would involve giving some participants in the trial a known ineffective treatment, thus exposing them to danger. This could be construed as a case of knowingly exposing participants in the trial to a risk for the sake of benefit to future patients or for the sake of benefit to society. If that were the case, it would violate one of the fundamental principles of research ethics. The fact is, however, that right now some people do not receive the care and treatments they need, and this will continue for quite some time into the future. This may be unjust all things considered, but there is little, if anything, we can do to change that in the foreseeable future. Specifically, if a trial is not carried out, newborns will be exposed to HIV without treatment in many developing countries. There is, given the way things are, nothing one can do that would change this fact either, at least in the foreseeable future. The alternative would be to give some women a therapy that might be effective against HIV transmission, at the same time as one can find out whether this short course therapy is really effective, and thus would offer a hope to avoid HIV transmission in the future. No treatments that ordinarily would be offered are withheld from the women taking part in the trial.

The alternatives one has to choose between are therefore:

1) Do nothing. All women in the country of the proposed trial who are now HIV positive would receive no treatment to prevent transmission, as well as all HIV positive women in the foreseeable future;

2) Do a clinical trial. This would mean that some women would receive a treatment that might be effective in reducing the chance of transmission, as well as the possibility of establishing that this treatment is effective, and thus prevent transmission in a substantial number of future cases.

In this situation, according to this consequentalist argument, the only ethically defensible course of action would be to do the trials, in violation of the Helsinki Declaration. The essential counter-argument to this position is that it is similar to the argument presented in favour of the Tuskegee and the Willowbrook studies, and which has been rejected by most commentators. The argument accepts that certain actions are wrong, irrespective of the consequences. The researchers involved in both of these trials defended it, arguing that the participants were no worse off in the trial than they would be if they did not take part in the trial. According to David Rothman:

> The Tuskegee study, the USPHS [U.S. Public Health Service] insisted, constituted a 'natural experiment' ... Macon County, USPHS maintained, was a 'ready made laboratory'. Even if the USPHS were to forego the opportunity to track syphilis of the Macon County blacks, it seemed certain that this poverty-stricken, isolated, and medically unserved population would never receive the only therapy that existed – a complicated, lengthy and somewhat dangerous, and not altogether effective treatment of mercury and the two arsenic compounds known as salvarsan. ... The project was ethical, the researchers could claim, because they would only be watching the inevitable. Since the subjects were not going to obtain treatment anyway, there was no reason to miss the opportunity to trace the effects of their infections.[23]

Similarly for the Willowbrook study: In this project the researchers gave the newly admitted children to an orphanage hepatitis infection using the argument that it was highly likely that they would be infected anyway because of the hygienic conditions of the place, and that it was better for them to be infected under controlled conditions. According to Rothman: "What harm or ethical violation would occur

---

[23] D.J. ROTHMAN, *Were Tuskegee & Willowbrook 'Studies in Nature'?*, in *Hastings Center Report* 12 (1982) 5-7.

by administering the virus oneself, observing the course of the disease, and, in this instance (but not in the Tuskegee one) attempting to find a cure?"

Rothman argues against the position taken by the researchers involved in these two studies. According to him, "there is an essential difference between taking advantage of *social*, as opposed to biological, conditions. ... Predictions of continued social deprivation .... tend to become self-fulfilling. ... Experiments that build upon social deprivation are likely to manipulate the consent of the subjects". And finally, according to Rothman, once researchers start such a research project they no longer are mere observers of the phenomena, but become "accomplices to the problem". When they start to recruit research subjects, one could argue that they have special obligations towards them, obligations that they do not have towards disadvantaged social groups in general.

If we generalise from Rothman's examination of these two cases, the main argument *against* the placebo trials is the following. It depends crucially on the acceptance of a principle that it is always wrong to do an action of a particular type, irrespective of the consequences: Giving a placebo to some of the women is a deliberate act of withholding a known effective treatment to identifiable individuals when one could easily provide that treatment. It would not for example represent an extraordinary expense to provide that treatment to the participants in the trial, and it would not add much to the budget of the trial as a whole. The argument that the women would receive no treatment if they were not part of the trial is not valid. There is a general obligation to provide effective, and in this case, life-saving treatment to people if they need it. One may nevertheless recognize that this ideal is not always fulfilled. In the US, for example, some people do not have insurance, and consequently do not always receive needed treatment, but this is recognized to be a flaw in the system. Similarly, because of economic conditions, many people in developing countries do not receive needed medical care. We *are* under an obligation to do what we can do rectify that situation, although we must also recognize that it is not always possible to do much about it. It is therefore quite another thing altogether to deliberately design a trial where some women would get an inferior treatment when we could easily do otherwise. An additional argument against the placebo trial would be that we have special obligations to participants in trials. Participants in clinical trials typically take some risk by agreeing to be randomised to one treatment of unknown benefit. In such a context we at least have the obligation to ensure that we do not knowingly expose them to an identifiable danger.

This argument presupposes that there are some actions that are wrong even though the consequences of doing these actions may be better than refraining from doing them. As is usual in arguments of this type, proponents of the argument need not argue that the action is right or wrong *whatever the consequences*. In the argument outlined above, for example, it is stated that it is wrong to knowingly withhold an effective treatment when one could easily provide it, pointing out that providing AZT in the trial would not add much expense to the trial. Given other types of consequences, one may reach a different conclusion. If, for example, one wanted to do a clinical trial in a developing country on the effects of Aspirin on survival after myocardial infarction, offering bypass surgery to trial participants may not be regarded as a treatment one could easily provide, given the need to build coronary care units and train and pay highly qualified staff. Offering state of the art antiretroviral therapy to trial participants may fall somewhere in between, costing $12-15.000 per year. Once initiated it would have to be provided for the rest of the patient's life.

There is an additional argument against an *obligation* to provide state of the art treatment in resource poor countries.[24] Crouch and Arras argue that rich countries can only be obligated to provide resources to poor countries if it can be shown that current economic imbalances are the result of exploitation of the resource poor countries in the past. Then one could argue that there exists an *obligation* to compensate for past injustices. Crouch and Arras argue that a general obligation to provide necessary resources to cover all HIV positive pregnant women in developing countries cannot be defended on any reasonable estimate of the magnitude of past injustice. Crouch and Arras also provide an argument against the position that there, because of a fiduciary relationship between researcher and research participant, exists a special obligation to provide treatment to the identifiable individuals in the trial.

---

[24] R.A. CROUCH & J.D. ARRAS, *AZT Trials and Tribulations, Hastings Center Report* 28 (1998) 26-33.

4.6. An Attempted Reconciliation of the Arguments

If it is the case that both the placebo and the non-placebo trials are subject to the ethical worry that one knowingly exposes one group of women to a treatment believed to be inferior for the sake of gaining knowledge which will be useful for the treatment of future patients, it does suggest that some of the principles in the current research ethics guidelines need to be revised. If one followed the strict interpretation of the Helsinki Declaration forbidding any risk to the research subjects justified solely in terms of societal benefit, or forbidding providing treatments known to be inferior, research that would be immensely valuable for developing countries cannot be carried out. That is, there are cases where reference to different economic conditions in different countries may be ethically justifiable. Specifically, if as is the case in the perinatal transmission studies, the following conditions are fulfilled, it would seem justifiable to carry out a trial in developing countries that is not carried out in the sponsoring country:

- The trial is the only way to gain useful knowledge for the host country.
- There is a reasonable likelihood that the results of the trial will be of benefit to the host country.
- The research subjects are not denied care or treatment they would ordinarily get in the country where the trial is carried out.

Let us briefly examine these conditions, noting the differences between the perinatal transmission studies and the Willowbrook and Tuskegee studies. If Rothman's arguments are correct, all three studies satisfy the third condition. If this were the only justification for carrying out the perinatal transmission studies, they would be subject to the same counter-arguments as the Willowbrook and Tuskegee studies. The perinatal transmission study, however, differs in one fundamental aspect. If this study is not carried out in the countries involved, an effective and affordable treatment will simply not be available for these countries in the foreseeable future. This is reflected in the first two conditions which, taken together with the third condition, could constitute a powerful argument in favour of conducting these trials. The Tuskegee and the Willowbrook studies were not primarily carried out for the benefit of the social groups involved in these studies, and it is also uncertain whether they were the only way to obtain useful knowledge. It should also be clear from my discussion that one can argue that the placebo controlled perinatal transmission studies satisfy all three conditions, whereas the non-placebo controlled trials may violate the first two conditions.

If this analysis is correct, it means that under certain circumstances it may be justifiable, contrary to the Helsinki Declaration, to carry out trials without the best current treatment for the control group. The UNAIDS guidance document on HIV vaccine trials takes a similar approach, and one might also want to include the considerations mentioned in that document. It specifies that care and treatment for HIV/AIDS and its associated complications should be provided to participants in HIV preventive vaccine trials, with the ideal being to provide the best proven therapy, and the minimum to provide the highest level of care attainable in the host country in light of the circumstances listed below. A comprehensive care package should be agreed upon through a host/community/sponsor dialogue which reaches consensus prior to initiation of a trial, taking into consideration the following:
- level of care and treatment available in the sponsor country
- highest level of care available in the host country
- highest level of treatment available in the host country, including the availability of antiretroviral therapy outside the research context in the host country
- availability of infrastructure to provide care and treatment in the context of research
- potential duration and sustainability of care and treatment for the trial participant.

The argument that under certain conditions one may justifiably provide less than the current best treatment, depends crucially on the condition that there is a reasonable likelihood that the result of the trial will be a benefit to the population where the trial took place. About this requirement there seems to be some agreement.[25] This means that it will be important to spell out the conditions under which there is a reasonable likelihood that the population will benefit.

[25] R.A. CROUCH & J.D. ARRAS, loc.cit; L.H. GLANTZ et al., Research in Developing Countries: Taking 'Benefit' Seriously, in Hastings Center Report 28 (1998) 38-42.

5

EPILOGUE

Human Experimentation

Paul T. Schotsmans

As all other parts in this book, the contributions on the ethics of human experimentation are meant to illustrate more particularly the European characteristics of the ethical debate. However, less than for the other two parts (physician-patient relationship and resource allocation in health care), a specific European perspective may be deductible. Human experimentation in medicine is indeed radically international and even radically intercontinental, as the contribution on HIV transmission of R. Lie illustrates. The reason why the planning committee of this Textbook decided to devote a full part on it, was therefore essentially the observation that research ethics is regularly neglected in this kind of publications. Bioethics makes us think at reproductive technologies, genetic engineering, transplantation medicine and medical decision making concerning the end of life, but human experimentation is rather minimally represented in publications and textbooks.

One of the reasons for this negligence may be the existence of a kind of self-evident procedural ethics, which accompanies since decades the efforts in human experimentation. That this was not always the case may be evident after reading J.N. Missa's contribution (he gives an insightful historical background helping us to understand how this was not always the first priority). Nowadays, the impression is created that research ethics is in the hands of some 'sub-specialists in bioethics', a special subgroup working in Research Ethics Committees (RECs) and establishing their own professional rules and norms. The planning committee of this European Textbook wanted to bring research ethics again in the middle of the (bio-) ethical concern, and essentially the concern of those who develop teaching projects in ethics.

Research ethics may be characterised by three major subjects. The function of Ethics Committees (local, regional, national or international), the protection of the autonomy of the research subject (the rule of informed consent and the status of research subjects, cf. M.L. Delfosse) and the development of a whole set of recommendations (see also M.L. Delfosse and R. Lie) are crucial for understanding what is going on in research ethics.

The first one – Ethics Committees – is essentially institutional: several countries in the world and also the international medical community (cf. World Medical Association) made the Ethics Committees a central locus of reference for the evaluation of research protocols. The problem is however the competency of these committees. It remains indeed a challenge to keep the members of these committees on "track" so that they evaluate research protocols with sufficient and adequate insight. Some (and I am very convinced by their arguments) even strongly question the competency of "local" Ethics Committees, a reaction essentially linked to the observation that their members are not fully trained in ethics. I hope that these contributions may help them to understand better the importance of their responsibilities. This should be indeed the main purpose of this section: the contribution of R. Lie for example may give an insight in the rationale behind randomised clinical trials (RCTs). From a theoretical and axiological point of view, he makes evidently clear that the conflict between individual and collective ethics creates a recurring challenge for every evaluation of a research protocol.

Research ethics should also clarify the different values and value patterns that guide human experimentation. M.L. Delfosse illustrates very well how the status of a research subject is different from the status of a patient in a classical physician-patient relationship. Other values that have to be weighed against each other, are the freedom and/or duty of research and the researcher (J. N. Missa), and several collective values coming into play when evaluating a research protocol (R. Lie).

A long way has been gone since medical doctors arbitrarily planned research activities with little respect for research subjects. As Missa made clear: "The true practice of informed consent implies the abandonment of medical paternalism." This practice has evolved to a structural and self-evident balance between the rights of research subjects on the one hand and the eventual improvement of medical practice and the furthering of scientific medical expertise on the other hand. Delfosse introduces here the notion of *solicitude* – a very specific European philosophical idea – as an exchange between two beings perceiving each other as equals, as sources of self-esteem, and links this notion to the Kantian test of universality.

And finally, research ethics has established more than any other discipline in Bioethics an "ensemble" of recommendations, guidelines and directives: they have become a cornerstone in the application of this kind of procedural ethics. They also function as specific tools and instruments for the sub-specialists in the field of medical research. We did not hesitate therefore to present the latest revision of the Helsinki Declaration (Edinburgh 2000), together with the European Directive on Human Experimentation. These two documents are a frame of reference for every kind of research ethics. As R. Lie illustrates, even some small changes in these recommendations, may have large implications. But more important is probably to observe how these recommendations brought an atmosphere of professionalism in the field: the guidelines represent a basic consensus and give a worldwide support to those who are functioning in this sub-area of Bioethics.

To conclude: research ethicists present their service to members of RECs in helping them to balance several values:
- freedom of research,
- duty to research,
- respect for the autonomy of the research subject,
- analysis of risks and benefits for the research subject or the balance between beneficence and 'do not harm' principles,
- special relationship between the physician as a researcher and the research subjects (cf. the notion of *solicitude* of Ricoeur),
- collective values as the furthering of medical knowledge and the amelioration of medical treatment, and
- as R. Lie makes clear: even the world wide solidarity with the poorest countries…

It is crucially important to develop these skills in discernment. Although it may be evidently clear that the international community has yet given very helpful guidelines, the unique challenge of ethics remains the continuing examination of how to keep these standards linked to basic value clarifications and value choices. Although we are aware that this is essentially an international and even intercontinental debate, European philosophical approaches may be helpful to stimulate this continuing self-examination of research ethics. I am convinced that this has been well illustrated by the contributions in this second part of the book. The invitation to continue this hermeneutic clarification also in the future, may even lead to a kind of research ethics, being more concerned with its presuppositions than with its applications.

WORLD MEDICAL ASSOCIATION DECLARATION OF HELSINKI

1.1. The Helsinki Declaration: Some Preliminary Remarks[1]

The Declaration of Helsinki is the most widely accepted code on medical research involving human subjects. It dates from 1964 and was conceived by the World Medical Association as a revision of the Nuremberg Code. The latter was written largely as a result of the atrocities of the Second World War. The formation of the World Medical Association (1947) was a response to the verdict of the Nuremberg trials, which followed the Second World War. During those trials, physicians and scientists were accused of murder and torture in the context of medical experiments in concentration camps. Since 1964, the Declaration of Helsinki has been revised four times and has become the cornerstone for biomedical research ethics. This international guideline places the well-being of the research subject in the forefront. It insists on weighing the benefits and the risks of the experiment against each other and proclaims the necessity to obtain informed consent either from the research subjects themselves or – in case of incompetence – from their legal representatives.

The changes made to the Helsinki Declaration in Edingburgh (2000) constitute more than a 'revision'. It can be considered the third version of the Declaration, following these of 1964 (Helsinki) and 1975 (Tokyo). In 1975 there were two major changes in the design and results of research protocols. Firstly, there was the creation of Ethics Committees, appointed independent committees for

---

[1] See the website of the *World Medical Association* (www.wma.net) and the *Bulletin of Medical Ethics* 162 (2000) 8-11.

ethical consideration, comment and guidance. Secondly, largely connected to the first, research papers could only be published after a
clearance by the Ethics Committee. The 1975 Declaration has been
amended three times: in Venice (1983), in Hong Kong (1989) and in
Somerset West (1996). The amendments were minor in comparison,
for instance about the consent of a minor, or about the recognition of
Ethics Committees by local law.

It is reasonable to call the Edinburgh revision a new version,
because only 3 of the 32 paragraphs did not change. The new Declaration of Helsinki is divided in three parts. First there is an introduction consisting of 9 guidelines. It is followed by 18 basic principles
for all kinds of medical research. Finally there are 5 additional principles for medical research combined with medical care. In general,
this version puts the research subjects' interest ahead of the interests
of the researcher and of society in the outcome of research. It also
places more emphasis on the assessment of risks and benefits. Some
paragraphs were substantially rewritten, especially on vulnerable
populations such as those not competent themselves to give consent
(A.8; B.24). Substantial rewording also extends the range of information that a Research Ethics Committee should review prior to giving
approval (B.13). Moreover, researchers must not only make publicly
available their results, whether positive or negative, but also conflicts of interests, institutional affiliations and sources of funding
(B.27). There are some completely new paragraphs too, e.g. a statement setting the Declaration in the context of national legislation
and regulatory requirements, that may not be allowed to reduce or
remove the protections provided in the Helsinki Declaration (A.9).
The most far-reaching new paragraph requires that patients after the
study have access to the best treatment identified by the study
(C.30). This statement is inserted primarily to prevent abuse of third
world populations by researchers who 'parachute' in, do a study,
and then flee from the country, leaving no improvement in health
care for the local population.

The European Directive is the legal translation of these provisions
by the World Medical Association. This legal transposition gives
more value to the old guidelines of professional ethics and to the
role of Ethics Committees within the member states. The Directive is
therefore symbolic for a new era in the European assessment of
human experimentation in medicine.

1.2. Ethical Principles for Medical Research Involving Human Subjects[2]

A. *Introduction*

1. The World Medical Association has developed the Declaration of Helsinki as a statement of ethical principles to provide guidance to physicians and other participants in medical research involving human subjects. Medical research involving human subjects includes research on identifiable human material or identifiable data.

2. It is the duty of the physician to promote and safeguard the health of the people. The physician's knowledge and conscience are dedicated to the fulfillment of this duty.

3. The Declaration of Geneva of the World Medical Association binds the physician with the words, "The health of my patient will be my first consideration", and the International Code of Medical Ethics declares that, "A physician shall act only in the patient's interest when providing medical care which might have the effect of weakening the physical and mental condition of the patient."

4. Medical progress is based on research which ultimately must rest in part on experimentation involving human subjects.

5. In medical research on human subjects, considerations related to the well-being of the human subject should take precedence over the interests of science and society.

6. The primary purpose of medical research involving human subjects is to improve prophylactic, diagnostic and therapeutic procedures and the understanding of the aetiology and pathogenesis of disease. Even the best proven prophylactic, diagnostic, and therapeutic methods must continuously be challenged through research for their effectiveness, efficiency, accessibility and quality.

[2] Adopted by the 18th WMA General Assembly Helsinki, Finland, June 1964 and amended by the 29th WMA General Assembly, Tokyo, Japan, October 1975; 35th WMA General Assembly, Venice, Italy, October 1983; 41st WMA General Assembly, Hong Kong, September 1989; 48th WMA General Assembly, Somerset West, Republic of South Africa, October 1996 and the 52nd WMA General Assembly, Edinburgh, Scotland, October 2000. (http://www.wma.net/e/policy/17c.pdf)

7. In current medical practice and in medical research, most prophylactic, diagnostic and therapeutic procedures involve risks and burdens.

8. Medical research is subject to ethical standards that promote respect for all human beings and protect their health and rights. Some research populations are vulnerable and need special protection. The particular needs of the economically and medically disadvantaged must be recognized. Special attention is also required for those who cannot give or refuse consent for themselves, for those who may be subject to giving consent under duress, for those who will not benefit personally from the research and for those for whom the research is combined with care.

9. Investigators should be aware of the ethical, legal and regulatory requirements for research on human subjects in their own countries as well as applicable international requirements. No national ethical, legal or regulatory requirement should be allowed to reduce or eliminate any of the protections for human subjects set forth in this Declaration.

B. *Basic Principles For All Medical Research*

10. It is the duty of the physician in medical research to protect the life, health, privacy, and dignity of the human subject.

11. Medical research involving human subjects must conform to generally accepted scientific principles, be based on a thorough knowledge of the scientific literature, other relevant sources of information, and on adequate laboratory and, where appropriate, animal experimentation.

12. Appropriate caution must be exercised in the conduct of research which may affect the environment, and the welfare of animals used for research must be respected.

13. The design and performance of each experimental procedure involving human subjects should be clearly formulated in an experimental protocol. This protocol should be submitted for consideration, comment, guidance, and where appropriate, approval to a specially appointed ethical review committee,

which must be independent of the investigator, the sponsor or any other kind of undue influence. This independent committee should be in conformity with the laws and regulations of the country in which the research experiment is performed. The committee has the right to monitor ongoing trials. The researcher has the obligation to provide monitoring information to the committee, especially any serious adverse events. The researcher should also submit to the committee, for review, information regarding funding, sponsors, institutional affiliations, other potential conflicts of interest and incentives for subjects.

14. The research protocol should always contain a statement of the ethical considerations involved and should indicate that there is compliance with the principles enunciated in this Declaration.

15. Medical research involving human subjects should be conducted only by scientifically qualified persons and under the supervision of a clinically competent medical person. The responsibility for the human subject must always rest with a medically qualified person and never rest on the subject of the research, even though the subject has given consent.

16. Every medical research project involving human subjects should be preceded by careful assessment of predictable risks and burdens in comparison with foreseeable benefits to the subject or to others. This does not preclude the participation of healthy volunteers in medical research. The design of all studies should be publicly available.

17. Physicians should abstain from engaging in research projects involving human subjects unless they are confident that the risks involved have been adequately assessed and can be satisfactorily managed. Physicians should cease any investigation if the risks are found to outweigh the potential benefits or if there is conclusive proof of positive and beneficial results.

18. Medical research involving human subjects should only be conducted if the importance of the objective outweighs the inherent risks and burdens to the subject. This is especially important when the human subjects are healthy volunteers.

19. Medical research is only justified if there is a reasonable likelihood that the populations in which the research is carried out stand to benefit from the results of the research.

20. The subjects must be volunteers and informed participants in the research project.

21. The right of research subjects to safeguard their integrity must always be respected. Every precaution should be taken to respect the privacy of the subject, the confidentiality of the patient's information and to minimize the impact of the study on the subject's physical and mental integrity and on the personality of the subject.

22. In any research on human beings, each potential subject must be adequately informed of the aims, methods, sources of funding, any possible conflicts of interest, institutional affiliations of the researcher, the anticipated benefits and potential risks of the study and the discomfort it may entail. The subject should be informed of the right to abstain from participation in the study or to withdraw consent to participate at any time without reprisal. After ensuring that the subject has understood the information, the physician should then obtain the subject's freely given informed consent, preferably in writing. If the consent cannot be obtained in writing, the non-written consent must be formally documented and witnessed.

23. When obtaining informed consent for the research project the physician should be particularly cautious if the subject is in a dependent relationship with the physician or may consent under duress. In that case the informed consent should be obtained by a well-informed physician who is not engaged in the investigation and who is completely independent of this relationship.

24. For a research subject who is legally incompetent, physically or mentally incapable of giving consent or is a legally incompetent minor, the investigator must obtain informed consent from the legally authorized representative in accordance with applicable law. These groups should not be included in research unless the research is necessary to promote the health of the population

represented and this research cannot instead be performed on legally competent persons.

25. When a subject deemed legally incompetent, such as a minor child, is able to give assent to decisions about participation in research, the investigator must obtain that assent in addition to the consent of the legally authorized representative.

26. Research on individuals from whom it is not possible to obtain consent, including proxy or advance consent, should be done only if the physical/mental condition that prevents obtaining informed consent is a necessary characteristic of the research population. The specific reasons for involving research subjects with a condition that renders them unable to give informed consent should be stated in the experimental protocol for consideration and approval of the review committee. The protocol should state that consent to remain in the research should be obtained as soon as possible from the individual or a legally authorized surrogate.

27. Both authors and publishers have ethical obligations. In publication of the results of research, the investigators are obliged to preserve the accuracy of the results. Negative as well as positive results should be published or otherwise publicly available. Sources of funding, institutional affiliations and any possible conflicts of interest should be declared in the publication. Reports of experimentation not in accordance with the principles laid down in this Declaration should not be accepted for publication.

C. *Additional Principles For Medical Research Combined With Medical Care*

28. The physician may combine medical research with medical care, only to the extent that the research is justified by its potential prophylactic, diagnostic or therapeutic value. When medical research is combined with medical care, additional standards apply to protect the patients who are research subjects.

29. The benefits, risks, burdens and effectiveness of a new method should be tested against those of the best current prophylactic,

diagnostic, and therapeutic methods. This does not exclude the use of placebo, or no treatment, in studies where no proven prophylactic, diagnostic or therapeutic method exists.

30. At the conclusion of the study, every patient entered into the study should be assured of access to the best proven prophylactic, diagnostic and therapeutic methods identified by the study.

31. The physician should fully inform the patient which aspects of the care are related to the research. The refusal of a patient to participate in a study must never interfere with the patient physician relationship.

32. In the treatment of a patient, where proven prophylactic, diagnostic and therapeutic methods do not exist or have been ineffective, the physician, with informed consent from the patient, must be free to use unproven or new prophylactic, diagnostic and therapeutic measures, if in the physician's judgement it offers hope of saving life, re-establishing health or alleviating suffering. Where possible, these measures should be made the object of research, designed to evaluate their safety and efficacy. In all cases, new information should be recorded and, where appropriate, published. The other relevant guidelines of this Declaration should be followed.

DIRECTIVE 2001/20/EC OF THE EUROPEAN PARLIAMENT AND OF THE COUNCIL OF 4 APRIL 2001[1]

On the approximation of the laws, regulations and administrative provisions of the Member States relating to the implementation of good clinical practice in the conduct of clinical trials on medicinal products for human use[2]

The European Parliament and the Council of the European Union,

Having regard to the Treaty establishing the European Community, and in particular Article 95 thereof,
Having regard to the proposal from the Commission[3],
Having regard to the opinion of the Economic and Social Committee[4],
Acting in accordance with the procedure laid down in Article 251 of the Treaty[5],

Whereas:

(1) Council Directive 65/65/EEC of 26 January 1965 on the approximation of provisions laid down by law, regulation or administrative action relating to medicinal products[6] requires that applications for authorisation to place a medicinal product on the market

---

[1] For an extensive comment on this Directive see H. Nys, *Analyse et commentaire de la directive 2001/20/CE concernant les bonnes pratiques cliniques dans la conduite d'essais cliniques de médicaments à usage humain à partir de la protection du sujet d'expérience,* in *Journal des Tribunaux* (in press).

[2] See http://europa.eu.int

[3] OJ C 306, 8.10.1997, p. 9 and OJ C 161, 8.6.1999, p. 5.

[4] OJ C 95, 30.3.1998, p. 1.

[5] Opinion of the European Parliament of 17 November 1998 (OJ C 379, 7. 12. 1998, p. 27). Council Common Position of 20 July 2000 (OJ C 300, 20.10.2000, p. 32) and Decision of the European Parliament of 12 December 2000. Council Decision of 26 February 2001.

[6] OJ 22, 9.2.1965, p. 1/65. Directive as last amended by Council Directive 93/39/EEC (OJ L 214, 24.8.1993, p. 22).

should be accompanied by a dossier containing particulars and documents relating to the results of tests and clinical trials carried out on the product. Council Directive 75/318/EEC of 20 May 1975 on the approximation of the laws of Member States relating to analytical, pharmaco-toxicological and clinical standards and protocols in respect of the testing of medicinal products[7] lays down uniform rules on the compilation of dossiers including their presentation.

(2) The accepted basis for the conduct of clinical trials in humans is founded in the protection of human rights and the dignity of the human being with regard to the application of biology and medicine, as for instance reflected in the 1996 version of the Helsinki Declaration. The clinical trial subject's protection is safeguarded through risk assessment based on the results of toxicological experiments prior to any clinical trial, screening by ethics committees and Member States' competent authorities, and rules on the protection of personal data.

(3) Persons who are incapable of giving legal consent to clinical trials should be given special protection. It is incumbent on the Member States to lay down rules to this effect. Such persons may not be included in clinical trials if the same results can be obtained using persons capable of giving consent. Normally these persons should be included in clinical trials only when there are grounds for expecting that the administering of the medicinal product would be of direct benefit to the patient, thereby outweighing the risks. However, there is a need for clinical trials involving children to improve the treatment available to them. Children represent a vulnerable population with developmental, physiological and psychological differences from adults, which make age- and development- related research important for their benefit. Medicinal products, including vaccines, for children need to be tested scientifically before widespread use. This can only be achieved by ensuring that medicinal products which are likely to be of significant clinical value for children are fully studied. The clinical trials required for this purpose should be carried out under conditions affording the best possible protection for the subjects. Criteria for the protection of children in clinical trials therefore need to be laid down.

(4) In the case of other persons incapable of giving their consent, such as persons with dementia, psychiatric patients, etc., inclusion in clinical trials in such cases should be on an even more

[7] OJ L 147, 9.6.1975, p. 1. Directive as last amended by Commission Directive 1999/83/EC (OJ L 243, 15.9.1999, p. 9).

restrictive basis. Medicinal products for trial may be administered to all such individuals only when there are grounds for assuming that the direct benefit to the patient outweighs the risks. Moreover, in such cases the written consent of the patient's legal representative, given in cooperation with the treating doctor, is necessary before participation in any such clinical trial.

(5) The notion of legal representative refers back to existing national law and consequently may include natural or legal persons, an authority and/or a body provided for by national law.

(6) In order to achieve optimum protection of health, obsolete or repetitive tests will not be carried out, whether within the Community or in third countries. The harmonisation of technical requirements for the development of medicinal products should therefore be pursued through the appropriate fora, in particular the International Conference on Harmonisation.

(7) For medicinal products falling within the scope of Part A of the Annex to Council Regulation (EEC) No 2309/93 of 22 July 1993 laying down Community procedures for the authorisation and supervision of medicinal products for human and veterinary use and establishing a European Agency for the Evaluation of Medicinal Products[8], which include products intended for gene therapy or cell therapy, prior scientific evaluation by the European Agency for the Evaluation of Medicinal Products (hereinafter referred to as the "Agency"), assisted by the Committee for Proprietary Medicinal Products, is mandatory before the Commission grants marketing authorisation. In the course of this evaluation, the said Committee may request full details of the results of the clinical trials on which the application for marketing authorisation is based and, consequently, on the manner in which these trials were conducted and the same Committee may go so far as to require the applicant for such authorisation to conduct further clinical trials. Provision must therefore be made to allow the Agency to have full information on the conduct of any clinical trial for such medicinal products.

(8) A single opinion for each Member State concerned reduces delay in the commencement of a trial without jeopardising the well-being of the people participating in the trial or excluding the possibility of rejecting it in specific sites.

(9) Information on the content, commencement and termination of a clinical trial should be available to the Member States where the trial takes place and all the other Member States should have access to the same information. A European database bringing

[8] OJ L 214, 24.8.1993, p. 1. Regulation as amended by Commission Regulation (EC) No 649/98 (OJ L 88, 24.3.1998, p. 7)

together this information should therefore be set up, with due regard for the rules of confidentiality.

(10) Clinical trials are a complex operation, generally lasting one or more years, usually involving numerous participants and several trial sites, often in different Member States. Member States' current practices diverge considerably on the rules on commencement and conduct of the clinical trials and the requirements for carrying them out vary widely. This therefore results in delays and complications detrimental to effective conduct of such trials in the Community. It is therefore necessary to simplify and harmonise the administrative provisions governing such trials by establishing a clear, transparent procedure and creating conditions conducive to effective coordination of such clinical trials in the Community by the authorities concerned.

(11) As a rule, authorisation should be implicit, i.e. if there has been a vote in favour by the Ethics Committee and the competent authority has not objected within a given period, it should be possible to begin the clinical trials. In exceptional cases raising especially complex problems, explicit written authorisation should, however, be required.

(12) The principles of good manufacturing practice should be applied to investigational medicinal products.

(13) Special provisions should be laid down for the labelling of these products.

(14) Non-commercial clinical trials conducted by researchers without the participation of the pharmaceuticals industry may be of great benefit to the patients concerned. The Directive should therefore take account of the special position of trials whose planning does not require particular manufacturing or packaging processes, if these trials are carried out with medicinal products with a marketing authorisation within the meaning of Directive 65/65/EEC, manufactured or imported in accordance with the provisions of Directives 75/319/EEC and 91/356/EEC, and on patients with the same characteristics as those covered by the indication specified in this marketing authorisation. Labelling of the investigational medicinal products intended for trials of this nature should be subject to simplified provisions laid down in the good manufacturing practice guidelines on investigational products and in Directive 91/356/EEC.

(15) The verification of compliance with the standards of good clinical practice and the need to subject data, information and documents to inspection in order to confirm that they have been properly generated, recorded and reported are essential in order to justify the involvement of human subjects in clinical trials.

(16) The person participating in a trial must consent to the scrutiny of personal information during inspection by competent authorities and properly authorised persons, provided that such personal information is treated as strictly confidential and is not made publicly available.

(17) This Directive is to apply without prejudice to Directive 95/46/EEC of the European Parliament and of the Council of 24 October 1995 on the protection of individuals with regard to the processing of personal data and on the free movement of such data[9].

(18) It is also necessary to make provision for the monitoring of adverse reactions occurring in clinical trials using Community surveillance (pharmacovigilance) procedures in order to ensure the immediate cessation of any clinical trial in which there is an unacceptable level of risk.

(19) The measures necessary for the implementation of this Directive should be adopted in accordance with Council Decision 1999/468/EC of 28 June 1999 laying down the procedures for the exercise of implementing powers conferred on the Commission[10],

Have adopted this directive:

Article 1: Scope

1. This Directive establishes specific provisions regarding the conduct of clinical trials, including multi-centre trials, on human subjects involving medicinal products as defined in Article 1 of Directive 65/65/EEC, in particular relating to the implementation of good clinical practice. This Directive does not apply to non-interventional trials.

2. Good clinical practice is a set of internationally recognised ethical and scientific quality requirements which must be observed for designing, conducting, recording and reporting clinical trials that involve the participation of human subjects. Compliance with this good practice provides assurance that the rights, safety and well-being of trial subjects are protected, and that the results of the clinical trials are credible.

[9] OJ L 281, 23.11.1995, p. 31.
[10] OJ L 184, 17.7.1999, p. 23.

3. The principles of good clinical practice and detailed guidelines in line with those principles shall be adopted and, if necessary, revised to take account of technical and scientific progress in accordance with the procedure referred to in Article 21 (2). These detailed guidelines shall be published by the Commission.
4. All clinical trials, including bioavailability and bioequivalence studies, shall be designed, conducted and reported in accordance with the principles of good clinical practice.

Article 2: Definitions

For the purposes of this Directive the following definitions shall apply:
(a) "clinical trial": any investigation in human subjects intended to discover or verify the clinical, pharmacological and/or other pharmacodynamic effects of one or more investigational medicinal product(s), and/or to identify any adverse reactions to one or more investigational medicinal product(s) and/or to study absorption, distribution, metabolism and excretion of one or more investigational medicinal product(s) with the object of ascertaining its (their) safety and/or efficacy; This includes clinical trials carried out in either one site or multiple sites, whether in one or more than one Member State;
(b) "multi-centre clinical trial": a clinical trial conducted according to a single protocol but at more than one site, and therefore by more than one investigator, in which the trial sites may be located in a single Member State, in a number of Member States and/or in Member States and third countries;
(c) "non-interventional trial": a study where the medicinal product(s) is (are) prescribed in the usual manner in accordance with the terms of the marketing authorisation. The assignment of the patient to a particular therapeutic strategy is not decided in advance by a trial protocol but falls within current practice and the prescription of the medicine is clearly separated from the decision to include the patient in the study. No additional diagnostic or monitoring procedures shall be applied to the patients and epidemiological methods shall be used for the analysis of collected data;
(d) "investigational medicinal product": a pharmaceutical form of an active substance or placebo being tested or used as a reference in a clinical trial, including products already with a marketing authorisation but used or assembled (formulated or packaged) in a way different from the authorised form, or when used for an unauthorised indication, or when used to gain further information about the authorised form;

(e) "sponsor": an individual, company, institution or organisation which takes responsibility for the initiation, management and/or financing of a clinical trial;

(f) "investigator": a doctor or a person following a profession agreed in the Member State for investigations because of the scientific background and the experience in patient care it requires. The investigator is responsible for the conduct of a clinical trial at a trial site. If a trial is conducted by a team of individuals at a trial site, the investigator is the leader responsible for the team and may be called the principal investigator;

(g) "investigator's brochure": a compilation of the clinical and non-clinical data on the investigational medicinal product or products which are relevant to the study of the product or products in human subjects;

(h) "protocol": a document that describes the objective(s), design, methodology, statistical considerations and organisation of a trial. The term protocol refers to the protocol, successive versions of the protocol and protocol amendments;

(i) "subject": an individual who participates in a clinical trial as either a recipient of the investigational medicinal product or a control;

(j) "informed consent": decision, which must be written, dated and signed, to take part in a clinical trial, taken freely after being duly informed of its nature, significance, implications and risks and appropriately documented, by any person capable of giving consent or, where the person is not capable of giving consent, by his or her legal representative; if the person concerned is unable to write, oral consent in the presence of at least one witness may be given in exceptional cases, as provided for in national legislation.

(k) "ethics committee": an independent body in a Member State, consisting of healthcare professionals and non-medical members, whose responsibility it is to protect the rights, safety and wellbeing of human subjects involved in a trial and to provide public assurance of that protection, by, among other things, expressing an opinion on the trial protocol, the suitability of the investigators and the adequacy of facilities, and on the methods and documents to be used to inform trial subjects and obtain their informed consent;

(l) "inspection": the act by a competent authority of conducting an official review of documents, facilities, records, quality assurance arrangements, and any other resources that are deemed by the competent authority to be related to the clinical trial and that may be located at the site of the trial, at the sponsor's and/or contract research organisation's facilities, or at other establishments which the competent authority sees fit to inspect;

(m) "adverse event": any untoward medical occurrence in a patient or clinical trial subject administered a medicinal product and which does not necessarily have a causal relationship with this treatment;

(n) "adverse reaction": all untoward and unintended responses to an investigational medicinal product related to any dose administered;

(o) "serious adverse event or serious adverse reaction": any untoward medical occurrence or effect that at any dose results in death, is life-threatening, requires hospitalisation or prolongation of existing hospitalisation, results in persistent or significant disability or incapacity, or is a congenital anomaly or birth defect;

(p) "unexpected adverse reaction": an adverse reaction, the nature or severity of which is not consistent with the applicable product information (e.g. investigator's brochure for an unauthorised investigational product or summary of product characteristics for an authorised product).

Article 3: Protection of Clinical Trial Subjects

1. This Directive shall apply without prejudice to the national provisions on the protection of clinical trial subjects if they are more comprehensive than the provisions of this Directive and consistent with the procedures and time-scales specified therein. Member States shall, insofar as they have not already done so, adopt detailed rules to protect from abuse individuals who are incapable of giving their informed consent.

2. A clinical trial may be undertaken only if, in particular:

   (a) the foreseeable risks and inconveniences have been weighed against the anticipated benefit for the individual trial subject and other present and future patients. A clinical trial may be initiated only if the Ethics Committee and/or the competent authority comes to the conclusion that the anticipated therapeutic and public health benefits justify the risks and may be continued only if compliance with this requirement is permanently monitored;

   (b) the trial subject or, when the person is not able to give informed consent, his legal representative has had the opportunity, in a prior interview with the investigator or a member of the investigating team, to understand the objectives, risks and inconveniences of the trial, and the conditions under which it is to be conducted and has also been informed of his right to withdraw from the trial at any time;

(c) the rights of the subject to physical and mental integrity, to privacy and to the protection of the data concerning him in accordance with Directive 95/46/EC are safeguarded;

(d) the trial subject or, when the person is not able to give informed consent, his legal representative has given his written consent after being informed of the nature, significance, implications and risks of the clinical trial; if the individual is unable to write, oral consent in the presence of at least one witness may be given in exceptional cases, as provided for in national legislation;

(e) the subject may without any resulting detriment withdraw from the clinical trial at any time by revoking his informed consent;

(f) provision has been made for insurance or indemnity to cover the liability of the investigator and sponsor.

3.   The medical care given to, and medical decisions made on behalf of, subjects shall be the responsibility of an appropriately qualified doctor or, where appropriate, of a qualified dentist.

4.   The subject shall be provided with a contact point where he may obtain further information.

Article 4: Clinical Trials on Minors

In addition to any other relevant restriction, a clinical trial on minors may be undertaken only if:

(a)   the informed consent of the parents or legal representative has been obtained; consent must represent the minor's presumed will and may be revoked at any time, without detriment to the minor;

(b)   the minor has received information according to its capacity of understanding, from staff with experience with minors, regarding the trial, the risks and the benefits;

(c)   the explicit wish of a minor who is capable of forming an opinion and assessing this information to refuse participation or to be withdrawn from the clinical trial at any time is considered by the investigator or where appropriate the principal investigator;

(d)   no incentives or financial inducements are given except compensation;

(e)   some direct benefit for the group of patients is obtained from the clinical trial and only where such research is essential to validate data obtained in clinical trials on persons able to give informed consent or by other research methods; additionally, such research should either relate directly to a clinical condition from which the minor concerned suffers or be of such a nature that it can only be carried out on minors;

(f) the corresponding scientific guidelines of the Agency have been fol-
     lowed;
(g) clinical trials have been designed to minimise pain, discomfort, fear
     and any other foreseeable risk in relation to the disease and devel-
     opmental stage; both the risk threshold and the degree of distress
     have to be specially defined and constantly monitored;
(h) the Ethics Committee, with paediatric expertise or after taking
     advice in clinical, ethical and psychosocial problems in the field of
     paediatrics, has endorsed the protocol; and
(i) the interests of the patient always prevail over those of science and
     society.

*Article 5: Clinical Trials on Incapacitated Adults not Able to Give Informed
     Legal Consent*

In the case of other persons incapable of giving informed legal consent,
all relevant requirements listed for persons capable of giving such consent shall apply. In addition to these requirements, inclusion in clinical
trials of incapacitated adults who have not given or not refused
informed consent before the onset of their incapacity shall be allowed
only if:
(a) the informed consent of the legal representative has been obtained;
     consent must represent the subject's presumed will and may be
     revoked at any time, without detriment to the subject;
(b) the person not able to give informed legal consent has received
     information according to his/her capacity of understanding regard-
     ing the trial, the risks and the benefits;
(c) the explicit wish of a subject who is capable of forming an opinion
     and assessing this information to refuse participation in, or to be
     withdrawn from, the clinical trial at any time is considered by the
     investigator or where appropriate the principal investigator;
(d) no incentives or financial inducements are given except compensa-
     tion;
(e) such research is essential to validate data obtained in clinical trials
     on persons able to give informed consent or by other research methods
     and relates directly to a life-threatening or debilitating clinical
     condition from which the incapacitated adult concerned suffers;
(f) clinical trials have been designed to minimise pain, discomfort, fear
     and any other foreseeable risk in relation to the disease and devel-
     opmental stage; both the risk threshold and the degree of distress
     shall be specially defined and constantly monitored;

(g) the Ethics Committee, with expertise in the relevant disease and the patient population concerned or after taking advice in clinical, ethical and psychosocial questions in the field of the relevant disease and patient population concerned, has endorsed the protocol;

(h) the interests of the patient always prevail over those of science and society; and

(i) there are grounds for expecting that administering the medicinal product to be tested will produce a benefit to the patient outweighing the risks or produce no risk at all.

Article 6: Ethics Committee

1. For the purposes of implementation of the clinical trials, Member States shall take the measures necessary for establishment and operation of Ethics Committees.

2. The Ethics Committee shall give its opinion, before a clinical trial commences, on any issue requested.

3. In preparing its opinion, the Ethics Committee shall consider, in particular:

    (a) the relevance of the clinical trial and the trial design;

    (b) whether the evaluation of the anticipated benefits and risks as required under Article 3(2)(a) is satisfactory and whether the conclusions are justified;

    (c) the protocol;

    (d) the suitability of the investigator and supporting staff;

    (e) the investigator's brochure;

    (f) the quality of the facilities;

    (g) the adequacy and completeness of the written information to be given and the procedure to be followed for the purpose of obtaining informed consent and the justification for the research on persons incapable of giving informed consent as regards the specific restrictions laid down in Article 3;

    (h) provision for indemnity or compensation in the event of injury or death attributable to a clinical trial;

    (i) any insurance or indemnity to cover the liability of the investigator and sponsor;

    (j) the amounts and, where appropriate, the arrangements for rewarding or compensating investigators and trial subjects and the relevant aspects of any agreement between the sponsor and the site;

    (k) the arrangements for the recruitment of subjects.

4. Notwithstanding the provisions of this Article, a Member State may decide that the competent authority it has designated for the purpose of Article 9 shall be responsible for the consideration of, and the giving of an opinion on, the matters referred to in paragraph 3(h), (i) and (j) of this Article. When a Member State avails itself of this provision, it shall notify the Commission, the other Member States and the Agency.

5. The Ethics Committee shall have a maximum of 60 days from the date of receipt of a valid application to give its reasoned opinion to the applicant and the competent authority in the Member State concerned.

6. Within the period of examination of the application for an opinion, the Ethics Committee may send a single request for information supplementary to that already supplied by the applicant. The period laid down in paragraph 5 shall be suspended until receipt of the supplementary information.

7. No extension to the 60-day period referred to in paragraph 5 shall be permissible except in the case of trials involving medicinal products for gene therapy or somatic cell therapy or medicinal products containing genetically modified organisms. In this case, an extension of a maximum of 30 days shall be permitted. For these products, this 90-day period may be extended by a further 90 days in the event of consultation of a group or a committee in accordance with the regulations and procedures of the Member States concerned. In the case of xenogenic cell therapy, there shall be no time limit to the authorisation period.

Article 7: Single Opinion

For multi-centre clinical trials limited to the territory of a single Member State, Member States shall establish a procedure providing, notwithstanding the number of Ethics Committees, for the adoption of a single opinion for that Member State.

In the case of multi-centre clinical trials carried out in more than one Member State simultaneously, a single opinion shall be given for each Member State concerned by the clinical trial.

Article 8: Detailed Guidance

The Commission, in consultation with Member States and interested parties, shall draw up and publish detailed guidance on the application format and documentation to be submitted in an application for an ethics committee opinion, in particular regarding the information that is given to subjects, and on the appropriate safeguards for the protection of personal data.

Article 9: Commencement of a Clinical Trial

1. Member States shall take the measures necessary to ensure that the procedure described in this Article is followed for commencement of a clinical trial. The sponsor may not start a clinical trial until the Ethics Committee has issued a favourable opinion and inasmuch as the competent authority of the Member State concerned has not informed the sponsor of any grounds for non-acceptance. The procedures to reach these decisions can be run in parallel or not, depending on the sponsor.

2. Before commencing any clinical trial, the sponsor shall be required to submit a valid request for authorisation to the competent authority of the Member State in which the sponsor plans to conduct the clinical trial.

3. If the competent authority of the Member State notifies the sponsor of grounds for non-acceptance, the sponsor may, on one occasion only, amend the content of the request referred to in paragraph 2 in order to take due account of the grounds given. If the sponsor fails to amend the request accordingly, the request shall be considered rejected and the clinical trial may not commence.

4. Consideration of a valid request for authorisation by the competent authority as stated in paragraph 2 shall be carried out as rapidly as possible and may not exceed 60 days. The Member States may lay down a shorter period than 60 days within their area of responsibility if that is in compliance with current practice. The competent authority can nevertheless notify the sponsor before the end of this period that it has no grounds for non-acceptance. No further extensions to the period referred to in the first subparagraph shall be permissible except in the case of trials involving the medicinal products listed in paragraph 6, for which an extension of a maximum of 30 days shall be permitted. For these products, this 90-day period may be extended by a further 90 days in the event of consultation of a group or a committee in accordance with the regulations and procedures of the Member States concerned. In the case of xenogenic cell therapy there shall be no time limit to the authorisation period.

5. Without prejudice to paragraph 6, written authorisation may be required before the commencement of clinical trials for such trials

on medicinal products which do not have a marketing authorisation within the meaning of Directive 65/65/EEC and are referred to in Part A of the Annex to Regulation (EEC) No 2309/93, and other medicinal products with special characteristics, such as medicinal products the active ingredient or active ingredients of which is or are a biological product or biological products of human or animal origin, or contains biological components of human or animal origin, or the manufacturing of which requires such components.

6.   Written authorisation shall be required before commencing clinical trials involving medicinal products for gene therapy, somatic cell therapy including xenogenic cell therapy and all medicinal products containing genetically modified organisms. No gene therapy trials may be carried out which result in modifications to the subject's germ line genetic identity.

7.   This authorisation shall be issued without prejudice to the application of Council Directives 90/219/EEC of 23 April 1990 on the contained use of genetically modified micro-organisms[11] and 90/220/EEC of 23 April 1990 on the deliberate release into the environment of genetically modified organisms[12].

8.   In consultation with Member States, the Commission shall draw up and publish detailed guidance on:

(a) the format and contents of the request referred to in paragraph 2 as well as the documentation to be submitted to support that request, on the quality and manufacture of the investigational medicinal product, any toxicological and pharmacological tests, the protocol and clinical information on the investigational medicinal product including the investigator's brochure;

(b) the presentation and content of the proposed amendment referred to in point (a) of Article 10 on substantial amendments made to the protocol;

(c) the declaration of the end of the clinical trial.

Article 10: Conduct of a Clinical Trial

Amendments may be made to the conduct of a clinical trial following the procedure described hereinafter:

---

[11] OJ L 117, 8.5.1990, p. 1. Directive as last amended by Directive 98/81/EC (OJ L 330, 5.12.1998, p. 13).

[12] OJ L 117, 8.5.1990, p. 15. Directive as last amended by Commission Directive 97/35/EC (OJ L 169, 27.6.1997, p. 72).

(a) after the commencement of the clinical trial, the sponsor may make amendments to the protocol. If those amendments are substantial and are likely to have an impact on the safety of the trial subjects or to change the interpretation of the scientific documents in support of the conduct of the trial, or if they are otherwise significant, the sponsor shall notify the competent authorities of the Member State or Member States concerned of the reasons for, and content of, these amendments and shall inform the ethics committee or committees concerned in accordance with Articles 6 and 9. On the basis of the details referred to in Article 6(3) and in accordance with Article 7, the Ethics Committee shall give an opinion within a maximum of 35 days of the date of receipt of the proposed amendment in good and due form. If this opinion is unfavourable, the sponsor may not implement the amendment to the protocol. If the opinion of the Ethics Committee is favourable and the competent authorities of the Member States have raised no grounds for non-acceptance of the abovementioned substantial amendments, the sponsor shall proceed to conduct the clinical trial following the amended protocol. Should this not be the case, the sponsor shall either take account of the grounds for non-acceptance and adapt the proposed amendment to the protocol accordingly or withdraw the proposed amendment;

(b) without prejudice to point (a), in the light of the circumstances, notably the occurrence of any new event relating to the conduct of the trial or the development of the investigational medicinal product where that new event is likely to affect the safety of the subjects, the sponsor and the investigator shall take appropriate urgent safety measures to protect the subjects against any immediate hazard. The sponsor shall forthwith inform the competent authorities of those new events and the measures taken and shall ensure that the Ethics Committee is notified at the same time;

(c) within 90 days of the end of a clinical trial the sponsor shall notify the competent authorities of the Member State or Member States concerned and the Ethics Committee that the clinical trial has ended. If the trial has to be terminated early, this period shall be reduced to 15 days and the reasons clearly explained.

Article 11: Exchange of Information

1. Member States in whose territory the clinical trial takes place shall enter in a European database, accessible only to the competent authorities of the Member States, the Agency and the Commission:

(a) extracts from the request for authorisation referred to in Article 9(2);

(b) any amendments made to the request, as provided for in Article 9(3);

(c) any amendments made to the protocol, as provided for in point a of Article 10;

(d) the favourable opinion of the Ethics Committee;

(e) the declaration of the end of the clinical trial; and

(f) a reference to the inspections carried out on conformity with good clinical practice.

2. At the substantiated request of any Member State, the Agency or the Commission, the competent authority to which the request for authorisation was submitted shall supply all further information concerning the clinical trial in question other than the data already in the European database.

3. In consultation with the Member States, the Commission shall draw up and publish detailed guidance on the relevant data to be included in this European database, which it operates with the assistance of the Agency, as well as the methods for electronic communication of the data. The detailed guidance thus drawn up shall ensure that the confidentiality of the data is strictly observed.

Article 12: Suspension of the Trial or Infringements

1. Where a Member State has objective grounds for considering that the conditions in the request for authorisation referred to in Article 9(2) are no longer met or has information raising doubts about the safety or scientific validity of the clinical trial, it may suspend or prohibit the clinical trial and shall notify the sponsor thereof. Before the Member State reaches its decision it shall, except where there is imminent risk, ask the sponsor and/or the investigator for their opinion, to be delivered within one week. In this case, the competent authority concerned shall forthwith inform the other competent authorities, the Ethics Committee concerned, the Agency and the Commission of its decision to suspend or prohibit the trial and of the reasons for the decision.

2. Where a competent authority has objective grounds for considering that the sponsor or the investigator or any other person involved in the conduct of the trial no longer meets the obligations laid down, it shall forthwith inform him thereof, indicating the course of action which he must take to remedy this state of affairs. The competent authority concerned shall forthwith inform the Ethics Committee,

the other competent authorities and the Commission of this course of action.

Article 13: Manufacture and Import of Investigational Medicinal Products

1. Member States shall take all appropriate measures to ensure that the manufacture or importation of investigational medicinal products is subject to the holding of authorisation. In order to obtain the authorisation, the applicant and, subsequently, the holder of the authorisation, shall meet at least the requirements defined in accordance with the procedure referred to in Article 21(2).

2. Member States shall take all appropriate measures to ensure that the holder of the authorisation referred to in paragraph 1 has permanently and continuously at his disposal the services of at least one qualified person who, in accordance with the conditions laid down in Article 23 of the second Council Directive 75/319/EEC of 20 May 1975 on the approximation of provisions laid down by law, regulation or administrative action relating to proprietary medicinal products[13], is responsible in particular for carrying out the duties specified in paragraph 3 of this Article.

3. Member States shall take all appropriate measures to ensure that the qualified person referred to in Article 21 of Directive 75/319/EEC, without prejudice to his relationship with the manufacturer or importer, is responsible, in the context of the procedures referred to in Article 25 of the said Directive, for ensuring:

    (a) in the case of investigational medicinal products manufactured in the Member State concerned, that each batch of medicinal products has been manufactured and checked in compliance with the requirements of Commission Directive 91/356/EEC of 13 June 1991 laying down the principles and guidelines of good manufacturing practice for medicinal products for human use[14], the product specification file and the information notified pursuant to Article 9(2) of this Directive;

    (b) in the case of investigational medicinal products manufactured in a third country, that each production batch has been manufactured and checked in accordance with standards of good manufacturing practice at least equivalent to those laid down in Commission Directive 91/356/EEC, in accordance with the

---

[13] OJ L 147, 9.6.1975, p. 13. Directive as last amended by Council Directive 93/39/EC (OJ L 214, 24.8.1993, p. 22).

[14] OJ L 193, 17.7.1991, p. 30

product specification file, and that each production batch has been checked in accordance with the information notified pursuant to Article 9(2) of this Directive;

(c) in the case of an investigational medicinal product which is a comparator product from a third country, and which has a marketing authorisation, where the documentation certifying that each production batch has been manufactured in conditions at least equivalent to the standards of good manufacturing practice referred to above cannot be obtained, that each production batch has undergone all relevant analyses, tests or checks necessary to confirm its quality in accordance with the information notified pursuant to Article 9(2) of this Directive. Detailed guidance on the elements to be taken into account when evaluating products with the object of releasing batches within the Community shall be drawn up pursuant to the good manufacturing practice guidelines, and in particular Annex 13 to the said guidelines. Such guidelines will be adopted in accordance with the procedure referred to in Article 21(2) of this Directive and published in accordance with Article 19a of Directive 75/319/EEC. Insofar as the provisions laid down in (a), (b) or (c) are complied with, investigational medicinal products shall not have to undergo any further checks if they are imported into another Member State together with batch release certification signed by the qualified person.

4. In all cases, the qualified person must certify in a register or equivalent document that each production batch satisfies the provisions of this Article. The said register or equivalent document shall be kept up to date as operations are carried out and shall remain at the disposal of the agents of the competent authority for the period specified in the provisions of the Member States concerned. This period shall in any event be not less than five years.

5. Any person engaging in activities as the qualified person referred to in Article 21 of Directive 75/319/EEC as regards investigational medicinal products at the time when this Directive is applied in the Member State where that person is, but without complying with the conditions laid down in Articles 23 and 24 of that Directive, shall be authorised to continue those activities in the Member State concerned.

Article 14: Labelling

The particulars to appear in at least the official language(s) of the Member State on the outer packaging of investigational medicinal products or, where there is no outer packaging, on the immediate packaging, shall be published by the Commission in the good manufacturing practice guidelines on investigational medicinal products adopted in accordance with Article 19a of Directive 75/319/EEC. In addition, these guidelines shall lay down adapted provisions relating to labelling for investigational medicinal products intended for clinical trials with the following characteristics:

- the planning of the trial does not require particular manufacturing or packaging processes;
- the trial is conducted with medicinal products with, in the Member States concerned by the study, a marketing authorisation within the meaning of Directive 65/65/EEC, manufactured or imported in accordance with the provisions of Directive 75/319/EEC;
- the patients participating in the trial have the same characteristics as those covered by the indication specified in the abovementioned authorisation.

Article 15: Verification of Compliance of Investigational Medicinal Products with Good Clinical and Manufacturing Practice

1. To verify compliance with the provisions on good clinical and manufacturing practice, Member States shall appoint inspectors to inspect the sites concerned by any clinical trial conducted, particularly the trial site or sites, the manufacturing site of the investigational medicinal product, any laboratory used for analyses in the clinical trial and/or the sponsor's premises. The inspections shall be conducted by the competent authority of the Member State concerned, which shall inform the Agency; they shall be carried out on behalf of the Community and the results shall be recognised by all the other Member States. These inspections shall be coordinated by the Agency, within the framework of its powers as provided for in Regulation (EEC) No 2309/93. A Member State may request assistance from another Member State in this matter.

2. Following inspection, an inspection report shall be prepared. It must be made available to the sponsor while safeguarding confidential aspects. It may be made available to the other Member States, to the Ethics Committee and to the Agency, at their reasoned request.

3. At the request of the Agency, within the framework of its powers as provided for in Regulation (EEC) No 2309/93, or of one of the Member States concerned, and following consultation with the Member States concerned, the Commission may request a new

inspection should verification of compliance with this Directive reveal differences between Member States.

4. Subject to any arrangements which may have been concluded between the Community and third countries, the Commission, upon receipt of a reasoned request from a Member State or on its own initiative, or a Member State may propose that the trial site and/or the sponsor's premises and/or the manufacturer established in a third country undergo an inspection. The inspection shall be carried out by duly qualified Community inspectors.

5. The detailed guidelines on the documentation relating to the clinical trial, which shall constitute the master file on the trial, archiving, qualifications of inspectors and inspection procedures to verify compliance of the clinical trial in question with this Directive shall be adopted and revised in accordance with the procedure referred to in Article 21(2).

Article 16: Notification of Adverse Events

1. The investigator shall report all serious adverse events immediately to the sponsor except for those that the protocol or investigator's brochure identifies as not requiring immediate reporting. The immediate report shall be followed by detailed, written reports. The immediate and follow-up reports shall identify subjects by unique code numbers assigned to the latter.

2. Adverse events and/or laboratory abnormalities identified in the protocol as critical to safety evaluations shall be reported to the sponsor according to the reporting requirements and within the time periods specified in the protocol.

3. For reported deaths of a subject, the investigator shall supply the sponsor and the Ethics Committee with any additional information requested.

4. The sponsor shall keep detailed records of all adverse events which are reported to him by the investigator or investigators. These records shall be submitted to the Member States in whose territory the clinical trial is being conducted, if they so request.

Article 17: Notification of Serious Adverse Reactions

1. (a) The sponsor shall ensure that all relevant information about suspected serious unexpected adverse reactions that are fatal or life-threatening is recorded and reported as soon as possible to the

competent authorities in all the Member States concerned, and to the Ethics Committee, and in any case no later than seven days after knowledge by the sponsor of such a case, and that relevant follow-up information is subsequently communicated within an additional eight days.

(b) All other suspected serious unexpected adverse reactions shall be reported to the competent authorities concerned and to the Ethics Committee concerned as soon as possible but within a maximum of fifteen days of first knowledge by the sponsor.

(c) Each Member State shall ensure that all suspected unexpected serious adverse reactions to an investigational medicinal product which are brought to its attention are recorded.

(d) The sponsor shall also inform all investigators.

2. Once a year throughout the clinical trial, the sponsor shall provide the Member States in whose territory the clinical trial is being conducted and the Ethics Committee with a listing of all suspected serious adverse reactions which have occurred over this period and a report of the subjects' safety.

3. (a) Each Member State shall see to it that all suspected unexpected serious adverse reactions to an investigational medicinal product which are brought to its attention are immediately entered in a European database to which, in accordance with Article 11(1), only the competent authorities of the Member States, the Agency and the Commission shall have access.

(b) The Agency shall make the information notified by the sponsor available to the competent authorities of the Member States.

Article 18: Guidance Concerning Reports

The Commission, in consultation with the Agency, Member States and interested parties, shall draw up and publish detailed guidance on the collection, verification and presentation of adverse event/reaction reports, together with decoding procedures for unexpected serious adverse reactions.

Article 19: General Provisions

This Directive is without prejudice to the civil and criminal liability of the sponsor or the investigator. To this end, the sponsor or a legal representative of the sponsor must be established in the Community. Unless Member States have established precise conditions for exceptional circumstances, investigational medicinal products and, as the case may be, the devices used for their administration shall be made available free of charge by the sponsor. The Member States shall inform the Commission of such conditions.

Article 20: Adaptation to Scientific and Technical Progress

This Directive shall be adapted to take account of scientific and technical progress in accordance with the procedure referred to in Article 21(2).

Article 21: Committee Procedure

1. The Commission shall be assisted by the Standing Committee on Medicinal Products for Human Use, set up by Article 2b of Directive 75/318/EEC (hereinafter referred to as the Committee).
2. Where reference is made to this paragraph, Articles 5 and 7 of Decision 1999/468/EC shall apply, having regard to the provisions of Article 8 thereof. The period referred to in Article 5(6) of Decision 1999/468/EC shall be set at three months.
3. The Committee shall adopt its rules of procedure.

Article 22: Application

1. Member States shall adopt and publish before 1 May 2003 the laws, regulations and administrative provisions necessary to comply with this Directive. They shall forthwith inform the Commission thereof. They shall apply these provisions at the latest with effect from 1 May 2004. When Member States adopt these provisions, they shall contain a reference to this Directive or shall be accompanied by such reference on the occasion of their official publication. The methods of making such reference shall be laid down by Member States.
2. Member States shall communicate to the Commission the text of the provisions of national law which they adopt in the field governed by this Directive.

Article 23: Entry into Force

This Directive shall enter into force on the day of its publication in the Official Journal of the European Communities.

Article 24: Addressees

This Directive is addressed to the Member States.

Done at Luxembourg, 4 April 2001.

For the European Parliament
The President
N. Fontaine

For the Council
The President
B. Rosengren

Part three

JUSTICE IN HEALTH CARE

INTRODUCTION

For years, the issue of justice was a marginal theme in bioethics. The principle of justice played a role in social ethics, but was not considered important in the micro-ethical debates of bioethics. The increasing possibilities in organ transplantation, however, played a decisive role in bringing it onto the bioethics agenda. The broad application of the transplantation technique led to a scarcity in the supply of transplants. This new situation forced ethicists to answer questions concerning their fair distribution: given the scarcity of organs, which patients were entitled to receive an organ from a donor? What could be the basis for a just organ allocation? In other words, ethicists were invited to re-think traditional theories of distributive justice in light of these new problems caused by the increase in medical-technological possibilities.

Nowadays, our health care systems are still faced with the problem of scarcity but it is the very basis of our health care systems that is affected, namely health care funding. The causes for this crisis are known: the application of expensive technological interventions in health care generate major costs as well as increased health care needs due to the proportional rise of the ageing population. Both have great impact on the required health care budgets. The subsequent allocation and rationing problems have serious consequences for day-to-day medical practice and for the lives of individual patients. Consider the following cases:[1]

---

[1] For a more extensive version of these cases, see W. DEKKERS, *Just Health Care. The Case of Waiting Lists*, p. 321-328 and P. BOITTE & B. CADORÉ, *The Allocation of Health Care Resources. Economic Constraints and Access to Health Care*, p. 299-320 in this volume.

Mrs. A is an enthusiastic hockey player. While playing hockey, her left knee is severely injured. Her general practitioner refers her to the orthopaedic surgeon at the hospital where she works as a nurse. The orthopaedic surgeon's first thought is a rupture of the anterior cruciate ligament, but to be sure of the diagnosis an arthroscopy is needed. The waiting time for this diagnostic procedure is about three weeks. After three weeks the diagnosis is confirmed. The most appropriate therapy is a reconstruction of the ruptured ligament. The waiting time for this kind of operation is twelve weeks. Mrs. A is disappointed about the waiting time, and has no choice but to accept it. Nine months after her knee injury (fifteen weeks of waiting and five months for revalidation) she can go back to work again.

A 60-year old woman that lives on minimal social security receives care in a cardiology ward. She constantly asks the doctors and nurses to be released from the hospital. After a profound discussion with the patient, the staff becomes aware of her numerous financial problems.

A 37-year old computer scientist has been fired from his job. He sets up as a private self-employed expert but is not very successful. He falls behind in his insurance contributions and has to live of his wife's earnings. He is admitted to the hospital for attempted suicide. He urgently calls for help from his wife and from the social security services.

These cases illustrate how far-reaching decisions on budget and allocation can be for individual cases (W. Dekkers). Therefore certain problems that arise in this context need serious consideration. On a general level, we state that policy-makers, and the general public, will have to decide how our societies should cope with the current crisis. This will imply policymaking both external and internal to the health care system, namely political choices concerning the total health care budget on the one hand and clear measures to optimise the use of available resources within health care on the other (rationing).

Before making choices in health care, however, the role of government in health care organisation must be spelled out. Traditionally, there are major differences in government participation in health care between the US and the European continent. Seeing health care as a private commodity, for example, is fundamentally different from including health care in the package of basic rights as it is the case in most European countries. These choices reflect basic values in democratic societies.

The contributions of this section aim at a clarification and careful analysis of the questions at hand. What are the objectives of our health care system and how is it shaped by the current crisis (P. Boitte & B. Cadoré)? Which are the different systems that are operational and what are the underlying values (Y. Denier & T. Meulenbergs)? Who will have to take the ultimate decisions (M. Defever) and what are the perspectives for the future (A. Vandevelde)?

RESOURCE ALLOCATION IN HEALTH CARE

Who will decide?

Mia Defever

1.1. Introduction

The start of the new millennium was enthusiastically celebrated all over the world. It was an occasion for exceptional festivities yet also for special reflection about the future, about *the road to take*. A Belgian Foundation brought fifty young people from different countries together to discuss the future, to outline society for the year 2025. Remarkably, the ethical debate in relation to health care was at the core of discussions. It was unanimously agreed that the future has to be ethical. Ethical reflections on an affordable health care system accessible for the total population and not only for the happy few took centre stage.[1] Apparently, ethics in health care is becoming a common concern, a priority in modelling the future. Why are ethical reflections on health care taking the limelight? What is happening to our health care systems?

1.2. Social Ethics

These issues of common concern look obvious. Health is a fundamental prerequisite for engaging in the different aspects of social life, for participating to the labour market, which requests creativity, flexibility and dynamic commitment. An excellent health status is

---

[1] *De toekomst moet ethisch zijn*, in *De Standaard*, 21 April 2000.

critical for an energetic response to the challenges of current life. Moreover, although *health care* is only but one aspect contributing to *health*, health care can do a lot to restore and support health. It is an achievement of modern medicine that it can prolong life where death would have been inevitable and can provide good quality of life to persons who would otherwise have been desperate.

Ethical reflections on health care, especially on *medical care*, are not new. Some of the issues discussed in medical ethics are as old as medical care itself. Ethical commitments to health care have grown in the past twenty years and have given way to outstanding expertise, to the development of highly recognised centres expressing a commonly concern about an appropriate and ethical sound answer to biomedical developments.[2] A closer look at the definitions teach us that medical ethics relates to the deep concern about what is ethically acceptable in approaching a person in ill health. Medical ethics is defined as the public theatre whereby, around the issues of life and death, health and illness, the fundamental values of a society are discussed.[3] Or, ethics are the reflection on human behaviour, on difficult situations and their related values and norms; the efforts to understand and analyse the image of the human being and to test this image on its humanity.[4] Of particular interest is an approach which takes the focus of ethical thinking beyond the controversial issues of health and health care and into the activities of daily care delivery. Each care procedure is a process of decision-making based on a value judgement. A value judgement about what is right for the patient in that particular situation, even in the absence of scientific evidence. The *ethical appeal* is emerging in all daily care activities, which are fundamental human relations.[5]

Three elements seem to be salient: Ethical reflection should lead to a more *decent* and compassionate relation with the patient, to an increase in the quality of attention to the sick person as opposed to a utilitarian reduction of the sick person to an object. Second, the

[2] M.A.M DE WACHTER, *Gezondheidsethiek: vragen vanuit de biomedische ontwikkelingen*, in *Tijdschrift voor Theologie* 26 (1986) 5-14.

[3] H.A. TEN HAVE, *Ethiek in de gezondheidszorg*, in *Ethiek en recht in de gezondheidszorg*, Deventer, 1990, p. 121.

[4] P. SPORKEN, *Ethiek en gezondheidszorg*, Baarn, 1979.

[5] P. SCHOTSMANS, *En de mens schiep de mens*, Kapellen, 1992.

ethical concerns are largely centred on *individual* events and *personal* situations. Third, ethics refers to social norms about what is appropriate behaviour. This means that the prevailing values and beliefs of a society mould the ethical reflection. In that respect, a two-dimensional aspect of biomedical ethics emerges. They are, on the one hand, solid concepts transcending ad-hoc or trivial reasoning but on the other hand, dynamic concepts which change over time due to a variety of factors. What is accepted at one moment in time was not accepted before and what is allowed in one society is forbidden in another.

However, what seems to be missing in those definitions is the concern about the health care *system* in which daily health care provision takes place, the ethical reflection beyond the individual events. The related literature is much less abundant and the research more recent. *Social ethics* in health care can be considered as a concept referring to the macro context of health care delivery. To put it simply, health care is using a mix of resources to cope with the health care needs of a population with the objective of reaching a certain outcome. But whose needs are we talking about? Who is defining these needs? On which principles will resource allocation be based? What are the criteria for evaluating outcome? The complex issues of needs, outcome and resource allocation are indubitably *ethical issues*. While discussing a semantic distinction between medical ethics and social ethics is essentially a pedantic issue, the field of social ethics in health care requires particular attention. Social ethics, sometimes called institutional ethics, goes beyond the questions of good and bad, allowed or not allowed, and focuses on the *fairness* and *justice* of the *system*.

In other words, *fairness* and *distributive justice* are at the core of this discussion. They are the key concepts for approaching the ethics of resource allocation. If health is such an important issue and if health care is instrumental for reaching that objective, then what is the commitment of a society to reach that goal when developing its health care system? What are the principles that guide the organisation and financing of health care? What are the distributive ethics? Ethical reflection on an individual medical problem is not possible without an understanding of the social-ethical dimension, e.g. what can decent patient care mean when that patient has no access to health care anyway?

1.3. Globalisation and Solidarity

Health care systems are not loose entities. They are determined by historical developments, and reflect the social, economic and political situation of a country. In that respect, the striking differences between the health care systems in the United States and Europe can be understood. The principles of distributive ethics of both systems are different. US health care systems are much more market-driven in comparison to European systems, where social insurance is prevalent.[6]

European nations have become welfare states through comprehensive yet expensive social security systems based on the principles of *solidarity* and *equity*, providing social benefits and social support in case of illness, impairment, poverty and unemployment. Jacques Delors, former President of the European Union, called Europe's welfare states "the third way of being of Europe", an improbable combination of personal freedom and public support in comparison with the United States and the former Soviet Union.[7] Europeans have, overall, been proud of their social security system, mainly operational by two different models, a National Health Service or 'Beveridge model', with the United Kingdom as an example, and a social security system or 'Bismarck model', with its origins in Germany and a variety of mixed formats, especially in the Southern European countries. Social solidarity as a distributive ethic has made health care services available, accessible and affordable for the major share of the population. However, today the fundamental paradigms of solidarity and social equity are increasingly debated, a process that is called *solidarity revisited*, reflecting a diminished willingness to pay for expensive social security, a shrinking of benefits, a less generous support system and an emphasis on personal responsibility for health and welfare. Questions are asked about the solidarity between the generations, among regions, between social classes, and between the sick and the healthy.[8]

---

[6] U. REINHARDT, *Accountable Health care: Is it Compatible with Social Solidarity?* London, 1997.

[7] Verbal communication by Prof. Chris Schutyser, *Secretary General of the Standing Committee of the Hospitals of the European Union.*

[8] *Choices in Health Care*, Report by the Ministry of Welfare, Health and Cultural Affairs, The Netherlands, Rijswijk, 1992

Moreover, it is repeatedly asked whether we are facing the end of the welfare state in the wake of globalisation. Globalisation refers to the internationalisation of the markets, to a world driven by economy. Globalisation has a persistent influence on politics, minimising the differences, emphasising similarities. It cannot be denied that the pressure from the economic unification is massive. Although globalisation entails a better world-market with fewer barriers and a booming economy, the danger is real that the successes favour selected parts of the population, the *haves*, to the disadvantage of the *have-nots*. The World Trade Organisation (WTO) is the main organisation putting economic globalisation into effect. For the WTO globalisation does not mean world government or the effective international development of policies aside from *trade* policies. There is no body comparable to the WTO to promote and protect public health and no global regulatory structure to assure that the market functions without doing undue harm to individuals. This brings us to the poignant principle of distributive justice among continents, among the developed and developing world. The WTO ran into serious difficulties at the Ministerial meeting in Seattle, in December 1999. A large part of the public protest against the WTO was aimed at its promotion of trade without attention of public health and other social concerns.[9] This clearly alludes to the collective ethical concern of people no longer accepting the neglect of social aspects in trade negotiations, or attention to the distributive ethics on a worldwide level.

The effects of globalisation on social security are also witnessed in Europe. The social safety net is shrinking to streamline economic collaboration and there is uneasiness about economics prevailing on politics, whereby an economic paradigm with less social concern could become dominant. Increasingly, similar to Japan and the United States, Europe relies on low-priced labour in Eastern Europe and third world countries. Those parts of Europe, not capable of following the globalisation rules, fear impoverishment, with an increase of people living below the poverty line. The gap between the rich and the poor seems poised to become larger within and among European countries.

It is encouraging to witness that politicians in office at the start of the new millennium express major concerns about the waning of the

---

[9] D. BANTA, *President's Message: Health Technology Assessment*, in *The Newsletter of The International Society of Technology Assessment in Health Care* 7/1 (2000) 4.

welfare state and are proposing systematic adjustments. A new architecture of the welfare state seems necessary since social security systems conceived decades ago were based on social configurations totally different from social life today. The age of retirement for example, fixed at 65 is at odds with current life expectancy at birth; people in industrialised countries expect to live past age 75 which is about 30 years longer than their ancestors did a hundred years ago, when the system of pensions was installed. The new concepts promulgate the *active welfare state* away from a passive support in case of needs, towards the creation of opportunities for active participation in society.[10] The traditional social protection is linked to the promotion of possibilities for active engagement. Such ideas are clearly emphasising ethical reflection on the organisation of society. It is a passionate plea for social concerns about the macro-economic organisation of Europe: an appeal for the *Social Europe* as a role model instead of the market model from the United States.

1.4. Health Care Reforms

Questioning the welfare state has major repercussions for health care. A clear message emerged from the European ministers of health, at an informal conference in Noordwijk, the Netherlands, already in 1991: *all countries of the European Community will need to limit their spending, to make choices in health care and to set priorities.* The urge to limit health care spending has led to important reform programmes.

Reform programmes are not unique for this decade; three waves of reforms have been witnessed. The first wave occurred after World War II. The main goal was to provide accessibility and availability of health care and universal and equitable coverage of services. All attention went to the hospital, perceived as the ultimate, sole and central provider of health care. A second wave of health care reforms was witnessed in the early 1970s. For the first time questions were asked about the rising health care costs in line with revolts against well-established institutions. Sociologists such as Ivan Illich[11], who pointed at iatrogenic diseases with the epigram, headed the attacks

---

[10] F. VANDENBROUCKE, *Europa als een actieve welvaartsstaat*, Den Uyl-Lecture, Amsterdam, 13 December 1999.

[11] I. ILLICH, *Medical Nemesis. The Expropriation of Health*, London, 1975.

on health care systems *"health care is bad for your health"*. Hospitals and medical technology lost their credibility. Substitution strategies were proposed. Reforms were predominantly structural and managerial. The current third wave of reforms started at the end of the 80s and continues to face the issue of an affordable system while preserving high quality care. The Organisation for Economical Cooperation and Development (OECD)[12] calls the current reforms, *evolutionary* reforms, an on-going reform process in search of the appropriate balance between costs and quality in an era of revolutionary developments of science and technology and shifts in society.[13]

Rationing seems to be at the core of current reform programmes. Rationing refers to limiting and restricting, to reduction and implosion of privileges that formerly were taken for granted, as evidenced in the organisation of social life. Although health care resources have in principle always been limited, at moments in time there has been an *illusion* of infinite resources. During the 1960s and early 1970s, whilst there were major advances in medical science and technology, governments gave little attention to expenditures and efficiency of health care systems. In retrospect, this may be explained by the ease with which health care was financed. Real incomes were rising and there was little resistance to increases in health care expenditure. The explicit attention of governments to the health care sector in the 1990s was dictated by the growing concern regarding the increasing *public deficits*, especially in the wake of the *Maastricht Treaty*, which specified that member states must reduce public deficits to 3% of the GNP by 1997. Controlling the public deficits by limiting health care expenditures became the first objective of reform programmes that were introduced in almost every European country. The urge to reach this objective by reform programmes prevailed over attention to a sound health care system itself.

[12] M.W. Raffel, *Health Care and Reform in Industrialised Countries*, Pennsylvania, 1997.

[13] *The Reform of Health Care Systems: A Review of Seventeen OECD Countries*, Health Policy Studies N° 5, Paris, 1994.

1.5. Health Care Reforms: A Response to Changes in Health Care and Society

At first glance, reforms to cope with limited resources seem an ethical paradox in itself. The services sector in Europe developed at the beginning of the last century as a result of the economic surplus. The pace of economic growth in the twentieth century had been remarkable. Between 1913 and 1989, the GDP per capita (adjusted for inflation) in OECD countries rose nearly four-fold, with especially a rapid growth in the quarter century following 1950.[14] Consequently, there was a legitimate reason to ask questions about the reasons for health care downsizing at a moment of economic expansion, about the willingness of society to invest in the health care sector. The situation however is much more complex, requesting a closer look at the determinants of current reform programmes.

A variety of intensive interrelated shifts, in both society and health care, lead to an increase in the demand for health care and an increase in its *utilisation* among all layers of the population. Four shifts are worth highlighting. In the first place, there are the shifts in social life, often radical and silent such as the demographic changes, including the ageing of the population and the increasing participation of women into the workforce. There is the growing autonomy among people and social groups, less bound by stringent rules from traditional institutions such as family, religion, neighbourhood, and social class. More people are living in single households, living alone with fewer opportunities for support by relatives in the case of illness. Secondly, developments in medical science and technology offer a myriad of new diagnostic and therapeutic possibilities. Before the early decades of the twentieth century, health gains in Europe depended predominantly on improvements in living standards and abundant food supplies. In the twentieth century, they increasingly mirror the powerful influence of advances in medical science and technology. For example, tissue engineered implants, the progress of Minimal Invasive Technology, the prospects of the human genome, medical imaging and the coming of age of e-health, the latter quoted

---

[14] R. PETRELLA, *Waarheen met de welvaartstaat?*, Conference at the seminar series De Ziekteverzekering Herbekeken: Beleidsopties voor gezondheidszorg, University of Leuven, 16 December 1998.

as being responsible for the most important mutation of Western societies since the Industrial Revolution. Third, there are the shifts in the burden of disease especially characterised by chronic degenerative diseases affecting quality of life. New diseases are at the forefront owing to the effects of environmental threats, such as air, water and chemicals leading to pollution, poisoning and related cancers; new emerging and re-emerging infections, such as AIDS and tuberculosis; and social and behavioural pathologies influenced by lifestyles such as violence and drug abuse. And finally, *patient behaviour is changing*. Patients have become critical *consumers* of health care, selecting, controlling, praising or reproving the services provided for, what Rudolf Klein is calling *the generalisation of middle class attitudes*.[15] Physicians seem more willing to give in to patient preferences even if the procedures are inappropriate. This increasing *consumerism* is especially witnessed among the more affluent health care consumers.[16]

1.6. Health Care Rationing

Policy makers are facing these growing medical possibilities and increasing demands while budgets allocated to health care are shrinking. Consequently, not everything that is scientifically feasible can be offered, and reform programmes focus on rationing, and priority setting in the process of resource allocation. Rationing and priority setting are intermingled concepts referring to choices in health care. Rationing has a more negative connotation, with a focus on the denial of services or potential benefits, on the exclusion from certain services. Priority on the other hand has a more positive connotation emphasising the extra benefit that, by preference, could be given to a certain group of the population or for a particular group of disease or for certain health care related activities.[17] But whatever the semantics of the concepts are, the unpleasant basic feeling is surfacing that choices and thus restrictions cannot be avoided.

---

[15] R. KLEIN, *Choices in Health care*, paper presented at the 58th European Health Policy Forum, Brussels, December 1993.

[16] R. SALTMAN, J. FIGUERAS & C. SAKELLARIDES, (eds.), *Critical Challenges for Health Care Reform in Europe*, Buckingham, 1998.

[17] A. EDGAR, S. SALEK, D. SHICKLE, & D. COHEN, *The Ethical QALY. Ethical Issues in Health care Resource Allocation*, Haslemere, 1998.

Rationing is often legitimised by an economic paradigm. Reform programmes should make the health care system more *efficient*, both at the macro-level (costs should not exceed a certain share of national resources), and at the micro-level (the mix of services should secure high quality health outcome at a minimal cost). A first paradox is immediately emerging. Reforming towards more efficiency is allegedly made because of inefficiency in the system, because of waste[18]. However, what expenditure is for policy makers is *income* for the large groups of persons and agencies involved in the health care industry. Physicians, managers, nurses, hospitals, pharmaceutical and medical technical companies make their income from delivering care or supplying the health care system. In opposition to the ideas of rationing, the provider groups complain about little appreciation and underpayment[19] and defend better patient care as an ethical imperative for increased funds. Ambivalence towards prioritisation reigns since choices might curtail a number of their vested interests, and privileges and strange alliances hampering the implementation of priority setting are being witnessed between traditional antagonists in health care. This brings us to the ethics of payment of providers and to the incentives that lead health care providers to over- or under-treatmentpatients – over-treatment is likely to happen when it generates more income.

In current rationing reforms, a greater accountability is requested from patients and emphasis is placed on responsibility for the personal health condition and for utilisation of health care resources. However, there is a danger that this emphasis on self-responsibility might favour the healthy and wealthy in society. Lifestyle diseases, for example those linked to behaviours such as smoking, inactivity, or inappropriate nutrition, have emerged in the solidarity debate, which tends to blame the diseased and to question entitlement to care, what Jan Blanpain called "the tyranny of the healthy".[20] Norway decided to place smokers at the bottom of the waiting list for surgical interventions. Questions arise such as: is someone entitled

---

[18] U. REINHARDT, *Accountable Health Care. Is it compatible with social solidarity?* London, 1997.

[19] *Ibid.*, p. 21.

[20] Verbal communication by Jan Blanpain, MD, Professor Emeritus at the University in Leuven, Belgium.

to receive blood when he refuses to donate blood? Is an alcoholic entitled to a liver transplant? This is controlling health care demand, but according to whose choices? Increasingly, the vocal, assertive patient, capable of defining his needs, sets norms for what is acceptable in health care. This is another ethical paradox invoking the interests of the weak, less articulate population groups, such as the frail elderly, the mentally ill, the poor, those suffering from chronic disease. In the Netherlands, the rich are uninsured and out of the system. In the US the poor are uninsured and out of the system. As already indicated, the middle class largely dominates society, and middle classes perceive solidarity as solidarity-for-me. The real risk groups are often ignored.[21]

1.7. Rationing and Government

The reluctance of governments to become engaged in a national debate on priority setting and, in particular, the ethical issues that underpin it, has been striking.[22] The guiding principles of clinical effectiveness and cost-effectiveness are at times juxtaposed to political effectiveness. Most of the choices in health care are choices that hurt and quite often politicians try to avoid them or avoid being explicit because the policy measures that result are unpopular. Therefore, policies may be implemented in a manner which looks impeccable on paper, but somehow in practice have allowed vested interests to creep in, so that the powerful, rather than the needy, benefit.[23]

The influence of politics is very often misunderstood. The state or government that is issuing policies is not a disinterested handler of public goods, but an actor in its own right, pursuing its own goals. The state is not a neutral arbiter among competing groups, but a self-interested actor, making alliances with other major interest groups, resulting in policies which are not necessarily in the public interest. In principle, the rationing of health care policy should be

[21] L. GUNNIG-SCHEPERS, *Why Choices in Health Care?*, paper presented at the 61st EHPF-Meeting, Choices in Health Care: The Problems of Implementation, Leuven, May 20-21, 1996

[22] M. McKEE & J. FIGUERAS, *Setting Priorities: Can Britain learn from Sweden?*, in *Rationing. Talk and Action in Health Care*, London, 1997, p. 203.

[23] C. BARKER, *The Health Care Policy Process*, London, 1996.

based on the analysis of *needs* and the ultimate goal in defining needs is to understand inequality[24]. Needs are located within the socio-cultural context of a given society, and cannot be understood without understanding the key values of that society.[25] However, because it is difficult to define needs and inequality, those concepts can be used in a perverse or cynical way leading to policies that increase instead of decrease inequality. Quite often vague definitions put forth, as are definitions with a specific purpose serving the interests of certain groups, such as a political party, a ministerial cabinet, an advisory council, a provider group, or supporting a policy.[26] A similar process arises when outcomes are considered. A holistic concept of outcomes has yet not been used. Outcome analysis is largely disease based and consequently rather fragmented, such as the evaluation of the reduction of a tumour due to therapeutic procedures, and not the increase in health status expressed in quality of life. Such kind of disease based outcome analysis has lead to vertical programmes of care provision and has reinforced the power of bureaucracies to determine priorities in allocating resources for diagnostic and therapeutic instruments.

1.8. Rationing in Health Care: Who should decide?

The fundamental questions in the process of rationing health care – whom should decide and on which criteria – seem to be very difficult. In practice clinicians, managers, and government officials take the bulk of rationing decisions but recently a variety of mechanisms have been proposed to involve larger groups of society.

Health economists have devoted substantial attention to the analysis of priority setting and there has been a trend to use evidence from economic evaluations in support of policy making, especially at the beginning of the priority setting approaches. However, increasingly, in different countries scepticism has grown regarding

---

[24] G. WALT, *Health Policy: an Introduction to Process and Power*, London, 1994.

[25] For a thoroughly analysis of health needs and health care needs see the contribution of Yvonne Denier and Tom Meulenbergs in this volume, p. 265-298.

[26] D. BLACK, *Deprivation and Health*, in *British Medical Journal* 307 (1993) 1603-1601.

about priority decisions based upon explicit economic criteria.[27] For example, the highly promoted Oregon model lost credibility.[28] The reason for the declining prevalence of economic evaluation seems to be the growing concern about the wider social, medical and political context within which priorities are made.[29] Choices relate to the complex reality of social life in which health and illness are intensely value-laden. Therefore, values interfere intensely in resource allocation to health care. Choices in health care seem to be at the crossroads of individual medical ethics and social ethics, where rational compromises seem to be difficult. Logical reasoning and ethical commitment with the objective of collective health gains looks perfectly feasible on paper. But the debate will undoubtedly be oriented in a particular direction fuelled by personal values, situations and experience, and by politics. As already indicated, policy making is not a rational process based on clear objectives, but a set of activities with a logic on its own made by people with emotions, driven both by public concerns and by individual objectives and emotions. The failure of major rationing committees such as the *Committee on Choices in Health Care* in the Netherlands and the Committee of the Canadian Medical Association is attributed to this genuine but misguiding belief in explicit, transparent and rational policy making.[30]

The public involvement in rationing health care has always been a question of special concern and at times there seemed to be a growing public interest in explicitly trying to define what types of health care might no longer be provided by public resources. A variety of mechanisms is being explored to develop public participation in programming rationing. In 1995 the Rationing Agenda Group (RAG)[31] was formed in the UK, to promote a continuing, broad and deep debate about rationing in the NHS. The RAG group consists of people from all parts of health care whose views on the substantive issues of rationing differ widely. The RAG as a whole is united on

---

[27] R. ROBINSON, *Limits to Rationality: Economics, Economists and Priority Setting*, in *Health Policy*, 49/1-2 (1999) 13-26.

[28] R. TER MEULEN & H. TEN HAVE (eds.), *Samen kiezen in de zorg, Het voorbeeld Oregon*, Baarn, 1993.

[29] R. ROBINSON, *Limits to Rationality: Economics, Economists and Priority Setting*, in *Health Policy* 49/1-2 (1999) 13-26.

[30] T. MARMOR & D. BOYUM, *Medical Care and Public Policy: The Benefits and Burdens of Asking Fundamental Questions*, in *Health Policy* 49/1-2 (1999) 27-43.

[31] B. NEW (ed.), *Rationing. Talk and Action in Health Care*, London, 1997.

only two points: that rationing is inevitable, and that the public must be involved in the debate about it. The Citizens' Jury experiment is another initiative in the United Kingdom led by the principle of active citizenship.[32] It was an effort to remedy to the weaknesses of other techniques of public involvement and is starting from questioning the difference between the public and the patient. A patient can be knowledgeable and able to evaluate the services provided for his ill health, since he is the consumer. Nevertheless, he being blinded by his own symptoms and condition may be the wrong advisor for allocating public resources. The Citizens' Jury experiment as yet cannot disclose advantages above other public involvement mechanisms in rationing decisions, but it clearly indicates the prevalence of *values* in assessing health care rationing.[33] What is considered right for one group might seem to be wrong for another. Of particular importance is a major analysis by Mossialos about the views and attitudes of the public in several European countries towards rationing and priority setting.[34] This study uses data from the Eurobarometer survey assessing attitudes of the public in six different European countries regarding rationing and prioritising.[35] The general results are reassuring and reflect the strength of support within the European region for the principle of equality in access to health care services and the role of government and public services to assure this access. The social solidarity paradigm still seems to exist, since the majority supported a universal health care system, even if for reasons of limited resources it has somehow to be restricted to basic packages.

1.9. Conclusion

It seems that less transparent approaches are favoured over open explanations of choices. Politicians view explicit prioritisation as politically dangerous.[36] Physicians are reluctant to be openly

---

[32] J. STEWART, E. KENDALL, & A. COOTE, *A Citizens' Jury*, London, 1994, p. 1-8.

[33] J. LEANGHAN, *Involving the Public in Rationing Decisions. The Experience of Citizens Juries*, in *Health Policy* 49/1-2 (1999) 45-62.

[34] E. MOSSIALOS & D. KING, *Citizens and Rationing: an Analysis of a European Survey*, in *Health Policy* 49/1-2 (1999) 75-135.

[35] International Research Associates (Europe), Eurobarometer 49, June 1998.

[36] D. HUNTER, *Desperately Seeking Solutions*, London, 1997.

involved in choices since their underlying professional ethic is still based on an individual relation with a patient, including having command of the resources they consider appropriate for treating that condition. Managers are often lobbying for expansion or survival of their institution, a process that is better served by implicit agreements than by open decisions. Public involvement can be risky because involved people often are subjective and uninformed.

The developing of rationing policies is a process in which input from all stakeholders, politicians, health administrators, physicians and the public is requested, since none of these on their own are well equiped to conduct the process to a proper end.[37] But the most important questions relate to the principles that will be used in the process of rationing and priority setting, to the values and paradigms that will be espoused, and to the distributive ethics that will be applied in developing and implementing health care rationing programmes.

Social ethics regarding choices and priority setting still have a long way to go to find their place in the rationing jungle.[38] The floor is therefore open for further investigation.

---

[37] Ibid., p. 36.
[38] This concept is quoted in E. MOSSIALOS & D. KING, Citizens and Rationing: an Analysis of a European Survey.

HEALTH CARE NEEDS AND DISTRIBUTIVE JUSTICE

Philosophical Remarks on the Organisation of Health Care Systems

Yvonne Denier & Tom Meulenbergs

2.1. Broadening the Bioethical Reflection

Fair allocation of health care resources is a relatively new topic in medical ethics. This is undoubtedly related to the origin and evolution of contemporary medical ethics, or bioethics. The development of bioethical thinking in the 1960s and 1970s has its origin in both clinical and biomedical research. Out of dissatisfaction with paternalism in the medical relationship, systematic reflection on the physician-patient relationship increases and the principle of respect for the patient's autonomy becomes an important value.[1] This evolution reflects a tendency towards emancipation of the patient and more equality in the physician-patient relationship. Next to this, reflection on the appropriate conditions of experiments with persons in biomedical research counts as the second field of origin of bioethics.

Answering the questions arising from the clinical and biomedical research, a cluster of four principles were developed: respect for autonomy, beneficence, non-maleficence and justice.[2] Today, these

---

[1] D.W. BROCK, *Broadening the Bioethics Agenda*, in *Kennedy Institute of Ethics Journal* 10/1 (2000) 21.

[2] In 1976, The National Commission for the Protection of Human Subjects of Biomedical and Behavioral Research, installed in accordance with the US National Research Act (1974), published *The Belmont Report*, where three principles were discerned: respect for persons, beneficence and justice. Tom Beauchamp and James Childress further elaborated this principle approach in five successive editions of

principles still determine the bioethical discourse. Even though being recognised as one of the basic tenets of bioethical thinking, the principle of justice has only been peripherally present in the actual biomedical reflections. A possible explanation is the typical and common perspective of bioethical thinking. Until today, the focal point of attention has been the quasi-intimate relationship between physician and patient.[3]

The nature of ethics on the one hand and the circumstances of health care, together with high technology developments in medical science on the other hand, forces bioethical thinking to reflect on matters of social and distributive justice. To free itself from one-sidedness, bioethics has to break through its restriction to reflection on the micro-level, and extend its attention to the ethical quality of decisions on the macro-level. With this, we follow Paul Ricoeur in his definition of ethics: "the pursuit of the good life together with and for others in a context of just and fair institutions".[4]

Broadening the bioethical reflection is not only important for bioethics as a theory but also for health care as a public system. Medicine cannot restrict its focus to the individual patient alone. As a public science she constantly moves in the field of tension between the individual and society. Not only the health care needs of an individual patient are important. Attention has to be paid to public health as well. Public health is the collective action by a community or society to protect or promote the health and welfare of its members.[5]

The first wave of attention to public health can be situated in the aftermath of the Industrial Revolution. As a consequence of this

---

their Principles of Biomedical Ethics where they formulate four basic principles: T.L. BEAUCHAMP & J.F. CHILDRESS, *Principles of Biomedical Ethics*, New York, 2001.

[3] However, there is an exception: the justice principle plays a prominent role in ethical reflections on organ transplantation. The medical-technological developments regarding organ transplantation have an obvious macro-ethical component that exceeds the intimacy of the physician-patient relationship. How to distribute, and assign scarce resources – in this case, the limited amount of organs available - is a matter of distributive justice and fairness. A. JONSEN, *The Birth of Bioethics*, New York, 1998, p. 217-223.

[4] "La visée de la bonne vie avec et pour autrui dans des institutions justes" in P. RICOEUR, *Soi-même comme un autre*, Paris, 1990, p. 202.

[5] J. DUFFY, *Public Health: History of Public Health*, in W.T. REICH (ed.), *Encyclopedia of Bioethics*, 2nd ed., New York, 1995, p. 2157.

revolution, societies as well as the medical establishment were confronted by a number of fundamental breaking points and changes, and as such also with new health problems. A public viewpoint is inherently linked to the paradigm of public health. In order to guarantee medical care for the individual patient, a wider perspective is necessary and the health of all members of the community and the well-being of the collective need to be taken into account. Nevertheless, the growing attention for the society as a whole by the concern for public health has to be understood as being in tension with the growing individualism of the 19th and 20th centuries.[6] The primacy of the individual seems to hinder an effective promotion of public health. The question arises whether pursuing public health can legitimise limiting individual freedom.[7]

During the last decennia, bioethical thinking has included relatively few topics related to the public perspective. This is rather remarkable since the public viewpoint is incorporated in the basic principles of the modern western welfare state. A possible explanation is the predominance of the principle of respect for autonomy vis-à-vis the other ethical principles of beneficence, non-maleficence and justice.[8] Analogous to the Industrial Revolution originating the public health movement, the medical revolution of technological, therapeutic and pharmacological possibilities can serve as the catalytic factor recalibrating the patterns of thought and introducing attention for the public perspective in bioethical thinking. The

---

[6] D.E. BEAUCHAMPS, *Public Health: Philosophy of Public Health*, in W.T. REICH (ed.), *Encyclopedia of Bioethics*, p. 2165.

[7] Cf. the discussion on autonomy and paternalism e.g. J. FEINBERG, *Legal Paternalism*, in ID., *Rights, Justice and the Bounds of Liberty*, Princeton, 1980, p. 110-129; J. FEINBERG, *Harm to Self. The Moral Limits of the Criminal Law*, New York, 1986; D.W. BROCK, *Paternalism and Promoting the Good*, in R.E. SARTORIUS (ed.), *Paternalism*, Minneapolis, 1983, p. 237-260; G. Dworkin, *The Theory and Practice of Autonomy*, Cambridge, 1988.

[8] Regarding the predominance of the principle of respect for autonomy, see e.g. the contributions of M. Patrão Neves, *The Identity of the Person, Autonomy and Responsibility*; and of F. ABEL and F. TORRALBA, *The Patient-Physician Relation within the Health Care Structure*. See also H. TEN HAVE, *Principlism. A Western European Appraisal*, in E.R. DUBOSE, R.P. HAMEL and L.J. O'CONNELL (eds.), *A Matter of Principle? Ferment in US Bioethics*, Valley Forge, 1994, p. 101-120; J.D. RENDORFF AND P. KEMP, *Basic Ethical Principles in European Bioethics and Biolaw*, Vol. I, Autonomy, Dignity, Integrity and Vulnerability, Copenhagen/Barcelona, especially p. 25-31 and p. 314; and P.R. WOLPE, *The Triumph of Autonomy in American Bioethics: A Sociological View*, in R. DEVRIES and J. SUBEDI (eds.), *Bioethics and Society: Constructing the Ethical Enterprise*, Upper Saddle River NJ, p. 38-59.

proliferation of these enhanced medical technologies is not merely an isolated fact but is related to the promotion of patient autonomy. The veneration of patient autonomy not only has major implications in the ethical deliberation process of issues such as euthanasia but also has important side effects on the demand for medical interventions. There tends to be an evolution of patients becoming more and more consumers rather than caretakers. Both the changing face of medicine and the rise of medical consumption have serious consequences for society: an increasing health care budget is only one among many.

All this comes in an era of a renewed sensitivity to political responsibility. After the economic crises and subsequent periods of recession during the 1970s and 1980s, the intensified attention of both the media and the public for what is happening in the public domain has forced politicians to behave more like good administrators in controlling the budget. Politicians are held accountable for any mismanagement of the state. They have to account for the way in which they administer public funds. Concerning the health care budget, policymakers are faced with a rise in costs due to expanded implementation of expensive medical technologies on the one hand and an intensified attention for the public interest on the other hand. Politicians are therefore urged to reform the health care system in such a way that the growing medical possibilities, the rising costs and the demands of patients are tuned.

Furthermore, the physician cannot neglect the importance of an overall view on health care. Obviously, the political problems extend beyond the individual physician's viewpoint. But while it is the physician's role to care and cure as much as possible, it is the duty of the policymakers to look at the overall health situation. This means that for policymakers the just society is the true patient. In order to guarantee the continuous delivery of good health care for all, they cannot limit their scope to the individual patient but have to concentrate on the organisation of a just health care system. This implies that the agenda of bioethicists and policymakers cannot solely be the physician's dictate. If the physician's dedication to his patients leads him time after time to an excessive share of health care resources, the individual physician might at the end find it impossible to perform his duty as a physician because of a collapsed health care system.

Developing and maintaining a just health care system does not happen arbitrarily. It is determined by a number of specific views regarding justice against the background of what is *necessary* to live a good and valuable life – i.e. in this case, what is necessary regarding health and health care. On a practical level, these views are reflected in a number of institutions and on a theoretical level in one or more theories of justice. These theories determine how just a particular health care system is, taking into account both the degree of access to health care and the allocation of health care resources. In the next part, we will make a philosophical analysis of health and health care needs, followed by a reflection on their meaning within the different theories of justice.

2.2. Health Care Needs and Contemporary Theories of Justice

The health needs of persons play an important role in determining just allocation of health care resources. What can we say about the concept of need? In general, the assertion that something is needed tends to create an impression of an altogether different quality, and to have a substantially greater moral impact, than an assertion that something is desired or preferred. This is because needs are likely to possess a more compelling characteristic than desires and preferences. This seems to be originated in the fact that a person has no control over what he needs and that he will suffer fundamental and crucial harm, in case of failure of meeting the need. Consequently, needs are likely to be treated with greater urgency and priority than desires and preferences. The priority of needs over desires and preferences is also described as the 'Principle of Precedence'.[9] It is, however, important not to claim too much for needs and to draw attention to the exceptions to the Principle of Precedence. Not every need complies with this principle. Harry Frankfurt distinguishes between three kinds of needs: free volitional needs, constrained volitional needs and non-volitional needs. A free volitional need is a need that derives from a voluntary desire for a certain end, e.g. the need for a racket when one wants to play tennis. A constrained volitional need is caused by an

---

[9] Defined and discussed in D. BRAYBROOKE, *Meeting Needs* (Studies in Moral, Political and Legal Philosophy), Princeton, 1987, p. 60-75; in H. FRANKFURT, *Necessity and Desire*, in ID., *The Importance of What We Care About*, Cambridge, 1988, p. 104-116; and in R.E. GOODIN, *Priority of Needs*, in *Philosophy and Phenomenological Research* 45 (1985) 615-625.

involuntary desire and continues to exist independently of the person's free will. An example of such a desire is jealousy or being in love. A non-volitional need is a need that exists fully independent from any desire whatsoever – such as the need for food or water. Because of the involuntary character only the last two types of needs comply with the Principle of Precedence. David Braybrooke distinguishes between 'basic course-of-life-needs' and 'adventitious needs': "The basic needs, or course-of-life-needs are the things that are necessary for the most fundamental projects, involved in living a human life, and which are essential to living or functioning normally. That is what distinguishes needs that are *basic* from nonbasic needs, desires, values and preferences, which need not be associated with normal functioning in the same way. In addition, it is often regarded essential or criteriological of the concept of basic need that it is associated with the concept of harm, such that if one's basic needs are not satisfied, one will be harmed in some crucial or fundamental way. Less urgent needs, which are not associated with harm in this way, are often called "adventitious needs".[10]

Basic or course-of-life needs are thus always of instrumental value for the projects involved in living a human life: "all necessities are in this respect conditional: nothing is needed except in virtue of being an indispensable condition for the attainment of a certain end".[11] When something is needed, it must therefore always be possible to specify what it is needed for. As such, meeting a particular need is not important in itself, but only as a necessary means to reach a certain end. The moral importance of the need thus always depends on the moral importance of the end. Being in good or reasonable health enables a person to carry out various life projects.[12] 'A health care system is a public service that determines who has access to what hinds of health care resources of servius on what basis'. As such, the importance of access to health care derives from the significance that is publicly ascribed to being in good health. Similarly, the content of health care results from a political consensus, based on the public significance of health care as a course-of-life-need.

---

[10] See H. FRANKFURT, *op. cit.*, p. 107-109; and D. BRAYBROOKE, *op. cit.*, p. 29-33 as explained by C. Wolf, *Theories of Justice: Human Needs*, in *Encyclopedia of Applied Ethics*, San Diego, 1998, vol. 4, p. 335-345, p. 336.

[11] H. FRANKFURT, *op. cit.*, p. 106.

[12] See also A. BUCHANAN, *Philosophic Perspectives on Access to Health Care*, in *The Mount Sinai Journal of Medicine* 64 (1997) 90-100, p. 91.

Essentially, needs can be met and through this they are different from desires. In being necessary for the most fundamental projects in living a normal human life, course-of-life needs contain basic archetypal needs such as food, shelter, and education as well as psychological needs such as the need for friendship and self-realisation. Important is the distinction between the possibility of immediate fulfilment of the archetypical basic needs and the impossibility of immediate fulfilment intrinsic to the second category. Society can immediately meet the need for food by providing food. The need for friendship cannot be met in the same manner, by for example giving him or her a friend. This would go against the meaning of true friendship. One wants to be recognised as friend, not only because one needs friends but also and primarily because of the appreciation of whom one is as a person. It is precisely this appreciation that cannot be fulfilled immediately but arises in and through a process of common experience and appreciation of personality and character. Thus, the framework of course-of-life needs contains a differentiated variety of needs, depending on whether or not they can be met immediately. This differentiation has important consequences for social policy. A situation wherein one can provide the means for immediate fulfilment of the needs of persons differs totally from a situation wherein providing the appropriate context is the only way towards possible fulfilment. Being in good health can be seen as a course-of-life need, only possibly fulfillable within the appropriate context. Indeed, being in good health enables a person to carry out most of his life projects. But whether one actually will enjoy a good health can however never be guaranteed. Many different factors such as genetic structure, natural and social environment, individual acts and negligence determine the actual health outcome. Therefore, social policy cannot instantaneously provide for a good health status. Access to good quality health care can, on the contrary, as an appropriate context providing for the best possible health status for all, be guaranteed. The need for a good health care system can be met if organised properly. Note that the need for a good health care system as a public institution differs from health as a course-of-life-need. The public health care institution is the result of a political consensus determined by the importance, publicly attributed to health and installed with a view to the common good, namely to meet as good as possible the individual course-of-life-needs of all.

The concept of need also contains a hierarchical differentiation. Some needs are morally more important than others, depending on the moral importance of the end. The need for a health care system in order to achieve the best possible health for all is considerably more important than a system distributing rackets enabling all to play tennis.

Which needs are hierarchically important and which are more trivial cannot be universally and uniformly determined. There is always a social context in which certain needs have more meaning than others. In some cultures one can have a need for a large family because of the social status attached to it while in other cultures having a large family does not play a significant role.

The historical perspective also plays an important role. Some needs evolve within the historical development of a society. In times when there was no organised national social security system, the size of a family had a far greater impact on the welfare of the people. With the development of a social security system the size of a family has lost its meaning in terms of the need for social security.

Nevertheless, some needs are independent from time and space. These entail the things that are necessary for the fundamental projects of *every* person. These needs are universal. Meeting these needs has significance for the survival of persons. As such, they differ from particular needs originating from specific wants and desires, i.e. adventitious needs, in that in the case of the former, having the need does not depend on the person's free will. Failure to meet the need causes fundamental and crucial harm. We consider health care needs as universal needs. Health care needs are not limited to the western welfare states, which have developed organised health care systems. The fact that many third world countries do not have a similar system that meets the health care needs of their citizens does not mean that these persons do not *have* these needs. Having the need does not depend on the existence of the system. Being in good health is of fundamental value for every person and eliminating or reducing barriers that undermine this value – such as disease, illness, or injury – is a positive obligation for every just society.

The acknowledgement of health care needs as universal needs has implications regarding the acknowledgement of the moral right to health care. The relationship between needs and rights is complicated since needs do not automatically create rights. Compare the difference between basic needs and adventitious needs and the difficulty in unequivocally determining which specific needs belong to which category. Furthermore, in determining the right to health care, one has to show that no competing claims with equal weight and of equal priority exist that would jeopardise the first claim. However complex this may be, rights are nevertheless in general perceived as an exceptionally powerful protection of what is considered to be of particularly important human interest. This proposition allows us to state that "because claims of basic needs typically have high priority and moral urgency, it can be argued that most persons have a right that at least their most basic needs should be met, and that those who possess more than they need have a corresponding obligation to see to it that the basic needs of others are met."[13] If we consider health care to be a course-of-life need, then, following Buchanan, we define the moral right to health care as "an obligation on the part of society as a whole, to ensure that everyone has access to some level of health care services"; that "the obligation is a very stringent one with exceptional moral force"; and that "to say that there is a moral right to health care is to say that access to health care is owed to those who have the right."[14]

A universal and a particular pillar structure the content of a health care system. The universal pillar is related to the need for good health as a course-of-life need. As argued above, this need is independent from time, space or socio-cultural context. The particular pillar, on the other hand, consists in meeting this need by the contingent development and particular design of a health care system based on political choices and public consensus. Different perspectives on justice and the role of the government determine this particular design. As such, it is related to time, space and socio-cultural context. Therefore, every particular design should be provisional and open to later revision. Against this background we want to sketch different possible designs for a health care system on the basis of four prominent theories of justice, i.e. libertarian, utilitarian, egalitarian and communitarian theory. Then, we will analyse two particular health care systems, namely the system in the US and the common pillars of the different European systems.

---

[13] C. WOLF, op. cit., p. 342.
[14] A. BUCHANAN, op. cit., p. 90.

2.2.1. *Libertarian Theory*

The first principle of libertarian theory is the right to private pro-perty. According to libertarianism, an absolute respect for the right to private property and for negative freedom constitutes the basis and guideline for the legitimate role of the state and for the basic principles of individual conduct.[15] Political institutions should only serve to protect this basic right.

The predominant version of libertarianism is the Entitlement Theory, developed and presented by Robert Nozick in *Anarchy, State and Utopia*.[16] Nozick understands justice in terms of the protection of rights or entitlements, in particular rights to liberty and private property.[17] Individuals have a property right in their own person and in the goods that they come to have through actions that con-form to 'the principle of justice in acquisition' and 'the principle of justice in transfer'. The first principle is based on Locke's idea of ini-tial acquisition and specifies the way in which an individual can come to own property without violating the rights of others. Nozick states that whatever the appropriate specification on acquiring pro-perty may be, it always has to include the 'Lockean Proviso'. One may acquire as many objects as one desires, on the condition that, firstly, one's acquisition does not worsen the condition of the other, in the sense that he is no longer capable of free use (without acquisition) of what he previously could use freely, and secondly that, if this never-theless would occur, one properly compensates the other. The second principle states that transfers of legitimate property – via sale,

---

[15] The libertarian concept of freedom signifies negative freedom, i.e. freedom from interference. One possesses negative freedom to the extent that in one's action one is not interfered by others. Positive freedom means a claim on something, the possibility to be someone, to pursue and realise a private goal in a certain manner, the possibility to be aware of choices and to be able to explain them in relation to ideas and goals. See: P. DASGUPTA, *An Inquiry into Well-Being and Destitution*, Oxford, 1993, p. 40-46, explaining Isaiah Berlin's distinction between positive and negative freedom as presented in I. BERLIN, *Two Concepts of Liberty*, in ID., *Four Essays on Lib-erty*, Oxford, 1969. Important concerning the difference between both concepts of lib-erty is that the former is individualistically understood. Negative freedom implies that the self-sufficient individual may not be hindered in his personal development. The starting point of the second conception of freedom is that an individual for his freedom needs society. This will be further developed in our analysis of fair-oppor-tunity egalitarianism.

[16] R. NOZICK, *Anarchy, State and Utopia*, New York, 1974.

[17] *Ibid.*, p. 149-182.

trade, gift or bequest – are justified as long as they happen voluntarily. The third principle is 'the principle of rectification' and guarantees a rectification of previous injustices, if any committed. A just society protects rights and property, allowing individuals to freely improve their circumstances. Note that within this framework distribution according to free market principles is an appropriate pattern for just distribution.

The absolute respect for individual freedom and property right leads to a form of strict procedural justice. Justice is not a matter of just *results* but of just *procedures*: "Whatever arises from a just situation by just steps is itself just."[18] A focus on the results would lead to systematic violation of individual freedom and the right to private property: "any principle of justice which demands a certain distributive end state or pattern of holding will require frequent and gross disruptions of individuals' holdings for the sake of maintaining that end state or pattern."[19] Consequently, Nozicks theory is strikingly anti-redistributive: "attempts to force anyone to contribute any part of his legitimate holdings to the welfare of others is a violation of that person's property rights, whether it is undertaken by private individuals or the state. On this view, coercively backed taxation to raise funds for welfare programs of any kind is literally theft."[20] Coerced redistribution would be an unjust redistribution of private property, by illegitimately considering it to be public property. This would mean sacrificing basic rights and liberties for the public interest.

Against the argument that an absolute respect for property rights would create immense poverty and a growing gap between rich and poor, libertarians argue for the difference between justice and charity. Morality comprises more than the non-violation of rights. Redistribution is legitimate only when voluntarily organised through the imperfect obligation of charity. Precisely because the obligation of charity is imperfect, those in need cannot claim fulfilment of their needs as a right: "While justice demands that we not be *forced* to contribute to the well-being of others, charity requires that we help even those who have no *right* to our aid."[21]

---

[18] *Ibid.*, p. 151.

[19] *Ibid.*, p. 13.

[20] See: A. BUCHANAN, *Justice: A Philosophical Review*, in E. E. SHELP (ed.), *Justice and Health Care* (Philosophy and Medicine 8), Dordrecht, 1981, p. 3-21, p.12.

[21] Allen Buchanan, explaining the libertarian perspective in A. BUCHANAN, *op. cit.*, p. 14.

This means that there is no moral right to health care.[22] According to the libertarian theory, rights only involve avoiding violation through interference and thus involve no more than the right to be left alone. Rights have nothing to do with providing services or goods that improve the well-being of all, that meet the basic needs and that as such offer protection to the poor and vulnerable. Libertarianism is 'a hands-off theory'. In this, libertarianism does not deny the existence of basic needs. However, meeting these needs and taking care for the distressed is not a matter of justice and thus not a legitimate obligation of society.[23]

As such, taxation in order to organise a health care system is a libertarian injustice. Even if one could show that health care contributes to individual freedom, it would still be irrelevant. Although, the importance of health care is not ignored by definition, it is only relevant within the framework of charity and moral virtuousness. Besides, nothing prevents an individual to take private health care insurance. With this, only a private health care system, i.e. a voluntary system of redistribution, can be legitimate. Libertarians support a health care system that is based on the free market ideal: distribution of health care services and goods are best left to the market operating through the principle of ability to pay.[24] There are no rights to health care and privatisation is a protected value.

2.2.2. Utilitarianism

Utilitarianism is probably the most well known form of consequentialism and has many variants, internally distinguished by a prefix.[25]

---

[22] "A basic human right to the delivery of health care, even to the delivery of a decent minimum of health care, does not exist. The difficulty with talking of such right should be apparent. It is difficult if not impossible both to respect the freedom of all and to achieve their long-range best interest." In T. ENGELHARDT, *The Foundations of Bioethics*, New York, 1986, p. 336.

[23] "It may well be unfeeling or unsympathetic not to provide such help [i.e. health care for the individuals injured], but it is another thing to show that one owes others such help in a way that would morally authorise state forces to redistribute resources, as one would collect funds owed in a debt. The natural lottery creates inequalities and places individuals at disadvantage without creating a straightforward obligation on the part of others to aid those in need." In T. ENGELHARDT, *op. cit.*, p. 340.

[24] See also: T. L. BEAUCHAMP & J. CHILDRESS, *Principles of Biomedical Ethics*, 5th ed., New York, Oxford University Press, 2001, p. 231.

[25] There is no contemporary canonical work or representative of utilitarianism. Contemporary utilitarianism is no uniform theory but a general approach to justice.

Common to all variants and contrary to libertarian theory, justice is exclusively seen in terms of the utility consequences of an act or rule. Justice is a matter of maximising utility and utility is defined as pleasure, satisfaction, happiness, welfare, realisation of preferences, et cetera. According to classic or overall utilitarianism an act or rule is just if it maximizes the aggregate utility. Aggregate utility is the sum of all individual utility experiences. According to average utilitarianism an act or rule is just when it maximises utility per capita. Average utility is the aggregate utility divided by the numbers of individual utility experiences. In both cases every person is one utility unit, so that 'each is to count for one and no one for more than one'. These units are fully equal but do not receive special protection. Utilitarianism could exclude certain individuals from health care entitlements if this would maximise utility, regardless of the value of health care for this particular individual.[26]

Act utilitarianism assesses a particular act in itself. An act is right when it maximises utility. According to rule utilitarianism an act is right when it complies with a rule, which if obeyed by all, will maximise utility over time. Mostly, both are in conflict: act utilitarianism does not maximise utility over time and following the rule can in individual cases lead to less than optimal utility results. In his article 'The Survival Lottery', John Harris proposes a scheme that would maximise total welfare by randomly selecting individuals in society, killing them and use their organs to save the life of several other individuals with organ failure. One donor person could thus save several lives and maximise utility for this act. Over time, utility will nevertheless diminish because of the reigning atmosphere of fear for selection. The rule of respect for bodily integrity then maximises

Within the framework of health care, the role of utilitarianism can be traced back to the question of what significance can or must be attributed to the consequences and efficiency of acts and rules within distributive problems of justice.

[26] Allen Buchanan provides a good example: "Consider Down syndrome. Individuals with this chromosomal disorder have a high incidence of cardiac and gastrointestinal defects, in addition to varying degrees of mental retardation. It might turn out that the way to maximize overall utility is to allow infants with Down syndrome to be removed from their parents' sight at birth, before attachments could deepen. If this were the case, then Utilitarianism would not justify a right to health care for all", in A. BUCHANAN, *Philosophic Perspectives on Access to Health Care: Distributive Justice in Health Care*, in *Mount Sinai Journal of Medicine* 64/2 (1997) 91-92.

utility over time by taking away that fear but results in individual cases in a lack of a sufficient amount of donor organs.[27] The difference between act and rule utilitarianism is important within a policy perspective since the latter offers an explanation for the justification of institutions. Institutional rules aim at maximising utility over time. A particular act that does not maximise utility at that particular moment can, thus, still be justified because it complies with the rule of an institution that maximises utility over time.

However refined, common to all variations of utilitarianism is that the value and significance of things or acts is measured by its utility value. From a rule-utilitarian perspective the moral significance of a health care system resides in the fact that it maximises utility. Many utilitarians support health care programs that protect public health and distribute equally basic health care based on the argument that it maximises utility: everybody benefits from the existence of such a system. Hence, the recognition of health care needs is derived from the extent in which a health care system maximises utility. Whether the total set of health care institutions indeed maximises utility will have to be shown by empirical evidence. With this, difficulties arise. One has to show that this particular system of health care institutions offering these particular services indeed maximises utility and that these services are best guaranteed if they are recognised as a right. One also has to show whether these services are best formulated as an equal right or not, at which point the benefits no longer outweigh the costs, which goods and services have priority and which not, et cetera. All this illustrates the complexity of the information problem that has to be solved in order to apply utilitarianism to the organisation of health care.[28]

Moreover, problems emerge when utilitarian principles are accepted as sufficient by themselves. The one-sided focus on utility consequences has problematic implications for the concept of individual rights. First of all, utilitarianism does not comprise a denial of the rights discourse. Utilitarian obligations of justice are correlative

---

[27] See J. HARRIS, *The Survival Lottery*, in *Philosophy* 50 (1975) p. 81-87; and P. SINGER, *Utility and the Survival Lottery*, in *Philosophy* 52 (1977) 218-222. Discussed in J. ELSTER, *Local Justice. How Institutions Allocate Scarce Goods and Necessary Burdens*, Cambridge, 1992, p. 190, 222.

[28] See: B. BARRY, *Theories of Justice* (A Treatise on Social Justice 1), London, 1989. See also: A. BUCHANAN, *op. cit.*, p. 15-16.

rights for individuals. Note, however, that these rights are *correlative* towards utility. They are derived rights. They only play a role within the context of a particular social arrangement that on a particular moment in time and under specific circumstances results in a maximisation of utility. Some refinement is offered in the difference between long-term and short-term utility: "However, if the justification of a system is that its protections *over time* maximise utility, then these rights can in principle override short-term utility calculations."[29] Still, individual rights have an undetermined, faint and fragile status when based upon utility maximisation. One could wonder whether rights that are correlative to the context of utility are rights at all. Contemporary rights theorists as Ronald Dworkin, define a right exactly as something that has priority over what maximises utility.[30] If the right to health care is to be understood as a claim that takes precedence over mere appeals to utility, then utilitarianism denies the existence of a right to health care. If, on the other hand, we mean by a right to health care a claim that is justified ultimately by appeal to the utility of the total set of health care institutions, then utilitarianism does include, and indeed may even require a right to health care. The first is an absolute right, the latter a correlative and thus derived right.

Furthermore, utilitarianism has problems with of just distribution issues. Overall and average utilitarianism do not take into account the just *distribution* of utility. Unequal distribution that maximizes utility is perfectly legitimate. Thus, it is possible that the rights of those with the greatest need, but with relatively low utility outcome, will be counted out. If one only has a right to health care to the extent that one increases total or average utility, the question arises what to do with Alzheimer or Persistent Vegetative State (PVS) patients or premature babies? This tends to the scapegoat mechanism where one individual is sacrificed in order to ensure 'the greatest happiness for the greatest number.' According to our spontaneous ethical intuitions, this course of action is fully unacceptable. From the utilitarian viewpoint, however, it can be deemed acceptable. It is doubtful whether this one-sided focus on utility fits in with our spontaneous

---

[29] T.L. BEAUCHAMP & J.F. CHILDRESS, *Principles of Biomedical Ethics*, 4th ed., New York, 1994., p. 335.

[30] See the concept of rights as trumps, as developed by R. DWORKIN, *Justice and Rights*, in ID., *Taking Rights Seriously*, London, 1977, p. xi and 81-96.

views on morality. After all, morality is also and perhaps primarily linked to the existence of moral prohibitions that limit our actions.[31] The way in which an end is achieved determines the morality of human conduct. The morality of society is to a great extent reflected in the way in which it treats the weak and the vulnerable. A society that for utility reasons neglects help to those most in need can hardly be called a just society. On the contrary, the morality of society resides to a large extent in its statement that not everything is taken into the utility calculus and that some values deserve absolute respect. Caring for the weak, the Alzheimer patient, the PVS patient, the premature is then not a matter of cost-benefit analysis but an inviolable starting point.

Because of its consequentialist nature utilitarianism is focused on trade-offs, efficiency, and deliberation and plays a legitimate role in the formation of policies of both macro- and micro-allocation. On the policy level of public institutions, attention for the consequences of measures is important because of the maintenance of the institutions themselves. On the individual level many would find it counter-intuitive to make enormous efforts whereby the results are so mini-mal that the act becomes meaningless.[32] Careful deliberation is an important factor in thinking about the organisation of health care. In coping with individual health care needs, one has to preserve the system from collapsing, and this in the name of individual as well as public interest: everybody benefits from maintaining the system so that one can save as many lives as possible.[33]

2.2.3. Egalitarianism

Classical libertarianism is devoted to the maximisation of liberty, utilitarianism to the maximisation of utility. Egalitarianism concentrates on equality as the baseline for justice. There are several variants of egalitarianism differing according to the answer to the question: equality of what? When applied to health care, the question

---

[31] See: S. HAMPSHIRE, Morality and Pessimism, in ID., Morality and Conflict, Oxford, 1983, p. 82-100.

[32] Also called the leaky-bucket argument. See: J. ELSTER, op. cit., p. 202, 228.

[33] Also see: IBID., p. 184-245; T.L. BEAUCHAMP & J.F. CHILDRESS Principles of Biomed-ical Ethics, 5th ed., p. 231; D.M. HAUSMAN & M.S. MCPHERSON, Economic Analysis and Moral Philosophy (Cambridge Surveys of Economic Literature), Cambridge, 1996, p. 101-115; W. KYMLICKA, Contemporary Political Philosophy. An Introduction, Oxford, 1990, p. 10-11.

becomes: what do we aim for? Equal welfare? Equal health status? Equal use of health care for equal need? Equal access to health care for equal need? Equal choice sets? Equal freedom? Depending on the answer, egalitarianism can be incorporated in several different theories and political models. A minimalist form of egalitarianism is used by the liberal rights-based theories and states equal freedom and equal political rights as the basis for a just society.[34] In contrast, strong egalitarianism demands actual equality of outcome, in this case equal health status. An intermediate variant and perhaps the most well known and discussed version of egalitarianism defends fair equality of opportunity as developed by John Rawls in his *Theory of Justice*. Norman Daniels has further developed the implications of this theory for health care ethics in his work *Just Health Care*.[35]

The concepts of positive freedom, equality and responsibility are central within the idea of fair equality of opportunity. The concept of positive freedom demands that persons are enabled to the fullest possible extent to choose independently and to realise their choices and hereby have been given a chance for personal development.[36] Consequently, social institutions affecting distribution should be organised in such a way as to enable each person to have a fair share of the normal range of opportunities available in society. The normal range of opportunities is determined by "the range of life plans that a person could reasonably hope to pursue, given his or her talents and skills."[37] In order to realise this positive freedom, it should be the means and opportunities that have to be equally distributed, not the results. Concerning the results, a clear distinction is being held between inequalities for which one is responsible and inequalities for which one is not responsible because they are independent of personal preferences. This second form of inequality is morally unacceptable and has to be adjusted. Inequality as a result of a deliberate and conscious choice for which one can be held responsible is morally legitimate.[38]

---

[34] Note that this involves equal *political* rights. Access to politics, suffrage, and equality before the law, social class, religion, and ethnicity should not be allowed to produce inequality. However, this does not involve equal *social* rights such as equal access to education and a social welfare and health care system. See also S. HELLSTEN, *Theories of Distributive Justice*, in *Encyclopedia of Applied Ethics*, vol. 1, San Diego, 1998, p. 815-828.

[35] N. DANIELS, *Just Health Care* (Studies in Philosophy and Policy), Cambridge, 1985.

[36] P. DASGUPTA, *op. cit.*, p. 40-46.

[37] See: T.L. BEAUCHAMP & J.F. CHILDRESS, *op. cit.*, p. 234; N. DANIELS, *op. cit.*, p. 26-42.

[38] See N. DANIELS, *op. cit.*, p. 38: "The immediate object of justice is not, then, happiness or the satisfaction of desires, though just institutions provide individuals with

The justice of social institutions is reflected in the attempts to counter the lack of opportunity caused by "unpredictable bad luck and misfortune over which the person has no meaningful control." To the extent that disease, disability or injury cause considerable and significant disadvantages and restrict the capacity to fulfil or pursue the individual life projects, justice demands the use of public health care resources to counter these morally arbitrary disadvantages and to restore to persons a fair chance to pursue their life plans, given his or her talents and skills.[39] According to the fair opportunity rule a just society cannot forsake fair allocation of health care resources. All citizens have a right to the resources related to this societal obligation. This means that equal access to health care in the sense that no one is legitimately prevented from obtaining health care must be guaranteed. It does however not imply that everyone has access to every available treatment or that one has a right to a good health outcome. The only demand is that persons be given a fair opportunity for a good outcome.

Within this framework goods have to be distributed according to the Rawlsian Difference Principle: we choose the principles of distribution that maximize the minimal situation, i.e. allocation should be so as to maximize the amount of primary goods held by the worst-off. This means that health policy would guarantee a safety net or minimum floor below which a person would not be allowed to fall. This complies with the weak egalitarian principle in the sense that equal access to *fundamental* health care resources has to be ensured.[40] Again, individual responsibility is an important element. The objective that all persons should have a maximum chance to self-realisation implies providing a threshold preventing persons to fall below a minimum of possibilities to lead a valuable life. Related to this, it

---

an acceptable framework within which they may pursue happiness. But in this pursuit, individuals remain responsible for the choice of their ends, so there is no injustice in not providing them with means sufficient reach extravagant ends." See also: T.L. BEAUCHAMP & J.F. CHILDRESS, *op. cit.*, p. 235-236: "The fair-opportunity rule states that no person should receive social benefits on the basis of undeserved advantageous properties (because no persons are responsible for having these properties) and that no persons should be denied social benefits on the basis of undeserved disadvantageous properties (because they are also not responsible for these properties)."

[39] N. DANIELS, *op. cit.*, chapter 3 and 4.

[40] See also T.L. BEAUCHAMP & J. L. CHILDRESS, *op. cit.*, p. 352.

may be expected from every person that he himself to the best of his ability makes the necessary effort to personal development.

The fair-opportunity perspective forms a liberal-egalitarian challenge to utilitarian and libertarian theories. Contrary to utilitarianism a person is anything but 'a drop in the ocean of overall social utility.' He is on the contrary always to be respected not merely as a means but also always as an end in itself.[41] Contrary to libertarian ethics, the fair-opportunity perspective defends a positive societal obligation to eliminate or reduce barriers that prevent fair equality of opportunity, an obligation that extends to programs that correct or compensate for disadvantages for which one is not responsible. The fair opportunity rule makes a plea for a moral right to health care according to which every individual irrespective of wealth or utility status has a right to equal access to health care.

Problems arise with the question of how much redistribution is required.[42] Up to which point of equality of opportunity do we have to go? What, for example, do we have to do with persons with a severely low health condition who probably will never reach the minimal level of fair opportunity because of this severely deteriorated health condition? Up to which point do we allocate health care resources? Health is affected by many factors outside health care such as access to health care, response to treatment, individual preferences and choices and other types of policies, such as educational policy, poverty policy, et cetera. It is not reasonable to expect from the health care system to constantly react to all the evolutions and differences following these factors. There are limits to what can reasonably be expected from the health care system. At a certain moment, the process of reducing inequalities has to stop. This happens on the boundary between the morally relevant and morally arbitrary differences. Therefore, the main question within the fair-opportunity perspective is which differences between persons are morally relevant and which are morally arbitrary? This is the difficult boundary between what is 'unfair' and what is 'unfortunate'.[43]

[41] J. ELSTER, op. cit, p. 224.

[42] See J. ELSTER, op. cit., p. 228, regarding the difference between non-envious egalitarianism ("divide equality up to the point where further equalisation would make some worse off without making anyone better off") and strongly envious egalitarianism ("insists on absolute equality even if it makes everyone worse off").

[43] See: T. ENGELHARDT, Health Care Allocation: Response to the Unjust, the Unfortunate and the Undesirable, in E.E. SHELP (ed.), op. cit., p. 121-137.

This line is not only difficult to determine – for instance, for what exactly is one held responsible?[44] The ultimate determination of the line also has immense consequences concerning the scope and content of the health care system. According to the libertarian perspective, very little belongs to the category 'unfair': only "maleficently or negligently caused setbacks to health justify the designation unfair, but other setbacks to health are matters of misfortune."[45] Whether one within this perspective can speak at all from a just health care system is disputable. If on the contrary, as a consequence of the uncertainty about what one is actually responsible for, such a broad definition is given to the category 'unfair' that too much is expected from the health care system and too little from the individual, then the risk arises that the system will not be able to maintain itself over a period of time.

Most people are in favour of some equitable definition of health care. However constructed, the demarcation between 'unfair' and 'unfortunate' is always linked to the deliberation between the demand of justice and the demand of efficiency. The demand of justice requires that everyone who is entitled to something should also receive it. The demand of efficiency focuses on avoiding as many free riders as possible. If one allows the demand of justice to determine the size of the health care domain, then the possibility of some free riders is automatically included. On the other hand, if one allows the demand of efficiency to be the prevailing principle, then there is a real possibility that one denies to a few persons something to which they are entitled.

2.2.4. *Communitarianism*

Communitarian theories criticise the individualism and formalism from the libertarian and liberal theories, as presented respectively by Nozick and Rawls. According to the communitarian critique these theories overemphasise autonomous individuals and their individual rights. The essential definition of an individual is not embedded

---

[44] For what is one *not* held responsible? Clear examples are, among others, race, gender, social and economic background, inborn talents and capacities. See Dworkin: results may be ambition-sensitive but not endowment-sensitive. The question arises to what extent one is responsible for ones preferences and ambitions (cf. the adaptive preferences of the contented slave). The problem again is: where to draw the line?

[45] T.L. BEAUCHAMP & J.F. CHILDRESS, *Principles of Biomedical Ethics*, 4th ed., p. 345.

in 'the right to be left alone', nor in the characteristic of being a rational agent. An individual is on the contrary always embedded in his
or her community, in the community ties that connect a society.
These community ties are necessary for welfare and well-being since
they are the foundation of *interindividual* responsibility and *solidarity*.
Hereby, solidarity is understood as "both a personal virtue of commitment and a principle of social morality based on the shared values of a group."[46]

Principles of justice are no abstract, uniform and universally valid
principles by which one can judge every society. Principles of justice
and normative standards do not develop outside the rules of a political community on an abstract, rational or natural level but evolve
within society itself. They are relative to social meanings and 'shared
understandings' of the members of society. Therefore, they are pluralistic, particular and derived from a various number of different
conceptions of the good, inherent to an equally various number of
moral communities. Communitarians do not develop a system of
justice; on the contrary, they describe the normative traditions existing within the community. Some communitarians, such as Alisdair
MacIntyre and Robert Bellah, go back to the normative traditions
from the past. Michael Walzer, on the other hand, states that we
ought to take a closer look at our present morality and see what is
latently present in our shared understandings of social goods, and
hidden in our concept and categories. Walzer is radically particularistic: "*Our* shared understandings: the vision is relevant to the social
world in which it was developed; it is not relevant, or necessarily, to
all social worlds."[47]

The significance of this particularism lies in its emphasis on the
fact that every person's ethical consciousness and sensitivity is
rooted in the particular domain of the concrete, ethical society in
which he or she lives. This particularism implies that needs are
determined within the community-derived standards of justice.
Applied to health care, this means that health care needs are relative
to social meanings and cannot be determined independently from
the concrete, ethical community. Strictly speaking, communitarian

---

[46] Ibid., p. 338.

[47] M. WALZER, *Spheres of Justice. A Defense of Pluralism and Equality*, s.l., 1983, p. xiv.
See also M.J. TRAPPENBURG, *Defining the Medical Sphere*, in *Cambridge Quarterly of
Health Care Ethics* 6 (1997) 416-434.

theory does not offer a foundation for moral rights to health care, universally and formally understood. This is closely connected to the criticism on violent universalism and to the concern that universalism is being abused to justify the condemnation of difference. Conversely, particularism becomes problematic if it deteriorates to relativism and thus excludes every possibility of moral critique, as clarified by the argument of the contented slave. This argument points to the lack of theoretical foundation to criticise traditionally and culturally embedded forms of oppression: "When forms of deprivations are culturally embedded, those who suffer them may be unable to desire or even to articulate what they need. People raised in a culture of slavery may be unable to imagine or hope for freedom and autonomy, but this would be a poor reason for us to accept that their circumstances are just and their needs adequately met."[48] The same goes for health care: despite the social context, the historical perspective and the fact that a health care system is the result of a public consensus, the universal moment cannot be excluded. There are moments of universal and objective recognition and thus of a 'must' that transcends the particularity of the own community. An example of such a moment is what could be called a moment of negative contrast-experience: a form of universal experience and intuition that certain things simply cannot be done or accepted. For example, allowing someone to starve on your doorstep, the genocide of innocent people, or allowing someone to die at the entrance of a hospital because he has no health insurance. According to Michael Walzer, it is the shared understanding of the members of the political community in the US that "care should be proportional to illness and not to wealth", derived from the "common appreciation of the importance of medical care."[49] It is important to note that even in being a shared understanding of a particular community, this opinion infers at the same time a universal moment: health care must be equally available for all.

However, for communitarian theories, it remains very difficult to evolve beyond a simple description of the plurality of moral communities and denotation of the shared understandings. These shared understandings within a community can be very diverse. Besides

---

[48] C. WOLF, *op. cit.*, p. 344.
[49] M. WALZER, *op. cit.*, p. 86, 90.

the shared idea of equality of access there exists in the US also the understanding that health care should be organised according to free market principles. The communitarian theory has no foundation for argumentation to demonstrate the superiority of one understanding over another.[50]

This outline of the four prominent theories of justice indicates the theoretical divergence of views on health care needs and on the moral right to health care. On the practical level, in matters of policy, different views belonging to different theories are being combined. In the next section, we will illustrate the foundations of the American health care system and of different European systems.

2.3. *The American and European Health Care Systems*

2.3.1. *The Four Objectives of a Health Care System*

Different kinds of health care systems are operational in the US and Europe. As mentioned above, the way in which health care needs are interpreted and valued in a concrete system does not by definition converge with one single theory of justice. In other words, no existing health care system is *purely* organised along the lines of a libertarian, utilitarian, egalitarian or communitarian theory. It is, however, possible to analyse the way in which the various health care systems combine different key-elements of different theories of justice. Related to this, four objectives can be circumscribed as points of reference for a just health care policy:[51] first, a just health care system should provide the best possible care for all; while secondly, guaranteeing equal access to health care; thirdly, maintaining freedom of choice on the part of health care provider and consumer; and fourthly, control the costs through cost containment programs, hereby promoting the public interests. However, trade-offs will have to be made. First, scarcity of resources demands that choices are made, and secondly it is the predominant sense of justice that

---

[50] See the discussion between Michael Walzer and Ronald Dworkin in *The New York Review of Books*, April, 14, and July, 21, 1983. Also discussed in: T. L. BEAUCHAMP & J. F. CHILDRESS, *Principles of Biomedical Ethics*, 4th ed., p. 339.

[51] In this we follow Beauchamp and Childress as well as Engelhardt, in ID., *Principles of Biomedical Ethics*, 5th ed., p. 230-231; H.T. Engelhardt, *op. cit.*, p. 337.

causes emphasis on one or more objectives. "Even gods and goddesses must choose to create one world rather than another", Engelhardt subtly notes.[52]

2.3.2. Three Systems of Health Care

Whether in a particular system equality of access will overrule the quality of the delivered care or the focus on cost-containment depends on how policymakers evaluate the conflicting values of freedom, equality, superior care and social efficiency. The evaluation of the various objectives and the subsequent trade-off reflects the underlying principles and theories of justice on which a particular policy is based. Various trade-offs are possible. Based on diverse compromises, a classification of health care systems can be indicated. Starting from the conflict between private and public property, the following threefold classification arises: (1) a free market system, (2) an egalitarian system, and (3) a two-tiered or mixed system of health care.[53]

In a *free market system of health care*, a trade-off is made in favour of negative freedom and social efficiency. A person should be free to enter in a trade relation with someone else. As mentioned, this focus on negative freedom and private property constitutes a form of procedural justice that excludes redistributive measures unless the individuals freely and explicitly choose for a redistribution of goods. Thus, health care is seen as a private commodity that can be traded on the market in exchange for other private goods. In a free market system, the provision of equal access for all is reduced to the provision of the possibility to participate in the health care market via the prevention of obstruction. Consequently, no equal basic health care will be provided but it is believed that in the long run this set up will demonstrate to be socially efficient by creating a surplus that also benefits the worst-off: "A free market economy, through maximising the freedom of those willing and able to participate, may create more resources than any other system and thus in the long run best advantage those most harmed through the natural lottery."[54]

---

[52] *Ibid.*, p. 369.

[53] Engelhardt uses this classification in *Ibid.*, p. 354-365 and in ID., *Health Care Allocations: Response to the Unjust, the Unfortunate and the Undesirable*, p. 121-124 and 128-131.

[54] ID., *The Foundations of Bioethics*, p. 357.

Besides, charity can also play a role in providing a safety net for the disadvantaged.

The American health care system originally was a pure free market system.[55] Medical care was provided only to individuals who either could cover the costs of health care themselves or who were offered aid through charity or philanthropy. Apart from charity, there was no safety net for the worst-off. Today, health policy proposals in the United States are still strikingly libertarian and market oriented; the market system remains the prevailing paradigm for health policy in the US[56] Federal and local governments still encourage religious communities and private hospitals to do charitable work to fill the urgent health care needs of the disadvantaged. An illustration of the influences of libertarian thinking on US health policy is the organisation of health insurance. Together with the Republic of South Africa, the United States is the only developed country in the world without compulsory health insurance that gives access to basic health care services. Patients are free to subscribe to a private health insurance or can obtain health insurance through their employer.[57] Health insurance being both private and voluntary entails the risk that the medical expenses of some patients are not covered because they are under- or uninsured against certain medical costs. For the United States this risk is confirmed: during the 1990s, the number of uninsured Americans increased from 36.3 million in 1990 to 43.9 million in 1998.[58] Since there is no universal health care insurance, persons who cannot afford to pay the insurance premium, risk to go without access to health care services since the provision of health care services is directly linked with someone's insurance status. In some cases, insurance companies refuse to insure the bad risks, i.e. persons with poor health or risky pre-existing conditions, hereby boldly neglecting considerations of social justice.[59] During the last decades, the costs of these insurance premiums

[55] *Ibid.*, p. 356.

[56] T.L. BEAUCHAMP & J.F. CHILDRESS, *op. cit.*, p. 231; see also H.T. ENGELHARDT, *Health Care Allocation: Response to the Unjust, the Unfortunate and the Undesirable*, p. 128.

[57] "More than 60% of the US population has employer-based health insurance coverage (...). Another 25% has either private health insurance unconnected to employment or some form of publicly supported health insurance." T.L. BEAUCHAMP & J.F. CHILDRESS, *op. cit.*, p. 240.

[58] S.A. SCHROEDER, *Health Policy 2001: Prospects for Expanding Health Care Insurance Coverage*, in *The New England Journal of Medicine* 344/11 (2001) 847.

[59] T.L. BEAUCHAMP & J.F. CHILDRESS, *op. cit.*, p. 240.

have substantially increased both for persons who rely upon employer based insurance programs as for those who buy insurance individually.[60] This significant increase in insurance premiums is worrying because health care insurance coverage is a determining factor for which care persons can claim or what type of health care they have access to. Lack of health insurance has both medical and financial consequences. Uninsured people are likely to refrain from needed care, even if the care is life saving, and high medical expenses cause bankruptcy in certain cases. The lack of universal health insurance has major implications for the actual health status of persons. Together with the rise of under- or uninsured Americans, there has been a significant deterioration of the health status within a number of vulnerable groups such as ethnic minorities, legal immigrants and children.

Next to the central focus on freedom, private property and the appreciation of health care as a private commodity, theorists argue that a market system of health care implicitly encourages social effi- ciency: "If some element of health care becomes too expensive or not worth as much as competing possible expenditure, individuals will engage in cost containment through not purchasing such health care, and its price tends to fall."[61] This assertion needs refining. First, the market system of health care failed to generate the required social efficiency. During the 1980s and 1990s, there was an exponential increase in health care expenditure.[62] Consequently, a fundamental reshuffle of costs was carried out, as indicated by Engelhardt. How- ever, even after these cost containment measures, the US health care expenditure largely exceeds the average health care expenditure of other developed countries where health care is less predominantly organised according to free market forces.[63] Secondly, the focus of

---

[60] R. KUTTNER, *Health Insurance Coverage*, in *The New England Journal of Medicine* 340/2 (1999) 163.

[61] H.T. ENGELHARDT, *The Foundation of Bioethics*, p. 357.

[62] In the period between 1988-1989, for example, the employer's contributions for health insurance coverage increased by 18 %. For more on this increase in health care expenditures, see R. KUTTNER, *The American Health Care System: Employer Sponsored Health Coverage*, in *New England Journal Of Medicine* 340/3 (1999) 248 ff.

[63] In 1997, the US's estimated total (public and private) expenditure on health was 13,7 % of the Gross Domestic Product (GDP). During the same period, the average expenditure on health in the EU countries was 7,3 % of GDP. See THE WORLD HEALTH REPORT 2000, *Health Systems: Improving Performance*, Geneva, World Health Organisa- tion, 2000, p. 192-195.

attention on cost-containment has turned out to compromise the freedom of choice within the health care system. The reshuffle of the costs and contributions included, among other things, cost sharing with employees in case of employer based health insurance and the introduction of 'managed care', i.e. a restriction of the available health care services. In managed care, private health care institutions, called Health Maintenance Organisations (HMOs), determine what health care services in which institutions people have access to. These measures, implying a deprivation of freedom of choice were imposed on patients by linking them with financial consequences. Because HMOs represent a collective of patients, they can negotiate reduced rates with health care providers who will accept to offer discounts in order to maintain access to patients.[64]

In addition to the existing system of managed care and the subsequent limitations on individual freedom, there is another characteristic of the US health care system that shows the weakening of the pure free market tendency, namely the guarantee of a minimum of health care for certain social groups by enrolling them in a public health insurance plan. Medicare and Medicaid are the most well known public health plans in the US. Their beneficiaries are respectively the elderly (over 65 years old), and the poor and disabled who are ineligible for the private insurance schemes. As a reaction to public concern about the universal accessibility of basic health care during the 1960s, these legislative initiatives aim at providing basic health care for society's most vulnerable groups. The above mentioned indicates that the US health care system is no longer a pure free market system. Although libertarian principles and the free market system still govern the paradigm in which the US health policy is designed, the availability of schemes that provide basic health care for the disadvantaged implies a distancing from the free market principle and the view that health care is a private good that can be exchanged for other goods. In combining elements from different perspectives, the US health care system can be qualified as a mixed or two-tiered system.

The opposite of a free market system is a strictly *egalitarian* system of health care. Here, the trade-off between the four objectives of a

---

[64] B.M. SMITH, *Trends in Health Care Coverage and Financing and Their Implications for Policy*, in *New England Journal Of Medicine* 337/14 (1997) 1000.

health care system is decided in favour of equal access to care or equal care for all depending on whether one applies to a weak or strong egalitarianism. Freedom of choice and social efficiency are, then, subordinated to the search for more equality in health care delivery. An egalitarian system clearly entails distributive elements because the provision of care ignores individual contributions to the costs of the health care system by, for example, using general taxation to finance health care. In practical terms, the egalitarian system is made operational in an inclusive health care system or 'unified system'[65] that provides equal health care to all regardless of the individual's financial, social or medical condition.

The United Kingdom's nationalised health care system was initially set up as a strictly egalitarian health care system; the purpose of the National Health Service (NHS) then was to provide equal care for all. Originally both finance and facilities were public. The NHS was financed mainly by state funds from general taxation. The actual level of health care funding is, then, under strict government budgetary control. This system of health care funding is referred to as the Beveridge Model according to the Beveridge Report (1944) that cleared the way for the NHS to be established in 1948. Apart from the health care funding, the central government also had control over the health care facilities. On the level of access, the NHS guaranteed universal access to health care services on the condition of the General Practitioner as entry point for medical care. At the beginning of the 1990s, however, Britain's NHS underwent fundamental reformation including among others more internal competition ('internal markets') and greater hospital autonomy as a response to efficiency problems and problems of quality of care. Since then, reformation of the NHS is a recurring theme on the political agenda due to problems waiting lists for non-urgent medical interventions as one of the most obvious. Additionally, countries with national health services have been introducing more and more market oriented elements, e.g. private contributions and co-payments. In other European countries, analogous circuits of state owned hospitals and private health care institutions appear and in primary care General Practitioners now often function in both public and private contexts. Alongside the UK, Ireland, the Scandinavian countries as well as Southern European countries

---

[65] T.L. BEAUCHAMP & J.F. CHILDRESS, op. cit., p. 376.

(Italy, Portugal and Spain; partly Greece) have nationalised health care systems. The overall result of these reformations is a greater degree of freedom from state control. Thereby, the inclusive and nationalised system is transformed into a two-tiered system of health care.[66]

Neither the egalitarian nor the free market systems of health care are static. The egalitarian system has incorporated a number of free market elements in order to eliminate problems of social efficiency and quality of care. The NHS, with its constant revisions is an archetypal example. The US-example of the organization of health care in a free market system shows that a safety net is built-in to guarantee a minimum access for the worst off. These reformations and changes show that both the free market and the egalitarian system have partially overcome their internal differences by evolving towards a two-tiered system.

A *two-tiered* or *mixed system* is a compromise between a free market and an egalitarian system of health care: "On the one hand, it provides at least some amount of health care for all, while on the other allowing those with resources to purchase additional health care."[67] In a two-tiered system, the weak egalitarian principle of equal access to fundamental health care resources is incorporated in the first tier of health care while at the same time freedom is promoted in a two-fold way. The first tier makes the egalitarian concept of positive freedom operational by offering people a decent minimum of health care that opens prospects for their personal development. The second tier acknowledges the libertarian concept of negative freedom since consumers are not obstructed to use private resources to provide themselves with whatever care they want.

The American as well as the various European systems have shifted towards a two-tiered system. In the US health care system the first tier of health care creates a safety net for the worst-off with public programs such as Medicare and Medicaid, while the extensive network of private facilities leave enough room for private initiatives funded by private resources. The European nationalised health care systems are converted into mixed systems by giving health care providers and patients more freedom while at the same time main-

[66] E. JAKUBOWSKI, *Health Care Systems in the EU: A Comparative Study*, Luxembourg, 1998, p. 22.

[67] H. T. ENGELHARDT, *op. cit.*, p. 361.

taining basic and affordable health care for all. Next to the nationalised systems of health care, there is another type of health care system operational in Europe, namely the social insurance or Bismarck
model that also incorporates two tiers of health care.[68] Following the
German blueprint, different modes of social insurance systems are
still operational throughout Europe. Among the countries that essentially have a system of social insurance are Austria, Belgium, France,
Greece, Luxembourg and The Netherlands. As the counterpart of the
Beveridge Model, funding under the social insurance model is organised through intermediary insurance funds that are largely independent from the government and often aligned with political or religious institutions or ideologies. In a social insurance system, the role
of the state is limited and there is more freedom of choice for both
patients and providers than in the original NHS. Patients have the
freedom to choose what health care insurance they subscribe to while
a number of health care institutions are privately owned. Access
to basic health care, the first tier of health care, remains assured
because health care insurance is compulsory. Furthermore, the private
insurance funds are not seeking profit: "the aim is to share the costs for
medical care between the sick and the well and to adjust for different
levels of ability to pay."[69] Lastly, social insurance focuses not only on
freedom of choice and basic and affordable health care but also on
social efficiency and cost containment. Private funds are merged and
the role of the state is growing because of budget control.[70]

2.3.3. Context and Community

As mentioned above, the European as well as the US health care systems have tried to reconcile the four different and sometimes contradictory goals of a health care system. The examples set by
the health care systems in the US and in Europe demonstrate
that a growing consensus is best achieved in a two-tiered system.[71]

---

[68] Referring to the German chancellor Bismarck who introduced the first system
of social insurance in 1883.

[69] E. JAKUBOWSKI, op. cit., p. 10.

[70] Ibid., p. 5.

[71] Beauchamp and Childress formulate their preferences for a combination of two
tiers of health care thus: "The best plan is likely to be the one that most coherently
promotes both values (i.e. efficiency, fairness and equity) and that insists on universal access to a decent minimum of health care", in T.L. BEAUCHAMP & J.F. CHILDRESS,
op. cit., p. 377.

Nevertheless, not all two-tiered health care systems are equal. The ultimate trade-off between the best possible care, equal access, social efficiency and freedom of choice, will determine how much public resources are to be at the disposal of the first tier of health care. Whether a two-tiered system can actually meet the health care needs of the disadvantaged depends to a large extent on how one translates 'a decent minimum of health care' on a practical level. Parallel to the President's Commission, Engelhardt suggests that the *de facto* meaning of basic health care depends to a large extent on public and social factors and on the outcome of the democratic deliberation process.[72] This implies a shift towards the communitarian theory, i.e. that shared understandings and social meanings play an important role in the discussion and deliberation on the construction of a health care system.

The American system seems to differ from its various European counterparts precisely on the issue of these underlying shared understandings. This is strongly suggested by the different roads the American and European systems have travelled. The American health care system, originally, was purely a free market system where only individual freedom was guaranteed. Throughout its history there have been moments where public concern was raised about the universal accessibility of basic health care and, particularly, about the right to health care of vulnerable groups. An example of such awareness is the State of Oregon's health plan, the first American plan to ration health care funds, that included measures to assure that the worst off have access to basic health care. The legislative initiatives of President Johnson and the US Congress in the 1960s that introduced the public insurance schemes of Medicare and Medicaid are also examples of this public concern. All together, the set-up of these public initiatives is however, relatively small compared with the rapid growth of the private based HMO's and managed care.[73] It is even so that the stringent rules of managed care are not active only in the employer based health care insurance programs but are expanded to the public programs as well.

The European health care systems that were created in the context of the welfare state, aimed at guaranteeing a number of basic social

---

[72] *Ibid.*, p. 362.
[73] C.M. CLANCY & M. DANIS, *Setting Priorities 'American Style'*, in A. COULTER & C. HAM, *The Global Challenge of Health Care Rationing*, Buckinham, 2000, p. 54.

rights. The right to basic health care is only one among several. Because of crises regarding the funding and problems with the quality of the services on offer, the European health care systems were forced to evolve towards a two-tiered system. As one can deduce from the example of the NHS in the UK, this process is still ongoing. It is important to note that these reformations do not question the guarantee of basic social rights but aim at translating these goals in practical and affordable solutions.

As stated by communitarian theory, shared understandings and social meanings play a central role in the design of societal institutions. Until today, the emphasis on individual rights and the right to private property are a determining factor in the US. Today, Americans hold the belief that health care should not be a top priority for government action.[74] In general, public support for government regulation of businesses and free enterprises and mixed public-private sectors such as health care, faded away to be replaced by widespread citizen distrust towards involvement of federal government in the private sector. This is rather remarkable evidence given the fact that during the last four decades there was substantial dissatisfaction with the American health care system and with the private health insurance and managed care industries.[75] These data however, confirm the American ethos of individual freedom where the right to private property has strong implications on all domains of private and public life and, moreover, for issues situated on the intersection of public involvement and private needs, such as the organisation and financing of a health care system.

Although our previous differentiation in nationalised and social insurance systems of health care has indicated that there is no such thing as a single European health care system, the various European systems have one common aim that differs from the shared understandings which shape the American health care system. The primary concern of the European systems is the neutralisation of the outcome of the natural and social lottery by sharing the costs for medical care between the sick and the healthy. This common aim can be explained through the close relationship between the culture and

---

[74] R.J. BLENDON & J. M. BENSON, *Americans' Views on Health Policy. A Fifty-Year Historical Perspective*, in *Health Affairs* 20/2 (2001) 43.

[75] *Ibid.*, p. 36-37.

the ethos of the different European countries where mutual solidarity and social responsibility take a central place as basic ethical principles of the welfare state.[76] This mechanism of solidarity reflects a consensus in the European countries that health care should not be left to a free market alone because one is convinced of the fact that costs of sickness are contingent and should therefore surmount the individual responsibility.[77] In addition to this, it is a widely accepted belief that access to health care may not be obstructed by a person's financial, social or familial background. These considerations are firmly fixed in the law since in the majority of the European countries access to health care is regarded as a constitutional right.[78]

---

[76] J.D. RENDORFF & P. KEMP, *op. cit.*, p. 56.

[77] E. JAKUBOWSKI, *op. cit.*, p.10.

[78] In particular, the right to health care is referred to in the Constitutions of Belgium, Greece, France, Italy, Luxembourg, the Netherlands, Portugal and Finland. In M.F. BUTT, J. KÜBERT & C.A. SCHULTZ, *Fundamental Social Rights in Europe* (Social Affairs Series 104), Luxembourg, p. 31.

THE ALLOCATION OF HEALTH CARE RESOURCES

Economic Constraints and Access to Health Care

Pierre Boitte & Bruno Cadoré

3.1. Preamble

In the American literature, or in the European literature that it directly inspires, the problem of allocation of health care resources is mainly directed to the justification of a fair distribution of the resources concerned. Such justification is needed either on the level of macro-allocation, on the level of micro-allocation, or on the intermediate level of the institution. At the level of macro-allocation, ethical reflection, which overlaps here conspicuously with political philosophy, consists of developing general theories in order to justify the existence of a fair health care system.[1] At the level of micro-allocation, ethical reflection is aimed at the development of rational criteria for making choices or decisions. These are intended to enable the most equitable possible individual access to health care services (for example, do acceptable ethical criteria exist to justify a patient not having access to an organ transplant?).[2] At the intermediate level, the question at hand is that of analysing the procedures used for the attribution of a rare commodity (for example, donors' grafts or sperm) at the 'local' level (a country, a region, a given institution) in accordance with normative principles, such as equality, time, status, need, merit, and efficiency.[3]

---

[1] N. DANIELS, *Just Health Care*, Cambridge, 1985.

[2] J-F. KILNER, *Who Lives? Who Dies?*, New Haven – London, 1990.

[3] J. ELSTER, *Local Justice*, New York, 1992 ; J. ELSTER, *Ethique des choix médicaux*, in J. ELSTER & N. HERPIN (éd.), *Ethique des choix médicaux*, Poitiers, 1992, p. 11-35.

A normative ethical concept is at work in each of these three scenarios: it is always a case of trying to "establish the way in which allocation practices depend on philosophical principles of distributive justice."[4] Ethical reflection has certainly proven necessary to the extent that it provides a sound basis for argument, in particular for the justification of the maintenance of a strong solidarity between the members of the same group regarding access to health care.[5] However, such a perspective appears as too restricted. In fact, the wager of a normative ethic is that a reasonably reached agreement on something defendable, such as justice, is a sufficient basis for certain collective actions intended to transform existing institutions and to inspire choices in the matter. From an ideal of equity some institutions and practices (a system of social protection, restriction of care for the oldest, economic constraints, generalised rationing of care...) certainly turn out to be open to criticism. In light of that ideal of equity, such practices reveal themselves to be unjust, e.g. the use of the age criteria to limit access to health care. Ethical reflection concentrates itself then on questions, such as what must be done so that these practices change, these institutions continue or, in short, so that the criticised situation inclines in the direction of the invoked ideal? The principles of distributive justice here keep largely silent, as their role does not consist of intruding immoderately in practice.

An ethical investigation therefore provides a first judgement on the degree of justice of a system, a decision or an institution. It thus precedes a more thorough and more systematic evaluation of the processes in action, which must, for example, mobilise the different social sciences. It is indeed the task of an empirical and descriptive analysis to facilitate a concrete judgement. With the support of an ethical approach conceived as an evaluation of reality, this *concrete* judgement (and thus not merely in principle) gives an evaluation of the situation and the evolution of care and health care systems hereby inspiring choices and actions. It seems, then, that the reality that these principles of justice must gauge – the equity of a system, of a decision, of an institution, partly escapes them, because the applied evaluative criteria prove to be only partially pertinent.

---

[4] J. ELSTER, *op. cit.*, p. 12.

[5] P. BOITTE, *Ethique, justice et santé. Allocation des ressources dans une société viellissante*, Montréal, 1995, p. 272.

We would therefore prefer, with regard to the question of allocation of resources, to adopt a different approach than the development of a normative ethic. This approach starts with the analysis of crisis situations, on the one hand, to examine them and to evaluate the significance of individual and collective practices and, on the other, to plant therein the seeds of a desirable transformation. Recourse to ethical reflection rests indeed on the hypothesis of a capacity for creativity in the human being faced with a crisis, with a view to invent new ways of assuming the tender care and solidarity that such a crisis requires of our communities. The perspective developed here therefore concerns the social and political component of the ethical intention, conceived as the peculiarly human quality of living on the horizon of meaning and of being capable of constituting this meaningfulness which characterises the human being as being human. In view of the general, individual and group interest that the health of a population represents (a human, demographic, economic and political interest all in one), the ethical evaluation of this reality may be very pertinent, at least if we admit its intrinsic creativity.

Our starting point is the hypothesis of an intrinsic connection between the supposed existence of an economic constraint and the current crisis of health care systems. The first point touches on the reasons for which the existence of this 'constraint' seems to us to invite criticism. A second point gives a statement of this crisis in our health care systems. A third point will illustrate that this crisis originates in a growing vulnerability of social systems, illustrated by the emblematic question of access to care. A fourth point describes the task of an ethical inquiry carried out in such a context and its subject matter. A fifth and last point finally addresses the question of how to assume an institutional and collective responsibility, taking into account the broad character of the situations under review.

3.2. Economic Constraint or Crisis in Health Care Systems?

The notion of economic constraint seems to have increasingly become not only an inevitable but also a primary element in any decision made concerning health care in as much that it limits the framework in which those decisions will be made. Sometimes it reduces the framework to the simple allowance for these financial limits. Blandly accepting such a limitation amounts to the immediate renunciation of any critical view as to the way in which that constraint functions in the framework of modern health care systems and, moreover, in the framework of the functioning of hospitals. It is therefore crucial to clarify this notion of constraint in any reflection exploring the influence of the budgetary limits on health care.

When we use the qualification of restraint, it is for the reason that spending on health care reached in the 1980s a level, deemed to be much too excessive. The costs for health care had to be contained and reduced at all costs for fear of a financial catastrophe. The paradox is that, during the same period, the health sector became a major element, if not the driving force, in the production of economic wealth, for instance by the development of hospitals as genuine production units. The political interventions of the 1980s, hoping to bring the development of social health expenditure under control using economic mechanisms, soon ran up against the very particularity of health care institutions, namely their sensitivity to the pressure of economic rationality. This observation is characterised by the fact that hospitals in particular do not respond (only) to precise health needs (as economists often think), in which case it would be enough to identify these needs, respond to them in some measure and limit them for the rest. In fact, hospitals, by meeting a need, quite often create a new need. The completely cured patient remains a potential care-consumer; the patient can always improve his state of health one way or another (we have only to think here of chronic illnesses due, for example, to an increase in human longevity). And we did not even mention *iatrogenic* phenomena.

There is the observation that medical supplies, still very abundant in our countries despite the numerous attempts towards rationalisation, attract health care requests, which appear to be inexhaustible. If collective health care consumption cannot be controlled, or only with serious difficulty and always only partially, by the government, this is because the main players in the growth of this consumption are to be found elsewhere. These players are, first, the health care institutions, themselves, increasingly linked to the producers of medical technology. A technological innovation is first the object of intense marketing around hospitals which, in turn, fall back upon social security in order to be able to 'sell' advanced technology. Another main player in this development is the social idea that highly valorises our hospitals: this explains the scale of the social need for medicine and contributes substantially to the type of medicine we have seen for at least a quarter of a century.[6]

If the constraint appears inevitable, it is so because of an inability to act from within on the conceptions and strategies of the main players in the development of health care spending. These players are, on the one hand, the hospitals and the multinational companies in the health care sector, very often acting in the name of the right to health care or the right to fair access to quality services. On the other hand, there are the care-consuming citizens, who become increasingly demanding in the name of these same rights.[7] The constraint therefore comes from the current impossibility of acting upon the deep imaginary, social, economic and political determinations that work towards the self-development of health as a central social institution in our societies. This affirmation then allows us to 'shift' the question of the constraint: it is less a case of a process imposing itself on the exterior of a health care system and more a case of a constitutive reality inherent in the health care system as such.

This 'constraint' – which could more correctly be entitled the 'health care system self-development process' – seems to be very persistent. The dynamics of the development of the health care sector within our societies will press ahead, since the public authorities find themselves powerless to regulate this spending. This illustrates the inability of the state to develop regulation in regard with health care institutions, what is very different for the trade and consumption of consumer goods which can be easily controlled by the simple setting up of technical mechanisms. The political discourse legitimating the 'constraint' that will limit health care spending fails in this task since it is not situated in a perspective of health improvement of individuals or the community. The latter perspective is the only pertinent way of proposing an inevitable and desirable restriction on certain expenses, on condition, however of proposing at the same time other initiatives intended to improve collective health. It is therefore time to evaluate today's health care systems from the angle of health promotion. We will show that the various discourses on the necessity of a 'constraint' for the health care systems,

---

[6] See L. SFEZ, *La santé parfaite*, Paris, 1995.

[7] For an analysis of different philosophical perspectives of health care needs and the right to health care, see the contribution of Y. Denier and T. Meulenbergs in this volume, p. 265-298.

whether economic, financial or budgetary, often prove to be ideological. Hereby, they neglect the groundwork of a critical analysis of the results produced in terms of health by the systems currently in place and refuse to consider the complexity and contradictions of reality.

3.3. Health Care Systems: a Critical Appraisal

The 'technical' responses to the progress of biomedical technoscience do not necessarily solve the health problems that they meant to eliminate. The crisis of the health care system is both linked to the relative inefficiency of these systems (3.3.1) and to their profound mutation (3.3.2).

3.3.1. Health Care Systems with Doubtful Efficiencies

The study Health in France presents a summary and compelling view of the structural weaknesses of the health care system in France and therefore could be a key for understanding similar systems.[8] Three major problems may be pinpointed. First, we have the problem of premature mortality.[9] This concerns 24 % of deaths in 1991, and avoidable mortality,[10] accounting for 52 % of early deaths over the same year. These deaths were mainly due to traffic accidents, suicides, cancer resulting out of the use of alcohol and tobacco, and cirrhosis and psychosis linked with alcoholism. Second, the incidence of chronic illnesses connected with lifestyle, increases each year. A distinction may be drawn here between the conditions connected with risk behaviour (alcoholism, tobacco consumption and drug addiction[11], sexually transmitted disease, AIDS, hepatitis, excessive speed, attempted suicide), psychological and social problems (mental and sleep disorders, use of psychotropic substances, suicide and attempted suicide, child abuse), chronic illnesses (men-

---

[8] Haut Comité pour la Santé Publique, La santé en France Vol. 1 , Paris, 1994, p. 75-171.

[9] Premature mortality is defined as "all deaths occurring before the age of 65", in Ibid., p. 76.

[10] The causes of avoidable mortality are defined as "those causes of death which, account being taken of the medical knowledge of the state of the health system, could have been avoided or at least reduced before the age of 65" in Ibid.

[11] Equally, the use of illegal toxic products (heroin, cocaine, cannabis, LSD, glues and solvents, tranquillisers, narcotics, anti-depressants and barbiturates).

tal illnesses, chronic somatic illnesses) and *iatrogenic* illnesses.[12] Third, there is the increasing problem of the vulnerable groups in society, in particular the unemployed, disadvantaged populations and young adults.

These kinds of problems explain why spending on public health improvement is experiencing difficulties. An analysis of the determinants of health and illness indicate that medical parameters alone are not sufficient to ensure the maintenance of health and, thus, that the individual therapeutic relation should leave far more room than it is the case at present for other practices "to obtain a maximum effect on the health of groups particularly exposed to an illness or to a handicap, and this at the best cost."[13]

Three indices, amongst others, originate from this relative inefficiency of health care systems. First, there is a lack of correlation between the means (number of doctors, hospital beds, etc.) and results in terms of health (the usual health indicators: life expectancy, expectancy of years of good health, infant or premature mortality rates, morbidity rate).[14] There are also enough variations between medical practices within any given country, or between comparable countries, without being able to show a difference in the prevalence of the problems at the origin of these practices. Finally, numerous medical practices exist that are not in accordance with the indications admitted by the international scientific community, or that have no demonstrable use to the patient. This concerns, for example, the unnecessary or irrelevant prescription of biological tests or complementary tests, in particular imaging, uselessly repeated systematic balance sheets, and prescription of dangerous, useless or unjustifiably expensive medication.

In short, consulting fewer doctors, taking less medication, undergoing fewer additional tests would still promote 'good health' for the majority of patients. Perhaps, it would even improve the health of others. Besides health care systems, other determinants also explain the quality of public health: lifestyle (diet, alcohol consump-

---

[12] Pathological effects provoked by medication or by a medical act with diagnostic or therapeutic intent resulting from an unforeseeable or inevitable fault, error or risk.

[13] *Ibid.*, p. 452.

[14] Japan also, currently with the longest life expectancy devotes amongst the lowest portion of its GNP to health care of all industrialised countries.

tion, tobacco, sexual behaviour), physical environment (work environment, atmospheric pollution, toxic industrial waste, various chemical substances) and, finally, the social environment (the lack of effective support and the lack of social activities, due, in particular, to a professional non-insertion or to poor working conditions).

If an ethical reflection on the allocation of resources wants to be relevant, it must take into account these important factors.

3.3.2. *Foreseeable and Uncertain Trends*

Furthermore, the probable mortality trends and technological innovations will enable us to foresee the evolution of health needs and health supply. They will also help to clarify the current crisis of the health care system, its probable transformation, and the reinforcement of a mainly ideological 'constraint' if nothing is done to take account of this reality and to change it.

The prospect of an ageing population looms ahead. Apart from the effects on mortality, the ageing society will also be confronted with an increase of chronic illnesses, as well as with a re-appearance of infectious diseases. Here, the elaboration of mechanisms for intergenerational solidarity is inevitable. At the same time, an integration of the treatment of chronically ill patients into the functioning of the current system is needed. Furthermore, the pathogenic characteristics of certain aspects of social evolution (the persistence of a high rate of unemployment, the effects of mechanisms of economic exclusion, the transformation of family structures) will induce health needs that will not be genuinely satisfied, except through the development of mechanisms to fight social exclusion.

The permanent technological innovation in the field of medicine may, in itself, brings potential ruptures on the organisation and practice of health care in so far as it incites a radical transformation of the health professions and encourages the emergence of a medicine of experts. Thus, medical imaging, new surgical techniques, the use of biotechnology, genetic therapy and functional substitution techniques (from renal dialysis to orthopaedic prostheses) can only reinforce the dynamics of the spread of technological innovation. New specialised professions will appear in medicine, biology, and information technology. They will change the traditional conception of the role of the doctor and the organisation of the corresponding work.

Despite past successes, despite the hopes for the future, medical practice has thus entered into a period of uncertainty. This uncertainty is incidentally illustrated by the increasing difficulties the physician-patient relationship is faced with. The general crisis of the health care system is reinforced by the negative effects of a 'policy of economic constraint'. When this policy is pursued, the scope of the challenges that need to be faced is not altered. Instead, the risk exists that there is a loss of confidence in the physician-patient relationship which would only hasten the gradual decay of the health care system.

Therefore, we want to illustrate in the following section that the erosion, which is already in progress, is itself linked to an increasing vulnerability of our social systems. It would be illusory that the present situation of health care could be changed without making reference to the more global evolution of our modern societies. The recurrent theme here is the problem of access to health care.

3.4. Access to Health Care as Illustrative for Social Vulnerability

In our ethical perspective, the clarification of the position of populations at risk in the health care setting is a useful method for the evaluation of the social character of our society.

First, it is necessary to understand the scale of the phenomenon under discussion: the difficult or impossible access for a considerable part of e.g. the Belgian and French populations to their health care system. In fact, even if the existence of an almost universal social insurance and a relatively homogeneous health care supply guaranteed a reasonably equitable access to qualitative health care services, increasing numbers of persons would experience difficulties in their access to the system. These difficulties are linked to phenomena of marginalisation that affect an extremely mixed population: young people without income, the unemployed, workers in low paid, high-risk jobs, single parents, immigrants, the elderly, HIV-positive patients, persons using hard drugs, etc. Reading documents issued for example by the social services of Belgian hospitals, provides a clear illustration of this fact. Every time the discussion on the development of human beings deeply affected in their physical being and in their dignity appears to become abstract, these specific cases can function as unique reminders.

A Belgian 60 year woman that lives on minimal social security receives care in a cardiology ward. She constantly asks the doctors and nurses to be released from the hospital. After a profound discussion with the patient, the staff becomes aware of her numerous financial problems.

A 37-year old Belgian computer scientist has been fired from his job. He sets up as a private self-employed expert but is not very successful. He falls behind in his mutual insurance contributions and has to live of his wife's earnings. He is admitted to the hospital for attempted suicide. He urgently calls for help from his wife and from the social security services.

A Belgian man, a chronic patient, had earnings of around € 2.500 per month. He finds his disposable income reduced overnight by about half while the usual charges and fees for his illness remain the same. He delays his heart operation as long as possible for lack of funds.

Security is deceptive, since the risk of slipping from a status of employment to a less favourable status, from one social status to a lower, has become greater for each one of us in this period of radical economic change. Besides the question of access, both the cost of health care provisions and the continuity of treatment pose problems. Even with access to health care, treatments are only partially refunded. Synthetic material, for example, is less and less refunded (e.g. dental work and optical prostheses). For the chronically ill this problem is crucial. They are confronted with numerous stays in hospital, long-term treatments, outpatient treatments and, sometimes, treatment at home. Because of this, chronically ill patients are faced with extremely large financial burdens. Furthermore, these health situations regularly have also a strong impact on the daily life of these persons: they have to give up work and accept a changed social position, can get into debt or are reduced to poverty. The problem of health care costs is becoming increasingly worrying: in France for instance, in 1994, "nearly a quarter of households in which at least one member is registered with the social security say they have dropped out of health care because of insufficient refunding".[15]

These two types of situations, non-access to care and financial difficulties, clearly indicate that access to health care is regulated around the insurability of the patient or the possibility of the latter to accept the financial burden of the costs of his/her hospitalisation.

---

[15] M. FOURDRIGNIER, *Les exclus de la santé*, in *Médecine de l'homme* 221/1 (1996) 20-27.

Efforts to improve the access to health care therefore proceed via a modification of these kinds of regulation. Economic, financial and budgetary 'constraints' will certainly not remedy this, because they constitute the main causes of this situation. In any case, such a modification would not fundamentally change the risk-factors, poverty or exclusion. In fact, the reflection on access to health care involves, beyond the analysis of the health care system, a broader reflection on precariousness and social inequality. This reflection also shows, that the problem becomes at once eminently ethical and eminently political.

The term 'precariousness' refers to extremely heterogeneous situations which display a triple rupture experienced by the person concerned: a rupture with functional daily activity, in particular employment; a relational rupture leading to gradual isolation; and, finally, a rupture in time perspective, the fact of having little or no future, make positive action seem all the more futile. This triple rupture reveals the dynamics of human situations that evolve towards social exclusion, situations that unfortunately multiply. The existence of such dynamics indicates a process of social vulnerability that very few persons can say with certainty that it will never affect them. These individual situations of precariousness are produced socially. They illustrate the exclusion resulting from social dynamics and therefore they require an analysis of the social structure in which such precariousness and exclusion originates. Besides, leading to a better understanding of the social processes at work, such an analysis would also allow us to avoid a double danger in the reflection on such situations: first, holding the socially excluded responsible for their own situation and, second, reacting with indignation instead of analysis like some do by crying out that it is all scandalous and that it has to be stopped !

It would lead us too far, to discuss this kind of social analysis in detail. We limit our discussion to the notion of social health inequality. This notion touches on inequalities with regard to death and illness. Heated debates move scientists to explore the nature, importance and causes of health inequalities in the developed countries. Taking into account health inequalities is no easy matter. Despite these difficulties, the persistence of social inequalities in health is, however, an incontestable phenomenon. In France, for instance, between 1981 and 1991, "whichever group of pathologies is considered, the inequalities in mortality between social categories have tended to increase".[16] At best, large discrepancies in health still remain between the best provided-for and the least well provided-for.

3.5. A Common Responsibility?

Until now, we have argued that the problem of constraint should be shifted towards the crisis of the health care system. We then called for an analysis of the components of this crisis and highlighted an increasing social vulnerability. Our analysis may raise some pessimism regarding the future of the purpose of health care systems which is: to ensure a high quality of life through good health for individuals and for the society, and, as for the current credibility of the values underlying that finality, the care for other persons, equity and solidarity. Our health care systems might therefore be said to be suffering from a twofold weakness: a practical vulnerability, which in turn is a sign of a more general cultural or anthropological vulnerability that concerns the society as a whole.

Against the backdrop of the slow maturation of the collective consciousness regarding human rights, solidarity was continuously defended since the end of World War II. This happened with the profound hope of improving the conditions and quality of life of the citizens of our societies. It served as the backbone of the functioning of our societies for half a century, a spinal column supported in its turn by the prodigious creation of wealth during the same period. It seems, nevertheless, that the profound belief in the necessity of social solidarity, which has been the scaffolding around the formidable construction of the doctrine of social security in Western Europe, is losing its hold.

This happens at a time when economic growth is slackening off, while individual demand for security and welfare, in particular regarding health, is more urgent than ever before. In short, the mechanisms of solidarity are currently being challenged and come under strong criticism. Now, the existence of a developed system of social protection – as has been proven during the first decades of its functioning – has had positive effects on the strengthening and quality of the social cohesion without which a social

---

[16] HAUT COMITÉ POUR LA SANTÉ PUBLIQUE, *op. cit.*, Vol. 2, p. 193

system would fall apart. A certain ethical quality of the social bond is therefore fundamentally called into question by the crisis of the health care system that has contributed, in its own way, to the production of social cohesion. In view of the inherent contradictions,[17] and the disintegration of the values and aims on which the health care system hitherto has been based, it seems necessary to describe this evolution.

The task of ethical reflection in this respect then consists of clarifying the necessary conditions from which to act in the field of health care so as to put a stop to the current erosion of the social bond. According to Emmanuel Levinas, this care for the quality of the social bond basically springs from the responsibility that each of us bears with regard to the rights of others. In fact, the claim made by our fellow man on our capacity for responsibility radically constitutes us in existence and freedom, as ethical subjects. This duty of care for others, this questioning by the mystery of the Other and the interpersonal relationship it involves, specifically structures the identity of each of us. A society preoccupied with fundamental rights, informed by a concern for justice, must therefore work towards acquiring the means to request this duty of 'solicitude'. The notions of 'equity' and 'solidarity' then can be understood as the political and collective translation of this undeniable responsibility in human brotherhood.[18] Here, the task of ethics is to remind us of the need to take these actions into account, if not actually try to breath fresh life into them. The supposition underlying such an affirmation is that it is possible to create room for debate and reflection with regard to the different choices that have already been made in order to erect a logic other than one which is structurally-imposed.

This task is carried out on the basis of a global evaluation of health care systems; it may take the following form. The desire for health and welfare that is increasingly coming to characterise our societies goes together with the impact of biomedical technoscience and the

[17] See 3.3. above.

[18] This approach is, of course, open to criticism. The issue at hand is to show that the ethical questions arising in health care require an in-depth reflection in terms of a political philosophy. Levinas' interest is to raise the question of justice from the most intimate aspect of the interpersonal relationship, based on the experience of an inverted initiative: the experience of the world is offered through the existence of others, the subject is not in the first instance free, but responsible. See on this point, e.g., B. CADORÉ, *L'expérience bioéthique de la responsibilité*, Montréal, 1994, p. 204.

resultant growing medicalisation of health. This congruence creates a very urgent need for health care and feeds a logic of omnipresent production due to the fact that care institutions are genuine economic production units, endowed with the capacity and autonomy to produce their own development. The medicalisation of health and the logic of economic production are now *de facto* two sides of the same reality, supported by a health care need that is largely artificial, given the contemporary attachment to health. This logic of auto-production of the health care institution, at once scientific and economic, increasingly turns the notions of equity or solidarity into moral alibis for the presumed goal of the institution: to heal both the individual and society.

In reality, however, the essential force at work in the evolution of health care systems originates more in the system's unfailing realisation of its own logic of auto-development than in a real concern for health or for social justice. The notion of solidarity is slowly losing its vitality and is replaced by an ideology of production and an increasing medicalization of health care systems. In light of this evolution, the hypothesis of a global counter-productivity of the health care institution becomes credible. This situation comes forth out of a double negligence. First, there is in health care practices a negation of the subject, patient and doctor alike. Second, we observe a rejection of a critical approach to health care in favour of the development of treatments as true objects of science and commerce. This double rejection makes health care institutions increasingly more vulnerable.

The rejection of the subject, which is an expression of a reduced concern for solidarity, corresponds with a reduction of the cultural, psychic and organic totality of the human person to a dimension where medicine is merely about objective and scientific facts. On the other hand, the medicalisation and commercialisation of health are without any doubt a sign that modern individuals are less apt to perceive their health outside the sphere of medicine. The consequence of this situation, more generally, is a kind of cultural split: on the anthropological level we move from a holistic conception of the body, of health and illness, to an objective, scientific approach. This is symbolic for the reduction of culture to the technoscientific dimension of the human body.

The necessary conditions for re-introducing an ethical dimension within this field therefore depend on a precondition: the critical questioning of the commercial and scientific evolution of health care. Only given this condition will we be able to consider desirable evolutions. Such a critical analysis would also, *ipso facto*, be a political challenge in the broadest meaning of the term.

3.6. Perspectives for Action

The notion of 'policy' adds to the analysis the collective dimension of all existence and all human action, as well as the legitimacy of collective plans intended to assume and set up a common 'good way of life'. This collective dimension points to the notion of public space. It is possible that our behaviour, our actions and other phenomena take on a new consistency within such a public space. Individual citizens, groups and communities should restart a debate on their social functioning. Only then a sincere evaluation of the quality of individual and collective life in a society will be conceivable and new possibilities may be imagined. At this moment, it rather seems that political action, as responsible action by the community toward itself, is greatly depreciated in our societies and is becoming increasingly reduced to the rationalisation of budgetary choices in order to produce maximum welfare. Following the absence of decisions in core areas of public life, the unresolved problems have piled up. Political institutions have proven to be incapable of preparing the changes that would open the debate on the multidimensional crisis with which we are now confronted, the crisis of health care systems being only one of its aspects.

Nonetheless, human beings are capable of recognising, acting and creating together. We therefore cannot argue that nothing can be done about the inequalities described but, on the contrary, that everything remains to be done so that the health of each becomes a communal concern, which is political in the broadest sense. The health of each person becomes then the one dimension that brings all citizens together in the fight against the process of social disaffiliation.

In the light of this ethical reflection two zones of action seem to be prior: first, at an intermediate level, among doctors, nurses and hospitals; second, on a more general level, the reflection about the necessity to develop an adequate health care policy.

3.6.1. *The Responsibility of the Hospital and its Medical Staff*

With regard to health care access, it seems that the responsibility of the medical staff and of the institutions in which they work is fully present, even if this turns out to be only a limited and partial responsibility. Given the current trends in society towards a greater degree of social vulnerability, it is urgent that the hospital ceases to be conceived by its managers (and, therefore, also by the health insurance companies) essentially as a place of a reduction of social deficits. Hospitals should become, much more than is now the case, key players in social cohesion. Maximum quality of health care must always be accessible for all those who need it. This implies more rather than less accessible health care services, or a reduction to a sort of minimum service in certain cases.

Faced with this tendency, it is essential that the medical staff, the social workers and the psychologists demonstrate their human qualities by a sincere care for their patients. Efforts are being made in this direction in many Belgian and French hospitals. One illustration of this is that an increasing number of hospital workers find it unacceptable that access is restricted only to those who have paid all their social security contributions.

Whatever the goodwill and generosity of those involved may be, the limits of professional possibilities soon appear to be reached. The hospitals have largely become technical platforms and are no longer the places of shelter that they originally were, even in times where the inefficiencies of medicine prevented them from offering more than professional compassion. And so, many people are now wondering: can the hospital, and should the hospital, respond to the shortcomings of society? We can reply to their worries with another question: is a negative answer the only possible answer?

Of course, hospital walls are not meant to protect those who work there and isolate them from outside realities. The hospital is primarily a social institution, mostly financed by public authorities and, as such, it can expect to find itself in the thick of the social problems of the day. The thousand-year history of the hospital constitutes a permanent reminder of the hospital's purpose in society, namely the care for the poor. Now, quite often, taking care of socially precarious patients is seen as opposed to high quality medicine and surgery. Short of bringing the failures to the attention of the responsible politicians, the hospital must learn how to return to its role of helping deprived and distressed persons.

Here again, initiatives are in place and are being developed in this direction. They call for ample creativity, imagination, tenacity and energy, first of course within the hospital itself (for example, the creation of a consultation platform enabling to become aware of situations of dispute, from a financial standpoint certainly, but also from a medical, administrative and social one). This must be followed by making associations with outside players: emergency medical care funds or special assistance funds, links with public hospitals, contacts with associations defending access to care for the 'sans papiers' (illegal immigrants); possible recourse to private initiatives in an attempt, to honour the values upheld by the clinic, etc. If hospitals really wish to place the patient at the centre of their action, it is important that they open up much more than it is currently the case. They should be able to accept and digest these social realities, which were hardly present only fifteen years ago. Why does each establishment not set up consultations for precarious situations, consultations that would respond to the health care needs of marginal patients? This could help to avoid the rejection of the sick, in particular by simplifying the previously exclusionary administrative procedures.

These initiatives are to be encouraged for their relevance and for the resistance that they symbolise against the fracturing of social structures. They would show that, in fact, medical and administrative staff, refuse to remain passive. They may prove that the individual responsibility of medical staff and hospital managers can keep alive the collective values at the foundation of post-war social protection, such as care, equity and solidarity. Finally, these initiatives can help to start the practical and symbolic democratisation of the hospital institution: is it not a case of expanding the services that the hospital must provide and of integrating the social concern to make it a place of humanity?

In this respect, why are public authorities not more encouraged by hospitals to take up this collective responsibility? Indeed, we are convinced that only a collective responsibility will be able to bring about a real progress in this matter.

3.6.2. Collective Responsibility for Health Care: the Need of Health Policy

Even if the health impact of their precariousness and their exclusion is undeniable, the situation of marginal patients is very often characterised by an accumulation of fragilities that have an impact on their health, but also on their relationship with their own body and with others. These weaknesses create problems for their involvement in social life, in particular regarding their access to a regular income, a steady job, fit accommodation, a satisfactory level of education. It seems obvious that medical services, e.g. regular consultations in the context of emergency services, hardly ever produce satisfactory solutions and provide only very partial answers to the overall problem of the precariousness, poverty or exclusion of these persons. It should without any doubt be possible not to become alienated, while remaining realistic, by the constraints but on the contrary make use of this experience to develop a creative reflection.[19] It is indeed more appropriate to speak about serious weaknesses in the functioning of our political structures in Western democracies, rather than calling the economic, financial and budgetary constraints inescapable. Indeed, these constraints refer to the technical dimension of the evolution of health care systems, while the problem of social inequalities in health essentially is related to our political systems.

The technical side of the question of access to health care concerns the debate on the role of the welfare state. It could be argued that the essential role of the welfare state in relation to the problem of exclusion in health care should be that of concentrating more on help for specific patients. At the same time, the obvious risk exists of being too closely directed to present help for the most vulnerable layers of the population, even if it is in their name that the politicians take the field. The French sociologist Dominique Schnapper has expressed this political danger to fight against exclusion before: "Social politics disqualifies those to whom it brings its support by giving them the status of people who need assistance. How do we get out of the circle that marks all kinds of policies against poverty in all known societies in history: aid the poor or excluded without branding him poor-excluded and straight away making it difficult for him to escape out of his condition?"[20]

In an attempt to answer this question, we could argue infinitely about the desirable level of income, aid, allowances and redistribution so as to allow the maintenance of this delicate balance between

---

[19] D. COHEN, *Richesse du monde, pauvreté des nations*, Paris, 1997, p. 125.

[20] D. SCHNAPPER, *Intégration et exclusion dans les sociétés modernes*, in S. PAUGAM, *L'exclusion : l'état des savoirs*, Paris, 1996 (cited by Cohen, *op. cit.*, p. 130).

de facto exclusion and confinement in new ghettos. However, these discussions concern the perfection of technical solutions that will be ineffective unless the political question is answered beforehand: how far must a society be prepared to go down the road of solidarity with regard to the most underprivileged of its members, that is, not only the excluded or the poor, but also the chronically ill, the senile, the mentally handicapped? Policymakers seldom ask this question without demagoguery and with a real desire to provide an answer. Which political alliances could rally modern Western societies around a plan for politically acceptable distribution? Is there any real will among the electors of the traditional parties, the famous middle class, to take up arms against these inequalities, and especially against the inequalities in health which, as we have seen, originate in the more visible inequalities of access to good accommodation, education, work, etc.? What is to be done in anticipation of the clear emergence of the political dimension of the provision of health care?

To set off on this course, we might recall how ill-suited the present system for caring for the needs of the population is, and this not only in the matter of access for the least well provided-for. Indeed, the essential objective of a health care system is not to dispense curative treatment but, first and foremost, to prevent disease. In this respect, it is a matter of public record that the health care system, taken as strictly curative, holds a minority share (roughly 15% to 20%) in the improvement of public health, considered from the viewpoint of mortality rates. Societal factors are recognised as eminently more responsible for the individual health paths (e.g. the gene pool, early years of life, hygiene, quality of nourishment and accommodation, socio-economic environment, social pressure, and the support from family and friends). The health of the individual then becomes an eminently public affair, requiring us to discuss health policy and not only the financing of health insurance. Such a development naturally requires the expansion of the field of representation in which our individual and collective beliefs and, finally, our values in the matter of health care are rooted. It may also require moving the current framework so as to reconfigure a frame, which certainly may represent a new type of coercion, but which takes better account of the reality and of the expressed human needs.

The question of change in our societal institutions will become unavoidable. Here, we must be aware of the fact that the institution of health and medicine is one of the central institutions of our societies. How can we express and represent the general interest? On the one hand, how do we transmute the values that articulate the individual interests emanating from the private sphere, e.g. the interest in being properly cared for when ill, and, on the other hand, the collective interests, e.g. the interest in having a society in good health? When we approach this problem in this way, collective health would no longer become a public commodity subject to the competition of private interests representing all the sectors that live from the development of medicine. A single figure in this respect: in France, more than EUR 1800 is spent per capita for curative treatment, and only EUR 40 per capita for prevention, school medicine and medicine at work.[21] There is clearly a growing gap between the understanding of the determinants of health and the priority that a technocratic management is prepared to give to health. Therefore, it is necessary to work as hard as we can to change the current frames of reference that allow this growing disjunction.

The social inequalities in health are among the least accepted consequences of general social inequality. What social policies must be devised that would lessen the inequalities of access to care? Quite certainly, policies that would be open for a serious debate about those at the margins of the current health care system. This would call into question the over-legitimisation of a Manager-and-Technician State – the necessities of the world economy – and would remind us to ask the most important political question: what kind of a society do we as a collective want to create together?

3.7. Conclusion

We developed a plea for a political approach to health care. We are convinced that this would give a stimulus to revitalise three fundamental values, namely care, equity and solidarity. To realise this, a critical examination of the constraints on medicine is inescapable. In view of the foregoing, the problem of the allocation of resources would best be approached, starting with the three following statements:

---

[21] J.-P. DAVANT, *La securité sociale continue à produire des dépenses inutiles*, in *Le Monde* 26-27/10/1997, p. 8.

- First, health care has become sick through the medicalisation of health. Contemporary health care would benefit from being rebalanced in the direction of health promotion in the name of the mission of general 'solicitude'.
- Second, growing technologisation has weakened medicine. To avoid blindness, a critical examination from the perspective of equity is absolutely necessary.
- Finally, a society in good health is a society in which the social bond is promoted. This social bond has an inherent creativity to promote health.

However, at least two very difficult problems remain. The first has to do with prevention. We have been talking about prevention for several years now, without noting any significant change in the matter. Some are developing the hypothesis that we are reluctant to give this problem priority, being essentially interested in our health, security and welfare. No ethically justified criterion nor any ministerial order can validly resolve this question: a cultural mutation proves to be necessary here. It is not only a matter of reflection on rights acquired in this field of social protection, but also of the way in which we engage our freedom in our representations of health, body and human life. From this viewpoint, it will be a long lasting journey where we are urged to join each other.

The second problem touches the health care system itself. Increasingly, the health care system contributes not only to expenditure but also participates in a logic of economic production. Here, the decisionmakers are not only the promoters of health: how will it be possible to redirect that logic of economic production in a new direction? Is this not the major source of our problems today?

The purpose of all this, namely a good health policy, in fact presupposes a double responsibility. First on the individual level: each one of us has to be as responsible as possible in our requests with regard to the systems for the provision of health care and with regard to our contribution to a collective provision for health for all.

Second on the collective level: since we would be committing ourselves to new social and cultural practices, one of our aims should be to promote the conditions of health, and another should be to remain critical towards our image of ideal and perfect health. Can human life ever avoid being marked by a certain tragic dimension? Should we not develop a serene, realistic pedagogy of health?

With this in mind, reflection should focus on the concrete social practices (associations, interest groups, half-way interfaces between technical medicine and the construction of representations of health, political action, etc.) in such a way as to take part in the initiative of shifting the question of constraint. With all due modesty, is it not possible to invent micro-realisations in which this new balance of health promotion would seek to emerge in the form of a communal medicine where the key players in health care would be the individual citizens themselves, where social groups would take valorised initiatives? All it would require are subjects capable of expressing their expectations, players susceptible to collective mobilisation, capable of articulating "their particularism of illness, their concern not to break with the universal values of reason and science, and their readiness to participate in the health care system".[22]

After all, it is often by daring to conceive Utopia that man discovers that, beyond the alienation of constraints, he remains fundamentally free and the leading actor of his own history.

---

[22] M. WIEVORKA, *Subjectivité du malade et action collective dans le domaine de santé*, in *Vous avez dit Santé?*, Paris, 1996, p. 111.

4

JUST HEALTH CARE

The Case of Waiting Lists

Wim Dekkers

4.1. Waiting lists

In discussions regarding just health care and a fair distribution of scarce health care resources, traditional principles such as distributive justice and solidarity play an important role. If scarcity cannot be eliminated, care must be rationed. One current method of regulation and rationing is the use waiting lists. Depending on the health care system, waiting lists exist in many West European countries. Long waiting lists have become normal in Dutch health care: for admission to a hospital, for all kinds of diagnostic and therapeutic procedures, for a new heart or a kidney, for care for a mentally handicapped person, for a place in a nursing home, for home care, etc. Waiting lists differ from region to region, from hospital to hospital, from one disease to another, and from one provision to another. Waiting lists were a key issue in the report of the Dutch Committee on Choices in Health Care (1992).[1] According to this committee, choices in health care are unavoidable and necessary. For making choices, the Committee on Choices in Health Care preferred a community-oriented approach in which individual rights and professional autonomy are limited in the interests of equity and solidarity in health care. Waiting lists may have a clear function in order to reach these goals.

---

[1] DUTCH COMMITTEE ON CHOICES IN HEALTH CARE, *Choices in Health Care*. Zoetermeer, 1992.

Waiting lists can be caused by an insufficient care delivery capacity, a lack of financial resources, personnel, or organs, or by inadequate management or a deficient health care organisation. However, they are not necessarily a sign of shortage of capacity, money or management. Often they function as a means of streamlining peaks and troughs in demand for care and the workload of a particular department. Waiting lists that are not too long are acceptable. Most people will accept a certain waiting time as long as they have been adequately examined and as long as they are informed about why they must wait. Waiting lists become problematic when the number of people becomes greater and the waiting period longer. The waiting list then loses its function as a planning instrument and becomes a means of selection through which rationing can be channelled.

Thus, waiting lists are a common phenomenon in health care and may have a clear function in rationing scarce health care resources, but rationing by means of waiting lists can lead to new problems. Waiting lists become a source of annoyance when the number of people waiting on a list increases and waiting periods become longer. In this regard it is worth mentioning that it is not easy for us, Westerners of the 21st century, to wait for something. The attitude (or virtue) of waiting and accepting a certain waiting time is not well developed in our fast-moving culture. Who in their right-mind chooses the longest queue in the supermarket? Who deliberately joins a line of cars? What, then, are the ways to by-pass waiting lists in health care?

4.2. Case

4.2.1. *Scenario 1*

Mrs. A, 40 years old, is married with two children of 14 and 12 years of age. Her husband works as a computer technician. Now that her children are older, Mrs. A. has resumed her previous job as an operation assistant in the regional hospital. She was asked to do so because of a severe shortage of capable operation personnel. One day a week the operation room is closed for that reason. Besides the fact that she likes her work very much, there is also a financial incentive to resume her old job because she and her family recently moved into a bigger house. Mrs. A is also an enthusiastic hockey player. While playing hockey, her left knee is severely injured. Her general practitioner refers her to the orthopaedic surgeon at the hospital where she works. The orthopaedic surgeon's first thought is a rupture of the anterior cruciate ligament, but to be sure of the diagnosis an arthroscopy is needed. The waiting time for this diagnostic procedure is about three weeks. After three weeks the diagnosis is confirmed. The most appropriate therapy is a reconstruction of the ruptured ligament. The waiting time for this kind of operation is twelve weeks. Mrs. A is disappointed about the waiting time, but has no choice but to accept it. Nine months after her knee injury (fifteen weeks of waiting and five months for revalidation) she can go back to work again.

4.2.2. *Scenario 2*

In this scenario Mrs. A does not accept the long waiting time. Her husband tells her to consult the Internet in order to have an overview of waiting lists in the region. It appears that 60 kilometres from where they live there is a hospital in which the waiting list for an arthroscopy and the necessary orthopaedic operation is one week and four weeks respectively. Mrs. A and her husband make an appointment with the orthopaedic surgeon of that hospital and is operated on there. Six months after her knee injury she can go back to work again.

4.2.3. *Scenario 3*

In this scenario Mrs. A informs the head of the operation room about her problems. Because of the existing lack of personnel he asks the board of the hospital for permission for a special arrangement for Mrs. A. She can by-pass the waiting list and consult the local orthopedic surgeon within one week. After four weeks she is operated on in her own hospital. Six months after her knee injury she can go back to work again.

4.3. Four Theories of Justice

As the above cases demonstrate, several ways exist to cope with waiting lists. Which of the three scenarios is correct from a moral perspective? What is just health care in this case? Does that depend entirely on the specific context of Mrs. A, or is it possible to consider this case from a more abstract point of view? What, then, are the criteria which are to be used in order to assess the three scenarios from a moral perspective? Not all of moral problems that this case raises can be analysed here. In this section I will focus on four current theories of justice: libertarianism, utilitarianism, egalitarism and communitarianism. The short presentation of each of these four theories has been mainly derived from another chapter in this volume.[2]

From a *libertarian* perspective, for example Nozick's Entitlement Theory, scenario 2 is probably the right one. Nozick understands justice in terms of the protection of rights or entitlements, in particular rights to liberty (and private property). Every patient should be respected as an autonomous and self-determining person. According to Nozick's theory, the claim of absolute respect for individual autonomy and freedom leads to the idea of a strictly procedural justice. Justice has to do with fair procedures instead of fair outcomes. Furthermore, the libertarian approach may be considered a "hands-off" perspective. From this perspective, Mrs. A has the absolute right to do whatever she can to achieve her goal, i.e. an operation as soon as possible. Nothing should prevent her from consulting the Internet to find the hospital with the shortest waiting lists and consulting the orthopaedic surgeon in that particular hospital. In a libertarian approach, delivery of health care is deemed to take place in a free market which every individual can enter freely. Thus scenario 2 fits best in a libertarian perspective. From that perspective, other people play a role only in a negative sense, i.e. as possible violators of one's own individual rights. Although Mrs. A definitely knows about the waiting list, she probably does not know about the specific needs and demands of other patients (some of whom may have the same knee problem). But even if she knew about the concrete situation of other patients, from a strong libertarian perspective this would not necessarily withhold her from exercising her own rights.

From a (classic or overall) *utilitarian* perspective, scenario 3 is probably the best one. Common to all forms of utilitarianism is that

---

[2] Y. DENIER & T. MEULENBERGS, *Health Care Needs and Distributive Justice. Philosophical Perspectives on the Organisation of Health Care Systems*, this volume.

justice is seen in the context of the utility of rules and actions. It is utility that is the basic criterion for the value of particular rules and actions. Justice is a matter of maximizing utility and utility is defined as pleasure, satisfaction, happiness, welfare, etc. From Jeremy Bentham's 'greatest happiness principle' it follows that "it is the greatest happiness of the greatest number that is the measure of right and wrong." Unlike in a libertarian approach, in a utilitarian perspective other people are reckoned with, but only insofar as certain actions affect their happiness and welfare. However, one of the biggest problems with the utilitarian approach is that it is difficult to assess a person's state of happiness, let alone the happiness of a greater number of people. Thus, the main question in the above case is whether there is empirical evidence for the claim that in scenario 3 utility is maximised. And, if the answer is affirmative, what does that mean? In this regard it is important to note that maximum utility (whatever that may be) can go hand in hand with seriously unequal distribution of health care resources among people. This is, for example, the case when the maximum utility of a group of ten people has not been distributed equally among them. Practically, an equal distribution of health care facilities is hardly possible at all. For then one should know the outcome of a certain waiting list for all people on that particular list. Moreover, widening the scope to all patients on all kinds of waiting lists, one should also know the outcome of a certain procedure for the happiness and well-being of any patient on any waiting list. This is not possible in practical terms. How should one distinguish, for example, between necessary care (a new donor heart or appropriate care for a severely mentally-handicapped family member) and less necessary care (a reconstruction of the anterior cruciate ligament)?[3] How should one distinguish between service with low priority and service with high priority? Answering questions of this type implies a thorough analysis of what it means for people to be on all kinds of waiting lists.

From an *egalitarian* perspective, equality is the baseline for justice. Depending on the answer to the question 'equality of what?', there are many different forms of egalitarianism. Let us focus on Rawls'

---

[3] "Necessity from the community point of view" is the first of the four criteria which have been proposed by the Dutch Committee Choices in Health Care to decide what health care provisions should be integrated in to the basic package. The other three criteria are effectiveness, efficiency, and individual responsibility.

theory of 'fair equality of opportunity.' The only demand of this theory is that persons be given a fair opportunity for a good outcome of a certain action or intervention. It does not imply that everyone must have access to every available medical intervention or that one has a right to a good health outcome. In this theory, positive freedom, equality, and responsibility are central notions. The notion of positive freedom means that people must have the maximum chance to make a personal choice. It seems as though scenario 2 fits best in this theory. However, a deliberate decision to wait for one's turn and not to speed up the operation (scenario 1) would also be in line with maximising individual freedom. Regarding the notion of equality, the 'fair opportunity' theory holds that the focus should be on equal distribution of means and chances rather than of outcomes (as in any utilitarian theory). Regarding the outcomes, the theory of 'fair equality of opportunity' makes a clear distinction between inequalities for which one is responsible and inequalities for which one is not responsible. Thus, again, if Mrs. A deliberately decides to wait and to accept inequality (of whatever sort and however it is assessed) between her and other patients, this inequality is morally acceptable. However, if Mrs. A was not aware of other possibilities (such as visiting another hospital or bypassing the waiting list in her own hospital) and accepted the waiting time because of a lack of information, this inequality would be unacceptable from a moral point of view. Situations like this one could easily lead to a dichotomy between two categories of people in our society. One group is not well-informed about all the ways in which individual rights can be exercised and has no option other than accepting waiting times. The other group always stays in front because they know how to express themselves and realise their own preferences.

Communitarian approaches criticise the libertarian emphasis on individual autonomy and individual rights. From a communitarian perspective, the essential characteristic of an individual person resides neither in "the right to be left alone" or a "hands-off" perspective nor in being a rational decision-maker. From a communitarian perspective, a human being is primarily a social being. The emphasis is on *inter*individual dependency, *inter*individual and societal responsibility and solidarity rather than on individual freedom and rights. The Dutch Committee on Choices in Health Care took such a community-oriented approach as a starting point for decision-making at the macro level. According to the Dutch Committee, health care may not solely be a function for the individual, but also for his or her place in the community, and thus for the community as a whole (p. 55). Health is defined as the ability to function normally in society rather than the absence of disease (the medical-professional approach) or the ability to reach one's own goals (the individual approach) (p. 50). To what scenario would such a communitarian approach lead in the above case? Would it be scenario 1 because solidarity with other patients in the same situation, waiting for one's turn, and the experience of being dependent on other people are highly valued? Or would it be scenario 3 because a shorter waiting time for Mrs. A would benefit the community as a whole? An argument for scenario 3 is that the long absence of Mrs. A. will further enlarge the capacity problems of the operation room and be damaging to the community as a whole. Any delay in her treatment will lead to a loss of working days and, thus, to a further increase of the waiting list.[4] Another conclusion to be drawn from this scenario is that non-medical criteria too may play a role in the place people have on a waiting list.

4.4. Conclusion

Attempts have been made to reduce waiting lists by increasing finances. Presently, however, there is growing evidence that waiting-list problems cannot and must not be solved solely by increasing finances, but through greater efficiency, responsible substitution, and strict admission criteria. Explicit rules and procedures are needed. Admission to and positions on the waiting list must be based on explicit criteria. A precondition for the development of such criteria is openness about the length of waiting lists in all kinds of health care areas. Waiting lists must be made public and be accessible for evaluation. Recently the Dutch Society of Hospitals (Nederlandse Vereniging van Ziekenhuizen) published a list of waiting lists on the Internet. A comparison between waiting lists is now possible and will lay the ground for indicating priorities for reducing or revising them. The Dutch newspaper *Algemeen Dagblad* developed a waiting-list service based on the same data.[5] The waiting time for an arthroscopic

---

[4] That is why scenario 3 also fits within Rawls' "maximin-principle."

[5] http://www.ad.nl/wachtlijsthulp

operation on the knee appears to range from 3 to 27 weeks. Yet few patients and general practitioners presently choose a hospital on the basis of such national or regional information. Patients still see their own general practitioner as the most important source of information about waiting lists.[6] The length of a waiting list is not indicative of the seriousness of the problem. Some patients deliberately choose the option of being treated at a later stage and are not waiting in the strict sense. Furthermore, a discrepancy exists between the fact that people feel they have to wait too long and the fact that they are not easily inclined to move to another hospital with a shorter waiting list. More research should be done on the preferences of actual patients who are hidden behind anonymous waiting lists.[7]

From the above description and short analysis of the case of Mrs. A one can learn that the level of micro-allocation (care for Mrs. A), the intermediate level of the institution (the hospital policy), and the level of macro-allocation (the problem of just health care) are intrinsically connected.[8] The moral problems that the case of Mrs. A raises can be understood only if one takes account of all societal questions relating to the fair allocation of scarce resources, including the underlying macro-ethical norms and values. As Defever argues, the floor is open for debate on social ethics in health care.[9] Furthermore, I believe that a communitarian approach rather than a libertarian, utilitarian or egalitarian approach is needed. The communitarian perspective within social ethics is particularly relevant because it highlights the humane (or inhumane) nature of the whole health care system, its social and cultural conditions and its underpinning presumptions and values.[10] The focus should be on solidarity rather than on individual autonomy and freedom of choice. What this means for the case of Mrs. A in particular, and for a fair system of waiting lists in general, deserves further scientific and social-ethical attention.

[6] M.A.A. SCHOOL, Informatie over toegangstijden, in Medisch Contact 56/43 (2001) 1587-1588.

[7] A.P. STOOP & W.B.F. BROUWER, De patiënt achter de cijfers, in Medisch Contact 56/44 (2001) 1610-1612.

[8] P. BOITTE & B. CADORÉ, From the 'Weak Argument of Constraint' to a Health Policy, this volume.

[9] M. DEFEVER, Who Will Decide?, this volume.

[10] M.AM. PIJNENBURG, Humane Health Care as a Theme for Social Ethics, in Medicine, Health Care and Philosophy 2002 [in press].

5

ARE THERE LIMITS TO SOLIDARITY WITH THE ELDERLY?

*Ruud Ter Meulen**

In most European countries health care, including care for the elderly, is based on the principle of solidarity. This principle is premised on deliberation and freely chosen unity among certain people, groups, or populations. It involves not only an awareness of unity, but also acceptance of the consequences of unity.[1] This choice was once limited to members of an individual's immediate group, for instance family, village, or social class. This 'group solidarity' played an important role in the history of health insurance: workers, employees, or civil servants united voluntarily in sickness funds to safeguard themselves against the financial risks of disease and physical or mental handicap. Solidarity was not limited to health insurance, but was a basic principle in other social security schemes as well, like pension systems, unemployment insurance, and disability insurance and workers' compensation.

In sociology and gerontology there is a debate as to whether solidarity, including solidarity across generations, still exists in our modern society.[2] In view of the breakdown of traditional bonds and groups, solidarity is said to have melted away as a unifying force

* The editors and publishers wish to thank The Hastings Center Report for permission to use this copyright material which was previously published as R. TER MEULEN, *Are There Limits To Solidarity With the Elderly?*, in *Hastings Center Report* 24/5 (1994) 36-38.

[1] *Choices in Health Care*, Report by the Ministry of Welfare, Health and Cultural Affairs, The Netherlands, Rijswijk, 1992, p. 56.

[2] M.L. JOHNSON, *Generational Relations under Review*, in D. HOBMAN (ed.), *Intergenerational Solidarity: Fact or Fiction?*, s.l., s.d..

within society. In fact, solidarity has not disappeared but rather has been transformed into another structure. The traditional solidarity of class and neighbourhood has given way to a new dependency on bureaucratic structures of the state and other social institutions (for example, insurance companies). Instead of the personal relations that were dominant in traditional society (horizontal dependency), individuals are nowadays dependent on each other by way of collective arrangements of the state (vertical dependency).[3] These arrangements safeguard individuals against the uncertainties of human existence, for example, as a result of natural causes (disease, handicaps) or social causes (loss of income).

Moreover, as society has changed into a loose community of individuals or small groups protected by the collective arrangements of the state, the old group solidarity of care and concern has been replaced by a new solidarity of interests that cuts across social categories. People now are sharing certain risks jointly with individuals belonging to other social categories out of clear self-interest. Such solidarity is not a consciously chosen unit with people in the same group, but a compulsory recognition of mutual self-interest enforced by the state. Nowadays, solidarity means the obligation to share the financial risks of illness and handicap with others not necessarily of one's own social group. In exchange for meeting their obligation to pay a premium, people have access to a broad package of health care services.

5.1. Blaming the Elderly?

Solidarity of interests is based on the principle of reciprocity: people share risks that are common to each other. The more commonplace the risk, the broader the base of solidarity. For uncommon risks or risks that are the result of irresponsible behaviour, there is only a narrow base. In an era of limited resources, general solidarity across interests groups is giving way to a tendency to blame those whose irresponsible behaviour or excessive claims for health care services effectively limit other's access to care.

---

[3] R. JANSWEIJER, *Individualization and Solidarity: An Effort to Clarify the Concepts* (in Dutch), in *Filosofie en Praktijk* 8 (1988) 26-36, p. 28.

It is unlikely that the elderly will be victimized in this way. Historically, attitudes toward the elderly have never been very positive and will almost inevitably become more negative in times of scarce resources. Because of their increasing demand for care and their dependency on others, the elderly are seen more and more as a burden on society. They occupy an increasing number of beds in the hospitals, which in some cases results in waiting lists for younger patients. Premiums for health insurance are rising, partly at least in order to pay the increasing costs of care for the elderly. The scarcity of institutional care and home care is putting pressure on families and neighbours to take care of dependent elderly persons informally.

For their part, elderly react to their situation with feelings of powerlessness and superfluity. This is particularly true in the Central European countries, where respect for the elderly is already low and will deteriorate further as they impose more burdens on society. The process is not unique to Eastern and Central Europe, however, for it can be noted in Western European Countries – for example, the United Kingdom, where respect for the elderly is rapid declining, partly because of their rising demand for care. The growing phenomenon of elder abuse in nearly all European countries is writing on the wall. The elderly also often feel that they are discriminated against covertly or even overtly (as for example happens in the British National Health System). Organizations of Dutch elderly point out, for instance, that the majority of waiting lists are for services that are important for the elderly, such as nursing home care, home care, cataract surgery, and hip replacements.

It would not be fair to blame the elderly for the scarcity of resources. The graying of the population is only partly responsible. Indeed, the alleged impact of demography on the demand for care is grossly exaggerated: focusing on the demographic process is a way of creating a myth, which hinders an insight into the real causes of the scarcity of resources. More important is the impact of medicalisation and individualization within society.

5.2. The Medicalisation of Old Age

Without blaming the victim, we must still rethink solidarity across generations. The increasing demand for care by the elderly is putting a heavy claim on the social resources for health care and on the willingness of younger generations to take care of their independent parents. Are the elderly entitled to all of our resources for health care or may we set some limits on what care they will perceive?

This problem emerges particularly in acute care medicine. There is a tendency to treat older and older patients with sophisticated medical technologies. The number of people over eighty or even ninety years of age who are getting open heart surgery, organ transplantation, or renal dialysis is increasing rapidly. These medical treatments do not simply prolong organic life, but are truly beneficial in restoring health and quality of life. A leading Dutch cardiologist said that "age is hardly an indication against cardiac surgery for patients who are in good condition."[4] In fact, the real 'problem' is that a growing number of the elderly are in very good condition and eligible for nearly all kinds of medical interventions even in their eighties or nineties.

This medicalisation of old age is driven by the dynamics of health care economics. This process can be noted, for example, in diagnostic technology: hospitals try to recover the costs of expensive diagnostic devices by an intensified use of them, particularly with the elderly. However, the increased use of diagnostic technologies is also a result of public demands. The inconveniences of old age are less readily accepted, at the same time that people are on a 'quest for certainty', that is, to rule out disease.[5]

Medicalisation will put increasing strains on intergenerational solidarity in two ways. First, under conditions of finite resources, it will hinder the access of younger patients to acute care services. This is already apparent in heart transplantation, where there is a scarcity of donor organs – i.e., scarcity that is not the result of a lack of financial resources (and thus that could be removed by greater efficiency or more money), but of other social or physical causes. The scarcity of donor organs, that is, arises out of individuals' lack of willingness to donate their organs or because of the nature of the organ procurement system. The same problem is coming up in intensive care units: though the elderly benefit from high technology procedures, they

---

[4] R.W. KOSTER, *Cardiology by Others* (in Dutch), in *Ouder worden nu '90*, Almere, 1990.

[5] P.J. VAN DER MAAS, *Aging and Public Health*, in J.F. SCHROOTS (ed.), *Health and Aging*, New York, 1988, p. 95-115, p. 110.

need more time to recover in ICU. The 'graying' of these units will result in limited access for younger persons who are in extreme need. For instance, in December 1990 a young child died in the Netherlands because there was no room area in ICUs, which were in large part occupied by elderly patients.

A second problem is that the increased use of acute care services will drain away resources from long-term care. In consequence, there will be a growing demand for informal care by family members or neighbours. Though many family members, particularly daughters, are willing to supply this care, there are limits to family care-givers' physical and emotional resources. While most adult children want solidarity with their parents, they do have their own life plans and their own children to care for.

5.3. Limits to the Elderly?

One of the most hotly debated proposals in the ethics of resource allocation is the notion of setting an age limit for acute care services. Well known (and controversial) are the ideas of Daniel Callahan, who opposes the medicalisation of old age and believes that, within the next twenty or thirty years, it may be necessary to set an age limit on the use of expensive, life-prolonging technology. He proposes instead that the emphasis be given to providing decent economic support and long-term and home care. There should be, that is, a shift from curing to caring beyond a certain age (he suggests the late seventies or early eighties as the time to draw the line), with the goal of insuring a good balance of resources between young and old and a limit to efforts to endlessly push back the frontiers of acute care medicine for the old.[6]

This proposal for the allocation of resources for the elderly has been strongly criticized as a kind of 'ageist' discrimination.[7] Gerontologists and liberal ethicists particularly have argued that every age has its own aims and that nobody can determine for another when his life has been completed or his 'natural life span' has been

---

[6] D. CALLAHAN, *Setting Limits: Medical Goals in an Aging Society*, New York, 1987.

[7] See, for example, R.H. BINSTOCK and S.G. POST (eds.), *Too Old for Health Care? Controversies in Medicine, Laws, Economics and Ethics*, Baltimore, 1991.

reached. There is no reason, they argue, to suppose that an old person values his life less than a younger one. When one considers only years of life instead of life alone, one shows no respect for the unique value of the human person, which is the moral basis for our society.

Nonetheless, there is some truth in the argument that people who are seventy-five years old have had a 'fair share' of life, or 'fair innings'.[8] In a situation in which treatment possibilities are limited and a choice must be made between a person who has had a fair share and one who has not, it would be reasonable to favour the latter. But we should be careful not to turn to such a decision into an official policy, which might reinforce a negative view of old age and the elderly in our society. Were that to happen, the elderly might take less responsibility themselves for their health and have a lower subjective evaluation of their health status. In the end, a policy of age rationing could result in more visits by the elderly to physicians, particularly general practitioners, and thus to an increase in the demand for care.

Apart from these concerns, there are serious doubts as to whether an age criterion will ever be accepted in modern society. Part of the process of individualization, referred to above, is the disappearance of traditional social relationships. Traditional values and structures of authority are replaced by relationships based on negotiation and equal respect. This process can be noted in the clinic (physician-patient relationship)[9], as well as in other social areas like the family, the school, and the workplace. Two important features of the negotiation process are that it presupposes no fixed rules or shared notions of the good and that age or generation are losing ground as criteria for social arrangements and relationships.[10] Such an 'age-irrelevant' society, as Bernice Neugarten styled it, is a perfect breeding ground for liberal ideologies that deny any special status to the elderly other than that they are equal to any other person in society.

---

[8] J. Harris, *The Value of Life*, London, 1985.

[9] H.R. Moody, *From Informed Consent to Negotiated Consent*, in *Gerontologist* 28 Supplement (1988) 64-70.

[10] H.R. Moody, *The Meaning of Life and the Meaning of Old Age*, in T.R. Cole & S.A. Gadow (eds.), *What Does It Mean to Grow Old? Reflections from the Humanities*, Durham, 1986, p. 9-40.

5.4. Access to Care

When there is a scarcity of resources, the better off will have more opportunities to buy a better quality of care or to jump waiting lists for scarce medical treatments. National governments, unwilling to make difficult choices in health care, are trying to increase personal financial responsibility for health care services, for instance by co-payments, compulsory deductibles, or compulsory additional private insurance. This shift from collective responsibility towards private responsibility fits very well with the retreat of the welfare state, the introduction of market forces, and a greater emphasis on freedom in the health care system. However, more freedom will inevitably result in greater inequalities in access to care. Particularly the elderly, many of them with low incomes and pensions, will be affected by such policies.

The introduction of such a two-tier system in health is often criticized as a danger to solidarity and equality, which for many European countries are basic values in their health care systems. However, provided that society is supplying an adequate package of health care services, to which all persons have equal access (unhindered by co-payments or other financial obstacles), persons who buy their own services exceeding this package do not offend any ethical principle in doing so.[11]

An important question is, of course, what is an adequate package of care services, particularly for the elderly? The answer to this question depends on society's values and expectations in regard to health care. An important value, which in spite of the individualization of society is still strongly adhered to in the Netherlands, is *humanitarian solidarity*. This kind of solidarity, which is based on the dignity of the human person whose existence is threatened by circumstances beyond their own control, particularly natural fate or unfair social structures.[12] Humanitarian solidarity should be the starting point for defining necessary care, as was advocated by the Committee on

---

[11] President's Commission for the Study of Ethical Problems in Medicine and Biomedical and Behavioral Research, *Securing Access to Health Care: A Report on the Ethical Implications of Differences in the Availability of Health Services*, Washington D.C., 1983, p. 20.

[12] GOVERNMENT COMMITTEE, *Choices in Health Care*, p. 57.

Choices in Health Care in the Netherlands. Care services for persons unable to care for themselves because of psychological handicaps, for example, Alzheimer disease, psychiatric disorders, or mental retardation, should have priority in the basic package. The remaining content (and extent) of the basic package should be given over to other kinds of long-term care (for example, home care), acute care services, and for less important health care services.

Defined this way, the basic package should be equally accessible to all, without financial constraints like co-payments or obligatory risks. A two-tier system based on the principle of humanitarian solidarity puts care, not cure, at the center of its efforts to provide an adequate level of health care. While cure has a permanent tendency to vanquish the barriers of illness and death, care has much more modest aspirations and is more selfcontaining.[13] Moreover, the emphasis on care can preserve respect for the human person that might be endangered by the need to set limits and the exclusion of acute services from the basic package. By securing access to long-term care services and limiting access to some acute care services, a two-tier system based on the principle of humanitarian solidarity might limit the medicalisation of old that is the most important threat to solidarity between the young and the old.

---

[13] D. CALLAHAN, *What Kind of Life? The Limits of Medical Progress*, New York, 1990, p. 145.

6

EPILOGUE

Justice in Health Care

Antoon Vandevelde

For a long time ethicists were mainly interested in personal moral dilemma's and in highly theoretical meta-ethical questions. All this changed in the 1970s, mainly after the publication of Rawls' *Theory of Justice*. The worldwide stagnation of the economy caused mass unemployment in the wealthy countries of Western Europe and Northern America and had even worse effects in the rest of the world. In these circumstances the general public as well as professional ethicists focused their attention on problems of distributive justice and on the design of new economic and political macro-structures. In the 1990s however, new concerns arouse slowly. With the downfall of communism in Eastern Europe, the question of economic institutions seemed settled: market solutions were supposed to be at hand for most economic problems and market failures had to be corrected by carefully devised government intervention. Declining population figures solved the most urgent unemployment problems in the West. The theme of economic justice was replaced by analysis of the influence of trust and social capital on economic performances. All this is quite interesting but it is also a clear sign that economic ethics has lost its critical edge.

At the same time however the interest in biomedical ethics started booming. Discussions about abortion, euthanasia, cloning and the limits of genetic engineering were covered at the front pages of newspapers. Less spectacular but at least as important is the fact that the whole of the health care sector is confronted with ever more urgent scarcity problems. In this way economic ethics regain a new actuality.

In her text Mia Defever shows that rationing and priority setting is the inevitable answer to scarcity problems in health care. I am not sure that this is mainly due to shrinking budgets allocated to health care. Surely these budgets are increasing in absolute terms, but it is true that the demands on behalf of patients and health care providers are increasing still more rapidly. However Defever is right in pointing out that public support for increased solidarity in the sphere of health care is considerable. She advocates a public debate among all stakeholders about rationing policies, but at the same time she warns that no party in this debate is completely disinterested. This seems to make transparent policy making in this field extremely difficult.

Yvonne Denier and Tom Meulenbergs draw attention to the different perspectives policy makers, patients, physicians and other care providers have on the problems raised by scarcity in health care. They analyse carefully the concept of needs and they argue for a rational health care policy that would give priority to needs above mere preferences or desires. Respect for the autonomy of the patient should not lead to medical overconsumption. However, the bulk of their text is devoted to a careful comparison between various theories of justice which could serve as as many standards for assessing the legitimacy of the institutions allocating health care resources. Libertarianism advocates a strict respect for individual freedom and the right to private property. This yields a private health care system, based upon voluntary insurance contracts. Poor people will have to rely on private charity. Neither do utilitarians acknowledge a genuine right to (access to) health care. They want to maximize aggregate utility. If the provision of health care to the worst off happens to increase social welfare, then it should be assured, but sacrificing the interests of a few people to the interest of all is considered to be recommendable. Egalitarianism tries – sometimes painfully – to eliminate inequalities for which individuals are not responsible without hampering too much the overall efficiency of the system. Communitarianism is in general favourable to a rather generous system of health care, but its precise shape should be determined by the common understandings within a particular community. No existing health care system is uniquely organised along the lines of one of these theories. A good system should provide at reasonable costs equal access to health care of good quality and freedom of choice on behalf of patients and providers. The authors argue that this can best be realised within a two-tiered or mixed system, a compromise between a free market and an egalitarian system of health care.

Pierre Boitte and Bruno Cadoré point out that there is no correlation at all between the quantity of resources absorbed by various health care systems and their results in terms of health indicators. They suppose that health care systems obey to an autonomous self-feeding logic that produces ever new medical needs. One always remains a potential consumer of care. Like Illich they warn against the threat of global counterproductivity of our overdeveloped health care systems. How to stop medical overconsumption? The authors explore several remedies. First of all, one should focus more on preventive than on curative medicine. Secondly there is the problem of what is commonly called 'moral hazard'. The occurrence of risks tends to increase by the very fact that they are insured. Economic theory tells us that this is due to overinsurance. Partial insurance would stimulate patients to be more careful and to avoid risky behaviour. However, this creates problems for chronically ill patients. Some of them become unable for the care and the medicines they need. In an unregulated market they risk to become the victims of adverse selection, so that they will be unable to get insured at all. Finally the authors call for a global reorientation of the health care system towards its intrinsic goals. This cannot be realised except on the base of a renewal of the sense of responsibility of all actors.

This part of the book is closed by two case studies. Wim Dekkers discusses rationing of health care by way of waiting lists. Queuing is generally associated to the principle of merit and is considered by most people as more fair than market solutions for scarcity problems, an auction for instance. It is however far from evident in our hasty culture. Ruud ter Meulen asks whether there are limits to solidarity with the elderly. He rejects age limits to care but adheres to a system inspired by humanitarian solidarity, emphasising care rather than cure for the aged. Some acute care services could be excluded from the basic package of social security, accessible to all without financial constraints. Definitely these kinds of proposals, however abstract they remain, are highly controversial in our society.

For the first time people in the most wealthy countries of the world face a perspective that is already very common in the poorer parts of the world, namely that people will have to die although a treatment for their disease is available, the only problem being that it is excessively expensive. Take the problem of pulmonary hypertension. Treatment is possible. It takes a long time and it has to be repeated frequently, but it lengthens the life of some people with some additional years and it improves the quality of their life. However one such treatment costs hundreds of thousands of Euros. Moreover this is not a unique case. General medical progress, improving the life prospects of considerable numbers of people, like with the discovery of antibiotics is not evident anymore. Maybe it is still possible for some tropical diseases, but we all know that people suffering from malaria or sleeping sickness do not have enough purchasing power to make medical research that could benefit them profitable. Consequently medical progress today benefits increasingly very small and very specific groups of patients in the richer parts of the world, suffering from rather uncommon types of disease.

So it is likely that policy makers, hospitals and physicians will have to face many analogous dilemma's as with pulmonary hypertension. In this respect patent law will be more and more contested. Clearly there is a logic behind the protection of new discoveries and inventions. It costs huge amounts of money to develop new medicines. Without intellectual property rights no pharmaceutical firm is able to engage in such a research. However, once an interesting new molecule has been found, its mass production is often relatively easy and cheap. Patent law increases prices of new medicines and seems to be particularly heartless towards poor people or countries, but maybe these people would even be worse off if patent law was abolished and the general pace of medical progress declining. Certainly public authorities are able to alleviate these problems by appealing to tax money, collected among the general public or by stimulating more encompassing (and more expensive) health insurances. However, in most countries health expenditures are already increasing much more rapidly than GNP per capita. Definitely, hard political choices will have to be made in this respect. Even taking into account that new treatments and advanced technological equipment become less expensive in the years after their introduction, it seems impossible to find solutions to these problems that are satisfying on all accounts and for all stakeholders.

EUROPEAN PERSPECTIVES ON HEALTH CARE ETHICS

A Selected Bibliography

B. Hansen & T. Meulenbergs

1. WORKS ON HEALTH CARE ETHICS

Comprehensive Introductions in Health Care Ethics

- BONDOLFI, A., BOMPIANI, A., DE WACHTER, M. & VIAFORA, C., *Vent'anni di bioetica: idee protagonisti istituzioni* [Twenty years of Bioethics], Padua, Fondazione Lanza, 1992.
- BONDOLFI, A. & MULLER, H., *Medizinische Ethik im ärztlichen Alltag* [Medical Ethics in Medical Practice], Zurich, 1999.
- HOTTOIS, G. & MISSA, J.-N., *Nouvelle encyclopédie de bioéthique: médecine, environnement, biotechnologie* [New Encyclopedia of Bioethics: Medicine, Environment, Biotechnology], Bruxelles, De Boeck Université, 2001.
- KAPPEL, K., *Medicinsk etik. En filosofisk diskussion af etiske grundprincipper* [Medical Ethics. A Philosophical Dicussion of Ethical Priciples], Copenhagen, Gyldendal, 1996.
- KEMP, P., LEBECH, M. & RENDTORFF, J.D., *Den bioetiske vending: en grundbog I bioetik* [The Bioethics Turn: A Basic Text in Bioethics], Copenhagen, Spektrum, 1997.
- KLINT JENSEN, K. & ANDERSEN, S., *Bioetik* [Bioethics], København, Rosinante, 1999.
- LOEWY, E., *Ethische Fragen in der Medizin* [Ethical Questions in Medicine], Wien, Springer Verlag, 1995.
- NIEKERK, K., *Teologi og Bioetik: den protestantisk-teologiske vurdering af bioteknologien i Norden 1972-1991* [Theology and Bioethics: The Protestant-Theological Evaluation of Biotechnology in the Nordic Countries 1972-1991] (Skrifter fra Center for Bioetik ved Aarhus Universitet, 1), Aarhus, Aarhus Universitetsforlag, 1994.

- PARKER, M. & DICKENSON, D. (eds.), *The Cambridge Medical Ethics Workbook. Case Studies, Commentaries and Activities*, Cambridge, Cambridge University Press, 2001.
- RENDTORFF, J. & KEMP, P. (eds.), *Basic Ethical Principles in European Bioethics and Biolaw*, 2 vol., Copenhagen, Centre for Ethics and Law, 2001.
- SGRECCIA, E., *Manuale di bioetica. Vol. 1, Fondamenti di etica biomedica* [Bioethics Handbook. Foundations of Biomedical Ethics], Milano, Vita e Pensiero, 1999.
- TEN HAVE, H.A.M.J., TER MEULEN, R.H.J. & VAN LEEUWEN, E., *Medische Ethiek* [Medical Ethics], Houten – Diegem, Bohn Stafleu van Loghum, 1998.
- TEN HAVE, H. & GORDIJN, B. (eds.), *Bioethics in a European Perspective*, Dordrecht, Kluwer Academic Publishers, 2001.

Works on the Physician-Patient Relationship

- COLONNA, L. & LACHAUX, B., *Le consentement en pratique clinique. La loi Huriet: dix ans après, bilan, enjeux, perspectives* [Consent in Clinical Practice. The Huriet-law: Ten years later, Results, Efforts and Perspectives], Paris, Flammarion, 2000.
- GUERIN, M., *Le généraliste et son patient* [The GP and his Patient], Paris, Flammarion, 1995.
- GRACIA, D. & PESET, J.L. (eds.), *The Ethics of Diagnosis*, Dordrecht, Kluwer, 1992.
- HOERNI, B., *L'autonomie en médecine: nouvelles relations entre les personnes malades et les personnes soignantes* [Autonomy in Medicine: New Relations between Sick Persons and Caregivers], Paris, Payot, 1991.
- HOERNI, B. & SAURY, R., *Le consentement: information, autonomie et decision en medicine* [Consent: Information, Autonomy and Decision-making in Medicine], Abrégés, Masson, 1998.
- MEYER, P., *L'irresponsabilité médicale* [Medical Irresponsibility], Paris, Grasset, 1993.
- MANSCHOT, H. & VERKERK, M. (red.), *Ethiek van de zorg. Een discussie* [Ethics of Care. A Discussion], Boom, Amsterdam – Meppel, 1994.
- RUYTER, K.W., SOLLBAKK, J.H. & FØRDE, R., *Medisinsk Etikk: en problembasert tilnærming* [Medical Ethics: A Problem-based Approach], Oslo, Gyldendal Akademisk Forlag, 2000.
- TRANOY, K.E., *Medisinsk etikk i vår tid* [Medical Ethics Today], Bergen – Sandviken, Fagbokforlaget, 1999.
- WIDDERSHOVEN, G., *Ethiek in de kliniek. Hedendaagse benaderingen in de gezondheidsethiek* [Ethics in the Clinic. Contemporary Approaches in Healthcare Ethics], Boom, Amsterdam – Meppel, 2000.

Works on Human Experimentation

- CAPOVILLA, E., *et al.*, *Etica e sperimentazione medica: da cavia a partner* [Ethics and Medical Experimentation: From Guinea Pig to Partner] (Quaderni di etica e medica), Padua, Fondzione Lanza Padua, 1992.
- DE DEYN, P. (ed.), *The Ethics of Animal and Human Experimentation*, London, John Libbey London – Paris – Rome, 1994.
- DELFOSSE, M-L., LADRIÈRE, J. *et al.*, *L'expérimentation médicale sur l'être humain: construire les normes, construire l'éthique* [Medical Experimentation on Human Beings: Creating Norms, Creating Ethics], Bruxelles, De Boeck – Wesmael, 1993.
- HOTTOIS, G., *Le paradigme bioéthique: une éthique pour la technoscience* [The Bioethics Paradigm: Ethics for Techno-Science], Bruxelles, De Boeck Université, 1990.
- LAROUCHE, J.-M., *Ethique de la recherche* [Research Ethics], Ethique Publique, 2000.
- LECOURT, D., *L'humain est-il expérimentable?* [Are Experiments on Humans Allowed?], Paris, Presses Universitaires de France, 2000.
- McNEIL, P.M., *The Ethics and Politics of Human Experimentation*, Cambridge, Cambridge University Press, 1993.
- MISSA, J.-N. (ed.), *Le devoir d'expérimenter* [The Duty to Experiment], Bruxelles, De Boeck Université, 1996.
- SIRNES, T. & SANDBERG, P., *Bioteknologiens etiske, juridiske og sosiale aspect: rapport fra et seminar arrangert av Innsatsområdet etikk* [The Ethical, Legal and Social Aspects of Biotechnology: A Seminar Report] (Innsatsområdet etikk skriftserie 3), Oslo, Innsatsområdet etikk, Universitetet i Oslo, 1999.
- TEN HAVE, H. & WELLIE, J., (ed.), *Ownership of the Human Body: Philosophical Considerations on the Use of the Human Body and its Parts in Healthcare* (Philosophy and Medicine, 59), Dordrecht, Kluwer, 1998.
- VAN DEN DALE, W. & MÜLLER-SALOMON, H., *Die Kontrolle der Forschung am Menschen durch Etikkommissionen* [Checking Human Experimentation by Ethics Committees], Stuttgart, Enke, 1990.

Works on Justice in Health Care

- BOITTE, P., *Ethique, justice et santé: Allocation des resources en soins dans une population vieillissante* [Ethics, Justice and Health: Resource Allocation and Care in an Aging Popolation], Artel, 1995.
- CASTIEL, D., *Equité et santé* [Equality and Health], Paris, Editions Ecole Nationale de la Santé Publique, 1995.
- *Choices in Healthcare*, Report by the Government Committee on Choices in Healthcare, The Netherlands, Rijswijk, Ministry of Welfare, Health and Cultural Affairs, 1992.

- DRACOPOULOU, S. (ed.), *Ethics and Values in Health Care Management*, London, Routledge, 1998.
- EDGAR, A., SALEK, S., *The Ethical Qualy. Ethical Issues in Healthcare Resource Allocations*, Haslemere, Euromed Communications, 1998.
- ELSTER, J., & HERPIN, N. (éds.), *Ethique des choix medicaux* [Ethics and Medical Choices], Poitiers, Observatoire du changement social en Europe occidentale, Actes Sud, 1992.
- JAKUBOWSKI, E., *Health Care Systems in the EU: A Comparative Study*, Luxembourg, European Parliament, 1998.
- LEMAIRE, F., RAMEIX, S. & DREYFUSS, D., *Accès aux soins et justice sociale* [Access to Care and Social Justice] (Sixième Journée d'Ethique Médicale Maurice Rapin, novembre 1996), Paris, Flammarion médecine-sciences, 1996.
- SCHERER, K. (ed.), *Justice: Interdisciplinary Perspectives*, Cambridge, Cambridge University Press, 1992.
- TER MEULEN, R., & TEN HAVE, H. (eds.), *Samen kiezen in de zorg. Het voorbeeld Oregon* [Joint Choices in Care. The Oregon Example], Baarn, Ambo, 1993.

2. PERIODICALS ON HEALTH CARE ETHICS

- *Bioethica Forum*, Schweizerische Gesellschaft für Biomedizinische Ethik, Basel (Switzerland)
- *Bioetica e Cultura*, Istituto Siciliano di Bioetica, Acireale (Italy)
- *Bulletin of Medical Ethics*, Royal Society of Medicine Publishing, London (UK)
- *Cahiers du Comité Consultatif National d'Éthique*, CCNE, Paris (France)
- *Cambridge Quarterly of Healtcare Ethics*, Cambridge University Press, Cambridge (UK)
- *Eidon: Revista de la fundación de ciencias de la salud*, Madrid (Spain)
- *Ethica Clinica: Revue francophone d'éthique des soins de santé*, Fédération des Institutions Hospitalières de Wallonie, Erpent (Belgium)
- *Ethical Perspectives/Ethische Perspectieven*, European Ethics Network/Overlegcentrum Christelijke Ethiek, Leuven (Belgium)
- *Ethik in der Medizin*, Springer-Verlag, Berlin (Germany)
- *Health Care Analysis*, Kluwer Academic Publishers, Dordrecht (The Netherlands)
- *Human Reproduction and Genetic Ethics*, European Bioethical Research, Edinburgh (UK)
- *Jahrbuch fürWissenschaft und Ethik*, de Gruyter, Berlin (Germany)
- *Journal of Medical Ethics*, BMJ Publishing Group, London (UK)
- *Laennec. Santé – Médecine – Étique*, Centre Laennec, Paris (France)
- *Medicina e Morale*, Milano, (Italy)

- *Medicine, Health Care and Philosophy. A European Journal,* Kluwer Academic Publishers, Dordrecht (The Netherlands)
- *Studies in Research Ethics,* Centre for Research Ethics, Göteborg University, Göteborg (Sweden)
- *Tijdschrift voor geneeskunde en ethiek,* Koninklijke Van Gorcum, Assen (The Netherlands)
- *Zeitschrift für Medizinischen Ethik,* Schwabenverlag, Stuttgart (Germany)

3. EUROPEAN ETHICS INSTITUTIONS

Supranational

- Council of Europe, Steering Committee on Bioethics, http:// www.legal.coe.int/bioethics/index_gb.html
- European Association of Centres of Medical Ethics http://www.eacmeweb.com
- European Group on Ethics in Science and Technology, http:// europa.eu.int/comm/european_group_ethics

National

- Belgium: Federal Consultative Committee for Bioethics, http:// www.health.fgov.be/bioeth
- Denmark: Danish Council of Ethics, http://www.etiskraad.dk
- Finland: National Research Ethics Council, http://www.minedu.fi/ asiant/neuvotte.html
- France: National Consultative Ethics Committee for Health and Life Sciences, http://www.ccne-ethique.org
- Germany: National Ethics Council, http://www.nationalerethikrat.de
- Italy: National Bioethics Committee, http://www.palazzochigi.it/ bioetica
- Luxembourg: National Consultative Ethics Commission
- Nordic Countries: Nordic Committee on Bioethics, http://www. ncbio.org
- Norway: The National Committees for Research Ethics, http:// www.etikkom.no
- Portugal: National Council for Ethics of the Life Sciences, http://www.cnecv.gov.pt

- The Netherlands: Health Council,
  http://www.gr.nl
- United Kingdom: The Nuffield Council on Bioethics,
  http:// www.nuffield.org/bioethics

CONTRIBUTORS

Francesc ABEL is honorary director of the Institut Borja de Bioètica, Barcelona, Spain.

Pierre BOITTE is director of the Centre d'Éthique Medicale and lecturer at the Medical School, Université Catholique de Lille, France.

Alberto BONDOLFI is professor in moral theology, Universität Zürich, Switzerland.

Bruno CADORÉ is past director of the Centre d'Éthique Medicale (1997-2001), Université Catholique de Lille, France. Presently, he is Prior of the French Dominican Province.

Wim DEKKERS is professor at the Department of Ethics, Philosophy and History of Medicine at the University Medical Centre, University of Nijmegen, The Netherlands.

Marie-Luce DELFOSSE is professor in philosophy at the Faculty of Philosophy and member of the Centre Interfacultaire Droit, Éthique et Sciences de la Santé, Facultés Universitaires Notre-Dame de Namur, Belgium

Mia DEFEVER is professor in medical sociology at the Faculty of Medicine, Katholieke Universiteit Leuven, Belgium, and director of 'European Health Policy Forum'.

Yvonne DENIER is research-fellow in moral philosophy at the Centre for Economics and Ethics and at the Institute of Philosophy, Katholieke Universiteit Leuven, Belgium

Maurice DE WACHTER is professor emeritus and former director of the Institute for Bioethics, Maastricht, The Netherlands.

Chris GASTMANS is professor in health care ethics at the Faculty of Medicine and member of the Centre for Biomedical Ethics and Law, Katholieke Universiteit Leuven, Belgium.

Bart HANSEN is research-fellow (F.W.O.-Vl.) in moral theology at the Faculty of Medicine and member of the Centre for Biomedical Ethics and Law, Katholieke Universiteit Leuven, Belgium.

Reidar K. LIE is professor in philosophy, University of Bergen, Norway.

Tom MEULENBERGS is research-fellow in moral philosophy at the Faculty of Medicine and member of the Centre for Biomedical Ethics and Law, Katholieke Universiteit Leuven, Belgium.

Jean-Noël MISSA is professor in philosophy at the Université Libre de Bruxelles, Belgium.

Paul T. SCHOTSMANS is professor in medical ethics at the Faculty of Medicine, Katholieke Universiteit Leuven, Belgium, member of the Board of Directors of the International Association of Bioethics, and president of the European Association of Centres of Medical Ethics.

Ruud TER MEULEN is professor in health care ethics and philosophy, and director of the Institute for Bioethics, Faculty of Health Care Studies, Maastricht University, The Netherlands.

Francesc TORRALBA is professor in philosophy at the Universitat Ramon Llull, Barcelona, Spain.

Maria PATRÃO-NEVES is professor in philosophy at the Universidade des Açores, Portugal.

Antoon VANDEVELDE is professor in moral philosophy at the Insitute of Philosophy and member of the Centre for Economics and Ethics at the Katholieke Universiteit Leuven, Belgium.

Johan VERSTRAETEN is professor in moral theology at the Katholieke Universiteit Leuven, Belgium, and director of the European Ethics Network.

Guy WIDDERSHOVEN is professor of health care ethics at the Faculty of Health Care Studies, Maastricht University, The Netherlands, and secretary-general of the European Association of Centres of Medical Ethics.

PRINTED ON PERMANENT PAPER • IMPRIME SUR PAPIER PERMANENT • GEDRUKT OP DUURZAAM PAPIER - ISO 9706

N.V. PEETERS S.A., KLEIN DALENSTRAAT 42, B-3020 HERENT